The Young Adolescent and the Middle School

a volume in
The Handbook of Research in Middle Level Education

Series Editor:
Vincent A. Anfara, Jr.
The University of Tennessee

The Handbook of Research in Middle Level Education

Vincent A. Anfara, Jr., Series Editor

The Handbook of Research in Middle Level Education (2001)
edited by Vincent A. Anfara, Jr.

Middle School Curriculum, Instruction, and Assessment (2002)
edited by Vincent A. Anfara, Jr. and Sandra L. Stacki

Leaders for a Movement: Professional Preparation and Development of Middle Level Teachers and Administrators (2003)
edited by P. Gayle Andrews and Vincent A. Anfara, Jr.

Reforming Middle Level Education: Considerations for Policymakers (2004)
edited by Sue C. Thompson

Making a Difference: Action Research in Middle Level Education (2005)
edited by Micki M. Caskey

The Young Adolescent and the Middle School (2007)
edited by Steven B. Mertens, Vincent A. Anfara, Jr., and Micki M. Caskey

The Young Adolescent and the Middle School

Edited by

Steven B. Mertens
CPRD, University of Illinois

Vincent A. Anfara, Jr.
The University of Tennessee

Micki M. Caskey
Portland State University

NMSA
National Middle School Association
Westerville, Ohio

IAP
INFORMATION AGE PUBLISHING

Charlotte, North Carolina • www.infoagepub.com

Library of Congress Cataloging-in-Publication Data

The young adolescent and the middle school / edited by Steven B. Mertens, Vincent A. Anfara, Jr.
p. cm. — (Handbook of research in middle level education)
Includes bibliographical references.
ISBN 978-1-59311-662-0 (pbk.) — ISBN 978-1-59311-663-7 (hardcover)
1. Middle school students—United States. 2. Junior high school students—United States. 3. Adolescence. I. Anfara, Vincent A. II. Mertens, Steven B.
LB1623.Y68 2007
373.180973—dc22

2007010737

ISBN 13: 978-1-59311-662-0 (pbk.)
ISBN 13: 978-1-59311-663-7 (hardcover)
ISBN 10: 1-59311-662-4 (pbk.)
ISBN 10: 1-59311-663-2 (hardcover)

Printed in the United States of America

MLER

MIDDLE LEVEL EDUCATION RESEARCH
SPECIAL INTEREST GROUP

The Handbook of Research in Middle Level Education is endorsed by the Middle Level Education Research Special Interest Group, an affiliate of the American Educational Research Association.

As stated in the organization's Constitution, the purpose of MLER is to improve, promote, and disseminate educational research reflecting early adolescence and middle-level education.

CONTENTS

INTRODUCTION

Vincent A. Anfara, Jr., Steven B. Mertens, and Micki M. Caskey

This volume of the *Handbook of Research in Middle Level Education* marks the sixth installment in the series. The Handbook series, begun in 2001 by Vince Anfara, the series editor, has addressed varying thematic issues important to middle level education research. The five prior volumes have examined current research on the status of the middle school concept (Anfara, 2001), curriculum, instruction, and assessment (Anfara & Stacki, 2002), the professional preparation of teachers and administrators (Andrews & Anfara, 2003), policy implications of middle level research (Thompson, 2004), and the role of action research in improving middle level education (Caskey, 2005). This volume, *The Young Adolescent and the Middle School,* focuses on the unique developmental needs of young adolescents and the role of the middle school in attending to these needs. The contributing authors in this volume address one of three developmental areas critical to young adolescents—physical development, intellectual/cognitive development, or social and personal development—and how these developmental characteristics affect the educational environment and the organization of middle schools.

This introductory chapter presents an overview of the middle school movement, briefly discussing the evolution of the movement, as well as providing descriptions of the seminal works that have guided the move-

The Young Adolescent and the Middle School
pp. ix–xxxiii

ment. We then follow with a discussion of the unique developmental characteristics of young adolescents. These characteristics were recognized and acknowledged over a century ago and much has been written addressing the varying physical, intellectual, and social development of this age group. Lastly, we provide a discussion of our review of the extant literature that deals with the concept of "developmentally appropriate" or "developmentally responsive" middle schools. Here we attempted to address the history of these terms and examine how they have been used in discussions of the education of young adolescents. This examination will assist readers as they advance through each of the chapters contained in this handbook and focus on the integrated nature of young adolescent developmental characteristics and their schooling.

THE MIDDLE SCHOOL MOVEMENT

In 1989, the Carnegie Council on Adolescent Development noted that, "young adolescents face significant turning points" (p. 8). While their report, *Turning Points: Preparing American Youth for the 21st Century,* set the stage for continuing discussion and debate on the nature and character of middle level education, the call for middle level reform was not new. Anthony Jackson (1990), the project director of the Carnegie Task Force, noted, "Nevertheless, some educators have commented that there is very little new in this report. 'We are already doing that' is a common response to many of the recommendations in *Turning Points* from schools across the nation" (p. 1).

The distinctive developmental characteristics of young adolescents—ages 10-14—was recognized over a century ago (Hall, 1904). Earlier reports called attention to the need for something different to happen in the way school in general was organized. Cognizant of this need, the Committee on College Entrance Requirements, commissioned by the National Education Association (1899), wrote, "the most necessary and far-reaching reforms in secondary education must begin in the seventh and eighth grades in our schools" (p. 659). This committee noted that the seventh grade was a "natural turning point in the pupil's life, as the age of adolescence demands new methods and [a] wiser direction" (p. 659). Over time, the developmental characteristics of young adolescents have come to include physical, intellectual, emotional/psychological, social, and moral/ethical development (Kellough & Kellough, 2003; Scales, 1991, 2003).

At the beginning of the last century, there was considerable debate on the merits of the existing eight years of elementary school and four years of secondary schooling (see Gruhn & Douglass, 1956). High dropout rates were blamed on the difficult transition from elementary to high school. The first response to the problematic eight-four organization of schools was the creation of the junior high. Appearing in the first decade of the twentieth century, junior highs were hailed for their ability to prevent dropouts and to prepare students for the job market. The hope was that the curriculum, as well as the students, would be invigorated by the new format.

At the beginning of the 1900s, psychologists, like G. Stanley Hall (1904), noted that schools needed to address the developmental needs of students. Hall's research influenced Americans to accept that the field of education should be grounded in psychology and that adolescence should be given scientific study. Van Til, Vars, and Lounsbury (1961) wrote that, "The development of the new science of individual differences in the early twentieth century provided another justification for the organization of the junior high" (p. 18). In 1918, the Commission on the Reorganization of Secondary Education recommended the new organization in its annual report:

> We, therefore, recommend a reorganization of the school system whereby the first six years shall be devoted to elementary education designed to meet the needs of pupils approximately 6 to 12 years of age, and the second six years to secondary education designed to meet the needs of pupils approximately 12 to 18 years of age. The six years devoted to secondary education may well be divided into two periods, which may be designated as the junior and senior periods. (pp. 12-13)

What is important to remember from this junior high period is the recognition and acknowledgement that schools were to understand and respond to the particular nature of the young adolescent while attempting to continue the influence of the home (see Koos, 1927). According to George and Alexander (2003), "the junior high emerged, originally, as an attempt to satisfy two goals: a richer curriculum than the elementary school was able to offer and a more personal atmosphere than the high school was able to develop" (p. 347). Indeed, the uniqueness of the student provided the foundation on which debates about the nature of the school program would flourish (see Cuban, 1992, for a more thorough treatment of the development of the junior high).

By the 1960s much of the literature on the junior high noted that such schools had turned into "miniature high schools" (Johnson, Dupuis, Musial, & Hall, 1994). Junior highs had become "pale imitations of senior high schools" (Grooms, 1967). The call to reform junior highs was heard as early as the 1920s, within 2 decades of their founding. While the junior high movement was an effort to separate young adolescents and to provide educational programs designed specifically for them, a knowledge base was not available to sustain the uniqueness of the reform movement; thus, the movement gradually gravitated toward a subject orientation, attempted to emulate the organization of the high school, and more closely imitated what had existed in the past (Lewis, 1992). Echoing this assessment, Alexander and George (1981) stated that "unequivocally, many junior high schools became in time almost duplicate copies of their senior high schools in terms of credit and grading systems, methods of teaching, time schedules and student activities, so that sixth graders in June became high school students in September without adequate readiness or maturity" (p. 11). In effect, aided by additional sociological and psychological research during the 1950s and 1960s (e.g., Bossing, 1954; Gruhn & Douglass, 1956; Lounsbury, 1960; Tanner, 1962), educators judged the junior high school organization as inappropriate for young people (ages 10-14) who are psychologically, socially, mentally, emotionally, and physically at a very different place than adolescents. Noar (1961), a junior high educator and advocate of adolescents, stated, "The junior high schools originally founded to meet the need for education on a level intermediate between elementary school and high school have generally been accused of falling short of helping children for whom they are designed" (p. 10). Not surprisingly, by the 1960s the call to reform the junior high had evolved into a call for the creation of the middle school.

It is precisely the uniqueness of these "in-between" years that led many educators, including Eichhorn (1966), to favor the creation of middle schools to serve students in transition from childhood to adolescence. According to Scales (1991), the distinctiveness of this developmental period is characterized by seven needs, including the need for: (1) positive social interaction with adults and peers, (2) structure and clear limits, (3) physical activity, (4) creative expression, (5) competence and achievement, (6) meaningful participation in both family and school, and (7) opportunities for self-definition. Or as Stevenson (1992) stated, "Every child wants to believe in himself or herself as a successful person; every youngster wants to be liked and respected; every youngster wants physical exercise and freedom to move; and youngsters want life to be just" (p. 123).

While middle schools had modest beginnings in the 1950s and early 1960s, their incredible growth in numbers began in the mid- and late-1960s. By the mid-1970s, most of the eastern United States had established programs and facilities that reflected the increased knowledge of the educational needs of young people 10 to 14 years of age. An altered school district organizational pattern—an elementary unit of kindergarten through Grade 5, a middle school grouping of Grades 6 through 8, and a high school unit of Grades 9 through 12—was initiated. Some school districts never fully adopted the idea of a middle school and retained many of their junior highs alongside middle schools that were newly created.

In the midst of this debate, the National Education Association (NEA) (1965) defined middle school as "The school which stands academically between elementary and high school, is housed separately (ideally in a building especially designed for this purpose), and offers at least three years of schooling beginning with either grade five or six" (p. 5). In 1995, the National Middle School Association (NMSA) defined middle schools as "mainly 6-8 schools, but also 5-8, 5-7, and 7-8; based on developmental needs (social and academic) of young adolescents, organized by interdisciplinary teams, with flexible organizational structures, using varied learning and teaching approaches" (p. 1).

Solidifying the Middle School Concept: The Need for a Clear Rationale

In 1969, the Council on the Emerging Adolescent Learner was established by the Association for Supervision and Curriculum Development (ASCD). That council was followed by both formal and informal working groups until 1974 when the Executive Council of ASCD appointed a group and charged them with "developing a paper for the Association identifying the rationale and significance of the American middle school and stressing the kinds of programs appropriate for emerging adolescent learners" (ASCD, 1975, p. v). In 1975, ASCD published *The Middle School We Need* that reasserted the need to develop schools around the needs and characteristics of young adolescents. From this, an increasing number of educators came to realize that the transition from childhood to adolescence required a program of continuous progress education and a broad and flexible curriculum, with appropriate instructional, guidance, and administrative support and implementation.

ASCD (1975) identified a number of variables that they deemed extremely important organizational considerations for the middle school. They viewed middle schools as "taking full cognizance of the dynamic physical, social, and intellectual changes that are occurring in young people during the 10- to 14-year-old span, and providing a program with the major purpose of creating a faciltative climate so that the transescents can understand themselves and the challenges that are occurring within and around them" (p. 6). ASCD suggested that middle schools provide opportunities for innovations and that such innovation might include team teaching, individualized instruction, flexible scheduling, and some form of continuous progress.

In 1973, the National Middle School Association (NMSA) was created. In a 1977 report of its Committee on Future Goals and Directions, the following set of goals for the middle school was presented and subsequently adopted by the association:

1. Every student should be well known as a person by at least one adult in the school who accepts responsibility for his/her guidance.
2. Every student should be helped to achieve optimum mastery of the skills of continued learning together with a commitment to their use and improvement.
3. Every student should have ample experiences designed to develop decision-making and problem-solving skills.
4. Every student should acquire a functional body of fundamental knowledge.
5. Every student should have opportunities to explore and develop interests in aesthetics, leisure, career, and other aspects of life. (p. 16)

Many schools were resistant to implementing the recommendations offered by NMSA or ASCD. In 1975, ASCD revealed that "the available research indicates a significant gap between the main tenets of the theoretical middle school concept proposed by leading middle school authorities and actual educational practices in most middle schools" (p. 3).

In 1982, NMSA released their first position statement, *This We Believe,* which examined the rationale for the middle school and provided a descriptive definition of a middle school. John Swaim, a past president of NMSA stated in the foreword of *This We Believe*, "Because the middle school concept has been implemented in a variety of different ways across the nation, the [National Middle School] Association felt that a clear and relatively complete statement was needed which would reflect the consensus views of the Association regarding the essential elements of middle school education" (p. 1). This position statement presented and discussed the ten essential elements of a "true" middle school

This We Believe has been revised twice, once in 1995 (with the subtitle, *Developmentally Responsive Middle Level Schools*) and again in 2003 (subtitled, *Successful Schools for Young Adolescents*). The 2003 version of this position statement set forth 14 essential elements or characteristics of a successful middle school, including several developmentally responsive characteristics such as curriculum that is relevant and challenging, students and teachers engaged in active learning, and assessment and evaluation programs that promote quality learning (NMSA, 2003).

In 1985, the National Association of Secondary School Principals (NASSP) released *An Agenda for Excellence at the Middle Level,* which described the most successful middle schools as being client oriented. Focusing on 12 areas (e.g., culture and climate, student development, school organization, curriculum, learning and instruction, transition, client-centeredness and connections) this document aimed at building school programs responsive to the needs of students. The dimension entitled "school organization" encourages:

> the smooth operation of the academic program, clear communication among teachers and administrators, and maximum teacher and student control over the quality of the learning environment. The organization of the school should contribute to a sense of belonging on the part of the people who work and learn there, and should mitigate against anonymity and alienation from the primary mission of the school. (NASSP Council on Middle Level Education, 1985, pp. 10-11)

In 1989, the Carnegie Council on Adolescent Development issued its seminal report *Turning Points: Preparing American Youth for the 21st Century* which noted that

> A volatile mismatch exists between the organization and curriculum of middle grade schools and the intellectual and emotional needs of young adolescents. Caught in a vortex of changing demands, the engagement of many youth in learning diminishes, and their rates of alienation, substance abuse, absenteeism, and dropping out of school begin to rise. (pp. 8-9)

In short, *Turning Points* challenged middle schools to be places where close, trusting relationships with adults and peers create a climate for personal growth and intellectual development. Recommendations specific to developmentally appropriate teaching and learning included the creation of small communities for learning, ensuring success for all students, and staffing schools with teachers who are expert at teaching young adolescents (Carnegie Council on Adolescent Development, 1989).

With this information in hand, some middle schools began changing the structure of their programs, adding such components as interdisciplinary teaming and advisory programs. Those most intimately involved with middle schools began referring to these reform components as the middle school concept or philosophy. The middle school movement was grounded in the reality that "the nature and education of young adolescents must be an integrated venture; physical, social, emotional, and intellectual development are each inexorably woven together in the fabric of early adolescent life" (Alexander & McEwin, 1989, p. 1).

George, Stevenson, Thomason, and Beane (1992) observed that something was different about *Turning Points* (1989). "Perhaps because of the public prestige associated with the members of the commission, and because of the quality of work previously completed by other Carnegie groups, *Turning Points* has received a great deal more public attention than earlier studies" (p. 12). Additionally, the Carnegie Council offered grants to 27 states that submitted competitive plans for middle school improvement. These grants helped turn the recommendations into reality—bridging the gap between theory and practice. Middle grades education was suddenly in the spotlight.

Alexander and McEwin (1989) reported that the number of schools organized in a Grade 6 through 8 configuration grew from 1,663 schools in 1970-1971 to 4,329 in 1986-1987—an increase of 160%. According to the National Center for Education Statistics (2000), the number of middle schools increased from 9,086 to 11,712 between 1987-1988 and 1993-1994. This amounts to approximately three middle schools for every junior high in existence. Of the approximately 41.6 million students in public schools in 1993-1994, 6.8 million were enrolled in middle schools. More recently, the organizational arrangements are approximately 1,535 middle schools that have fifth through eighth grades, 9,035 that house sixth through eighth grades, and 2,657 that contain only seventh and eighth grades (NCES, 2003).

Ten years after the publication of *Turning Points*, *Turning Points 2000* (Jackson & Davis, 2000) provided practitioners with "more flesh on the bone" guidance in attempting to implement the middle school concept. A striking, but needed, departure from the original *Turning Points* (Carnegie Council on Adolescent Development, 1989), this publication places more emphasis on curriculum, instruction, and assessment. Some, though, have characterized its recommendations as "less progressive," especially in relation to its lack of emphasis on advisory and exploratory and its heightened emphasis on standards-based curriculum (Brown & Saltman, 2005). While the original report called for teaching a "core of common knowledge," *Turning Points 2000* goes into great detail regarding curriculum, instruction, and assessment that are developmentally appropriate. "Ensuring the success of *every* student" is now the overarching goal for Carnegie's recommendations for exemplary middle schools. This change helps to emphasize the fact that the reform model was never meant to be a smorgasbord from which middle school practitioners could pick and choose.

In 2003, NMSA revised and expanded its position statement in *This We Believe: Successful Schools for Young Adolescents*. In addition to the six characteristics introduced in the second edition (NMSA, 1995), two new characteristics—courageous, collaborative leadership and students and teachers engaged in active learning—were added. In addition to updating its position statement, NMSA decided that there was a need for an accompanying volume describing the research supporting the tenets of *This We Believe*. *Research and Resources in Support of This We Believe* (Anfara, Andrews, Hough, Mertens, Mizelle, & White, 2003) was written by the NMSA Research Committee (now Research Advisory Board) and summarized the existing research, in addition to providing annotated bibliographies and resources for practitioners interested in implementing the middle school concept.

Most recently, *Breaking Ranks in the Middle: Strategies for Leading Middle Level Reform* (2006) was published by the National Association of Secondary School Principals (NASSP) as a follow up to their highly acclaimed, *Breaking Ranks II* (NASSP, 2004) which contained a set of national recommendations for reforming American high schools. The nine strategies and 30 recommendations that form the core of *Breaking Ranks in the Middle* are similar to those in *Breaking Ranks II,* but are grounded in the middle school philosophy. A commission of middle level practitioners and experts had an active hand in developing the book, which includes a number of full-length profiles and vignettes of schools that have attempted to successfully implement its recommendations.

Collectively, these reports, based on a myriad of philosophical, ideological, and political arguments, support a very consistent collection of ideas about what constitutes a "good middle school"—interdisciplinary teaming, small learning communities, flexible scheduling, advisory periods, among others. While it seems common sense to assume that schools would respond to the needs of their students and create developmentally appropriate learning environments, it is evident from the history of middle level reform that schools are slow to change. Capelluti and Stokes (1991) reminded:

> Although there is considerable knowledge about the characteristics and interests of early adolescents, this information has not at all times been reflected in what and how we teach these students. These differences are, in fact, the foundation upon which the middle school level is based. It is this uniqueness that provides the rationale and justification for creating a middle level school as a distinct entity within a school system. (p. iii)

While much attention has been afforded both elementary and secondary levels of schooling, more interest (and the necessary resources) must be given to the education of young adolescents at this critical period in their development, inclusive of cognitive and affective needs. Let us turn now to an examination of these developmental characteristics.

DEVELOPMENTAL CHARACTERISTICS OF YOUNG ADOLESCENTS

In *This We Believe* (1982, 1995, 2003), the National Middle School Association consistently articulated that schools for young adolescents must be developmentally appropriate. In a similar vein, Lipsitz (1984) maintained that "to succeed with young adolescents, schools must be responsive to their developmental needs" (p. 6). In delineating these developmental needs, one runs the risk of over generalization and over simplification. Addressing this concern, Kellough and Kellough (2003) noted that generalizations could be risky; however, researchers, experts, and practitioners have come to agree upon a set of common developmental characteristics that prove useful to understanding youth between the ages of 10 to 14.

Typically, these developmental characteristics are organized and described in five categories: physical, intellectual, emotional/psychological, social, and moral/ethical. Scales (2003) emphasizes that "the categories to which these developmental characteristics are assigned—psychological development rather than social, emotional, or cognitive rather than moral—are sometimes relatively arbitrary (pp. 43-44). Therefore, it is important to recognize that the characteristics contained in each of these categories are interconnected and have implications to developmentally appropriate practice.

Physical Development

Rapid and uneven changes in physical development exemplify young adolescence (California State Department of Education, 1987; Kellough & Kellough, 2003; Scales, 2003). Young adolescents experience accelerated physical development marked by increases in weight, height, heart size, lung capacity, and muscular strength. In addition, they have uneven muscle and bone development, which can result in the lack of coordination and awkwardness. Bones may lack the protection of covering muscles and supporting tendons leading to actual "growing pains." Young adolescents often feel disadvantaged due to varied rates of maturity and feel uncomfortable about the differences in maturity by gender (Simmons & Blyth, 1987). For example, girls tend to mature one to two years earlier than boys do (Caissy, 1994). Young adolescents are also concerned about noticeable changes such as the development of secondary sex characteristics and increases in nose size, protruding ears, and long arms. Their digestive systems are often overtaxed with large quantities of improper or unusual foods. Further, they are physically vulnerable because they may adopt poor health habits or engage in risky experimentation with drugs and sexual activity.

Intellectual Development

Young adolescents display a wide range of individual intellectual development (California State Department of Education, 1987; Kellough & Kellough, 2003; Manning, 2002; Milgram, 1992; Scales, 2003) and begin the transition from concrete to abstract thought processes (Elkind, 1974; Flavell, 1963; Piaget, 1952, 1960). Though intellectual changes are less visible than physical, they are just as profound (Stevenson, 2002; Van Hoose, Strahan, & L'Esperance, 2001). During these years, young adolescents develop their reasoning and problem-solving skills, become appreciative of more sophisticated levels of humor, and understand subtle nuances and idiosyncrasies. They are inclined to consider ideological issues, formulate and defend a position, and challenge adult authority (Stevenson). They are capable of interpreting broad concepts and traditional wisdom expressed through sayings, axioms, and aphorisms (Kellough & Kellough). Many are egocentric, intensely curious, and experience metacognition for the first time.

Young adolescents draw on their individual experiences and background knowledge to make sense of the world around them, yet their schema differs from those of adults (Piaget, 1960). Similarly, they may be less interested in conventional academic subjects and want to explore those topics they consider interesting and useful. They are most interested in participating in real life experiences such as service learning. The changes in intellectual development allow young adolescents to think about the future as well as anticipate and develop personal goals (Kellough & Kellough, 2003).

Moral/Ethical Development

With regard to moral/ethical development, young adolescents are generally idealistic and possess a strong sense of fairness. As they progress through stages of moral development (Kohlberg, 1983), young adolescents reconcile their understanding of people who care about them (Roney, 2005). They transition from self-interest to considering the feelings and rights of others, making them interested in participatory democracy. This age group often shows compassion for disadvantaged individuals and groups and exhibits concern for animals and environmental problems. It is during this period of human development that young adolescents form personal values, which tend to be in harmony with their parent's values. They begin to consider moral matters in shades of grey rather than in black and white. They also face hard moral and ethical questions but are often unprepared to cope with the complexities.

Ironically, while they are aware of flaws in others, they are often slow to acknowledge their own (Scales, 2003). Finally, young adolescents are reflective, introspective, and analytical about their thoughts and feelings.

Emotional/Psychological Development

Changes in emotional/psychological development lead young adolescents to experience mood swings often characterized by peaks of intensity and unpredictability (Caissy, 1994). They may exhibit erratic and inconsistent behavior—feeling anxious and fearful, or brave and bold (Kellough & Kellough, 2003). Feelings can often shift between superiority and inferiority. During this time, young adolescents seek independence and an adult identity (Erikson, 1993; Scales, 2003). This search for identity and self-discovery can lead young adolescents to be easily offended and be sensitive to criticism of personal shortcomings. At this age, they seek their own identity and acceptance even in the midst of intense peer-group relationships (Kellough & Kellough). Many young adolescents feel psychologically at risk because they as they face so much diversity in relation to self and others (Scales). Much of this is attributed to chemical and hormonal imbalances that trigger frightening and poorly understood emotions. This is why it is not uncommon to observe childish behavior patterns, exaggeration of simple occurrences, and vulnerability to naive opinions and one-sided arguments among young adolescents.

Social Development

Young adolescents have a strong need to belong to a group (Scales, 2003). Changes in social development cause young adolescents to experience traumatic conflicts because of opposing loyalties to peer group and family (Manning, 2002). This is why they experiment with new slang and behaviors as they search for a social position within their group (Caissy, 1994). Young adolescents model behavior after older, esteemed students or non-parent adults (Scales), and want to make their own choices, but still rely on family values for critical and/or final decisions (Manning). Often, they overreact to situations, ridicule others, express embarrassment, and feel rejection (Scales). It is important that they seek positive social relationships with members of the same and opposite sex under the guidance of caring and trustworthy adults. These changes can put young adolescents at risk of becoming socially vulnerable because the influence of media and negative experiences with adults and peers may compromise their emergent ideals and values (Scales). A heightened sense of the negative impact of young adolescent behavior on parents and teachers is apparent, and young adolescents are quick to realize the thin edge between tolerance and rejection. Feelings of adult rejection can drive the adolescent into the relatively secure, but sometimes negative and risky, social environment of peer group.

We turn now to the next section of this introduction. Here we look at how the developmental needs of young adolescents influence the organization and educational program of the middle school. We begin this last section with a critical examination of what many of the early writers offered regarding developmentally appropriate practices.

DEVELOPMENTALLY RESPONSIVE MIDDLE GRADES SCHOOLS

After focusing our discussion on the middle school and the young adolescent our challenge is to examine how these two intersect in the practices and organization of "developmentally appropriate" or "developmentally responsive" middle schools. Essentially, we need to address what it means to be "developmentally responsive." Though this phrase has been widely used, we are less certain that a common definition is widely held. The National Middle School Association included this phrase in the subtitle to an earlier version of its position statement, *This We Believe: Developmentally Responsive Middle Level Schools*, published in 1995. A serious concern is that the definition and translation of this phrase to teaching, learning, and organizing students for schooling have been less than sufficient. This position is supported by Manning (1993) who wrote:

> Researchers and writers have suggested that learners' developmental levels should provide the basis for school curricular and instructional practices, as well as the overall teaching-learning environment. While developmental psychologists have offered insightful theories about physical, psychosocial and cognitive development, the process of translating them into practice has been somewhat slow, especially beyond the elementary school years. (p. iii)

To begin our journey of trying to understand how the nature of young adolescence affects schooling, we need to turn our attention to many of the early writers who spoke very clearly on this issue. Indeed, the interrelationship between learner and school were fundamental to the question of school effectiveness according to writers like Donald Eichhorn, M. Ann Grooms, John Lounsbury, Gordon Vars, James Bondi, and William Alexander, to name only a few. From the early 1960s to the 1980s, middle grades scholars noted that much was known about who these young adolescents are, but questions remained about what teachers should know about them, what practices should be employed to facilitate teaching and learning, and what structures need to be created to establish an appropriate learning environment. They advised those interested in middle grades education to consider the school's relationship with the learner by carefully examining two factors: the school environment and the educational program. The middle school should serve the unique physical, psychosocial and cognitive needs of young adolescents by providing developmentally appropriate curriculum and instruction, and environmental experiences. A brief review of these two factors follows.

Focusing on the school environment, Eichhorn (1980) noted four qualities that he deemed essential to addressing the needs of the young adolescent. These included: (1) a fluid, but structured atmosphere, (2) a friendly climate, (3) an active and dynamic climate, and (4) an emphasis on learning. On the first of these qualities, Eichhorn wrote:

> The mercurial nature of the transescent learner requires a fluid but structured atmosphere. It should provide students with the security of structure, but it should be sufficiently elastic to permit students to explore learning and socialization in a manner consistent with individual needs. Since youth in the middle years are seeking greater independence, there should be provisions for activities that allow students to accept challenges and for help in meeting those challenges. (p. 67)

Eichhorn (1980), noting that friendliness is a needed element in the school climate, stated "When a friendly relationship exists, the increased interaction between teachers, administrators, counselors, secretaries, and custodians enables students to develop needed competencies to meet successfully their emotional peaks and valleys" (p. 67). In essence, he called on the teachers, administrators, and staff to model good human relations.

Eichhorn (1980) goes on to discuss that the school climate should be active and dynamic. A variety of learning experiences should be provided as young adolescents pursue their curiosity and grow intellectually. It is desirable to have flexibility that will permit students to avail themselves of learning activities at the time of actual need. Finally, an aura of learning (i.e., academic emphasis) should permeate the school. Bondi (1972) noted, "The general atmosphere relating to students should be one of recognizing that each student is in the process of becoming a better functioning, more mature human being. Each should be treated and accepted as a responsible individual" (p. 9). Pumerantz and Galano (1972) characterized the middle school climate as "free and flexible." They emphasized that students and teachers should move away from the rigid time allotments and qualities like teacher and textbook domination of learning.

The second factor involves the middle schools' educational program. In order to be developmentally responsive, this factor is characterized as:

(1) facilitating the acquisition of essential learning skills in a sequential and individual manner, (2) showing the interrelationships of knowledge, (3) exploratory, and (4) concerned about personal development through appropriate guidance and counseling.

According to Eichhorn (1980), Grooms (1967), Alexander and Williams (1965), Howard and Stoumbis (1970), and Bondi (1972), the educational program should be characterized by the acquisition of essential learning skills in a sequential and individual manner. Alexander, Williams, Compton, Hines, and Prescott (1968) were insistent that systematic instruction must be provided in all middle schools and at all levels in English, mathematics, science, and social studies. This call for a core curriculum or common learnings (see Lounsbury & Vars, 1978; Vars, 1969) was linked with the need to respond to the diverse achievement levels, cognitive styles, and varied competencies and interests that characterize young adolescent learners. Howard and Stoumbis commented, "The program of the middle school must be especially designed to serve the educational needs of a school population that has a wide range of differences in many traits" (p. 247).

The call for essential learning skills also included skills that foster continued learning (Lounsbury & Vars, 1978). These included reading, listening, asking questions, viewing visual aids, using library tools and resources, observing the natural and social environment, organizing information, generalizing from observations and readings, evaluating information and opinions, and problem solving.

Another common element of the educational program deals with the interrelationships of knowledge and the presentation (teaching) of skills and concepts in a practical problem-solving context to enhance learning. Students should be involved in learning in a peer relationship that aids socialization. The exploration of content is also an important element. Elective, exploratory, and activity programs permit student to explore their interests.

The fourth element involves personal development. The developmentally responsive middle school provides for guidance and counseling through advisory programs, curriculum, and specialized help. According to Alexander et al. (1968), personal development included counseling and referral, development of values, health and physical development, individual interests (a pattern of special-interest activities that includes exploratory experiences, laboratory courses, and the activity program).

Brunetti (1969) reported that the implications that student developmental characteristics have for the middle school program result in "a rejection of standardized curricula, grouping practices, and instructional methods. Most recent developments have emphasized a program of exploratory experiences centered in a flexible curriculum" (p. 2). According-ing to Brunetti, the middle school should provide two kinds of experiences for its students: those common to all students, and those experiences that are highly individualized and diverse. In so doing, the middle school stresses the continual development of fundamental skills and aids in the beginnings of specialization.

Grooms (1967) and Pumerantz and Galano (1972) noted that the content of the curricula differs in that it is determined by students and professional staff members rather than by tradition, textbooks, and courses of study. It is intended to encourage student inquiry, problem analysis, and decision making. The curricula should stress student investigation, questioning, conception of new approaches, evaluation of possible courses of action, and decisions as to which procedures to follow.

Alexander and Williams (1965) stressed individualized instruction, nongrading, diagnostic services to permit divergence from standard programs by individuals, scheduling of pupils to special instructional centers, and use of individually paced materials such as programmed learning. They called for program of common learning that focuses on social studies, languages, mathematics, science, and the fine arts. Further, they recommended a strong exploratory program along with health and physical education that would be designed especially for students of this age. Plainly, students would not move at the same speed through content to be learned.

More recent scholarship (Irvin, 1992; Manning, 1993) concerning the nature of developmental responsiveness is consistent with the early writings, which noted that middle level educators must consider young adolescents' unique developmental needs when planning learning experiences. Young adolescents should be provided with:

- Opportunities to work cooperatively in groups (meeting social needs);
- Vehicles for connecting new information to what is already known, thus helping them feel more confident about their learning ability and about their own experiences (meeting intellectual and emotional needs);
- Experiences in abstract thinking that help them move gradually and successfully from concrete to abstract levels of reasoning (meeting intellectual needs);
- Opportunities to move and change activities (meeting physical needs);
- Experiences designed to help them feel better about themselves as learners (meeting socioemotional needs); and

- Motivation to learn through use of strategies that heighten their curiosity about learning (meeting intellectual needs) (Irvin).

Later literature (Beane, 1990; Manning, 1993; National Association of Secondary School Principals, 1993) reiterated that developmentally appropriate middle level school curricula should focus on skills and attitudes such as communicating, computing and researching; reflective thinking; identifying and judging the morality of problem situations; problem-solving; valuing; forming self-concept and self-esteem; developing social action skills (e.g., acting on a problem situation both individually and collectively); and searching for completeness and meaning. Students should acquire skills needed for continued learning (reading, listening, research); organizing for action (planning, group process, leadership); understanding the universality of the human condition (personal fulfillment in various times, places and conditions); understanding cultures and differences among peoples; artistic expression (art, music, dance); systematic study of change and its effect on society; and productive thinking, systematic reasoning and evaluation of information. The curriculum should challenge students at their respective ability levels, providing a clear articulation between elementary and secondary levels, and responds to the immediate concerns of the young adolescent learner. Attempting to connect the theoretical knowledge of young adolescent development with the world of practice in middle schools, prompts a focus on the implications for teaching and learning that are grounded in young adolescents' developmental needs.

Implications for Practice

Physical development

Because physical characteristics can affect learning, teachers are encouraged to discuss with students the natural developmental changes that are common to the human experience (Van Hoose et al., 2001; Wiles & Bondi, 2001; Wiles, Bondi, & Wiles, 2006). In addition to needing information about these physical changes, young adolescents need frequent opportunities for physical movement accompanied by rest and change of activity (George & Alexander, 1993). Competition between early and late maturing students needs to be minimized; instead, schools should offer educational experiences in nutrition, exercise, and other healthful behaviors. Further, schools should provide appropriate instruction on drugs use, pregnancy, and sexually transmitted diseases. Young adolescents need access to accurate sources of information about how their bodies are changing and differences between their changes and their peers. Classroom teachers need to provide active learning experiences—role-playing, simulations, and service learning rather than passive activities and provide learning experiences that promote student involvement and collaboration.

Intellectual Development

When planning instruction for young adolescents, teachers need to consider their varying intellectual development and individual differences by providing learning experiences that are appropriate for students' cognitive levels. Young adolescents "have their own ideas, and for us to have a true intellectual relationship with them, we need to understand and respect how they think" (Stevenson, 2002, p. 97). Teachers need to provide a continuum of learning experiences to address the variability among students. Concrete thinkers require teachers to scaffold learning experiences, while abstract thinkers need opportunities to experience higher order thinking skills and cause-effect relationships (Wiles & Bondi, 2001). Teachers are encouraged to provide authentic learning experience for students (e.g., analysis and synthesis of data, problem solving, and experimentation), and allow students to explore the reasons for school and home rules. Stevenson notes:

> Early adolescent intellectual development is enhanced when youngsters actively explore their world by having first hand interactions with people and objects in their environment: talking, working with adults and classmates, using objects such as tools, and organizing personal experience. They construct their knowledge (schemas) through such experiences. (p. 100)

All educators should recognize students' changing interests and adapt educational experiences accordingly, as well as understand the connection between intellectual and moral reasoning.

Moral/Ethical Development

Rather than critique young adolescent moral development, middle grades educators need to understand the complexities of moral development and capitalize on the relationship between intellectual and moral reasoning. For example, when teachers are planning they need to address both higher order thinking skills and higher levels of moral reasoning. In doing so, teachers should provide opportunities for students to consider moral and ethical dilemmas in social and personal situations. Teachers should also provide opportunities for students to explore concepts of justice and equity, and they should provide opportunities for students to examine issues such as racism, sexism, and discrimination (see Van Hoose et al.; Wiles & Bondi, 2001).

Emotional/Psychological Development

Schools are encouraged to provide young adolescents with opportunities to form relationships with adults who understand and are willing to support their development. It is incumbent on caring adults to help young adolescents understand that shifting allegiances are normal developmental occurrences. Adults should serve as role models demonstrating the importance of friendships for positive psychological development. Adults can help young adolescents understand that self-esteem affects nearly all aspects of their development. Therefore, schools must provide opportunities through curricular experiences, organizational patterns, instructional approaches, exploratory programs, and advisory programs to foster success and build students' self-esteem.

Social Development

Because of the dramatic social changes, one can readily understand the difficulty teachers and parents experience when working with young adolescents who are becoming closely associated with new peer groups. All adults charged with the education and well-being of young adolescents must influence them in positive and constructive ways. To do this, adults must understand the importance of young adolescent friendships and the impact on their positive social development. In fact, parents and teachers can help young adolescents to understand that their pursuits of freedom and independence should not lead to dangerous or unsafe practices. To help young adolescents handle social situations, teachers are encouraged to provide educational experiences such as role-plays, simulations, and debates. It is also important to recognize gender differences in socialization and friendship formation without generalizing or stereotyping. Schools can plan gender responsive social situations or collaborative interactions to address this emergent social growth.

CONCLUSION

"The education of young adolescents must be an integrative venture: physical, social, emotional, and intellectual development are inexorably woven together in the fabric of early adolescent life" (NASSP, 1989, p.1). The middle school movement emerged due to the recognition and acknowledgement that young adolescents had unique developmental needs. Over the past century, this educational movement has attempted to implement restructuring and reform efforts to provide young adolescents with a more developmentally appropriate learning experience and environment. To what extent have middle schools and the recommendations offered by various educational organizations and researchers met the developmental—physical, intellectual, and social—needs of young adolescents? It is our hope that the contributing authors in this volume will answer to some extent this fundamental and ever-present question.

ORGANIZATION OF THE HANDBOOK

The chapters in this volume address one of three areas critical to young adolescent development: physical, intellectual/cognitive, or social and personal. The first three chapters focus on the physical development of young adolescents. Mulhall discusses the issue of health integration and discusses the benefits of heath practices that promote high performing middle grades schools. In chapter 2, Fisher and Madeson address a much overlooked topic, that of young adolescents and sport and physical activity. Their chapter examines the psychological implications and effects of these activities on young adolescent development. Caskey and Ruben (chapter 3) review neuroscience research literature that is relevant to young adolescent brain development and report the findings for access by academics and practitioners.

Chapters 4 through 7 address varying aspects of the intellectual/cognitive development of young adolescents. Falk-Ross (chapter 4) examines the role of language in literacy achievement, specifically how it occurs in classroom interaction routines, language patterns and its relationship to content reading, and ways to address challenges for struggling readers. The degree to which the middle level learner and the middle level school "fit" directly impacts students' motivation, performance, and behavior is discussed in chapter 5 by Bishop, Allen-Malley, and Brinegar. This qualitative study of student perceptions examines a middle school team employing an integrative curriculum model. In chapter 6, Tomlinson and Murphy deal with the often controversial topic of gifted learning; they discuss the challenges faced by young adolescents who, while highly able academically, share the same developmental issues as all other middle grades students. Mee's case study in chapter 7 explores students' perceptions of the influences of Socratic Seminar on their motivation for learning. Four characteristics of motivation are examined—attention, relevancy, confidence, and satisfaction.

Aspects of young adolescent social or personal development are examined in the chapters in the last section. Anderman and Leake (chapter 8) review empirical research examining middle school students' sense of belonging in social groups and their sense of connectedness to others. Characteristics of school and family settings that are likely to promote a sense of belonging are also described. The unique characteristics that middle school counselors must possess in order to be developmentally and contextually responsive to young adolescent needs are discussed by Akos in chapter 9. Brinthaupt, Lipka, and Wallace (chapter 10) review and critically analyze the research literature relevant to the alignment of student self and identity characteristics with middle school practices. They examine the extent to which developmentally appropriate practices, in-school and out-of-school programs, and characteristics and qualities of teachers, administrators, and support staff align with the self and identity needs of young adolescents. Chapter 11, by Brown and Leaman, presents theories and research that describe how ethnically diverse adolescents' search for identity is influenced by the majority culture, school experiences, and their own ethnic backgrounds. Research focusing on immigrant and refugee students in middle school settings is discussed by Virture (chapter 12) where he also highlights the ways organizational structures and cultural characteristics impact the processes of acculturation and student identity development. Employing a mixed methods design, Spielhagen (chapter 13) explores single-sex academic classes in a small middle school to examine perceptions of this organization approach and to explore the extent to which the reform affected student achievement. Issues related to the transition from middle school to high school are discussed by Smith and Lim (chapter 14). Employing a transformative research process, they examine student expectations and experiences in the academic, social, organization, and school support aspects of the middle/high school transition. Through an in-depth case study, Rishel (chapter 15) tackles the difficult topic of young adolescent suicide. She discusses how home and school problems contributed to a cycle of despair, depression, and suicide and how the middle school educational setting can ameliorate these effects. In chapter 16, Vagle presents a theoretical discussion of the qualities middle school teachers must possess in order to create both dignified and democratic classrooms. Lastly, Schoolwide Positive Behavior Support, a research-based framework, for addressing the numerous challenges to healthy social development during the middle school years, is examined and discussed by Borgmeier (chapter 17).

Collectively, these chapters provide middle school advocates, practitioners, and policy makers with research focusing on the physical, intellectual/cognitive, and social and personal development of young adolescents.

REFERENCES

Alexander, W., & George, P. (1981). *The exemplary middle school.* New York: Holt, Reinhart, and Winston.

Alexander, W., & McEwin, C. (1989). *Schools in the middle: Progress* 1968-1988. *NASSP schools in the middle: A report on trends and practices*. Reston, VA: National Association of Secondary School Principals.

Alexander, W. M., & Williams, E. L. (1965). Schools for the middle years. *Educational Leadership, 23*(3), 217-223.

Alexander, W. M., Williams, E. L., Compton, M., Hines, V. A., & Prescott, D. (1968). *The emergent middle school*. New York: Holt.

Andrews, P. G., & Anfara, V. A., Jr. (Eds.). (2003). *The handbook of research in middle level education: Vol. 3. Leaders for a movement: Professional preparation and development of middle level teachers and administrators*. Greenwich, CT: Information Age Publishing.

Anfara, V. A., Jr. (Ed.). (2001). *The handbook of research in middle level education*. Greenwich, CT: Information Age Publishing.

Anfara, V. A., Jr., Andrews, P. G., Hough, D. L., Mertens, S. B., Mizelle, N. B., & White, G. P. (2003). *Research and resources in support of This We Believe*. Westerville, OH: National Middle School Association.

Anfara, V. A., Jr., & Stacki, S. L. (Eds.). (2002). *The handbook of research in middle level education: Vol. 2. Middle school curriculum, instruction, and assessment*. Greenwich, CT: Information Age Publishing.

Association for Supervision and Curriculum Development. (1975). *The middle school we need*. Washington, DC: Author.

Beane, J. A. (1990). *Affect in the curriculum: Toward democracy, dignity, and diversity*. New York: Teacher College Press.

Bondi, J. (1972). *Developing middle schools: A guidebook*. New York: MSS Information Corporation.

Bossing, N. (1954). A junior high designed for tomorrow. *The ClearingHouse, 9*, 3-7.

Brown, E. R., & Saltman, K. J. (Eds.). (2005). *The critical middle school reader*. New York: Routledge.

Brunetti, F. (1969).The school in the middle—A search for new direction. *School Planning Laboratory Reports*, 2.

Caissy, G. A. (1994). *Early adolescents: Understanding the 10 to 15 year olds*. Reading, MA: Perseus Books.

California State Department of Education. (1987). *Caught in the middle: Educational reform for young adolescents in California public schools*. Sacramento, CA: Author.

Capelluti, J., & Stokes, D. (1991). *Middle level education programs, policies, and practices*. Reston, VA: National Association of Secondary School Principals.

Carnegie Council on Adolescent Development. (1989). *Turning points: Preparing American youth for the 21st century*. New York: Carnegie Corporation of New York.

Caskey, M. M. (Ed.). (2005). *The handbook of research in middle level education: Vol. 5. Making a difference: Action research in middle level education*. Greenwich, CT: Information Age Publishing.

Commission on the Reorganization of Secondary Education. (1918). *Cardinal principles of secondary education*. Washington, DC: Department of the Interior, Bureau of Education.

Cuban, L. (1992). What happens to reforms that last? The case of the junior high school. *American Educational Research Journal, 29*(1), 227-251.

Eichhorn, D. (1966). *The middle school.* New York: Center for Applied Research in Education.

Eichhorn, D. H. (1980). The school. In M. Johnson (Ed.), *Toward adolescence: The Middle school years* (pp. 56-73). Chicago: University of Chicago Press.

Elkind, D. (1974). *Children and adolescents: Interpretative essay on Jean Piaget.* New York: Oxford University Press.

Erikson, E. (1993). *Childhood and society* (reissue ed.). New York: W. W. Norton.

Flavell, J. H. (1963). *The developmental psychology of Jean Piaget.* Princeton, NJ: Van Nostrand Reinhold.

George, P. S., & Alexander, W. M. (1993). *The exemplary middle school* (2nd ed.). Fort Worth, TX: Harcourt Brace.

George, P. S., & Alexander, W. M. (2003). *The exemplary middle school* (3rd ed.). Belmont, CA: Wadsworth/Thomson Learning.

George, P., Stevenson, C., Thomason, J., & Beane, J. (1992). *The middle school: And beyond.* Alexandria, VA: Association for Supervision and Curriculum Development.

Grooms, M. (1967). *Perspectives on the middle school.* Cincinnati, OH: Merrill.

Gruhn, W., & Douglass, H. (1956). *The modern junior high school* (2nd ed.). New York: Ronald Press.

Hall, G. (1904). *Adolescence: Its psychology and its relations to physiology, anthropology, sociology, sex, crime, religion and education*. New York: Appleton & Co.

Howard, A. W., & Stoumbis, G. C. (1970). *The junior high and middle school: Issues and practices*. Scranton, OH: Intext Educational.

Irvin, J. L. (1992). *Transforming middle level education: Perspectives and possibilities*. Boston: Allyn & Bacon.

Jackson, A. (1990). From knowledge to practice: Implementing the recommendations of *Turning Points. Middle School Journal, 21*(3), 1-3.

Jackson, A. W., & Davis, G. (2000). *Turning points 2000: Educating adolescents in the 21st century.* New York: Teachers College Press.

Johnson, J., Dupuis, Y., Musial, D., & Hall, G. (1994). *Introduction to the foundations of American education.* Needham Heights, MA: Allyn & Bacon.

Kellough, R. D., & Kellough, N. G. (2003). *Teaching young adolescents: A guide to methods and resources* (4th ed.). Upper Saddle River, NJ: Merrill Prentice Hall.

Kohlberg, L. (1983). *The psychology of moral development.* New York: Harper & Row.

Koos, L. (1927). *The junior high school.* Boston, MA: Ginn.

Lewis, A. (1992). Middle schools come to age. *Education Digest, 58*(2), 4-7.

Lipsitz, J. (1984). *Successful schools for young adolescents.* New Brunswick, NJ: Transaction Books.

Lounsbury, J. (1960). How the junior high school came to be. *Educational Leadership, 18,* 145- 47.

Lounsbury, J. H., & Vars, G. F. (1978). *A curriculum for the middle school years*. New York: Harper & Row.

Manning, M. L. (1993). *Developmentally appropriate middle level schools.* Wheaton, MD: Association for Childhood Educational International.

Manning, M. L. (2002). *Developmentally appropriate middle level schools* (2nd ed.). Olney, MD: Association for Childhood Education International.

Milgram, J. (1992). A portrait of diversity: The middle level student. In J. Irvin, (Ed.), *Transforming middle level education: Perspectives and possibilities* (pp. 16-27). Needham Heights, MA: Allyn & Bacon.

National Association of Secondary School Principals Council on Middle Level Education. (1985). *An agenda for excellence at the middle level*. Reston, VA: National Association of Secondary School Principals.

National Association of Secondary School Principals. (1989). *Middle level educators' responsibilities for intellectual development*. Reston, VA: Author.

National Association of Secondary School Principals. (1993). *Achieving excellence through middle level curriculum*. Reston, VA: Author.

National Association of Secondary School Principals. (2004). *Breaking ranks II: Strategies for leading high school reform*. Reston, VA: Author.

National Association of Secondary School Principals. (2006). *Breaking ranks in the middle: Strategies for leading middle level reform*. Reston, VA: Author.

National Center for Education Statistics. (2000). *In the middle: Characteristics of public schools with a focus on middle schools*. Washington, DC: U.S. Department of Education.

National Center for Education Statistics. (2003). *Core of common data, 2003*. Washington, DC U.S. Department of Education.

National Education Association. (1899). *Journal of proceedings and addresses*. Denver, CO: Author.

National Education Association. (1965). *Middle schools*. Washington, DC: Author.

National Middle School Association. (1977). Report of the NMSA Committee on Future Goals and Directions. *Middle School Journal, 8*, 16.

National Middle School Association. (1982). *This we believe*. Columbus, OH: Author.

National Middle School Association. (1995). *This we believe: Developmentally responsive middle schools*. Columbus, OH: Author.

National Middle School Association. (2003). *This we believe: Successful schools for young adolescents*. Westerville, OH: Author.

Noar, G. (1961). *Junior high school: Today and tomorrow*. Englewood Cliffs, NJ: Prentice Hall.

Piaget, J. (1952). *The origins of intelligence in children*. New York: International University Press.

Piaget, J. (1960). *The child's conception of the world*. Atlantic Highlands, NJ: Humanities Press.

Pumerantz, P., & Galano, R. W. (1972). *Establishing interdisciplinary programs in the middle school*. West Nyack, NY: Parker.

Roney, K. (2005). Young adolescent development. In V. A. Anfara, Jr., G. Andrews, & S. B. Mertens (Eds.), *The encyclopedia of middle grades education* (pp. 397-401). Greenwich, CT: Information Age Publishing.

Scales, P. (1991). *A portrait of young adolescents in the 1990s: Implications for promoting healthy growth and development*. Minneapolis, MN: Search Institute/Center for Early Adolescence.

Scales, P. C. (2003). Characteristics of young adolescents. In National Middle School Association, *This we believe: Successful schools for young adolescents* (pp. 43-51). Westerville, OH: National Middle School Association.

Simmons, R., & Blyth, D. A. (1987). *Moving into adolescence: The impact of pubertal change and the school context.* New York: Aldine de Gruyter Press.

Stevenson, C. (1992). *Teaching ten to fourteen year olds.* White Plains, NY: Longman.

Stevenson, C. (2002). *Teaching ten to fourteen year olds* (3rd ed.). Boston: Allyn & Bacon.

Tanner, J. (1962). *Growth at adolescence.* Oxford, England: Blackwell Scientific Publications.

Thompson, S. C. (Ed.). (2004). *The handbook of research in middle level education: Vol. 4. Reforming middle level education: Considerations for policymakers.* Greenwich, CT: Information Age Publishing.

Van Hoose, J., Strahan, D., & L'Esperance, M. (2001). *Promoting harmony: Young adolescent development and school practices.* Westerville, OH: National Middle School Association.

Van Til, W., Vars, G., & Lounsbury, J. (1961). *Modern education for the junior high school years.*Indianapolis, IN: Bobbs-Merill.

Vars, G. F. (1969). A contemporary view of the core curriculum. In G. F. Vars (Ed.), *Common learnings: Core and interdisciplinary team approaches* (pp. 5-18). Scranton, PA: International Textbook.

Wiles, J., & Bondi, J. (2001). *The new American middle school: Educating preadolescents in an era of change* (3rd ed.). Upper Saddle River, NJ: Pearson Prentice Hall.

Wiles, J., Bondi, J., & Wiles, M. T. (2006). *The essential middle school* (4th ed.). Upper Saddle River, NJ: Pearson Prentice Hall.

CHAPTER 1

HEALTH PROMOTING, HIGH PERFORMING MIDDLE LEVEL SCHOOLS

The Interrelationships and Integration of Health and Education for Young Adolescent Success and Well-Being

Peter F. Mulhall

ABSTRACT

The positive relationship between health and education suggests that they are highly integrated. Whether better educated people are more likely to engage in health promoting behaviors or healthy people have the personal resources to attain a higher levels of education is unclear. However, research continuously shows that young adolescence is the time when most children begin making decisions regarding health behaviors as well as their aspirations and expectations about their education and sense of future. Middle level schools can play an integral role in helping young adolescents navigate the challenges and vulnerabilities confronting them as they pass through

The Young Adolescent and the Middle School
pp. 1–26

this phase in life. Based on the current educational and health status of young adolescents to date, neither system has been successful in meeting their needs. This chapter describes the relationships between health and education, vulnerabilities and developmental challenges of young adolescents, the numerous and narrowly focused strategies that view health and education independently, and recommended researched-based programs, policies, and practices that integrate health and education in an effort to maximize the likelihood for improving middle level schools for students, teachers, and families.

"Good health supports successful learning. Successful learning supports health. Education and health are inseparable."

—Desmond O'Byrne (World Health Organization, 2004)

BACKGROUND

The critical role of middle level schools, typically Grades 5-8, in the transformation of children to adolescence and on to adulthood has been widely recognized in the research literature (Jackson & Davis, 2000; Takanishi & Hamburg, 1997). Middle level schools serve young adolescents as they initiate their solo and collective journeys through biological, social, emotional and ecological changes that will lead them into adolescence and adulthood within a cultural context that was unimaginable even a decade ago. The journey is far more complex than most adults know and vulnerabilities and risks are ever present. Although middle level schools are only one of the critical links in this transformation, policymakers, educators, and researchers are compelled to ask hard questions regarding how the American middle schools are doing, if we are doing what is best for the young adolescent, or if school is in any way contributing to their problems. And what does research and best practice tell us what we should be doing to help young adolescents navigate this critical period in life? Educational attainment and health-promoting behaviors are two major developmental transitions that young adolescents must successfully navigate to find their way into adulthood. Many problem behaviors such as alcohol and tobacco use, staying out late, aggression, and sexual experimentation are related to the fact that society says youth who engage in them are not old enough, and if they get caught they are considered "status offenders." To that end, this chapter examines the relationship between health promotion and academic success relative to the role of middle level schools as they prepare students to become healthy, productive citizens.

We begin with an initial understanding that health goes beyond one's physical well-being. "Health is a state of complete physical, mental, and social well-being and not merely the absence of disease or infirmity" (World Health Organization, 1946). Middle level schools have a major role in health promotion, which combines educational and environmental supports for actions and conditions of living conducive to health (Green & Kreuter, 1990.) Finally and more specifically, a health-promoting school is one that constantly strengthens its capacity as a healthy setting for living, learning, and working. A health-promoting school is a place where all members of the school community work together to provide students with integrated and positive experiences and structures that promote and protect their health (Boddington & Hull, 1996). A health-promoting middle level school not only includes both the formal and informal curricula in health, but ensures a safe and healthy school environment, the provision of appropriate health services, and the involvement of the family and wider community in efforts to promote health. Its ultimate goal is to support young adolescents in the adoption and sustaining of health promoting behaviors including healthy diet, exercise, coping skills, recreation and avoidance of health compromising behaviors such as alcohol, tobacco, and drug use; unsafe sex; and reckless and harmful behaviors.

As nebulous as the concepts of health and health promotion seem, the definition of a well-educated or highly-educated individual is even more vague, and often part of a contentious debate among educators, policymakers, parents, and the private sector (Kohn, 2003; National Center on Education and the Economy, 2007). Most school districts define their goals for an educated student in their mission and vision statement with grandiose adjectives such as productive citizens, life-long learners, responsible decision makers, and engaged citizen, while others use terms such as an individual who has intelligent self-direction, wisdom, knowledge of the truth, critical thinking skills, and of course, the attainment of a high score on an alphabet soup of standardized tests ranging from CAT, ISAT, ITBS, NASS, ACT, SAT, and GRE. Some groups prefer to identify an educated person by a series of milestones they accomplish ranging from middle school and high school graduation, attending a post-secondary education, vocational or trade school, and professional or graduate school. Then, of course, accomplishing these milestones alone does not tell the whole story since a high school diploma from an affluent suburban high school is very different from a Graduate Education Development degree (GED), and an undergraduate degree from a open enrollment university is not likely to be equated with an Ivy League degree. Under No Child Left Behind (NCLB), the United States appears to be using a test score definition of an educated person, as almost all students are required to take a series of exams at various grade levels and subject matter, along with a number of pre-college exams designed to determine student readiness and preparation for postsecondary education. In middle level schools, all students must take math, reading, and science tests under NCLB.

A recent appraisal of the U.S. educational system was delineated in *Tough Choices or Tough Times,* published by the National Center on Education and the Economy (2007), which made compelling and alarming arguments for the impact of globalization on the American economy and future workers. The report describes the current status of the U.S. educational system and recommends massive changes ranging from universal preschool education, personal competitiveness accounts, high stakes testing, high levels of literacy, high school completion in Grade 10, and increased teacher quality. Their definition of an educated person is defined in terms of completing rigorous national standards that would enable the U.S. workforce to continue to compete with countries such as China and India, who have surging economies and massive workforce development efforts well underway.

Now that we have broadly discussed the concepts of health and education, we will continue to move downstream, so to speak, by briefly exploring the importance and impacts that health and education have on a person's economic, social, and physical well-being, including life satisfaction, morbidity, and mortality. The net result is that research supports the supposition that one's health status and educational attainment are inextricably linked to a high quality life in modern society. Specifically, research demonstrates that the value of education and educational success are major markers for economic sufficiency, higher wages, and positive health (Lleras-Muney, 2005; Mirowsky & Ross, 2003; Winkleby, Jatulis, Frank, & Fortmann, 1992). Study after study show that higher levels of educational attainment result in greater annual earnings, with high school dropouts earning $15,000 less than individuals with an associate's degree and nearly $30,000 less that those with bachelor's degree (Webster & Bishaw, 2006). One of the most compelling documents regarding the status of youth and young adults was published by W. T. Grant Foundation in 1988 and was recently updated in 2001 known as *The Forgotten Half Revisited* (Halperin, 2001) which continues to make a compelling case that adolescents and young adults who don't attend college continue to fall behind in terms of average salary, social status, and a variety of quality of life indicators. Moreover, the benefits of attaining a high quality education, on average, goes far beyond the income level to include greater life satisfaction, home ownership, employment with access to health care and retirement benefits, more likely to participate in health promoting behaviors, and broader engagement in community service and civil society (Halperin). Although *The Forgotten Half Revisited* and other studies focus on the status of high school students and young adults, it is well established that decisions and motivation for education often begin at the middle grades years where the confluence of self, sense of future, academic and social skills, and health behaviors are germinated. Nonetheless, the relationship between level of education and economic payoff is irrefutable. Although it is not clear whether better educated people are healthier because of the health attitudes and behaviors they adopt or whether are able to attain a higher level of education because of better health. One health economist who studied the relationship between education and longevity concluded: "If you want to improve health, you get more return by investing in education than by investing in medical care" (Kolata, 2007). It appears that the combination of good health and higher levels of education are interactive and synergistic, and ultimately improve the quality of life for all citizens.

Another approach in the identification and definition of what it means to be healthy and educated are constructs that reflect the consequences of poor health and health-comprising behavior and lack of education. School failure, health care costs, accidents, disease, disability, dropouts, income, infant mortality, and low test scores are widely used indicators of how healthy or how effective schools and communities are at the state or national levels (Chen & Kaplan, 2003; Zaza, Briss, & Harris, 2005). More specifically, these consequences are most often described or understood in terms of their relationship to the colossal costs and resources that individuals, businesses, local, state, and federal governments pay for these services, as well the comparisons that are often made relative to health and achievement disparities, access for high-quality health care, and the political polemics associated with each issue. We will now focus on young adolescence and middle level schools as a critical time and place where health and education problems manifest, but also provides an extraordinary opportunity to intervene.

YOUNG ADOLESCENT RISK AND VULNERABILITIES

The question then becomes "What do these macro and micro social, health care, and economic factors have to do with middle grades education in the United States?" To backward-assess the major health and educational outcomes described above, the focus on middle level schools appears relevant due to the well-established national trends that show that young adolescence (middle school years) is the time when significant numbers of students begin to lag behind academically and disengage from school (Roderick, 1994; U.S. Department of Education, National Center for Education Statistics, 2005). Internationally, U.S. elementary school students' achievement scores appear to demonstrate academic comparability on reading, math, and science scores that are highly ranked above the international averages (U.S. Department of Education, National Center for Education Statistics). However, for American young adolescents attending middle level and high schools, that trend moves in the opposite direction. As a result, critics of middle level schools have characterized them as "pathways to failure," "weak links in the educational system," or places of mediocrity (New York City Coalition for Educational Justice, 2007; Yecke, 2003).

Similarly, young adolescence is a time when student health and health behaviors become increasing problematic. Although there has been a lot written in recent years about obesity and asthma problems among children and young adolescents, the major health risks and behaviors include the experimentation and use of tobacco, alcohol, drug use, sexual activity, aggressive behaviors, and even gambling. For example, 6% of eighth grade students are regular smokers (Substance Abuse and Mental Health Services Administration, SAMHSA, 2003), and a 2002 national survey reports sizeable numbers of adolescent drug users who report first use of alcohol (39%), marijuana (18%), inhalants (10%), and hallucinogens (4.5%), before the age of 15 (SAMHSA, 2002) These patterns are quite disconcerting since research shows that early onset of drug use increases associated personal and social problems, and in particular, the increased chance of the individual becoming addicted to substances (SAMHSA, 2003).

Young adolescence is also a time when youth experience puberty and become interested in the opposite sex and sexual experimentation. In a recent study of sexual behaviors among early and middle adolescent youth, 9% of girls and 8% of boys reported they had vaginal intercourse, and 12% of girls and 10% of boys report having oral sex (Bersamin, Walker, Fisher, & Grube, 2006). Finally, research has found that young adolescence is the time that children manifest mental health problems. A recent study reported that 50% of all serious adult psychiatric issues—depression, anxiety, and substance abuse—begin at 14 years old, which is typically eighth grade (Kessler, Berglund, Demler, Jin, Merikangas, & Walters, 2005).

These health risks and behaviors are predominantly related to a number of developmental, social, emotional, intellectual, and cultural factors, such as the onset of puberty, increased autonomy and decision making, and the preeminence of peers and the popular culture which can positively and negatively influence young adolescents' decisions and behaviors. Many young adolescents can gain access to alcohol, tobacco, and drugs, conceive and bear children, earn or have access to discretionary money, and follow the crowd regardless of the potential risks or dangers at hand. They begin to understand the world in new ways with a cognitive complexity and emotions that include love, hate, insincerity, and hypocrisy.

Although these challenges have been described and documented all the way back to the turn of the twentieth century, it was the Carnegie Council on Adolescent Development's *Turning Points* document in 1989 which profoundly stated young adolescence is the last best chance to choose a path toward productive and fulfilling lives. Many argue that this "turning point" is a time of risk for all youth, but others have estimated that between 25-50% are at high risk because of family, economic, or educational circumstances (Carnegie Council on Adolescent Development, 1989).

Therefore, one of the most compelling questions that should be asked is "Is there a common denominator that appears to influence young adolescents to disengage from school or engage in destructive and health compromising behaviors?" Although we recognize there is no magic bullet to understanding young adolescent challenges, over two decades of research on risk and protective factors has aided our understanding of adolescent problem behaviors that generally begin in the middle grade years (Hawkins, Catalano, & Miller, 1992; Hays, Hays, & Mulhall, 2003). For example, the Add Health study was a large longitudinal cohort of 12,118 adolescents in Grades 7-12, and reported that three key protective factors shield youth against multiple problem behaviors: parental family connectedness, perceived school connectedness, and parent expectations regarding school achievement. Numerous risk factors ranged from access to substances and guns, extended work hours, repeating a grade, and early sexual debut (Resnick et al., 1997). Two of the three protective factors are directly related to education and the other relates to family, which in turn, is likely to directly and indirectly influence student attitudes toward school.

A well-established finding from adolescent health research is that many of these health-compromising behaviors among young adolescents are interrelated or overlapping (Jessor & Jessor, 1977). That is, young adolescents appear to engage in clusters of problem behaviors over time, which further exacerbates their risks for academic disengagement and poor health habits and behaviors. This widely known risk profile, which was documented nearly 30 years ago, was graphically displayed by Dr. Cheryl Perry at the University of Minnesota when she wrote a seminal article that integrated adolescent health, education, and behavioral issues as three concentric circles that describe their interrelatedness and commonalities (see Figure 1.1). Each circle reflects a set of youth problems focused on health, mental health, and role failure within each of the three dimensions with an overlapping area that contributes to multiple and more seri-

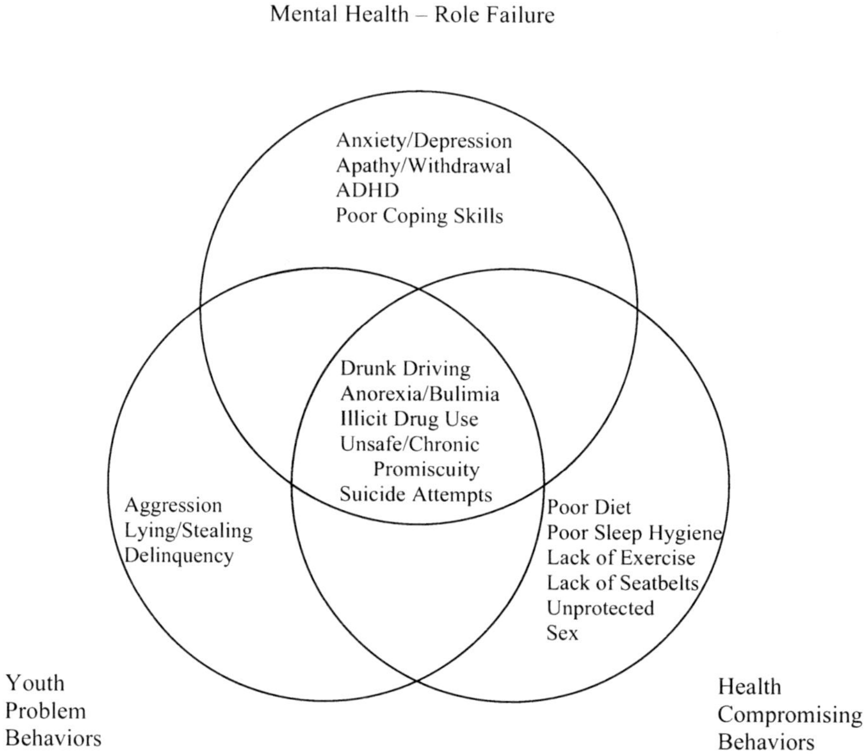

Source: Adapted from Perry (1984).

Figure 1.1. Interrelatedness of the physical, behavioral, and social-emotional domains.

ous problem behaviors. Similarly, Wheaton and his colleagues called the combination of school disengagement, mental health problems, and engaging in delinquent or deviant behaviors "change reactions" that produce a sequence of negative behaviors and outcomes (Wheaton & Gotlib, 1997).

Another interesting but not-so-surprising finding relating to the challenge of young adolescents is the fact that problem behaviors are not limited exclusively to so called "bad" or "troubled" kids. That is, problem behaviors are not the sole realm of young adolescents from disadvantaged, minority, or single parent families. In fact, in a series of studies by Luthar and her colleagues at Columbia University, they identified a number of risk factors associated with middle and high school students living in middle class and the affluent suburbs of the New York metro area. She reported indices of maladjustment that were worse than inner city, disadvantaged youth, resulting in higher anxiety, depression, sexual activity, and substance use, which she believes reflects adolescent efforts to self-medicate due to loneliness and high expectations (Luthar & Becker, 2002).

The culture and confusion of young adolescence appears at times to engulf parents' and schools' judgment, as recently portrayed in a *New York Times* editorial, "Middle school girls gone wild." Mr. Lawrence Downes describes a middle school talent show he attended in suburban New York with his sixth grade daughter. He watched in amazement as team of sixth, seventh, and eighth grade girls dressed and danced in provocative ways to a song that would make most parents blush in mixed adult company, never mind Mr. Downes with his 10-year daughter. He noted parents and the school appeared to be fully complicit in what he called the eroticization of young adolescent girls. The astonished reporter went on to say:

> Suburban parents dote and hover over their children, micromanaging their appointments and shielding them in helmets, kneepads, and thick layers of SUV steel. But they allow the culture of boy-toy sexuality to bore unchecked into their little one's ears and eyeballs, displace their nimble and growing brains, impoverishing the sense of wider possibilities in life. (Downes, 2006)

Culturally, young adolescents are increasingly exposed to the healthy and unhealthy sides of society-based access and "in your face" mass media, music, targeted marketing to tweens and teens, and ever-present peer competition and desire to be more grown up than they are. Seemingly, the most vulnerable appear to be the most susceptible. The age of innocence appears to be diminishing for many of today's young adolescents. Cell phones, iPods, World Wide Web, and My Space connect and expose youth to a vastly different world. Along with this increased exposure and faux sophistication of the world, there is a noticeable naiveté of skills and maturity that make them vulnerable to purveyors of every imaginable vice including high-risk, casual sex, alcohol and drugs, gambling, violence, and barbarism. An empirical example of culture run amok was described in a recent Rand Corporation study that found that adolescents who listened to music with degrading sexual lyrics were more likely to engage in intercourse and progress in sexual activity compared to youth who listened to nondegrading music (Martino, Collins, Elliott, Strachman, Kanouse, & Berry, 2006). These problems are often exacerbated in families or circumstances where parents are unwilling or unable to serve as the primary adult caretakers or provide anticipatory guidance necessary for healthy development (Hawkins et al., 1992).

We also know that young adolescents view the world through their youthful and unadulterated eyes of invulnerability, longevity, and instrumentality. They are risk takers, adrenaline junkies who believe that they will live forever and that bad things cannot happen to them. Adolescent brain research shows that many youth have high octane, supercharged brains geared toward risk taking and adventure, but lack perspective of their own vulnerability, which makes them prime candidates in a number of dangerous circumstances. High speed driving, binge drinking, risky sexual behavior, "stupid human tricks," emotional recklessness, and delinquent behavior are but a few of the more common health-related compromising behaviors that produce unintended consequences to themselves and others. Finally, it should be noted that some young adolescents are not overwhelmed during this period in life, but almost all have struggles, concerns, and worries related to puberty, academic pressures, peer groups, obtaining resources, adult interactions, changing schools, and a variety of developmental challenges that can positively or negatively influence their short and long term health and well-being.

How do Middle Level Schools Contribute or Exacerbate Health and Education Problems for Young Adolescents?

Middle level schools, like other levels of schooling, have a long history of implementing programs, policies, and practices that create more problems than they solve, hurt more students than they help, or unwittingly undermine student motivation and legitimate authority. To my knowledge, educators do not have their own version of medicine's Hippocratic Oath that proclaims "First, you will do no harm." Moreover, educational research does not have a corpus of validated literature that guides programs, policies, and practices regarding what works and what does not in a particular school and community setting (Berliner, 2002; Meier & Wood, 2004). Education practice is bound by experience and tradition rather than empirically-based methods. In addition, many educational practices, although not exclusive to middle level schools, are potentially damaging to young adolescents given the developmental and transition issues that are salient at this age. In medicine, these would be considered iatrogenic practices (i.e., unintended side affects of the practice) that are often based on good intentions, crisis intervention, or political expediency rather than empirical research. Some people would argue that certain practices would be considered negligent if their impacts could be well substantiated. A few examples of unhealthy or problem policies and practices are described below.

Zero Tolerance Policies

Zero tolerance policies, which are often state- or district-mandated, have become more of the rule than exception in most school districts throughout the United States. Zero tolerance policies are designed to protect and ensure safe schools for students, but there is no substantive evidence that they do either (American Bar Association, 2000). The major problem associated with zero tolerance is that the punishment is designed for students who intentionally violate policies, but the same punishment is meted out regardless of circumstance or intention. Carrying a gun to school often has the same penalty as carrying a pocketknife, and it treats first graders the same as high school students. Moreover, the most-often penalized are minorities, the poor, and students with mental health issues (Civil Rights Project, 2000).

There is no evidence or rationale for how or why Zero Tolerance Polices should increase school safety (Skiba, Reynolds, Graham, Sheras, Conoley, & Garcia-Vazquez, 2006). No one would argue that serious problem makers who threaten the health and well-being of a school should be stopped, but zero tolerance policies are complicated by the fact that no one problem has a single or simple cause or solution. Students who are expelled miss school at a time when academic work is accelerating, creating additional falling behind and being out of the school setting hurts both academics and social development. Young adolescents need to be in school learning in a constructive way. It is well known that middle level schools generally have the highest rates of disciplinary actions in a school district, which suggests that that there are numerous opportunities to intervene and minimize problem behaviors and promote healthy behavior.

Tracking Students for Teacher and Curriculum Expediency

Tracking students in middle level schools often creates a developmentally hazardous condition for many young adolescents. This highly-charged practice is designed to assist teachers and students by improving and ensuring a good match between student ability and instructions (Mulkey, Catsambis, Steelman, & Crain, 2005). The problem results from the unintended consequences from students placed in the lowest tracks. The problem with tracking students is both overt and covert. Research has found that students in lower tracks rarely get out of that track, have new, low quality, and/or inexperienced teachers, use inferior learning materials, receive poorer instructions, and have greater teacher turnover (Oakes, 2005). In addition, it is believed that tracking negatively affects student motivation, effort, and self-esteem, which eventually leads to further disengagement and dropping out of school. Not surprisingly, low educational tracks most often enroll poor minorities and English language learners (Oakes).

More covert are the images, perceptions, and interactions of lower tracked students compared to the upper tracked students; this may create deeper and profound feelings of superiority, resentment, and even racism. Given the sensitive nature and vulnerable feelings of young adolescents, many middle level schools have worked hard to reduce or eliminate tracking at their schools, but it remains a contentious issue among parents, teachers, and the public.

The Presidential Physical Fitness Test

One of the oldest and widely despised practices in middle school and high school that appears to negatively influence children in multiple ways is The President's Physical Fitness Tests, conducted in thousands of schools across the country (President's Challenge Physical Fitness Test, 2006). This fitness test is based on a post-WWII educational practice that continues today. The President's Physical Fitness Test is a nationally normed test based on thousands of school-age youth (10-17 years old) completing a series of five fitness related events. Students obtain the President's Award if they attain the 85th percentile in all five events, and the National Award if they reach the 50th percentile. Students receive a Participation Award if they complete all five tests and score below the 50th percentile. The fact remains that performance on the President's test for young adolescents is most likely attributed to students' age and stage of physical development, not some level of physical fitness based on physical training. Competing for awards that young adolescents have little control over creates winners and losers, particularly in light of the fact that research-based physical education curricula use health-related fitness activities that have demonstrated positive results (McKenzie, Sallis, Prochaska, Conway, Marshall, & Rosengard, 2004).

SOCIAL PROMOTION

One of the most insidious problems faced by schools districts, students, and families is the practice of social promotions. The evidence of this issue has been the subject of research and debate for the past decade and the results suggest that both social promotion and retention have serious downsides. Promoting students who have not met the standards or qualifications just makes them fall further behind; retaining students, particularly in the middle level grades, produces no academic improvement and starts a downward spiral toward dropping out (Nagaoka, & Roderick 2004). Most middle level students who are falling behind or failing also have been at the lowest end of the achievement ladder since entering school. We also know that by ensuring that students enter middle level school with the pre-requisite skills, they can succeed if the middle level school provides appropriate opportunities to learn and the necessary resources and supports for success. There are numerous examples of low income and minority students achieving at high levels if they are provided rich and supportive school environments (Borman & Overman, 2004).

Other Potential Problem Policies and Practices

A number of other policies and practices remain questionable in terms of their best interest for young adolescents. These include tolerance for bullying and sexual harassment, teaching to tests, after-school programs for "dummies," overemphasis on competitive sports, requiring group showers, behavioral management by embarrassment and intimidation, and many others. The value and utility of these practices reflect tradition, personal experience, neglect, legislation, expediency, and lack of resources to support students rather than sincere efforts to motivate or promote student learning, health, and success.

WHAT DOES RESEARCH TELL US ABOUT BUILDING HEALTH PROMOTING, HIGH PERFORMING MIDDLE LEVEL SCHOOLS?

The next major set of questions relates to the roles of the middle level school in terms of: What can it contribute to the academic and health outcomes? Can we make middle level schools responsible for attaining high levels of academic performance or adopting health promoting behaviors? Can schools' influence on students' health and education be supported equally without negatively affecting the other? Of course, middle level schools alone cannot be held responsible for behavioral and education outcomes such as tobacco use, voting behavior, paying taxes, arrest records, disease and disabilities, job performance, community service, or ACT scores. In fact, many educators, policymakers, parents, and politicians argue that schools are in the business of educating our youth, and health-related issues are the responsibility of external factors such as the family, physicians, and hospitals. After all, the NCLB legislation specifically requires that schools only target the academic side of student outcomes, and nothing else appears salient (Meier & Wood, 2004). However, as described earlier, research has demonstrated the intricate relationship between health and education, suggesting that it is difficult to have one without the other. In summary, we cannot attain these two qualities without addressing schools and we cannot have an educated society without addressing health. Although the middle level schools cannot be solely responsible for the health and education of children and adolescents in the United States, they do have a major and timely role that is only marginally meeting these goals and expectations.

Health Promoting, High Performing Middle Level Schools (HP^2)

Middle levels schools must both be health promoting and high performing to meet the developmental and health needs of young adolescents and the demands of a rigorous and relevant academic program. Illustratively, we have conceptualized HP^2 as a 2×2 matrix that shows the relationship between health-promoting and academically high-performing schools (see Table 1.1). Research and practice must build programs, policies, and practices reflected in the upper left quadrant of the table. Middle level schools must first and foremost be health promoting by asking the question, "Are our programs, policies, and practices supporting health behaviors and a healthy school environment as broadly defined for the needs and developmental challenges of young adolescents?" We extend this understanding by proposing that schools create healthy environments that promote high-quality academic and student learning. Student learning in an unhealthy, unsafe, hostile, or dangerous environment will unnecessarily create health and behavioral problems with short- and long-term unintended consequences. Middle level schools with high levels of academic pressure but lacking health promoting characteristics often breed student cheating, drug abuse, bullying, hopelessness, mental health problems, and drop outs. Although the high performing, unhealthy schools are not well delineated or described in the research literature, anecdotal examples abound and are widely described in the media with stories about widespread cheating, physical health problems, bullying, suicide, and of course, school violence. Schools that appear to promote health, but do not challenge young adolescent learning, are doing a major disservice to students and families. The middle level school that coddles young adolescents with low academic expectations is often the way American middle schools are portrayed by critics (Yecke, 2003). Finally, unhealthy and low-performing schools should be shut down or reconstituted.

Although research on this HP^2 framework is more conceptually defined than empirically derived at this point, several studies have begun to differentiate and understand the relationships for a HP^2 middle level school using these multiple dimensions. For example, the educational research group at the University of Chicago characterized academic press (high performance) and high support (health-promoting) at an optimal dosage to support and improve student learning. They studied over

Table 1.1. A Framework for Health Promoting, High Performing Middle Level Schools (HP²)

		Health Promoting Middle Level schools	
		High	*Low*
High Performing Middle Level Schools	*High*	Health promoting and high performing schools	High performing & low health promoting schools
	Low	Health promoting and low performing schools	Low health promoting & low performing schools

30,000 young adolescents (6th and 8th graders) in Chicago public schools and found that high expectations (academic press) and high levels of support were both necessary and sufficient to improve academic achievement (Lee & Smith, 1999). If either dimension was low, student achievement did not improve. Academic press has been be characterized and operationalized using multiple constructs including common goals and objectives, academic standards, homework, teacher demandingness, teacher expectations, time on tasks, high stakes testing, and academic rigor (Brown, Anfara, & Roney, 2004; Lee & Smith). Similarly, a number of other studies of middle level schools and students have examined climate, engagement, attachment and motivation, and teacher support demonstrating positive academic, mental health, and behavioral outcomes (Felner, Jackson, Kasak, Mulhall, Brand, & Flowers, 1997; Mertens & Flowers, 2003; Reddy, Rhodes, & Mulhall, 2003; Roeser, Eccles, & Sameroff, 1998). Some researchers have also found and made distinctions between academic and behavioral engagement whereby students may really like school, teachers, and their friends, but are not highly engaged (interested or motivated) in the academic side of school (Stipek, 2001).

The middle school reform movement has been advocating for healthy and high performing schools settings for young adolescents for nearly 100 years. However, most middle level reform efforts have focused on student academic and affective well-being, and less so on programs and services that are health promoting. To that end, the elements of the framework for a HP^2 middle level school has been proposed and described by a number of reform efforts including the National Middle School Association's *This We Believe*, Carnegie Corporation's *Turning Points*, and multiple comprehensive schools reform models such as Talent Development, Middle Start, and AIM for Middle Grades Results. More recently, the National Forum to Accelerate Middle Grades Reform (2007) distilled these reform efforts into three major goals for middle grades schools to promote academic excellence, developmental appropriateness, and social equity. However, the ways in which these reforms are defined, operationalized, implemented, and assessed vary quite dramatically from school to school. After 10 years of supporting middle level reform in a number of states, the Carnegie Corporation's *Turning Points* initiative concluded that structural changes in middle level schools, as difficult as they are, were not adequate to improve classroom teaching and learning, and subsequently student achievement outcomes (Jackson & Davis, 2000). To that end, major emphasis should be been placed on improving the instructional and teaching practices of teachers and school staff that can engage and support high quality student learning. In fact, it is easy to define or describe a healthy and high performing middle level school, but it is enormously challenging to move a school, district, or state to full scale implementation with fidelity and demonstrated effectiveness.

Direct curriculum initiatives to improve student health and create healthy schools have also struggled for access and time in the classroom. The school health education movement also dates back to the late 1800s with the great immigration movement as mandatory, universal education integrated disparate families and cultures from across the world. Health-promoting middle level schools have been equally challenged with only modest evidence that comprehensive health education demonstrated reductions or delays in health compromising behaviors and improvement in positive health behaviors. There are literally dozens of health-related curriculums that have been developed and implemented into middle schools, addressing drug abuse, HIV, obesity, suicide, and other "pathologies on the front page." Most curriculums are issue-specific since research and funding are targeted by problem behavior, and a comprehensive health education curriculum has not, to my knowledge, been funded since the early 1980's. Most recent school health efforts have focused on structural and organizational efforts to provide necessary services to students and their family in a school or school-linked settings such as Comprehensive School Health Programs, Full Service Schools, School Mental Health Project, and Healthy Schools Initiatives. Each has overlapping goals and objectives for high-performing and health-promoting middle level schools. More recently, HP^2 approaches have begun to address psycho-social dimensions designed to influence both student health and education by targeting practices, climate, and culture for healthy learning and health promotion. Two research-based efforts promoted under these approaches include social-emotional learning and goal mastery learning. There is a lot of talk about the relationship between education and health, but rarely do we see funded initiatives focusing on health promoting structures, services, and curriculum that are fully integrated into schools that have high expectations for student outcomes.

Health education has long held that school health programs hold the potential for educating students regarding health promoting behaviors and meeting most student health service needs. The Division of Adolescent and School Health at the Centers for Disease Control and Prevention has been the leading advocate for health promotion and services in schools using the eight components of the Comprehensive School Health Program (CSHP) (Allensworth, Lawson, Nicholson, & Wyche, 1997). The eight components include health and physical education, healthy school environment, health services, health promotion for staff and faculty, family and community involvement, nutrition services and counseling, and psychological and social services (Allensworth et al.). Historically, CDC efforts predominately focus on classroom-based health and physical education, but have more recently targeted food and nutrition services and policies as they relate to the obesity epidemic. To our knowledge there are no recent evaluation studies of the CSHP because of the complexity and challenges associated with full implementation. The potential effectiveness of the CSHP remains mostly conceptual in that these are the components that schools should be implementing, but little is known whether they are, and if so, if they make any difference in the health and academic success of students.

Another widely described and supported health promoting school initiative is the School Mental Health Project, which seeks to understand a range of learners in schools and targets barriers to healthy, educational development (Adelman & Taylor, 1994). The multiplicity of students that walk through the front door of a school are viewed in three categories: (1) motivated and ready to learn; (2) not motivated to learn, lacking prerequisite skills, and different learning styles and rates; and (3) avoidant or very deficient and has a major disability or health problem (Adelman & Taylor). This approach works across a middle level school by providing support, mental health, individualized instruction, and parental services in partnership with community-based health and human service organizations. Full-service schools and school-based clinics would include a number, but not all, of the program elements of the School Mental Health Project.

The area of biobehavioral research relative to educational and learning practices is emerging and may assist middle level schools to become HP^2. A rapidly emerging area of research is the study of the brain and learning as well as how schools can promote and support high quality student learning (Bransford, Brown, & Cocking, 2000). The brain is the great mediator between the internal and external worlds, serving as the central processing unit for thinking, feeling, and acting. Young adolescent emotions play an enormous role in how students feel about themselves and the world, which means that every individual needs to learn how to understand, manage, and use their own emotions and integrate those emotions into their daily living. In addition to learning about learning, acquisition, and use of knowledge, the field of socioemotional learning has exploded in both the private and public sectors, based on Daniel Goleman's *Emotional Intelligence: Why It Can Matter More Than IQ* (Goleman, 1995). The fundamental premise of EI is that a person's emotional intelligence, not his or her intelligence quotient, has a greater role in school and workplace success. Recently, the state of Illinois adopted social-emotional learning (SEL) standards that are now part of their state learning standards (Illinois State Board of Education, 2006). SEL is characterized into broad competencies that predict positive academic, social, and behavioral outcomes (Durlak & Weissberg, 2007; Hawkins, 1997). The four major SEL competencies include:

1. Self awareness (emotions, self-perception efficacy, needs, value and spirituality);
2. Social awareness (empathy, respect, perspective taking, and appreciating diversity);
3. Responsible decision making (problem solving, reflection, personal, moral and ethical responsibility); and
4. Relationship management (communication, relationship building, working cooperatively, negotiation, conflict management, seeking and providing help).

Some of the best thinking regarding SEL is done by Dr. Roger Weissberg and his staff at the Collaborative for Academic and Social and Emotional Learning (CASEL) at the University of Illinois at Chicago. Dr. Weissberg and his staff are an international resource for schools, districts, and countries around the world, and CASEL and local mental health and educational professionals are supporting the implementation of the recently adopted social-emotional learning standards in Illinois (Illinois State Board of Education, 2006). In fact, Dr. Weissberg and Dr. Joseph Durlak at Loyola recently completed a meta-analysis of over 300 youth development programs, which finds that youth who participate in these types of activities actually achieve at a higher level academically, socially, and emotionally than youth who do not participant in these types of programs (Durlak & Weissberg, 2007).

SEL programs and practices also are found in a number of "canned" curriculums that are widely available from commercial and research outlets. However, CASEL has cataloged and documented a large number of SEL programs using a *Consumer Reports* rating approach for assessing their effectiveness, strengths, and limitations (CASEL, 2006). However, most educators and researchers recognize that a curriculum alone does not assure a school and teachers are providing appropriate SEL instruction and experiences, and that greater emphasis needs to be placed on integrating SEL practices throughout the curriculum, school, and student and teacher interactions. Getting whole schools to adopt and implement SEL practices creates a school culture and climate that addresses the unique SEL needs of young adolescents.

Another research-based approach for HP^2 middle level schools is the use of a cognitive evaluation theory or goal-mastery structure for academic achievement and health behaviors (Roeser, Eccles, & Sameroff, 1998). Cognitive evaluation theory is an extension of social learning, achievement motivation, and attribution theories examining how individuals view the world and interpret their own and others behavior (Ames, 1992; Ryan & Deci, 2000). This work evolves from research findings that cognitive beliefs about a task or behavior are greatly influenced by whether the behavior is viewed as internally or externally controlled or stable or unstable. If a student attributes a behavior to his or her abilities that are perceived to be stable and uncontrollable ("I'm bad at math," or "I'm a terrible baseball player," or "I hate to write"), it is not likely they will believe they are capable of improving or resolving the issue. If the school curriculum or teacher states that a student attribute is stable or uncontrollable ("You're stupid"), there is little likelihood for a young adolescent to find a way to extricate oneself from this belief. By contrast, if a student believes his/her behavior is internal and controllable, they are likely work at that behavior and sustain their effort and motivation ("I can exercise enough to be healthy", "I can pass this Algebra course").

This motivational pattern has been widely studied in academic achievement (perceptions of ability versus effort, internal versus external control) and more recently has received attention from physical and nutrition educators as goals focus on participation, goal setting, and sustained lifetime effort rather than athletic performance and prowess. In fact, the cornerstone of the "new" physical education programs (in contrast to the President's Challenge Physical Fitness Tests), promoted in many middle level schools is based on increasing student motivation for lifetime fitness and physical activity through goal setting, effort, and intrinsic motivation, while minimizing natural competition that exists among students this age group (Carroll & Loumidis, 2001; Treasure & Roberts, 2001). Research shows that if students understand they do not have to be the greatest runner or tennis player to gain the health benefits of physical activity, they are more likely to participate and sustain behavior over time (McKenzie et al., 2004). Regardless of the subject matter, cognitive evaluation theory uses teaching and instructional methods for competence and confidence. To that end, schools need to teach and students need to learn to help them develop attributions of their behaviors that promote willingness to take risks, try hard, master tasks, and persevere based on curriculum and instruction that promotes this type of learning.

Unfortunately, the degree to which these programs, policies and practices are currently implemented in middle level schools is unknown. Much has been written about improving middle level schools, but little empirical data supports the full implementation of a HP^2 middle level school. As might be expected, the educational profession focuses on academics and the health profession focuses on health education and services. Rarely do the two professions give each other the attention, time and resources to make each other successful. We suggest that by implementing only one side of this dichotomy, schools will miss the major mechanisms for meeting the needs and attaining desired outcomes for young adolescents. A comprehensive, multi-level approach using a combination of programs, policies, and practices that balance health promotion and academic rigor needs to be implemented in all middle level schools. To that end, we present a list of empirically supported and pragmatically demonstrated programs, policies, and practices for creating a HP^2 middle level school.

Research-based practices for a health promoting, high performing middle level school include:

I. Structural and Organizational

- A School Leadership Team, which includes parents and citizens, that provides guidance and direction for the middle level school.
- Small communities for learning based on interdisciplinary teams that are not more than 75-125 students per team.
- Engage faculty and staff in a continuous quality improvement process for multiple levels of school operations—curriculum, teacher selection, promotions, discipline, school climate, and so forth.
- Employ highly qualified teachers with certifications, experiences, and commitment to working with young adolescents.

II. Curriculum, Instruction, and Assessment

- Authentic curriculum, instruction, and assessment that allows students to master state standards using developmentally appropriate and goal oriented approaches.
- Provide multiple methods for assessment that engage student, parents, and teachers.
- Provide exploratory and experiential courses that allow students to learn and try out an array educational, occupational, and recreational activities.

- Engage families and communities in ways to support learning and health promotion at home and at school.

III. School Culture and Climate

- Implement a school transition program for students and parents as they enter middle school and as they prepare to enter high school.
- Teacher and student advisement programs that monitor student progress and provide appropriate adult guidance.
- Establish, promote, and support a culture of self-determination and success for all students.
- Respect cultural diversity and differences among students and teachers.
- The curriculum should contain life and social skills with major emphasis on communication, conflict resolution, cultural differences, and socioemotional learning and skills.

IV. Health Education, Promotion, and Services

- Provide extensive in- and out-of-school intramural, extracurricular programs, and service learning experiences, driven by student and community interests.
- Health and physical education must be provided to students every semester while students are enrolled in middle school, with a special emphasis on sexuality; alcohol, tobacco, and other drugs; mental health; and related community-relevant issues.
- Develop Student Assistance Teams to identify and address students and families with special challenges, crises, or requiring extra supports.
- School-based or school-linked health and social services for students and families with special needs and challenges.
- Use food, health, and social services as ways to teach and experience health-promoting, educated consumer behavior.
- Develop and/or adopt a health promotion and employee assistance program for faculty and staff.

CONCLUSION

The health and education of American children and youth are increasingly and rapidly becoming high stakes issues recognized through their costs and consequences that burden an individual, family, community, and society as a whole. Middle level schools have enormous challenges and unfulfilled potential to address these issues given the developmental, cultural, and biological transformations that occur in young adolescents. Although health and educational research needs to continue to understand the complexities of a HP^2 middle level school, we certainly know enough about what most middle level schools should and should not be doing (Adelman & Taylor, 1994; Allensworth et al., 1997; Jackson & Davis, 2000). We can begin by ending the unhealthy and problem policies and practices, whether it is tracking students in school, coercive discipline policies, unhealthy lunches and snacks, or the President's Physical Fitness Tests. Recommendations for making a HP^2 middle level school have been widely discussed and disseminated in both the research and professional practice literature. Several studies of middle grades reform such as Turning Points and Middle Start have found that, when done with high levels of fidelity, whole school reform probably captures the multiple dimensions of a HP^2 middle level schools with the greatest clarity, but the process of instituting these practices remains elusive. However, it should also be noted that teachers and school districts alone cannot provide the programs, polices, and practices necessary to create a HP^2 middle level school, but truly requires a community of committed people and organizations. Schools must partner with parents, cultural groups, community-based organizations, health departments, hospitals, universities, mental health services, businesses, and a variety of community resources, if available. We also recognize that some communities, particularly in rural and urban communities, may not have many of these partnering organizations and resources, and may have to go to the regional or state level to access these services. To that end, school-community stakeholders must be creative and entrepreneurial to bring these resources and supports to schools. A school with a mission and vision can delineate what a HP^2 middle level school-community should look like, but only leadership, resources, and staff commitment can make it happen.

REFERENCES

Ames, C. (1992). Classrooms: Goals, structure and student motivation. *Journal of Educational Psychology, 84*, 261-271.

Adelman, H. S., & Taylor, L. (1994). *On understanding intervention in psychology and education*. Westport CT: Praeger.

Allensworth, D., Lawson, E., Nicholson, L., & Wyche, J. (Eds.). (1997). *Schools and health: Our nation's investment*. (Committee on Comprehensive School Health Programs in Grades K-12, Institute of Medicine). Washington DC: National Academy Press.

American Bar Association. (2000). *Zero tolerance policy.* (ABA Juvenile Justice Policies). Retrieved January 14, 2007, from http://www.abanet.org/crimjust/juvjus/zerotolreport.html

Berliner, D. C. (2002). Educational research: The hardest science of all. *Educational Researcher, 31*(8), 18-20.

Bersamin, M. M., Walker, S., Fisher, D. A., & Grube, J. W. (2006). Correlates of oral sex and vaginal intercourse in early and middle adolescence. *Journal of Research on Adolescence, 16(1),* 59-68.

Boddingon, N., & Hull, T. (1996). *The health promoting school.* London: Forbes.

Borman, G. D., & Overman, L. T. (2004). Academic resilience in mathematics among poor and minority students. *Elementary School Journal, 104*(3), 177-195.

Bransford, J. D., Brown, A. L., & Cocking, R. R. (2000). *How people learn: Brain, mind, experience, and schools.* Washington, DC: National Academy Press.

Brown, K. M., Anfara, V. A., Jr., & Roney, K. (2004). Student achievement in high performing, suburban middle schools and low performing urban middle schools: Plausible explanation for the differences. *Education and Urban Society, 36*(4), 428-456.

Chen, Z. Y., & Kaplan, H. B. (2003). School failure in early adolescence and status attainment in middle adulthood: A longitudinal study. *Sociology of Education, 76,* 110-127.

Civil Rights Project. (2000). *Opportunities suspended: The devastating consequences of zero tolerance and school discipline.* Cambridge, MA: Harvard University. Retrieved January 31, 2007, from http://www.civilrightsproject.harvard.edu/research/discipline/opport_suspended.php

Carnegie Council on Adolescent Development. (1989). *Turning points: Preparing American youth for the 21st century.* New York: Carnegie Corporation of New York.

Carroll, B., & Loumidis, J. (2001). Children's perceived competence and enjoyment in physical education and physical activity outside of school. *European Physical Education Review,* 7(1), 24-43.

Collaborative for Academic, Social, and Emotional Learning. (2006). *Safe and sound: An educational leader's guide to evidence-based social and emotional learning programs.* Retrieved January 29, 2007, from http://www.casel.org/downloads/Safe_and_Sound_ILedition.pdf

Downes, L. (2006, December 29). Middle school girls gone wild. *New York Times.* Retrieved December 30, 2006, from http://www.nytimes.com

Durlak, J., & Weissberg, R. (2007). *The impact of afterschool programs that promote social and emotional learning.* Chicago: Collaborative for Academic, Social, and Emotional Learning.

Felner, R. D., Jackson, A. J., Kasak, D., Mulhall, P., Brand, S., & Flowers, N. (1997). The impact of school reform for the middle years: Longitudinal study of a network engaged in Turning Points-based comprehensive school transformation. *Phi Delta Kappan, 78,* 528-532, 541-550.

Goleman, D. (1995). *Emotional intelligence: Why it can matter more than IQ.* New York: Bantam.

Green L., & Kreuter, M. (1990). Health promotion as a public health strategy for the "1990s." *Annual Review of Public Health, 11*, 313-334.

Halperin, S. (2001). *The forgotten half revisited. American youth and young families, 1988-2008*. Washington, DC: American Youth Policy Forum.

Hawkins, J. D. (1997). Academic performance and school success: Sources and consequences. In R. P. Weissberg, T. P. Gullotta, R. L. Hampton, B. A. Tryan, & G. R. Adams (Eds.), *Healthy children 2010: Enhancing children's wellness* (pp. 278-306). Thousand Oaks, CA: Sage.

Hawkins, D., Catalano, R. C., & Miller, J. Y. (1992). Risk and protective factors for alcohol and other drug problems in adolescence and early adulthood: Implications for substance abuse prevention. *Psychological Bulletin, 11*(1), 64-105.

Hays, S. P., Hays, C. E., & Mulhall, P. (2003). Community risk and protective factors and adolescent substance abuse. *Journal of Primary Prevention, 24*(2), 125-142.

Illinois State Board of Education. (2006). *Illinois social emotional learning standards.* Retrieved December 5, 2006, from http://www.isbe.net/ils/social_emotional/standards.htm

Jackson, A., & Davis, G. (2000). *Turning points 2000: Educating adolescence in the 21st century.* New York: Teachers College Press.

Jessor, R. J., & Jessor, S. L. (1977). *Problem behavior and psychological development: A longitudinal study of youth*. New York: Academic Press.

Kessler, R. C., Berglund, P., Demler, O., Jin, R., Merikangas, D. R., & Walters, E. E. (2005). Lifetime prevalence and age-of-onset distributions of DSM-IV disorders in the National Comorbidity Survey Replication. *Archives of General Psychiatry, 62*, 768.

Kohn, A. (2003). What does it mean to be well-educated? *Principal Leadership, 3*(7), 24-28.

Kolata, G. (2007, January 3). A surprising secret to a long life: Stay in school. *New York Times*. Retrieved January 3, 2007, from http://www.nytimes.com.

Lee, V. E., & Smith, J. B. (1999). Social support and academic achievement: The role of academic press. *American Educational Research Journal, 36*, 4, 907-945.

Lleras-Muney, A. (2005). The relationship between education and adult mortality in the United States. *Review of Economic Studies, 72*(1), 189–221.

Luthar, S. S., & Becker, B. E. (2002). Privileged but pressured? A study of affluent youth. *Child Development, 73*(5), 1593-1610.

Martino, S. C., Collins, R. L., Elliott, M. N., Strachman, A., Kanouse, D. E., & Berry, S. B. (2006). Exposure to degrading versus non-degrading music lyrics and sexual behaviors among youth. *Pediatrics, 118*(2), 430-441.

McKenzie, T. L., Sallis, J. F., Prochaska, J., Conway, T. L., Marshall, S. J., & Rosengard, P. (2004). Evaluation of a two year middle school physical education intervention: M-SPAN. *Medicine and Science in Sport and Exercise, 36*(8), 382-388.

Mertens, S., & Flowers, N. (2003). Middle school practices improve student achievement in high poverty schools. *Middle School Journal, 35*(1), 33-43.

Meier, D., & Wood, G. (Eds.). (2004). *Many children left behind: How the No Child Left Behind Act is damaging our children and our schools*. Boston: Beacon Press.

Mirowosky, J., & Ross, C. E. (2003). *Education, social status and health*. New York: Aldine Publishers.

Mulkey, L. M., Catsambis, S., Steelman, L.C., & Crain, R. L. (2005). The long term effects of ability grouping in mathematics: A national investigation. *Social Psychology of Education, 8*, 137-177.

Nagaoka, J., & Roderick, M. (2004). *Ending social promotion: The effects of retention*. Chicago: Consortium on Chicago School Research.

National Center on Education and the Economy. (2007). *Tough choices or tough times: The report of the new commission on the skills of the American workforce*. San-Francisco: Jossey-Bass.

National Forum to Accelerate Middle Grades Reform. (2007). *Vision statement*. Retrieved January 30, 2007, from http://www.mgforum.org/about/vision.asp

National Middle School Association. (2003). *This we believe: Successful schools for young adolescents*. Columbus, OH: Author.

New York City Coalition for Education Justice. (2007, January 16). *New York City's middle grade schools: Platforms for success or pathways for failure*. Retrieved January 12, 2007, from http://www.annenberginstitute.org/CIP/publications/NYC_MiddleGradeSchools_Report.pdf

Oakes, J. (2005). *Keeping track: How schools structure inequality* (2nd ed.) New Haven, CT: Yale University Press.

Perry. C. (1984). Health promotion at school: Expanding the potential for prevention. *School Psychology Review, 13*, 141-149.

President's Challenge Physical Fitness Tests. (2006). Retrieved January 15, 2007, from http://www.presidentschallenge.org/educators/program_details/physical_fitness_test.aspx

Reddy, R., Rhodes, J. E., & Mulhall, P. F. (2003). The influence of teacher support on student adjustment in middle school years: A latent growth curve study. *Development and Psychopathology, 15*, 119-138.

Resnick, M. D., Bearman, P. S., Blum, W., Bauman, K. E., Harris, K. M., Jones, J., et al. (1997). Protecting adolescents from harm: Finding from the National Longitudinal Study on Adolescent Health. *Journal of the American Medical Association, 278*(10), 828-832.

Roderick, M. (1994). *The path to dropping out: Evidence for intervention*. Westport, CT: Auburn House.

Roeser, R. W., Eccles, J. S., & Sameroff, A. J. (1998). Academic and emotional functioning in early adolescence: Longitudinal relations, patterns and prediction by experience in middle school. *Development and Psychopathology, 10*, 321-352.

Ryan, R. M., & Deci, E. L. (2000). Self determination theory and facilitation of intrinsic motivation, social development, and well-being. *American Psychologist, 55*, 68-78.

Skiba, R., Reynolds, C. R., Graham, S., Sheras, P., Conoley, J. C., & Garcia-Vazquez, E. (2006). *Are zero tolerance polices effective in the schools? An evidentiary review and recommendations.* (A report by the American Psychological Association's Zero Tolerance Task Force). Retrieved January 30, 2007, from http://www.apa.org/releases/ZTTFReportBODRevisions5-15.pdf

Substance Abuse and Mental Health Services Administration. (2002). *National Survey on Drug Use & Health: Detailed tables*. Retrieved June 20, 2005, from http://www.oas.samhsa.gov/nhsda/2k2nsduh/html/Sect4seTabs1to76.htm

Substance Abuse and Mental Health Services Administration. (2003). *Substance abuse and mental health data archive: List of available quick tables for the National Survey of Drug Use and Health, 2002*. Retrieved June 20, 2005, from http://webapp.icpsr.umich.edu/quicktables/quickconfig.do?nsduh02_druguse

Stipek, D. (2001). Good instruction is motivating. In A. Wigfield & J. S. Eccles (Eds.), *Development of achievement motivation* (pp. 310-332). San Diego, CA: Academic Press.

Takanishi, R., & Hamburg, D. A. (1997). *Preparing adolescents for the twenty-first century: Challenges facing Europe and the United States.* London: Cambridge University Press.

Treasure, D. C., & Roberts, G. C. (2001). Students' perceptions of motivational climate, achievement beliefs and satisfaction in physical education. *Research Quarterly for Exercise and Sport, 72*(2), 165-175.

U.S. Department of Education, National Center for Education Statistics. (2005). *The condition of education 2005* (NCES 2005-094). Washington, DC: U.S. Government Printing Office.

Webster, F. H., & Bishaw, A. (2006). *U.S. Census Bureau, American community survey reports, income, earning and poverty: Data from the 2005 American community survey.* Washington, DC: U.S. Government Printing Office.

Wheaton, B., & Gotlib, I. H. (1997). Trajectories and turning points over the life course: Course and themes. In I. H. Gotlib & B. Wheaton (Eds.), *Stress and adversity over the life course: Trajectories and turning points* (pp. 1-25). Cambridge: Cambridge University Press.

Winkleby, M. A., Jatulis, D. E., Frank, E., & Fortmann, S. P. (1992). Socioeconomic status and health: How education, income and occupation contribute to risk factors for cardiovascular disease. *American Journal of Public Health, 82*(6), 816-820.

World Health Organization. (1946). *Constitution of the World Health Organization*. Geneva: Author. Retrieved January 5, 2007, from http://www.who.int/about/en/

World Health Organization. (2004). *Local action: Creating health promoting schools*. (Information series on school health). Geneva: Author.

Yecke, C. P. (2003). *The war against excellence: The rising tide of mediocrity in America's middle level schools.* Westport, CT: Praeger Press.

Zasa, S., Briss, P. A., & Harris, K. W. (2005). *A guide to community preventive services: What works to promote health*? London: Oxford University Press.

CHAPTER 2

"PUT ME IN, COACH"

The Psychology of Sport and Physical Activity for Young Adolescents

Leslee A. Fisher and Melissa N. Madeson

ABSTRACT

Young adolescents face several critical issues in the twenty-first century including bullying and harassment, teen pregnancy, and alcohol and drug abuse (Crockett, 2003). There are also 3 times as many obese youth today as there were 20 years ago (National Middle School Association, 2006). In this chapter, we discuss how sport and physical activity can provide opportunities for young adolescents to combat the stresses they face in everyday life by learning how to exercise and feed their bodies properly, become "good sports," and watch out for the warning signs of inappropriate coaching and exercise behaviors. Literature in sport and exercise psychology related to 6 major topics is reviewed. It is our hope that educators, parents, coaches, and administrators will make a concerted effort to structure sport and physical activities for young adolescents so that they can develop into healthy sportspersons for a lifetime.

The Young Adolescent and the Middle School
pp. 27–45

INTRODUCTION

At a recent "Future of School Psychology" national conference, the keynote speaker Deborah Crockett (2003) noted several critical psychosocial issues children face as they move into the twenty-first century. These include but are not limited to: poverty, violence, bullying and harassment, teen pregnancy and sexual behavior, alcohol and drug abuse, mental health issues and services, diversity and tolerance, education, and technology. While not mentioned in her talk, another critical issue facing children today is the threefold increase in obesity over the last twenty years (National Middle School Association, 2006). Sport and physical activity can provide opportunities for young adolescents to combat the stresses they face in everyday life by teaching them how to feed their bodies properly, help them acquire mature "character" behaviors like good sportspersonship, take on leadership roles, and decrease behaviors related to unwanted pregnancies and the use of illegal drugs (Women's Sports Foundation, 2006). This does not happen automatically, however. Educators, parents, coaches, and administrators must make a concerted effort to structure sport and physical activities so that they contain such "character-building" emphases.

In this chapter, we summarize the sport psychology literature on six major topics related to young adolescent sport and physical activity participation: (a) why young adolescents participate in sport (e.g., participation motivation patterns); (b) childhood obesity and physical inactivity; (c) the importance of friends and social support; (d) the role of coaches in young adolescents' lives; (e) potential overuse issues related to sport and physical activity participation (e.g., stress/burnout/overtraining/eating and injury issues); and (f) effective training programs for young adolescents.[1] Each is discussed in turn. Like many of our sport psychology colleagues (see, for example, Weiss & Williams, 2004), we use an interactionist or social cognitive perspective to understand and explain these issues. Those advocating this perspective posit that individual behavior is best understood by examining both individual differences (e.g., traits, perceptions) and the social environment (e.g., how significant others impact the individual) and how these factors interact to create sport and physical activity behavior.

Why Do Young Adolescents Participate in Sport? Participation Motivation Patterns

According to Weinberg and Gould (2003), at least 45 million children participate in sport in the United States. However, there are a great number of youth sport participants who drop out by the age of 12 years (State of Michigan, 1976). What researchers discovered is that these phenomena are related. In other words, perhaps the reason children drop out of sport is that sport stops satisfying the initial participation motivation children had when they undertook sport in the first place.

For example, Weiss and Williams (2004) synthesized a number of studies undertaken during the 1970s and 1980s related to sport participation motivation and dropout. They put forward three very highly consistent findings related to why children participate in sport: "(a) to develop or demonstrate *physical competence or adequacy* (e.g., learn and improve skills, be physically fit, get stronger, achieve goals), (b) to attain *social acceptance and approval* (e.g., make friends, feel part of a group, receive coach/parent approval), and (c) to *enjoy experiences* related to sport involvement (i.e., have fun, feel excited)" (p. 224). Among the reasons listed for discontinuing sport participation were "lack of fun, issues with the coach, time commitment required, lack of playing time, overemphasis on winning, and greater interest in other activities" (p. 225). As Weiss and Williams and Weinberg and Gould (2003) surmise, perhaps kids drop out of sport when they are no longer learning and improving their physical skills (e.g., feel physically incompetent), are no longer making friends or feeling a part of a group (e.g., do not feel socially accepted or approved of), and are not enjoying their sport experiences anymore.

In terms of perceived competence—defined as one's beliefs about his/her ability in a given domain—researchers propose that children ages 8 to 13 are able to distinguish between and within many specific competency domains including athletics/the physical domain, academics, and the social domain. They are also able to assess their own general level of self-worth in such domains (Harter, 1982, 1985; Weiss & Williams, 2004). By young adolescence (from ages 10-14 years), Weiss and Williams advise that three additional perceptions emerge which are critical to young adolescent development. These include close friendships, romantic relationships, and work/job competence.

In organized sport, it appears that young adolescents use friend or peer comparison and peer evaluation in addition to coach evaluation when trying to determine how skilled they are. This is different than the evaluations used by both younger children and older adolescents; in fact, younger children rely on parental feedback to judge their own physical competence while older adolescents use self-referenced information (i.e., how they compared to their last performance) (Weiss & Williams, 2004). In terms of connecting theory and research with practice, Weiss and Williams recommend four major strategies for enhancing motivation in youth sport and physical activity: (a) structuring the sport and physical activity experience so that it is fun; (b) creating a mastery motivational climate;

(c) maximizing social support; and (d) helping children help themselves. Such strategies need to be informed by the growing concern among parents and educators that our nation is full of overweight, inactive young adolescents.

Childhood Obesity: The Importance of Physical Activity

The United States—and many other parts of the world—face the serious and growing health problem of obesity. This problem is spreading rapidly among youth and is occurring in children at younger and younger ages. Obesity is a chronic condition defined by an excess of body fat (Pi-Sunyer, 2000). It can be diagnosed and measured using several different methods including underwater weighing, bioelectrical impedance analysis (BIA), and the less invasive procedure of weight-to-height ratios.

For children and young adolescents who are still growing the Centers for Disease Control and Prevention (CDCP) provides growth charts to define healthy and overweight levels. Adolescents with a body mass index (BMI) for age at or above the 95th percentile of the CDCP growth charts are considered overweight (U.S. Department of Health & Human Services, 2004). The CDCP's most recent report (2003)—related to data from 1999-2002—indicates that 15.8% of 6-11-year-olds and 16.1% of adolescents (12-19 years) are overweight. These statistics have become dramatically worse over time. In fact, between the National Health and Nutrition Examination Survey (NHANES) III (1994-1998) and the NHANES IV (1999-2000) studies, the percentage of overweight youth rose from 11.3% to 15.3% for 6-11-year-olds and from 10.5% to 15.5% for adolescent's ages 12-19 years (U.S. Department of Health & Human Services, 2000).

These statistics are frightening considering the consequences associated with being overweight and/or obese. Overweight youth are not only at increased risk for becoming obese adults, they are more likely to experience immediate health problems such as hypertension, high levels of blood lipids, glucose intolerance, and orthopedic complications due to excess stress and strain on limbs (Dietz, 1998). The psychological and social effects of childhood overweight and obesity can include low self-esteem and problems with social interaction and body image. (Neumark-Sztainer, 1999). Obese adults—which are what obese youth are likely to become—are at risk for a wide range of adverse health conditions which often create financial strain for families, communities, and health care systems. Conditions such as hypertension, increased levels of cholesterol, Type 2 diabetes, coronary heart disease, stroke, gallbladder disease, osteoarthritis, sleep apnea and respiratory problems as well as increased risk of endometrial, breast and colon cancers are all associated with increased body weight (U.S. Department of Health and Human Services, 1996). It is clearly important to treat the obesity epidemic in children and young adolescents to stem its spread in these future adults.

To treat obesity early, it is important to understand its cause. While comprised of an interaction between genetics, metabolism, behavior, environment and culture (Sallis, Simmons-Morton, Stone, Corbin, Epstein, & Faucette, 1992), obesity is ultimately the result of an energy imbalance related to consuming too many calories and not expending enough energy. The CDCP advocates that behavior and environment play the largest roles in causing young adolescents to become overweight and obese and are, therefore, the greatest areas for prevention and treatment (U.S. Department of Health and Human Services, 2000). The most effective way to overcome the obesity epidemic is by preventing childhood obesity from developing through the creation of nutritious eating plans and physical activity habits at an early age (Caroli & Lagravinese, 2002). This is critical because it may become more difficult, uncomfortable and/or potentially embarrassing for sedentary and overweight youth to participate as they get older. In fact, it can become a vicious cycle because being overweight is usually accompanied by a decreased level of physical activity leading to even more weight gain. Researchers conclude that once children become overweight or obese, it is unlikely that they will ever return to a normal weight (Armstrong et al., 2003). Conversely, active children and adolescents are more likely to be active adults.

How Important Are Friends and Social Support?

Social support can help in getting young adolescents to participate in sport and physical activity. According to Sallis and Patrick (1994), it is necessary to focus attention on youth physical activity not only to promote health and well-being during adolescence, but to instill healthy habits that will last a lifetime. Social support is critical in the development of such skills (King, 1994). Social support is defined as "an exchange of resources between at least two individuals perceived by the provider or the recipient to be intended to enhance the well-being of the recipient" (Shumaker & Brownell, 1984, p. 13, as cited in Weinberg & Gould, 2003, p. 163). It can be provided by friends/peers, family members, and school staff through three main avenues: (a) *informational, motivational and emotional support* such as watching a practice, talking about game strategy, or discussing physical activity; (b) *instrumental and direct support,* which involves taking part in the activity by providing transportation, equipment, or financial aid; and (c) *observational support* via modeling healthy behaviors (Sallis, Taylor, Dowda, Freedson, & Pate, 2002).

Several studies have not only examined the influence of social support on physical activity levels in adolescents, but have made the distinction between familial and friend support. Both friend and family support are significantly correlated with physical activity among youth (Duncan, Duncan, & Strycker, 2005). However, peer support appears to play a more critical role for female adolescents (Prochaska, Rodgers, & Sallis, 2002; Sallis et al., 2002; Springer, Kelder, & Hoelscher, 2006). Specifically, researchers found that adolescent girls who had physically active friends were more likely to be physically active themselves (Voorhees, Birnbaum, Johnson & Saksvig, 2005). In fact, the frequency of activity with friends was the most significant predictor of participants' own activity; conversely, girls who were less frequently active with friends were less physically active overall. This suggests that encouraging young adolescent girls to participate in sport or physical activity with a close friend or social network may be an especially effective way to increase levels of activity among this population.

In terms of young adolescent boys, sport ability may be a moderating factor of how influential peer support is in determining sport participation. Sport ability appears to be a strong component of how young adolescent boys are accepted, admired, and, therefore, supported by peers. It appears that many boys engage in sport participation as a way to develop social relationships and gain peer acceptance which is so important during this stage in life. Weiss and colleagues (Weiss & Chaumeton, 1992; Weiss & Ferrer-Caja, 2002) found that affiliation motives (e.g., a need for other people, including the dimensions of social comparison, emotional support, positive stimulation and attention) were as strong at influencing youth to become involved in sport as achievement motives were. They also found that gaining social acceptance and approval was one of the three main incentives for young athletes to become involved in sport. In these studies, social acceptance and approval included the specific reasons of being with friends, making new friends, feeling like part of a group, social recognition, approval from parents and coaches, social status, team spirit and atmosphere (Weiss & Ferrer-Caja).

In terms of young adolescent social status, research has shown that athletic ability determines social status in a peer group for males, but that physical appearance is the strongest indicator of social status for girls (Chase & Drummer, 1992). So, while social support from peers may influence young adolescents to get involved in sport (e.g., affiliation motivation), an individual's success and ability within the sport (e.g., achievement motivation) may determine whether or not one receives social support and peer acceptance within that sport. A more recent review of literature on youth sport participation concluded that—whatever the motivation—there is good reason to encourage young adolescents to participate in sport because it has a positive effect on their social well-being. Pirrie (2003) stated that sport "can help increase the self-esteem of individuals, build community spirit, increase social interaction, improve health and fitness, and give young people a purposeful activity, reducing the temptation to anti-social behavior"(p. 184). This makes intuitive sense because as children develop and become adolescents, an increasing amount of time is spent with friends rather than family. Therefore, opinions and habits of peers become more and more important (Monteymayor, 1983). Duncan et al. (2005) proposed that peer support in sport may serve as a factor in social integration or companionship (participating together), emotional support (encouragement), informational support (learning about a sport or physical activity), and instrumental support (sharing equipment or transportation). Further, peers provide a sense of self-worth, value, or esteem which improves self-efficacy in performing a specific sport skill or physical activity task.

Peer support is supported in Physical Education class research as well. Duncan et al. (2005) reported that "companionship and esteem support provided by friends in physical education classes influenced the level of positive affect related to physical activity and choices to participate in physical activity" (p. 7). Companionship and esteem support provided in the form of verbal encouragement friends give has been found to be the most significant variable related to vigorous physical activity (Springer et al., 2006). According to the results, however, all forms of support (friend and family encouragement and participation) play an important role in the physical activity levels of adolescent girls.

It is clear that all forms of social support provided by a significant other can be a critical factor for increasing the level of participation in physical activity among an increasingly sedentary cohort of young adolescents. It should be encouraging to know that increasing levels of physical activity within this group may be possible through family member encouragement, social networks, and positive peer influences. This means that physical activity class instructors could allow young adolescents to play on teams with friends instead of dispersing social networks and creating feelings of isolation and individualism. Families can choose to participate in recreational events that involve more vigorous activity such as going on bike rides rather than to the movies. Parents can encourage children to join sport teams with friends or try a new activity to make friends. Physical activity needs to be fun for children and adolescents so they will enjoy it, participate more frequently, and continue to do it throughout their lifespan. Social support from coaches is another way to make physical activity enjoyable and sustainable throughout life.

The Role of Coaches in Young Adolescents' Lives

Youth sports play an important role in the lives of many children and adolescents and are a large part of American culture and society. Over 35 million children and adolescents between the ages of 6 and 16 years are involved in some form of organized youth sport activity (Leonard, 1998). McCallister, Blinde, and Weiss (2000) put forward that this time in an individual's life is a critical period for learning appropriate social values, life skills, and forming a solid foundation for the adult world. Because of this, social, emotional, and physical growth through sport participation is critical to general health and development and should be monitored closely. While many individuals influence the learning and development of a child or adolescent in youth sport, the coach occupies a key position within this context. In fact, some suggest that "the youth sport coach may in fact be the most significant individual in determining the values and life skills that children learn through participation" (Steelman, 1995, p.16). Coaches are in unique positions of influence and authority and their personal values or philosophies about sport are likely to directly impact the life experience of young adolescent athletes they are coaching.

In this vein, coaches can have either a positive or negative impact on athletes as they practice and compete. Sport participation becomes a place of learning, development, exploration and growth with the coach-as-model and leader throughout this process. Smith and Smoll (1996) contend that coaches not only have a central role in the athletic arena, but also influence outside areas of an adolescent's life. Research has demonstrated that coaches can teach fair play, respect for others, cooperation, decision-making, teamwork, skill development, leadership, and even moral development through participation in youth sport (Barnett, Smoll, & Smith, 1992). On the other hand, the same influence of a coach can result in harmful effects of undue stress and tension, low levels of moral reasoning, overemphasis on winning, low self-esteem, disregard for opponent/lack of respect for others, cheating, and internalizing adult norms prematurely (Decker & Lasley, 1995). In one group of multisport 7-19 year-olds, 60% of the drop-outs did so because of factors that were the responsibility of the coach (Orlick, 1974). Burton and Martens (1986) also found that "conflict of interest" was the most frequently cited reason for dropping out of youth sport. This negative coaching impact not only harms the social, moral, and psychological development of young athletes, it may cause them to drop out and quit participating in sport altogether which, in turn, harms physical health and development.

Indeed, young athletes tend to remember and internalize the relationships developed in sport and how they were treated, not the outcome of the games or season records. Smith and Smoll (1997) found that win-loss records did not relate to psychosocial outcome measures but coaching behavior did. This research demonstrated that positive outcomes were reported when coaches provided high levels of positive reinforcement for performance and effort, gave encouragement and instruction after mistakes, and valued fun and personal improvement over winning. Smith and Smoll advised that athletes with coaches providing these actions and behaviors liked coaches more, had more fun playing, and liked their teammates more. On the other hand, while punitive and hostile actions made up only 1.5% of the coded behaviors in this research, they correlated more strongly and negatively with athlete attitudes than any other coaching behavior recorded. This indicates the detrimental effects even the smallest amount of poor coaching can have on athlete attitudes, emotions, and development.

Because of the way that youth sport is structured in our society, those with the most power and influence (e.g., coaches) are usually unpaid, untrained volunteers (e.g., parents) and/or former athletes or general enthusiasts of the sport. Many have the technical knowledge and skill acquisition needed to teach a particular sport, but not the formal training in social-psychological health and development for young athletes (Smith & Smoll, 1997). As a result, they may imitate coaching behaviors seen on television or develop coach philosophies and values based on personal experiences. These behaviors, philosophies, and values may not be appropriate or suitable for youth sports as they do not focus on age-appropriate instruction or the health, growth and development of the whole person. Many also use fitness activities like running, push-ups and sit-ups as punishment; while this may be one of the most effective strategies for changing a person's behavior in the short-term—and we do not advocate its use—punishment can have the most long-term damaging consequences. For example, many young adolescents who experience this type of punishment in sport may not want to run, do sit-ups or push-ups as adults because of the negative association.

Smith and colleagues (Smith, Smoll, & Curtis, 1979) have done extensive research within the youth sport setting to develop a coach training program to meet the needs of young athletes and overcome many of the problems mentioned above. The Coach Effectiveness Training (CET) program is based on five critical principles for effective youth sport experience: (a) an emphasis on the developmental sports model which highlights having fun, satisfaction, camaraderie, learning skills, increasing self-esteem, and reducing fear of failure over the professional sports model which considers financial gain and winning the most important outcomes of sport; (b) a "positive approach" to coaching which includes reinforcement, encouragement, sound technical instruction, and a high level of interpersonal attraction between coaches and athletes; (c) creating norms that require athletes' mutual obligations to help and support each other such as teamwork, commitment, cohesion, and a collective group atmosphere; (d) assigning team roles and responsibilities that involve athletes in decisions and team rules providing clear limits, structure, and guidelines within a sport context; and (e) teaching coaches to self-monitor, increase awareness of their actions, and obtain behavioral feedback from an outside source for effective adjustment and personal development.

The effects of this training program have demonstrated that coaches can change behaviors, standards, and actions to provide young athletes with an optimal sport experience. When the CET program was initially tested, Smith, Smoll, and Curtis (1979) found that trained coaches had a positive effect on the sport experiences of 10-15 year-old athletes. In fact, after a single 3-hour CET workshop, athletes evaluated the trained coaches significantly higher than the non-trained coaches after a baseball season. Further, trained coaches created more cohesive teams and an increase in self-esteem in athletes who reported low self-esteem prior to sport participation. Recent research has supported these findings, demonstrating that trained coaches provide more support which positively influences children with low-self-esteem (Smith & Smoll, 1997). These results are encouraging for the future of youth sport athletics and will hopefully generate interest and excitement among both those who currently coach and those who wish to coach in the future.

In summary, youth sport coaches must realize the impact they have on a large number of young lives. At this level, the coach's influence can permeate every area of young adolescent's life and may even extend into his/her future growth and development. Whether a coach is a volunteer parent, sport enthusiast or a paid employee, s/he must take the job seriously and truly care about the future of his/her athletes. With a little extra knowledge, effort, and training, coaches can do more than complete a season on the field—they can positively impact the course of young adolescents' lives perhaps forever.

Potential Overuse Issues in Sport and Physical Activity

Even with appropriate training, the simple fact is that some youth have negative experiences related to their sport and physical activity participation. Questions that educators, coaches and parents need to ask themselves to ensure that this risk is minimized include: When is exercise and sport participation unhealthy for young adolescents? What kinds of issues arise when young athletes display disordered eating patterns? How much exercise is too much? What symptoms do "distressed" athletes display?

When does it get so bad that a young adolescent would drop out of sport? Research related to eating disorders and disordered eating patterns, exercise addiction, stress and burnout as well as overtraining and injuries are discussed in this section.

Eating Disorders

Many athletes engage in exercise and weight loss techniques in order to improve performance. However, some can go too far with their caloric restriction and excessive exercise. According to the fourth edition of the *Diagnostic and Statistical Manual of Mental Disorders* (DSM-IV) (American Psychiatric Association, 1994), the most common forms of eating disorders are anorexia nervosa and bulimia nervosa. The four criteria for anorexia nervosa are: (a) weight loss of 15% below normal body weight or refusal to maintain normal body weight, (b) an intense fear of becoming fat, (c) body image disturbance, and (d) the absence of three consecutive menstrual cycles (see pp. 544-545 for more detailed information). This disease is characterized by low body weight and fat. Contrary to popular media accounts, it is a condition related to low self-esteem and "confirmed negativity condition" (Claude-Pierre, 1997) and not an obsession with appearance. This condition is like having a "civil war in the mind" (p. 37); there is a constant stream of negativity playing like a tape in the victim's mind, telling one to harm oneself or what a "worthless human being" one is.

In contrast, bulimia nervosa is characterized by "binging" and "purging" (American Psychiatric Association, 1994, pp. 549-550). "Binging" is taking in massive amounts of food while "purging" is getting rid of those calories either through vomiting or excessive exercise. The five criteria for diagnosis are: (a) recurring incidences of "binge" eating, (b) feeling a lack of control during binges, (c) regular "purging" (d) two binges a week for three months, and (e) persistent and heightened concern with body shape and weight (see pp. 549-550 for more detailed information). This disease is characterized by average or slightly above average body weight and fat. It is not uncommon for an individual suffering from bulimia to eat large quantities of food in a single sitting—often up to 10,000 calories—and then vomit it up because of feelings of guilt and shame. Athletes can also get into the vicious cycle of engaging in behaviors that do not meet all the criteria for eating disorders but can be termed "disordered eating/exercise behaviors" such as excessive exercise, fasting and the use of laxatives or enemas to rid the body of consumed calories. Obviously, these unhealthy behaviors are not ones any adult working with adolescents should encourage.

Exercise Addiction

Excessive exercise can often coincide with an eating disorder. Exercise can be defined as excessive or "addictive" when it moves from important and central to controlling and dominating in one's life (Murphy, 1995). The basic characteristics of exercise addiction are: (a) a belief that one needs the activity to cope and cannot live without it; and (b) s/he experiences withdrawal symptoms if/when deprived of it. Two important points to remember about exercise addiction are that it is brought on when a planned workout is missed and when withdrawal symptoms such as anxiety, restlessness, headaches, apathy, sluggishness, tension, irritability and guilt are evidenced when that happens. Reasons for engaging in the activity often change as well; what were once good reasons to engage in physical exercise (e.g., to get fitter as a member of a team, to lose weight) shift to exercising because one wants to avoid feeling guilty if a planned exercise session is missed.

Stress, Burnout, and Overtraining

Overtraining occurs when young athletes do not get the appropriate amount of rest for the amount of workload their bodies are being asked to do (Murphy, 1995). For example, the deliberate strategy of exposing athletes to higher and higher training loads in the form of aerobic and/or anaerobic work and then tapering off prior to competition is healthy; this is called periodization, overload or overwork. However, when athletes are asked to periodize without a taper or rest period that follows—allowing their bodies to recover and build muscle tissue—this can lead to overtraining and overtraining syndrome. Overtraining syndrome occurs when athletes are exposed to repeated overwork sessions with a total lack of rest cycles. Physical signs of overtraining can include a higher resting heart rate upon waking up and higher or lower than normal blood pressure. Psychological symptoms of overtraining can include feelings of depersonalization and lack of control and emotional exhaustion and frustration. This is often the end result of overtraining, most appropriately referred to as staleness. Staleness can lead to burnout and withdrawal from sport if athletes do not get the physical and emotional rest they need to adequately recover from such overtraining.

Injuries in Young Adolescents

A final negative experience that can happen to young athletes is suffering from an injury. Weinberg and Gould (2003) recommended that, on average, more than 10,000 children and adults are injured in sport and physical activity contexts every year. Anderson and Williams (1988) contended that stress is one psychological factor that influences these injury occurrences. Other precursors to injury include personality factors like introversion-extroversion, self-concept and tough-mindedness as well as a history of stressors in athletes' lives and their coping resources. Whether or not young athletes perceive physical activity and sport participation as threatening is also important, as are the attentional distractions and increased state anxiety, which can occur. The good news is that young athletes can be taught psychological skills training—specifically the use of psychological coping skills and imagery—to ease the recovery process.

Researchers advocate that psychological coping strategies such as goal-setting, positive self-talk, relaxation training, and imagery can be helpful to teach athletes to use in their rehabilitation from sport injury (Weinberg & Gould, 2003). For example, athletes can be taught to create both short- and long-term goals for lifting weights in rehabilitation, can be shown anatomical models of knees/ankles/shoulders/the injured body part and aided in creating an imagery script which "knits" the tear or break back together, can be introduced to and practice progressive muscle relaxation prior to rehabilitation and imagery, and can switch out negative self-talk statements for positive ones related to healing and getting even stronger than before their injury. Social support via talking to other injured athletes has also been shown to speed injury recovery (Gould, Udry, Bridges & Beck, 1997).

CONCLUSIONS AND FUTURE DIRECTIONS

The decline in physical activity among children has occurred in homes, schools, and communities and is a major contributing factor to the rise in obesity. In our opinion, there are two major reasons for this change: schools are dropping physical education from their curriculums and children are engaging in less physical activity and more sedentary pursuits such as television watching and video game–playing. An additional contributing factor can be living in an unsafe neighborhood as Crockett (2003) noted in her keynote address related to the future of school psychology and the critical issues children face as they move into the twenty-first century. Living in dangerous neighborhoods deters children from playing outdoors, visiting parks for recreation, and walking or riding bikes for transportation leading to sedentary lifestyles and inactive leisure choices (Lindquist, Reynolds, & Goran, 1999).

It is no surprise, therefore, that young adolescents are not getting adequate amounts of physical activity and are becoming an obese generation. Researchers propose that obese youth have significantly lower levels of physical activity self-efficacy and report that they are less confident in their ability to overcome barriers to physical activity, ask parents to provide opportunities for physical activity, and choose physically active pursuits over sedentary ones (Trost, Kerr, Ward & Pate, 2001). This is in line with social-cognitive theory, which states that self-efficacy perceptions are derived from four main sources of information: past performance, vicarious experience (modeling), verbal persuasion, and physiological state (Bandura, 1986). So how can educators help this generation increase levels of physical activity so that they can overcome a future destined to poor health?

While many government programs such as *Healthy People 2010* (U.S. Department of health and Human Services, 2000) have already taken action to set goals and guidelines to promote physical activity, healthy eating, and decreased levels of obesity, the physical activity problem should be approached from every angle. Parents need to take responsibility in the home by providing the necessary support and interventions for children. Communities and neighborhoods must fight together to provide parks, recreational and sport opportunities in safe environments for children and families to become involved. Educators and school administrators need to defend physical education and sport programs and understand the importance and relevance of keeping these programs alive in spite of budget deficits and staffing constraints. If government programs, communities, schools, and parents work together, the rise in physical inactivity and obesity among youth can be stopped so that this next generation can be a group of active and healthy individuals who continue to engage in positive habits in the future.

Boon and Clydesdale (2005) put forward that sport and physical activity interventions for young adolescents should be: (a) enjoyable; (b) allow children to experience success; (c) provide opportunities to observe similar or influential others performing physical activity; (d) include verbal encouragement and positive feedback; and (e) decrease participants' anxiety/fears associated with physical activity by eliminating grading and competition. Specifically, walking and moderate-intensity exercise programs allow young adolescents to experience success, see results and stay motivated to remain physically active. Pedometers and activity or goal colanders are excellent ways for them (and parents, schools, and health professionals) to track physical activity and record progress and success. The use of an activity calendar with adolescents can inspire them to exercise and serve as a visual reminder to maintain exercise efforts (Yackel, 2003). An activity calendar lists specific exercises, sports or activities to participate in and a space can be provided for stickers to mark off the accomplished activity.

Parents also play an important role in modeling influential behavior and habits for their adolescent children. In fact, parental physical activity is shown to be strongly and positively correlated with child physical activity (Fogelholm, Nuutinen, Myohanen, & Saatela, 1999) and many parents serve as their children's' youth sport coaches. Parents can provide positive feedback and encouragement which is vitally important to continued participation. They can also provide tangible interventions such as the above mentioned activity calendars as well as working out with their children. They can even take part in sport programs with their young adolescents in neighborhoods or communities if such activities are available.

Coaches (who are also often teachers) are perhaps the most critical in making sure that young adolescents develop into good sportspersons. According the Wormeli (2006), there are at least three ways to keep young adolescents engaged in any curriculum. These overlap with many of the suggestions for quality programs listed above and include: (a) providing frequent and specific feedback; (b) making it vivid; and (c) priming their brains. There is also a young adolescent sport curriculum available through the Character Education Partnership (George Lucas Educational Foundation [GLEF] Staff, 2004) which contains character development principles that apply to sport and life. The curriculum has foundational exercises which focus on self-worth and building the following concepts and skills through participation in sport: (a) working hard and actively helping others because both make you feel good about yourself; (b) being positive with others because people perform and learn better in a positive environment; (c) being positive with yourself because what you are thinking generally affects your behavior or performance; (d) recognizing harmful or distracting thoughts and changing them to helpful ones so our chance of success improves; (e) setting goals to attain success daily and build self-worth; (f) for better results, concentrating on the details of a task, not the outcome; (g) visualizing successfully completing a task to improve chances of success; and (h) meditating to relax and control thoughts, feelings, and actions. As is evident, the GLEF Staff curriculum focuses on building skills, which teach students to be "good thinkers" well beyond their playing time. The "GoGirlGo" Program from the Women's Sports Foundation (www.womenssportsfoundation.com) is another curriculum-based program that is available as well.

Young adolescents are our future. At present, many are suffering from the epidemic of obesity and a lack of physical activity commensurate with the amount of calories they consume. Sport and physical education programs systematically designed with young adolescent psychosocial development as a foundation can be an excellent way to change this pattern. The creation of lifelong fitness habits and good sportspersonship via such programs can transfer over into many spheres of young adolescents' lives. It is our hope that as a result, we can create healthier future generations to come.

ACKNOWLEDGMENT

The authors would like to thank the editors for their helpful suggestions related to this chapter.

NOTE

1. It is important to note that many sport psychology researchers who conduct studies using middle-school students also include students from the upper-elementary and lower-high school grades (ages 10-14 years). In other words, these researchers often do not make the distinction between "youth sport participants," "youth and adolescent sport participants," and "young adolescent" sport participants.

REFERENCES

American Psychiatric Association. (1994). *Diagnostic and statistical manual of mental disorders* (4th ed.). Washington, DC: Author.

Armstrong, J., Dorosty, A. R., Emmett, P. M., Ness, A., Rogers, I., Steer, C., et al. (2003). Early life risk factors for later obesity in contemporary children. *Proceedings of the Nutrition Society, 62,* 2A.

Anderson, M. B., & Williams, J. M. (1988). A model of stress and athletic injury: Prediction and prevention. *Journal of Sport & Exercise Psychology, 10,* 294-306.

Barnett, N. P., Smoll, F. L., & Smith, R. E. (1992). Effects of enhancing coach-athlete relationships on youth sport attrition. *The Sport Psychologist, 6(2),* 111-127.

Bandura, A. (1986). *Social foundations of thought and action: A social-cognitive theory.* Englewood Cliffs, NJ: Prentice Hall.

Boon, C., & Clydesdale, F. (2005). A review of childhood and adolescent obesity interventions. *Critical Reviews in Food Science and Nutrition, 45,* 511-525.

Burton, D., & Martens, R. (1986). Ruined by their own goals: An exploratory investigation into why kids drop out of wrestling. *Journal of Sport Psychology, 8,* 183-197.

Caroli, M., & Lagravinese, D. (2002). Prevention of obesity. *Nutrition Research, 22,* 221-226.

Centers for Disease Control and Prevention. (2003). Physical activity levels among children aged 9-13 years—United States, 2002. *Morbidity Weekly Report, 33,* 785-788.

Chase, M. A., & Drummer, G. M. (1992). The role of sports as a social status determinant for children. *Research Quarterly for Exercise and Sport, 5,* 210-223.

Claude-Pierre, P. (1997). *The secret language of eating disorders.* New York: Times Books (Random House).

Crockett, D. (2003). *Critical issues facing children in the 2000's (*Future of School Psychology Conference Keynote). Retrieved September 18, 2006, from http://www.indiana.edu\futures\crockett.ppt

Decker D., & Lasley, K. (1995). Participation in youth sports, gender, and the moral point of view. *The Physical Educator, 52*(1), 14-21.

Dietz, W. H. (1998). Health consequences of obesity in youth: Childhood predictors of adult disease. *Pediatrics, 101,* 518-525.

Duncan, S. C., Duncan, T. E., & Strycker, L. A. (2005). Sources and types of social support in youth physical activity. *Health Psychology, 24*(1), 3-10.

Fogelholm, M., Nuutinen, O., Myohanen, E., & Saatela, T. (1999). Parent-child relationship of physical activity patterns and obesity. *International Journal of Obesity Related Metabolic Disorders, 23,* 1262-1268.

George Lucas Educational Foundation Staff. (2004). *What coaches can do*. Retrieved September 17, 2006, from http://www.educationworld.com/a_issues/soapbox/soapbox005.shtml

Gould, D., Udry, E., Bridges, D., & Beck, L. (1997). Psychological strategies for helping elite athletes cope with season-ending injuries. *Athletic Therapy Today, 2*(4), 50-53.

Harter, S. (1982). The perceived competence scale for children. *Child Development, 53*(1), 87-97.

Harter, S. (1985). *Manual for the self-perception profile for children*. Denver, CO: University of Denver.

King, A. C. (1994). Clinical and community interventions to promote and support physical activity participation. In R. Dishman (Ed.), *Advances in exercise adherence* (pp. 183-212). Champaign, IL: Human Kinetics.

Leonard, W. M. (1998). *A sociological perspective of sport* (5th ed.). Boston: Allyn & Bacon.

Lindquist D., Reynolds, K. D., & Goran, M. I. (1999). Sociocultural determinants of physical activity among children. *Preventive Medicine, 29*(4), 305-312.

McCallister, S. G., Blinde, E. M., & Weiss, W. M. (2000). Teaching values and implementing philosophies: Dilemmas of the youth sport coach. *Physical Educator, 57*(1), 35-45.

Montemayor, R. (1983). Parents and adolescents in conflict: All families some of the time and some families most of the time. *Journal of Early Adolescence, 3*(1), 83-103.

Murphy, S. (1995). *Sport psychology interventions*. Champaign, IL: Human Kinetics.

National Middle School Association. (2006). *Exploring essential components: Physical activity, nutrition, and the young adolescent.* Retrieved September 18, 2006, from http://www.nmsa.org

Neumark-Sztainer, D. (1999). The weight dilemma: A range of philosophical perspectives. *International Journal of Obesity Related Metabolism Disorders, 23*(8), S31-S37.

Orlick, T. D. (1974). The athletic dropout—a high price of inefficiency. *Canadian Association for Health, Physical Education, and Recreation Journal, 41*(2), 21-27.

Pirrie, A. (2003). Spoilsport: On sport and attainment. *Educational Research, 45,* 181-203.

Pi-Sunyer, F. X. (2000). Obesity: Criteria and classification. *Proceedings of the Nutrition Society, 59,* 505-509.

Prochaska, J. J., Rodgers, M. W., & Sallis, J. F. (2002). Association of parent and peer support with adolescent physical activity. *Research Quarterly Exercise and Sport, 73*, 206-210.

Sallis, J. F., & Patrick, K. (1994). Physical activity guidelines for adolescents: Consensus statement. *Pediatric Exercise Science, 6*, 302-314.

Sallis, J. F., Simons-Morton, B. G., Stone, E. J., Corbin, C. B., Epstein, L. H., & Faucette, N. (1992). Determinants of physical activity and interventions in youth. *Medicine and Science in Sports and Exercise, 24*, S248-S257.

Sallis, J. F., Taylor, W. C., Dowda, M., Freedson, P. S., & Pate, R. R. (2002). Correlates of vigorous physical activity for children in grades 1 through 12: Comparing parent-reported and objectively measured physical activity. *Pediatric Exercise Science, 14*(1), 30-44.

Smith, R. E., & Smoll, F. L. (1996). *Children and youth in sport: A biopsychosocial perspective.* New York: McGraw Hill.

Smith, R. E., & Smoll, F. L. (1997). Coaching the coaches: Youth sports as a scientific and applied behavioral setting. *Current Directions in Psychological Science, 6*(1), 16-21.

Smith, R. E., Smoll, F. L., & Curtis, B. (1979). Coach effectiveness training: A cognitive-behavioral approach to enhancing relationship skills in youth sport coaches. *Journal of Sport Psychology, 1*(1), 59-75.

Spinger, A. E., Kelder, S. H., & Hoelscher, D. M. (2006). Social support, physical activity and sedentary behavior among 6th grade girls: A cross-sectional study. *International Journal of Behavioral Nutrition and Physical Activity, 3*(8), 8-18.

State of Michigan. (1976). *Joint legislative study on youth sports programs. Phase 2.* East Lansing, MI: Author.

Steelman, T. (1995). Enhancing the youth sports experience through coaching. *Parks and Recreation, 29*(11), 14-17.

Trost, S. G., Kerr, L. M., Ward, D. S., & Pate, R. R. (2001). Physical activity and determinants of physical activity in obese and non-obese children. *InternationalJournal of Obesity, 25*, 822-829.

U.S. Department of Health and Human Services. (1996). *Physical activity and health: A report of the surgeon general.* Retrieved October 9, 2005, from http://www.hhs.gov/children/index.shtml

U.S. Department of Health and Human Services. (2000). *Healthy people 2010.* Washington, DC: Author.

Voorhees, C. C., Birnbaum, A., Johnson, C. C., & Saksvig, B. (2005). The role of peer social network factors and physical activity in adolescent girls. *American Journal of Health Behavior, 29*, 183-190.

Weinberg, R. S., & Gould, D. (2003). *Foundations of sport & exercise psychology* (3rd ed.). Champaign, IL: Human Kinetics.

Weiss, M. R., & Chaumeton, N. (1992). Motivational orientations in sport. In T. S. Horn (Ed.), *Advances in sport psychology* (pp. 61-99). Champaign, IL: Human Kinetics.

Weiss, M. R., & Ferrer-Caja, E. (2002). Motivational orientations and sport behavior. In T. S. Horn (Ed.), *Advances in sport psychology* (2nd ed., pp. 101-183). Champaign, IL: Human Kinetics.

Weiss, M. R., & Williams, L. (2004). The *why* of youth sport involvement: A developmental perspective on motivational processes. In M. R. Weiss (Ed.), *Developmental sport and exercise psychology: A lifespan perspective* (pp. 223-268). Morgantown, WV: Fitness Information Technology.

Women's Sports Foundation. (2006). *The "GoGirlGo" program*. Retrieved September 18, 2006, from http://www.womenssportsfoundation.com

Wormeli, R. (2006). *Ten-to-fourteen-year-olds commonly demonstrate the best and worst ways to keep middle schoolers engaged.* Retrieved September 18, 2006, from http://www.education-world.com/a_issues/chat/chat153.shtml

Yackel, E. E. (2003). An activity calendar program for children who are overweight. *Pediatric Nursing, 29(1),* 17-22.

CHAPTER 3

UNDER CONSTRUCTION

The Young Adolescent Brain

Micki M. Caskey and Barbara Ruben

ABSTRACT

Young adolescence is a period of considerable developmental change. Middle grades educators and academics are usually aware of the physical, intellectual, psychological, emotional, social, and moral characteristics of young adolescents; however, they often seek additional information about young adolescent development. One area in particular—brain development—captures the attention of practitioners and neuroscientists alike. This chapter reviews neuroscience research literature that is relevant to young adolescent brain development and reports the findings for access by academics and practitioners. The chapter provides information about the human brain, an overview of early research studies on adolescent brain development, a description of neuroimaging advances, a synthesis of recent neuroscience research specific to the brain development of young adolescents, and a discussion of the dynamic nature of science, current brain research findings, and of suggestions for educators.

The Young Adolescent and the Middle School
pp. 47–72

INTRODUCTION

Understanding and responding to the unique developmental characteristics of young adolescents—10- to 14-year-olds—has been a central and enduring focus of middle grades education. At the beginning of the twentieth century, Hall (1904) acknowledged that young adolescence was a distinctive developmental stage. The Carnegie Council on Adolescent Development (1989) referred to young adolescence as a critical transition time—a "turning point"—in human development. Leaders in middle grades education (Alexander & George, 1981; Association for Supervision and Curriculum Development, 1975; Eichhorn, 1966; Lipsitz, 1984; Lounsbury & Vars, 1978; National Association of Secondary School Principals Council on Middle Level Education, 1985; National Middle School Association, 1982, 1995, 2003) and advocates (Jackson & Davis, 2000) offered recommendations and forwarded positions to support this specific age group. Scales (2003) described the considerable physical, intellectual, psychological, emotional, social, and moral developmental changes that young adolescents experience during this period. Not surprisingly, researchers (e.g., Blakemore & Choudhury, 2006; Giedd, 2004) have found that young adolescence is also a significant time for human brain development.

News regarding how the human brain develops from childhood to adulthood captures the interest of middle grades practitioners, parents, and others. This interest comes from their desire to understand the characteristics and needs of young adolescents. Educators access information about the developing brain via media and print formats including the Web (e.g., National Institute of Health Office of Science Education, n.d.; Society for Neuroscience, n.d.), television broadcasts (e.g., ABC News Special, 1999; PBS, 2002), educational video tapes (e.g., Video Journal, 1997), weekly news magazines (e.g., *Newsweek*, *Time*) and articles in educational journals (e.g., *Educational Leadership*, *Middle School Journal*, *Phi Delta Kappan*). With this greater access to information, teachers need to assume greater responsibility for the selection of reliable sources. Teachers need to be wary of those who move too quickly to make the link between brain research and educational practice such as entrepreneurs who develop market-driven "brain-compatible" products (Davis, 2000). Bruer (1999) also cautioned educators about the content of brain-based education literature that "formulate bold statements about brain science and education that are speculative at best and often far removed from neuroscientific fact" (p. 650). This chapter, however, synthesizes recent brain research findings with the intention of providing credible rather speculative information about young adolescent brain development.

Neuroscience is the study of the nervous system including the brain, spinal cord, and networks of neurons throughout the body (Society for Neuroscience, 2006). Due to advances in neuroscience technology, researchers can now study the complex and distinct changes in the brain that occur during young adolescence. Blakemore and Choudhury (2006) noted that "empirical research on cognitive and neural development during puberty and adolescents is in its initial phases" (p. 296). Neuroscientists are conducting numerous studies on specific areas of the brain including the prefrontal cortex, amygdala, and hippocampus (Casey, Giedd, & Thomas, 2000; Giedd, 2004; Geidd et al., 1999; Giedd et al., 2006; Killgore, Oki, & Yurgelun-Todd, 2000; Killgore & Yurgelun-Todd, 2004; Yurgelun-Todd & Killgore, 2006). Preliminary findings reveal differences in the development and function of the adolescent brain and the adult brain. What is most interesting for scientists (Bloom, Beale, & Kupfer, 2003; Dahl, 2003, 2004; Giedd) is the potential relationship between brain processes and human behavior. This potential relationship is also of compelling interest to teachers, parents, and others who work with young adolescents.

Research is beginning to show how brain development influences the physical, cognitive, and emotional development of adolescents (Dahl, 2004). Educators need an awareness of these developmental factors to understand and effectively teach young adolescents. To keep current with findings from the sciences, including neuroscience, teachers need reliable information.

The purpose of this chapter is twofold: (1) to review the neuroscience research literature pertinent to young adolescent brain development, and (2) to make the findings of neuroscience accessible to academics and practitioners. This chapter includes background information about the human brain, an overview of the early experiments on adolescent brains, advances in imaging technology, a synthesis of recent neuroscience research specific to the brain development of young adolescents, and a discussion of science, current brain research findings, and suggestions for educators.

BACKGROUND: THE HUMAN BRAIN

The brain is a complex organ that controls bodily functions including heart rate, movement, emotion, memory, and learning. Weighing about three pounds, an adult human brain consists of three divisions: the forebrain, midbrain, and hindbrain (National Institute of Neurological Disorders and Stroke, 2001). For clarity, neuroscientists describe the brain structures and their functions independently (see Appendix); however, it is imperative to recognize the interdependent nature and complexity of the brain. The hindbrain consists of the cerebellum, brain stem, and upper part of the spinal cord that work collectively to regulate vital bodily functions. The cerebellum is responsible for balance, posture, coordination of muscles; it also stores procedural memory associated with routine movements. Connecting the brain and spinal cord, the brain stem controls autonomic functions such as respiration and circulation. The smallest division, the midbrain, handles voluntary movements and some sensory processes. The largest and most developed of these divisions is the forebrain, which includes the cerebrum, cerebral cortex, and inner brain structures (e.g., thalamus, hypothalamus). The forebrain is responsible for cognitive or mental processes—knowing, thinking, reasoning, and remembering as well as sensorimotor functions. Since cognitive function and development are of primary importance to educators, additional detail about the cerebrum, cerebral cortex, and inner brain structures follows.

Cerebrum and Cerebral Cortex

The cerebrum and cerebral cortex are "the structures that operate at the conscious level" (Wolfe, 2001, p. 31). A deep fissure splits the cerebrum, the outermost part of the brain, into left and right cerebral hemispheres. These hemispheres communicate with each other through a network of nerves at the base of the fissure (corpus callosum). Covering the cerebral hemispheres is a thin, wrinkled, outer layer—the cerebral cortex. Approximately two millimeters in thickness, the cerebral cortex is where "most of the information processing in the brain takes place" (National Institute of Neurological Disorders and Stroke, 2001, p. 5). The cerebral cortex consists of four main sections—the occipital, temporal, parietal, and frontal lobes (see Figure 3.1). Named according to the adjacent skull bones, each lobe resides in a different part of the brain. Situated at the back of the brain, the occipital lobes process visual information from the eyes. Located above the ears and near the temples, the temporal lobes process auditory stimuli. Parts of the temporal lobes specialize in hearing, comprehending language, speech, and auditory memory; other parts appear to integrate memories and sensations (Society for Neuroscience, 2006). The parietal lobes rest between the occipital and frontal lobes and process sensory information—temperature, taste, touch, spatial awareness, and orientation. Positioned at the very front of the brain are the frontal lobes, which handle sensorimotor and complex cognitive tasks. Within each frontal lobe is the motor cortex that directs muscular movement and interacts with Broca's area of the temporal lobes

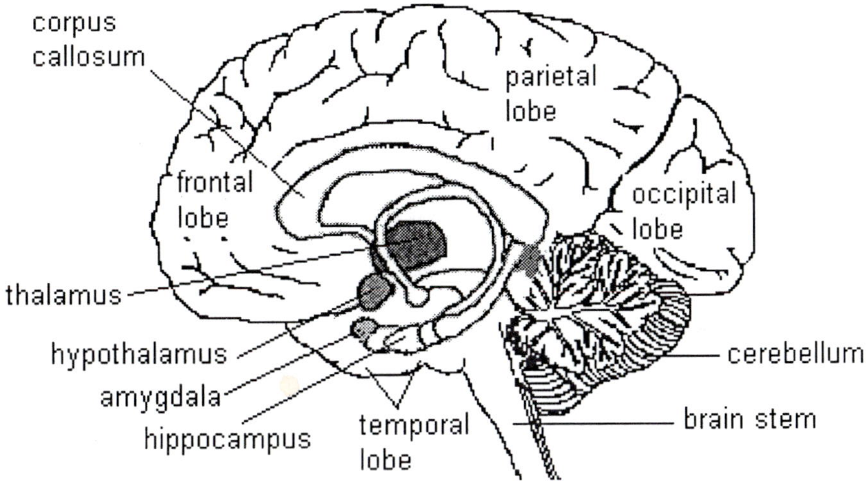

Figure 3.1. Medial view of brain lobes and inner brain structures.

to create speech. Additionally, the frontal lobes are the source of thought processes—thinking about the present, planning, focusing attention, reflecting on the past, reasoning, and problem solving. Though general agreement about the function of the cerebrum and cerebral cortex exists, scientists acknowledge that much more needs to be understood about their functions including coordination across the cerebral hemispheres and among the cerebral lobes.

Inner Brain Structures

Operating at the unconscious level are inner brain structures, which include, but are not limited to, the thalamus, hypothalamus, amygdala, hippocampus, and basal ganglia. Neuroscientists report that these structures have both distinct and interrelated functions. Situated deep within the brain (near the brainstem) are two small structures, the thalamus and hypothalamus, which regulate sensory perception and bodily functions (see Figure 3.1). Acting as a relay station, the thalamus receives sensory input and sends it to the cerebral cortex (Wolfe, 2001) and other areas of the brain. Adjacent to the thalamus, the hypothalamus regulates body temperature, nutrient needs, sleep, sex drive, and the "fight or flight" response to danger. Located near the thalamus and hypothalamus, is a small structure, the amygdala. The amygdala plays a vital role in emotional learning (Society of Neuroscience, 2006) and is also associated with "fight-or-flight" survival response. When the thalamus receives sensory input, it relays that information to the cerebral cortex and to the amygdala. If the amygdala senses that the input is dangerous, it sends a signal to the hypothalamus to speed up the heart rate, raise the blood pressure, and go into survival mode. The amygdala communicates with another inner structure, the hippocampus. The hippocampus is responsible for holding memories of the immediate past as well as dispatching these memories to the cerebral cortex for long-term storage (Wolfe).

The amygdala and hippocampus play an integral role in the regulation and expression of emotional memory. The basal ganglia—neural cells surrounding the thalamus—are also involved in emotion. The basal ganglia have a central role in movement and muscle tone as well as mediate higher cognitive functions, attention, and emotion (Giedd, 2004). Collectively, these inner structures "not only determine our emotional state, they also modify our perceptions and responses depending on that state, and allow us to initiate movements without thinking about them" (National Institute of Neurological Disorders and Stroke, 2001, p. 5). These inner brain structures are particularly relevant when examining the research about adolescent brain development.

Neurons

To acquire a basic understanding of human brain development, including those of young adolescents, prompts an explanation of the brain at the cellular level. Humans are born with over 100 billion neurons—highly specialized cells for information transmission. Each neuron consists of a cell body, dendrites (thousands of branch-like projections), and an axon that work together to receive, process, and transmit information using electrical and chemical signals. The end of the axon branches out into a terminal where electrical impulses launch into the synapse—a physical space between two neurons. Electrical impulses from one neuron convert to chemicals (neuron transmitters) that move through the synapse to receptors on dendrites from other neurons and where they convert back to electrical impulses. This process, neurotransmission, can be accelerated by the presence of myelin—a fatty substance that forms a sheath over the axon. Myelination, the formation of myelin around the axon, speeds the neurotransmission as much as 100 times faster than unmyelinated axons (Giedd, 2004).

Gray Matter

Gray matter is neural tissue composed of neurons that have axons with no myelin covering. Two major categories of gray matter are cortical (cerebral cortex) and subcortical (inside the cerebral cortex) (Giedd, 2004). Throughout childhood, gray matter grows through a process called arborization (branching out) to form multiple connections (Giedd). Conversely, gray matter decreases through a process known as neural pruning—when the brain prunes away unused neural pathways. Neural pruning occurs at certain periods of brain development and across specific regions of the brain.

White Matter

White matter is neural tissue that contains neurons with myelinated axons. It is called white matter because myelin is white. One of the primary areas of white matter in the brain is the corpus callosum, which connects the left and right hemispheres. The corpus callosum is a complex cluster of approximately 200 million myelinated axons. Not only does the corpus callosum coordinate left and right hemispheres, but it is also involved in memory storage, retrieval, attention, arousal, language and auditory functions.

ADOLESCENT BRAIN DEVELOPMENT: EARLY RESEARCH

Blakemore and Choudhury (2006) reviewed the early research on adolescent brain development, which they characterized as a relatively new area of research. Beginning in the 1950s, scientists began investigating the effects of environmental stimulation on normal brain development. Using animal experimentation, these pioneering researchers focused on the early childhood period. Not until the late 1960s and 1970s did research on post-mortem human brains uncover evidence of continued development of the brain after early childhood. By the late 1970 and 1980s, post-mortem experimentation documented that "the prefrontal cortex of the brain undergoes significant changes during puberty and adolescence (p. 296). Despite the limited number of autopsies on normal adolescent brains, the early research studies revealed two key changes: (1) neural pruning during adolescence, and (2) myelination of axons in the frontal cortex. In future decades, newer technologies would confirm these preliminary findings.

ADVANCES IN IMAGING TECHNOLOGY

Recent advances in neuroimaging technology allow researchers to view the structures and functions of the living human brain. Though scientists continue to conduct autopsies on human brain tissue to investigate brain abnormalities and diseases (Wolfe, 2001), they are increasingly using modern imaging methods including computerized tomography (CT or CAT scans), positron emission tomography (PET), and magnetic resonance imaging (MRI and fMRI) to study the human brain. To grasp how researchers are using these technologies to uncover the developmental mysteries of the young adolescent brain, a brief description of each follows.

Developed in the 1970s, neuroscientists and medical researchers use computerized tomography (CT) to scan a static image of the brain. A CT scan (sometimes referred to as CAT scan) takes a series of two-dimensional x-rays from different angles and uses computer processing to generate a cross-section or three-dimensional image. These scans can detect and pinpoint abnormalities such as lesions and tumors.

During this same period, neuroscientists began working on the development of techniques to monitor the brain's functions—metabolic and mental processes. One important technique, positron emission tomography (PET) scanning, measures blood flow or energy consumption in the brain (Society for Neuroscience, 2006). The technique entails the injection of a radioactive compound into the bloodstream that the PET scanner can detect in different regions of the brain (National Institute on Drug Abuse, 1996)—while a person performs a task. The PET scanner captures two- or three-dimensional images of the brain allowing researchers to discover which regions are expending energy. The PET scanning technique facilitates medical diagnoses (e.g., cancer) and studies of brain development (Chugani, 1998).

Two other neuroimaging techniques, magnetic resonance imaging (MRI) and functional magnetic resonance imaging (fMRI) provide high-quality, three-dimensional images of human organs without x-rays or radioactive compounds (Society for Neuroscience, 2006). An MRI uses radiofrequency waves and strong magnetic fields to form clear images of internal organs and tissues (RadiologyInfo, 2005a). Similar to PET scans, scientists use MRIs to locate brain abnormalities—tumors and lesions. An fMRI uses magnetic resonance imagery to measure the rapid and minute metabolic changes in the brain, which allows researchers to map brain activity and determine precisely which part of the brain handles critical functions (RadiologyInfo, 2005b). Not only do fMRIs produce high-resolution images of neural activity, but also are noninvasive instruments, which make them ideal for brain development research. Giedd (2004) notes that magnetic resonance imaging "has helped to launch a new era of adolescent neuroscience" (p. 78).

YOUNG ADOLESCENT BRAIN DEVELOPMENT

The young adolescent brain is under construction. To begin to grasp the complexity of the changes, neuroscientists are studying the structural and functional aspects of the developing human brain. Specific studies concerning the adolescent brain are increasing noticeably—growing from two published papers in 1990 to more than 150 research papers in 2005 (Monastersky, 2007). The following sections synthesize a selection of research findings related to (a) brain size, (b) gray matter and neural pruning, (c) white matter, (d) amygdala and hippocampus, and (e) effects of high-risk behaviors, specifically alcohol and cannabis use, on the brain.

Brain Size

The young adolescent brain is almost the size of an adult brain. By age six, the brain is approximately 95% of its adult size (Giedd et al., 2006). In their ongoing longitudinal study of healthy youth brains, Giedd and his colleagues determined that the total size of the brain remains fairly stable from ages 6 to 20, although various subcomponents of the brain undergo dynamic changes. Giedd (2004) and his team at the Child Psychiatry Branch of the National Institute of Mental Health acquired 329 scans from a sample of 95 males and 66 females. Taken approximately every 2 years, the MRI scans captured images of the subjects who ranged in age from 4 to 20. Within 2 years, Giedd et al. had expanded the data set to approximately 4,000 scans from 2,000 subjects. Analyses of scanned images occurred at imaging centers throughout the world. Results indicated the adolescent brain size differed by gender with male brains on average being 9% larger than female brains. They found that brain size peaks on average at 11.5 years for females and at 14.5 years for males. Giedd cautioned, "Differences in total brain size should not be interpreted as imparting any sort of functional advantage or disadvantage. However, differences in trajectories of brain size may be relevant to understanding some cognitive or behavioral differences" (p. 155). Though total brain size change is minimal, the proportion of gray matter decreases due to neural pruning while during the same period white matter increases due to myelination.

Gray Matter

As mentioned, gray matter consists of the neurons without myelin and exists in both the cerebral cortex (the outer covering of the brain) and subcortical areas (inside the cortex). Throughout childhood the gray matter grows through a process called arborization or branching out in to multiple connections (Giedd, 2004). During young adolescence, this branching stops in certain parts of the brain and the brain starts to prune away some connections of the gray matter. Giedd observed, "The thickening and thinning of cortical gray matter is thought to reflect changes in the size and complexity of neurons, not a change in the actual number" (p. 82). Gray matter changes are non-linear and occur unevenly across regions of the brain.

The refinement of gray matter also differs between males and females (Giedd, 2004; Giedd et al., 2006). Giedd et al. (1999) found that the frontal lobe of the brain (sensorimotor and cognitive functions) reaches maximum volume at age 11 in girls and 12.1 in boys. His studies showed that the temporal lobe (auditory processing and memory center) did not reach its peak until age 16.7 in girls and age 16.2 in boys, while the parietal lobe (related to touch) reached its peak at age 10.2 in girls and age 11.8 in boys. Giedd (2004) noted that the last area to reach maximum volume is the dorsolateral prefrontal cortex—the part of the brain "linked to inhibit impulses, weigh consequences of decisions, prioritize, and strategize" (p. 83). His research revealed that this vital part of the prefrontal cortex did not reach adult levels until 20 or more years of age.

Neural Pruning

Pruning of the gray matter, as aforementioned, occurs at different times in different sections of the brain. Neuroscientists do not fully understand how or why the brain goes through the neural pruning process. One hypothesis is that the brain prunes away unused connections giving rise to a "use it or lose it" premise. Giedd (2004) explained, "Those connections that are used will survive and flourish, whereas those connections that are not used will wither and die. If this hypothesis is correct, the activities of the teen may have a powerful influence on the ultimate physical structure of the brain" (pp. 82-83). What neuroscientists know is that young adolescent brains experience structural changes due to arborization and neural pruning processes.

White Matter

The white matter in the brain increases throughout childhood and adolescence (Giedd, 2004; Geidd et al., 1999; Giedd et al., 2006). "The white matter increases are roughly linear and the slope of the increase is approximately the same in the four major lobes of the brain" (Giedd, 2004, p. 80). As described previously, white matter is brain tissue with myelinated axons. The corpus callosum—the most prominent white matter component of the brain—also increases during young adolescence. It grows an average 1.3% per year throughout childhood and adolescence (Giedd, 2004). Further, Silveri, Rohan, Pimentel, Gruber, Rosso, and Yurgelun-Todd (2006) cited an earlier study that concluded that white matter increases to as much as 10% within a two year span during adolescence.

Silveri et al. (2006) looked at the relationship between brain's white matter activity and young adolescents' impulse control. Using fMRI scans, they studied the brain tissue of 21 healthy young adolescents (mean = 12.3 ± 2.9 years). The researchers examined the directional activity of the youths' corpus callosum during the completion of various cognitive and behavioral assessments (e.g., Bar-On Emotional Quotient Inventory-Youth Version, Stroop Color-Word Interference Test). Silveri et al. found that cognitive performance significantly improved with age. The corpus collosum's function was significantly different for boys and girls, though findings revealed no gender-related difference in the young adolescents' impulse control or cognitive performance. In this small sample, the researchers noted differences in both the development and function of the corpus callosum, which was not evident in the young adolescents' behavior. Notably, Silveri et al.'s study supports previous research findings of gender-specific differences in structural and functional brain development during adolescence (Giedd, 2002; Yurgelon-Todd, Killgore, & Young, 2002).

Yurgelun-Todd et al. (2002) studied the cerebral tissues of 30 healthy adolescents (ages 13-17) to determine whether changes in the ratio of white and gray matter are associated with improved cognitive performance. Data revealed a correlation between increased volume of white matter and the speed of information processing with improved verbal skills for the 10 boys. No such correlation was evident for the 20 girls, leading researchers to speculate that girls' brain tissue matured at an earlier developmental age. Importantly, Yurgelun-Todd, Killgore, and Young confirmed that chronological age correlates with greater verbal ability for both boys and girls. Further, they asserted that white matter volume and processing speed were consistent with earlier research that increased myelination of axons produced faster neurotransmission and "more efficient processing of information" (p. 751). They also noted decreases in gray matter volume and density during adolescence, which has been associated with neural pruning.

Due to consistency across findings, researchers (e.g., Blakemore & Choudhury, 2006; Casey, Giedd, & Thomas, 2000; Dahl, 2004; Giedd, 2004) agree on three critical points related to the developing adolescent brain. First, the total volume of the brain is relatively unchanged after age 5 or 6. Second, there is a significant decrease in gray matter after age 12 due to neural pruning—associated with more efficient neural circuitry. Third, white matter increases throughout childhood and young adulthood due to myelination—associated with information processing speed. Researchers speculate that improved cognitive performance coincides with the changes in gray matter and white matter. Additionally, they note differences in the brain development of girls and boys during young adolescence.

Amygdala and Hippocampus

Neuroscientists report that certain parts of the brain—the amygdala and hippocampus— go through dramatic gender-specific changes during the young adolescent years (Casey, Giedd, & Thomas, 2000; Giedd et al. 2006). These regions of the brain, as noted previously, play a major role in emotion, language, and memory. The amygdala, known as the brain's fear center, increases in size in young adolescent boys. The hippocampus, most associated with memory, increases in volume in young adolescent girls. Researchers continue to consider how gender and chronological ages affect the development of the adolescent brain.

Killgore, Oki, and Yurgelun-Todd (2000) studied the interaction of the amygdala and prefrontal cortex of the brain during the introduction of emotional stimuli. To identify developmental and gender differences in affective processing, the researchers examined subjects' fMRI brain scans. Nineteen children and adolescents ranging in age from 9 to17 (mean = 13.5 ± 2.1) viewed photographs of fearful faces while positioned inside an fMRI machine. Researchers identified differences in the responses of girls (n = 10) and boys (n = 9). They found that girls progressively increased the use of the prefrontal cortex relative to the amygdala when processing responses to emotional stimuli. In contrast, boys increased their dependence on the amygdala for processing emotional stimuli across young adolescence. In this small sample, the researchers concluded that boys by age 17 were still not utilizing the prefrontal cortex to help process emotion to the extent of an adult.

In a subsequent study, Yurgelun-Todd, Killgore, and Cintron (2003) examined developmental changes in amygdala and hippocampus volume related to cognitive performance of adolescents. Subjects included 37 healthy adolescents, 24 girls and 13 boys, ranging in age from 12 to 17 (mean = 14.6 ± 1.5). After completing a series of cognitive assessments (e.g., WRAT-R, WAIS-R), the subjects underwent structural MRI scanning. Researchers found that chronological age during adolescence correlated significantly with improved cognitive performance. Though chronological age did not correlate with hippocampus volume, the researchers found a significant correlation between age and amygdala volume. When researchers examined the data by gender, they detected better cognitive performances in boys—especially verbal tasks—correlated with greater amygdala volume. However, in girls, there was a limited structure-volume association excepting a negative correlation with math task performance and hippocampus volume. Regression analyses showed that amygdala volumes alone predicted the cognitive performances of boys, whereas in girls' cognitive performances hippocampus volume was also a factor. Adding to a growing body of evidence, Yurgelun-Todd, Killgore, and Cintron concluded that amygdala volume contributes to learning and memory.

In another study of response to facial affect, Killgore and Yurgelun-Todd (2004) investigated the processing of the prefrontal cortex and the amygdala across developmental age and gender. Using a cross-sectional design, the researchers scanned specific regions of the brains of 29 subjects, including 7 young adolescents (9 to 12 yrs.), 12 adolescents (13 to 17 yrs.) and 10 young adults (20 to 29 yrs.). Similar to other studies, the subjects underwent fMRI while completing a task requiring the perception of fearful faces. Killgore and Yurgelun-Todd reported significant differences in the function of the right and left amygdala. The amygdala function in boys and girls of the adolescent period (13-17 yrs.) was significantly more asymmetric (i.e., greater activation of the right amygdala) than that of young adolescents and young adults. In other words, amygdala activation was not a linear model of development.

In this study, scans of adolescent boys also showed dominant use of the right prefrontal cortex that was not evident in scans of adolescent girls. Killgore and Yurgelun-Todd noted that such activation "has been associated with a tendency to react more negatively to affectively charged stimuli" (p. 385). They continued

> While we emphasize that there is no evidence of causal relationship between observed patterns of brain activation and general social behavior, the greater propensity for adolescents to seek out novel stimulation and engage in greater risk-taking behavior is particularly interesting in light of our current findings. (p. 386)

Killgore and Yurgelun-Todd's findings have prompted questions regarding possible neurobiological explanations for the risky behaviors that often characterize adolescence.

Effects of High-Risk Behaviors

Young adolescents are at a particularly vulnerable time for participation in high-risk behaviors. A number of researchers examined the consequences of substance abuse on young adolescent brain development. Two substances commonly abused by young adolescents are alcohol and cannabis (i.e., marijuana).

Alcohol Use

Alcohol use among young and older adolescents remains a serious high-risk behavior. In 2004, the National Institute on Drug Abuse (2005) conducted a large-scale study of adolescent substance abuse among approximately 49,500 students—including about 17,400 eighth graders—in public and private schools. Forty-four percent of these eighth graders reported alcohol consumption—more than a few sips. Such early alcohol consumption has had serious repercussions. Hill (2004) explained, "The earlier an adolescent begins regular drinking of alcohol, the higher the level of misuse and alcohol dependence" (p. 246). Similarly, Brown and Tapert (2004) noted, "Youth that begin drinking alcohol before age 14, have a 41% chance of developing alcohol dependence during their lifetime compared to individuals who wait to the legal dinking age of 21 when lifetime risk reduced to 10%"(p. 235). Additionally, early alcohol abuse has been connected to conduct disorder, antisocial personality disorder, and nicotine dependence. Illicit drug abuse and addiction have also been shown to be higher among youth that drink early.

Brown and Tapert (2004) conducted a series of longitudinal studies about the effect of alcohol use disorders on cognitive performance of 15- to 16-year-olds. Subjects included adolescents with alcohol use disorders and those identified as non-abusers, who had been matched for age, gender, socioeconomic status, and family history. Baseline findings indicated that those adolescents diagnosed with alcohol use disorders used fewer strategies to learn new information and had reduced memory skill capacity than nonabusers. Subsequently, the subjects' cognitive skills were reevaluated at two intervals (4 and 8 years). The cognitive performance of adolescents who continued to abuse alcohol and experience alcohol withdrawal symptoms deteriorated relative to their own baseline data and the performance of nonabusing peers. Overall Brown and Tapert found that the longer an adolescent abuses alcohol, the poorer they score on working memory, visual-spatial functioning, and attention tasks. They acknowledged that what remains unknown is if the brains of heavy drinking adolescents can recover full cognitive functioning.

Other researchers focused on the effect of adolescent alcohol abuse on the physical structure of the brain. Using MRI technology, Bellis et al. (2000) scanned the brains of 36 adolescents—12 diagnosed with alcohol abuse disorder and 24 nonabusers. In this small sample, hippocampal volumes were significantly smaller in adolescents with alcohol use disorders. Further, the researchers noted that earlier the onset of heavy drinking and greater the quantity of alcohol was correlated with smaller size of the hippocampus. Bellis et al. concluded that the adolescent hippocampus might be particularly susceptible to the adverse effects of alcohol.

A complicating or mitigating factor is the young adolescent brain is still under construction; it does not receive the same physiological cues about excessive alcohol intake. Spear (2004) reported that the adolescent brains are less sensitive to the sedation and temperature regulation effects of alcohol. Unlike the adult brain, when young adolescents binge drink they do not get the message to stop. Therefore, they keep drinking far beyond when adults would lose consciousness and stop poisoning their bodies.

Cannabis Use

As evidenced in National Institute on Drug Abuse (2005) study, cannabis is the most prevalently used illicit drug among adolescents. As noted previously, researchers survey public and private school students, including about 17,400 eighth graders and 16,800 10th graders. The findings indicated that more than 16% of eighth graders and 35% of 10th graders reported the use of cannabis.

Researchers have also begun to examine the detrimental effects of cannabis use on adolescents. Jacobsen, Mencl, Westerveld, and Pugh (2004) conducted a pilot study concerning cannabis use and cognitive function of 21 adolescents ranging in age from 15 to 18. The subjects included cannabis users ($n = 7$), tobacco smokers ($n = 7$), and a comparison group of nonusers ($n = 7$). Cannabis users in the study reported their use began at age 13.8 (± 1.9). While the subjects attempted the completion of working memory tasks, the researchers scanned the adolescents' brains using fMRI technology. While none of the subjects was under the influence of cannabis during the cognitive assessment, they identified themselves as frequent cannabis users. Cannabis users were unable to sustain attention or perform a working memory task as accurately as the comparison group. Jacobson et al. found that "performance accuracy of cannabis users was significantly lower than that of non-smokers while performance accuracy of smokers did not differ from that of non-smokers" (p. 388). In a related part of the study, Jacobson et al. looked specifically at the subjects' hippocampus and observed that cannabis users failed to deactivate their right hippocampus during the performance of memory tasks. The researchers speculated that deactivation of the right hippocampus is associated with impaired memory. This small study offers preliminary evidence regarding the damaging effects of cannabis use for young and older adolescents.

Neuroscientists hypothesize that because youths' brains are more plastic, recovery is more likely. Nevertheless, researchers are concerned that the neurotoxic damage of alcohol (Brown & Tapert, 2004; Hill, 2004) and cannabis (Jacobsen et al., 2004) might severely interfere with essential neuromaturation of the brain, which should be taking place during healthy adolescent development.

DISCUSSION

Similar to young adolescent brain, the field of neuroscience is developing. Certainly, scientists do not fully understand the developing brain though they are able to detect considerable changes in the cerebral cortex, gray and white matter, and inner brain structures. Giedd (2004) reminded us, "Direct data on the relationship on the brain changes ... and the behavior changes of type described for teens has not been established" (p. 83). He continued, "Brain structure goes through explosive changes during the teen years. The connection between these structural changes and behavioral changes is only beginning to be elucidated" (p. 83). As a discipline, neuroscience is relatively young.

Science: Changing and Dynamic

By its very nature, science is changing and dynamic. Gould (1981) noted that scientists "refute older ideas in the light of a different view about the nature of things" (p. 322). Scientists posit ideas, test hypotheses, and develop theories that are subject to further investigation and can be supported or debunked. In the case studies of the human brain, newer research methods including instrumentation and exacting analyses help to uncover flaws of earlier theories. A few examples help to explicate the changing nature of science.

In nineteenth-century Europe, Paul Broca, a neurological clinician and researcher advanced the theory of craniometry—measurement of the cranium—as an indication of human intelligence. While scientists debated the findings, both academic journals and popular press disseminated the results. At the time, many scientists and the public viewed the theory of craniometry as a "rigorous and respectable science" (Gould, 1981, p. 25). However, by the twentieth-century, scientific and public acceptance of craniometry had ended. Craniometry's rise and fall from favor in the scientific community exemplifies how theories can evolve over time.

Another theory that gained and lost support was brain periodization—a theory of human brain growth stages. Epstein (1978) theorized that the brain undergoes alternating periods of growth spurts and growth plateaus from birth to adolescence. He hypothesized that five major brain growth stages occurred at ages 3-10 months, 2-4 years, 6-8 years, 10-12 years, and 14-16 years in 85% of children and suggested that no brain growth took place during the intervals between these stages. Epstein's findings spawned interest in brain periodization and possible reorganization of middle grades education (Epstein & Toepfer, 1978). At a National Middle School Association's annual conference, Epstein presented his theory, which grabbed the attention of middle school leaders and practitioners alike. The National Middle School Association (1982) referenced brain growth periodization in their initial position statement, *This We Believe,* when describing young adolescents' intellectual characteristics.

> Students at the middle level are pressured, often excessively, to succeed academically. The early stages of the transition (age 10-12 years) are usually characterized by success in initiating new and higher level cognitive processes because of the brain growth experienced by most youngsters during this time. Conversely, many 12 to 14 year olds may experience problem if expectations for continued development of higher thinking skills are held when a plateau in brain growth exists. (p. 11)

Middle grades educators (Brazee, 1983; Hester & Hester, 1983; Strahan, 1985; Strahan & Toepfer, 1984) wrote articles about brain periodization and its implications for practice. While some called for curricular changes to "avoid the introduction of new, higher level cognitive skills" (Hester & Hester, p. 6) and instructional methods that present information at students' existing skill level (e.g., Epstein & Toepfer, 1978), others argued against interpretations that suggested "memorization be used extensively as a learning tool during plateau periods" (Brazee, p. 8) or a return to rote learning. Concurrently, researchers criticized Epstein's research methods and analyses (Gould, 1981; Pellegrini, 1984) or warned against classroom application of brain periodization theory (McQueen, 1984; Pellegrini). Following these criticisms and challenges, support and interest in brain periodization dissipated. With the exception of an occasional attack on middle schools (Yecke, 2003), brain periodization theory's short-lived appearance had a negligible effect on middle grades education (Brazee).

Educators need to bear in mind that science, as a discipline of inquiry, is evolving—changing and dynamic. They must refrain from jumping too quickly on the brain-compatible products bandwagon (Davis, 2000) or from advocating educational policy based on speculation (Bruer, 1999). When considering the recent brain research findings, educators need to access credible reports that explicate the results, think carefully about the implications, and act judiciously.

Summary of Current Brain Research Findings

General agreement exists in the field of neuroscience regarding brain development. Researchers (e.g., Giedd, 2004; Giedd et al., 1999) concur that the brain experiences considerable neural development throughout young adolescence (10-14 years old). Following a period of arborization (growth), gray matter decreases significantly. Decreasing amounts of gray matter is associated with neural pruning (reduction), which "is believed to be essential for the fine-tuning of functional networks of brain tissue" (Blakemore & Choudhury, 2006, p. 297). In other words, neural pruning appears to eliminate unused connections and solidify brain circuitry. Researchers hypothesize that this growth and pruning is an important stage of brain development. Giedd asserted that the "use it or lose it" adage applies to brain development. Another significant developmental change is the increased production of white matter throughout childhood and adolescence. Neuroscientists (Giedd; Giedd et al.) attribute this increase to myelination—the formation of myelin that insulates the axons of some neurons. They report that the process of myelination increases the speed of the neurotransmission—the transmission of electrical impulses from neuron to neuron. Consistently, research studies provide evidence that the young adolescent brain experiences increases in white matter and decreases in gray matter (Blakemore & Choudhury).

Specific regions of the brain also undergo considerable change during young adolescence. Neuroimaging studies allow researchers (e.g., Giedd, 2004; Giedd et al., 1999) to conclude that the prefrontal cortex—the area of the brain that handles executive functions including planning, reasoning, anticipating consequences, sustaining attention, and making decisions—is not fully developed in young adolescents. Similarly, researchers (Killgore et al., 2000; Killgore & Yurgelun-Todd, 2004) note that neither of the prefrontal cortex and amygdala is fully mature in young adolescents. This lack of development is important since the prefrontal cortex and the amygdala operate in concert to act as a thermostat or surge protector for emotions. Likewise, brain researchers (Yurgelun-Todd et al., 2003) find that the hippocampus, which functions in learning, memory, and emotion, is not yet mature. Furthermore, numerous researchers (Blakemore & Choudhury, 2006; Casey et al., 2000; Dahl, 2004; Giedd; Yurgelon-Todd, Killgore, & Cintron) confirm the existence of specific differences in the brain development of girls and boys.

Neuroscientists continue to explore how brain structures and functions relate to young adolescents' abilities. Though neuroscientists (e.g., Giedd, 2004) admit that they do not fully understand the connection between brain development and young adolescent behavior, they are continuing their research. For instance, one group of researchers (Rosso,

Young, Femia, & Yurgelon-Todd, 2004) examined how adolescents' frontal lobe function affects their cognitive, emotional, and social capabilities. They discerned an association between adolescents' social anxiety levels and abstract reasoning skills, while acknowledging the need to verify these findings in their ongoing study. Other researchers (Shaw et al., 2006) studied how intellectual ability relates to the development of the cortex. They demonstrated that intelligence (as measured by IQ) is related to the cortical development in children and adolescents. Results of such studies prompted the call for "further research, preferably with input by multiple disciplines including educational researchers, cognitive scientists, and neuroscientists" (Blakemore & Choudhury, 2006, p. 307). Ongoing longitudinal and multidisciplinary research can potentially elucidate the connections between brain development and young adolescent ability.

Suggestions for Educators

The emergence of brain research suggests intriguing possibilities to educators, especially those who work with young adolescents (Caskey & Ruben, 2003). Middle grades practitioners can benefit from learning what neuroscientists are discovering about human brain development (Wilson & Horch, 2002). While learning about brain development, Bruer (2002) cautioned against the misuse or misinterpretation of science, which creates the impression that tomorrow's brain-imaging study will explain what to do with teenagers this weekend. Neuroscientists also remind the public through dissemination of their research that hypotheses concerning the connection between the development of the brain and young adolescent behavior are still under investigation. Therefore, it is imperative that educators seek reliable sources of information and avoid premature or speculative interpretations of research findings.

Middle grades teachers are uniquely positioned to share recent findings about the young adolescent brain with their students and empower them as partners in the learning process (Caskey & Ruben, 2003). These teachers can tap an array of trustworthy resources including print, web-based, and video (digital and VHS) materials to provide background information and enhance instruction. Among the most accessible print documents are *Know Your Brain: Brain Basics* (National Institute of Neurological Disorders and Stroke, 2001), *Brain Facts. A Primer on the Brain and Nervous System* (Society for Neuroscience, 2006), and *Teenage Brain: A Work in Progress* (National Institute of Mental Health, 2001). Complimentary copies and PDF versions of these publications are available. A number of educational websites provide accurate content, lesson plans, and other instructional resources. Among the most comprehensive are those sponsored by the Society for Neuroscience (n.d.), the National Institute of Health Office of Science Education (n.d.), and the Canadian Institutes of Health Research: Institute of Neurosciences, Mental Health and Addiction (n.d.). Videos such as those produced by PBS (2002) or ABC (1999) are other sources of reliable information and are often available from public or educational libraries. Following descriptions and instructional lessons regarding brain structures and functions, teachers can provide time for classroom discussion about brain development. Using resources from the National Institute on Drug Abuse for Teens (n.d.), educators can also teach young adolescents about negative influences on the brain—the detrimental impact of alcohol, drug, and tobacco. Additionally, educators can emphasize the positive influences on young adolescents' developing brains including the importance of nutrition, hydration, physical activity, and sleep.

Middle grades principals as educational leaders can schedule time for teachers to become acquainted with information concerning brain development. By providing professional development opportunities for middle grades teachers, principals communicate the importance of brain development research. Similarly, they may be positioned to allocate funds for securing educational resources or materials (such as those referenced above) for professional development sessions and/or classroom use. Furthermore, middle grades principals can sponsor brain awareness forums for parents and the school community.

Teacher educators, especially those who prepare future middle grades teachers, can become knowledgeable about young adolescent brain development. After expanding their own understanding, teacher educators can provide educative experiences for preservice and inservice educators. For example, they can guide undergraduate and graduate students to access, retrieve, and comprehend research literature concerning the developing brain. Additionally—as a public service—they can share information with schools, parent groups, or other community members who care about young adolescents.

Many middle grades teachers, principals, and teacher educators are aware that young adolescence is a momentous developmental period. They regularly seek information that helps them to respond to the unique developmental characteristics of young adolescents. At this time, educators must appreciate that young adolescence is also a significant time for brain development and recognize that the young adolescent brain is under construction.

APPENDIX: GLOSSARY OF BRAIN TERMINOLOGY[1]

Amygdala—structure in the brain that plays a central role in emotional learning, particularly within the context of fear.

Axon—fiber like extension of a neuron by which it sends information to target cells.

Broca's Area—brain region located in the frontal lobe of the left hemisphere that is important for the production of speech.

Cerebellum—large structure located at the roof of the hindbrain that helps control the coordination of movement.

Cerebral cortex—outermost layer of the cerebral hemispheres of the brain, which is largely responsible for conscious experience, including perception, emotion, thought, and planning.

Corpus Callosum—large bundle of nerve fibers linking the left and right cerebral hemispheres.

Dendrite—tree-like extension of the neuron cell body, which is the primary site for receiving and integrating information from other neurons.

Forebrain—largest part of the brain, which includes the cerebral cortex and basal ganglia. The forebrain is credited with the highest intellectual functions.

Frontal lobe—one of the four divisions of each hemisphere of the cerebral cortex. The frontal lobe has a role in controlling movement and in the planning and coordinating of behavior.

Hippocampus—structure in the brain, which functions in learning, memory, and emotion.

Hypothalamus—complex brain structure with various functions, including regulating the activities of internal organs, monitoring information from the autonomic nervous system, controlling the pituitary gland, and regulating sleep and appetite.

Myelin—compact fatty material that surrounds and insulates the axons of some neurons.

Neuron—nerve cell specialized for the transmission of information and characterized by long, fibrous projections called axons and shorter, branchlike projections called dendrites.

Neurotransmitter—chemical released by neurons at a synapse for the purpose of relaying information to other neurons via receptors.

Occipital lobe—one of the four subdivisions of the cerebral cortex. The occipital lobe plays a role in processing visual information.

Parietal lobe—one of the four subdivisions of the cerebral cortex. The parietal lobe plays a role in sensory processes, attention, and language.

Synapse—a physical gap between two neurons that functions as the site of information transfer from one neuron to another.

Temporal lobe—one of the four major subdivisions of each hemisphere of the cerebral cortex. The temporal lobe functions in auditory perception, speech, and complex visual perceptions.

Thalamus—structure in deep within the brain, which is the key relay station for sensory information flowing into the brain. The thalamus filters out information of particular importance from the mass of signals entering the brain.

NOTE

1. Glossary is adapted from Society for Neuroscience (2006).

REFERENCES

ABC News Special. (1999). *Teens: What makes them tick.* [Videotape]. American Broadcasting Companies.

Alexander, W., & George, P. (1981). *The exemplary middle school.* New York: Holt, Reinhart, and Winston.

Association for Supervision and Curriculum Development. (1975). *The middle school we need.* Washington, DC: Author.

Bellis, M. D., Clark, D. B., Beers, S. R., Soloff, P. H., Boring, A. M., Hall, J., et al. (2000). Hippocampal volume in adolescent-onset alcohol use disorders. *American Journal of Psychiatry, 157*, 737-744.

Blakemore, S., & Choudhury, S. (2006). Development of the adolescent brain: Implications for executive function and social cognition. *Journal of Child Psychology and Psychiatry, 47*(3/4), 296-312.

Bloom, F. E., Beale, M. F., & Kupfer, D. J. (Eds.). (2003). *The Dana guide to brain health.* New York: The Free Press.

Brazee, E. N. (1983). Brain periodization—Challenge not justification. *Middle School Journal, 15*(1) 8-9, 30.

Brown, S. A., & Tapert, S. A. (2004). Adolescence and the trajectory of alcohol use: Basic to clinical studies. New York Academy of Sciences. In R. E. Dahl & L. P. Spear (Eds.), *Annals of The New York Academy of Sciences: Vol. 1021. Adolescent brain development: Period of vulnerabilities and opportunities* (pp. 234-244). New York: The New York Academy of Sciences.

Bruer, J. T. (1999). In search of brain-based education. *Phi Delta Kappan, 80*(9), 648-657.

Bruer. J. T. (2002). Interview: John Bruer. In PBS *Frontline: Inside the teenage brain.* [Videotape]. Charlotte, NC: PBS Video.

Canadian Institutes of Health Research: Institute of Neurosciences, Mental Health and Addiction. (n.d.) *The brain from top to bottom.* Retrieved November 30, 2006, from http://thebrain.mcgill.ca/flash/index_d.html#

Carnegie Council on Adolescent Development. (1989). *Turning points: Preparing American youth for the 21st century*. New York: Carnegie Corporation of New York.

Casey, B. J., Giedd, J. N., & Thomas, K. M. (2000). Structural and functional brain development and its relation to cognitive development. *Biological Psychology, 54*, 241-257.

Caskey, M. M., & Ruben, B. (2003). Awakening adolescent brains. *Middle Matters, 12*(1), 4-5.

Chugani, H. T. (1998). A critical period of brain development: Studies of cerebral glucose utilization with PET. *Preventive Medicine, 27*, 184-188.

Dahl, R. E. (2003). Beyond raging hormones: The tinderbox in the teenage brain. *Cerebrum: The Dana Forum on Brain Science, 5*(3), 7-22.

Dahl, R. E. (2004). Adolescent brain development: A period of vulnerabilities and opportunities. Keynote address. In R. E. Dahl & L. P. Spear (Eds.), *Annals of The New York Academy of Sciences: Vol. 1021. Adolescent brain development: Period of vulnerabilities and opportunities* (pp. 1-22). New York: The New York Academy of Sciences.

Davis, S. M. (2000). Look before you leap: Concerns about "brain-based' products and approaches. *Childhood Education, 77*(2), 100-101.

Eichhorn, D. (1966). *The middle school*. New York: Center for Applied Research in Education.

Epstein, H. T. (1978). Growth spurts during brain development: Implications for educational policy and practice. In J. S. Chall & A. F. Mirsky (Eds.), *Education and the brain* (pp. 343-370). Chicago: University of Chicago Press.

Epstein, H. T., & Toepfer, C. F., Jr. (1978). A neuroscience basis for reorganizing middle grades education. *Educational Leadership, 35*(8), 656-658, 660.

Giedd, J. N. (2004). Structural magnetic imaging of the adolescent brain. In R. E. Dahl & L. P. Spear (Eds.), *Annals of The New York Academy of Sciences: Vol. 1021. Adolescent brain development: Period of vulnerabilities and opportunities* (pp. 77-85). New York: The New York Academy of Sciences.

Giedd, J. N., Blumenthal, J., Jeffries, N. O., Castellanos, F. X., Liu, H., Zijdenbos, A., et al. (1999). Brain development during childhood and adolescence: A longitudinal MRI study. *Nature Neuroscience, 2*(10), 861-863.

Giedd, J. N., Clasen, L. S., Lenroot, R., Greenstein, D., Wallace, G. L., Ordaz, S., et al. (2006). Puberty-related influence on brain development. *Molecular and Cellular Endocrinology*, 254-255, 154-162.

Gould, S. J. (1981). *The mismeasure of man*. New York: W. W. Norton.

Hall, G. S. (1904). *Adolescence: Its psychology and its relation to physiology, anthropology, sociology, sex, crime, religion, and education*. New York: Appleton.

Hester, J. P., & Hester, P. J. (1983). Brain research and the middle school curriculum. *Middle School Journal, 15*(1) 4-7, 30.

Hill, S. Y. (2004). Trajectories of alcohol use and electrophysiological and morphological indices of brain development: Distinguishing causes from consequences. In R. E. Dahl & L. P. Spear (Eds.), *Annals of The New York Academy of Sciences: Vol. 1021. Adolescent brain development: Period of vulnerabilities and opportunities* (pp. 245-259). New York: The New York Academy of Sciences.

Jackson, A. W., & Davis, G. (2000). *Turning points 2000: Educating adolescents in the 21st century.* New York: Teachers College Press.

Jacobsen, L. K., Mencl, W. E., Westerveld, M., & Pugh, K. R. (2004). Impact of cannabis use on brain function in adolescents. In R. E. Dahl & L. P. Spear (Eds.), *Annals of The New York Academy of Sciences: Vol. 1021. Adolescent brain development: Period of vulnerabilities and opportunities* (pp. 384-390). New York: The New York Academy of Sciences.

Killgore, W. D. S., Oki, M., & Yurgelun-Todd, D. A. (2000). Sex-specific developmental changes in amygdala response to affective faces. *Neuroreport, 12*(2), 427-433.

Killgore, W. D. S., & Yurgelun-Todd, D. A. (2004). Sex-related developmental differences in the lateralized activation of the prefrontal cortex and amygdala during perception of facile affect. *Perceptual and Motor Skills, 99*, 371-391.

Lipsitz, J. (1984). *Successful schools for young adolescents.* New Brunswick, NJ: Transaction Books.

Lounsbury, J. H., & Vars, G. F. (1978). *A curriculum for the middle school years.* New York: Harper & Row.

McQueen, R. (1984). Spurts and plateaus in brain growth: A critique of the claims of Herman Epstein. *Educational Leadership, 41*(5), 66-69, 71.

Monastersky, R. (2007, January 12). Who's minding the teenage brain? *The Chronicle of Higher Education, 53*(19), 14.

National Association of Secondary School Principals Council on Middle Level Education. (1985). *An agenda for excellence at the middle level.* Reston, V A: National Association of Secondary School Principals.

National Institute on Drug Abuse. (1996). *The basis of brain imaging. NIDA notes: Special report: Brain imaging research,* 11(5). Retrieved November 30, 2006, from http://www.nida.nih.gov/NIDA_Notes/NNVol11N5/Basics.html

National Institute on Drug Abuse. (2005). *Monitoring the future: National results on adolescent drug use. Overview of key findings.* Washington, DC: National Institutes of Health, U.S. Department of Health and Human Services. Retrieved November 15, 2006, from http://www.drugabuse.gov/PDF/overview2004.pdf

National Institute on Drug Abuse for Teens. (n.d.) *The science behind drug abuse.* Retrieved December 10, 2006, from http://teens.drugabuse.gov/

National Institute of Health Office of Science Education. (n.d.). *NIH Office of Science Education.* Retrieved December 15, 2006, from http://science.education.nih.gov/

National Institute of Neurological Disorders and Stroke. (2001). *Know your brain: Brain basics* (NIH Publication No. 01-3440a). Bethesda, MD: National Institutes of Health, U.S. Department of Health and Human Services.

National Middle School Association. (1982). *This we believe.* Columbus, OH: Author.

National Middle School Association. (1995). *This we believe: Developmentally responsive middle level schools.* Columbus, OH: Author.

National Middle School Association. (2003). *This we believe: Successful schools for young adolescents.* Westerville, OH: Author.

Pellegrini, A. D. (1984). Some questions about the basic tenets of brain periodization research. *Journal of Instructional Psychology, 11*, 165-169.

PBS. (2002). *Frontline: Inside the teenage brain.* [Videotape]. Charlotte, NC: PBS Video.

RadiologyInfo. (2005a). *Magnetic resonance imaging (MRI)—Head.* Retrieved November 10, 2006, from http://www.radiologyinfo.org/en/pdf/headmr.pdf

RadiologyInfo. (2005b). *Functional MR imaging (fMRI)—Brain.* Retrieved November 10, 2006, from http://www.radiologyinfo.org/en/pdf/fmribrain.pdf

Rosso, I. M., Young, A. D., Femia, L. A., & Yurgelon-Todd, D. A. (2004). Cognitive and emotional components of frontal lobe functioning in childhood and adolescents. In R. E. Dahl & L. P. Spear (Eds.), *Annals of The New York Academy of Sciences: Vol. 1021. Adolescent brain development: Period of vulnerabilities and opportunities* (pp. 355-361). New York: The New York Academy of Sciences.

Scales, P. C. (2003). Characteristics of young adolescents. In National Middle School Association, *This we believe: Successful schools for young adolescents* (pp. 43-51). Westerville, OH: National Middle School Association.

Shaw, P., Greenstein, D., Lerch, J., Clasen, L., Lenroot, R., Gogtay, N., et al. (2006). Intellectual ability and cortical development in children and adolescents. *Nature, 440*(30), 676-679.

Silveri, M. M., Rohan, M. L., Pimentel, P. J., Gruber, S. A., Rosso, I. M., & Yurgelun-Todd, D. A. (2006). Sex differences in the relationship between white matter microstructure and impulsivity in adolescents. *Magnetic Resonance Imaging, 24*, 833-841.

Society for Neuroscience. (2006). *Brain facts. A primer on the brain and nervous system.* (5th ed.). Washington, DC: Author.

Society for Neuroscience. (n.d.). *Neuroscience resources for the classroom.* Retrieved December 29, 2006, from ttp://web.sfn.org/BAW/SfNResources/SFN%20 resources.html

Spear, L. P. (2004). Adolescence and the trajectory of alcohol use. In R. E. Dahl & L. P. Spear (Eds.), *Annals of The New York Academy of Sciences: Vol. 1021. Adolescent brain development: Period of vulnerabilities and opportunities* (pp. 202-205). New York: The New York Academy of Sciences.

Strahan, D. B. (1985). Brain growth spurts and middle grades curriculum: Readiness remains the issue. *Middle School Journal, 16*(2), 11-13.

Strahan, D. B., & Toepfer, C. F., Jr. (1984). Transescent thinking: Renewed rationale for exploratory learning. *Middle School Journal, 15*(2), 8-11.

Wilson, L. M., & Horch, H. W. (2002). Implications of brain research for teaching young adolescents. *Middle School Journal, 34*(5), 57-61.

Wolfe, P. (2001) *Brain matters: Translating the brain research to the classroom.* Alexandria, VA: Association for Supervision and Curriculum Development.

Video Journal. (1997). *Bringing brain research into classroom practice.* [Videotape]. Salt Lake City, UT: Linton Professional Development Corporation.

Yecke, C. P. (2003). *The war against excellence: The rising tide of mediocrity in America's middle schools.* Westport, CT: Praeger.

Yurgelun-Todd, D. A., & Killgore, W. D. S. (2006). Fear-related activity in the prefrontal cortex increases with age during adolescence: A preliminary fMRI study. *Neuroscience Letters, 406*, 194-199.

Yurgelun-Todd, D. A., Killgore, W. D. S., & Cintron, C. B. (2003). Cognitive correlates of medial temporal lobe development across adolescence: A magnetic resonance imaging study. *Perceptual and Motor Skills, 96*, 3-17.

Yurgelun-Todd, D. A., Killgore, W. D. S., & Young, A. D. (2002). Sex differences in cerebral tissue volume and cognitive performance during adolescence. *Psychological Reports, 91*, 743-757.

CHAPTER 4

LANGUAGE FACTORS IN LITERACY ACHIEVEMENT OF YOUNG ADOLESCENTS

Francine Falk-Ross

ABSTRACT

The role of language as it occurs in classroom interaction routines and reading instruction activities is considered with a focus on middle level students' literacy achievement. This chapter will examine teachers' language patterns in discourse as it relates to content reading. Factors derived from language differences and cultural influences on language are discussed as they affect literacy development and instruction in schools with diverse student populations. The challenges for struggling readers with language difficulties are considered for literacy modifications and collaborative teaching methods. Lastly, the language of technology and media in supporting language and literacy connections is reviewed.

Middle grade students occupy a unique set of school experiences as they enter the transitional period between the nurturing, protected atmosphere of the elementary grades and the tracked, focused environment of the secondary grades. These young adolescents, usually in Grades 5-8, are

The Young Adolescent and the Middle School
pp. 73–89

caught "in the middle" and require reading and writing activities that reflect the transitional nature of their lives and the differentiated nature of their educational needs (Atwell, 1998; Carroll, 2004; National Middle School Association, NMSA, 2003).

In general, the bulk of reading activities in the middle school classroom and reading assignments for independent work occurs in the content areas such as science, math, history, and health. In these classes, young adolescents are challenged to integrate new information into existing background knowledge creating new schema organizations and situation models to remember facts and generate reflective comments. This process is difficult to master without a solid foundation in vocabulary knowledge to comprehend the message and literacy strategies to decode the text. Successful learners must master five essential components of proficient reading, including vocabulary, comprehension, word identification, fluency, and listening skills (National Reading Panel, 2000; Richgels, 2004), all of which are based on language elements. Students who can express their ideas through oral language have an advantage over those who have do not have this ability (Catts & Kamhi, 2004; Gee, 2001; Vukelich, Christie, & Enz, 2002). Those who do not have appropriate language bases will benefit from the opportunity for preparation and rehearsal through oral language in classroom literacy activities (Falk-Ross, 2002; Friend & Bursuck, 2005). Another important factor is that teachers' perceptions of students' language variation in educational contexts that influence the types of assessment and instruction that occur in the classroom (Haig & Oliver, 2003). Therefore, in middle level education, where high levels of literacy achievement are at the heart of content area learning, a strong language base is the lifeblood, which keeps the system of learning fluid through the foundational reading, writing, and thinking tasks that characterize all learning activities.

Close readings of government initiatives and assessments (e.g., U.S. Department of Education, 2002), national standards (e.g., International Reading Association, 2003; Jackson & Davis, 2000; NMSA, 2003) and educational statistics (e.g., National Center for Education Statistics, 2004) mandate that educators consider students' individual learning needs that stem from cultural and linguistic diversity. Yet, in the hustle to keep students' achievement high and programs of instruction viable, this foundational element is often not given the attention it deserves (Nystrand, 2006) nor is talking viewed as a part of reading and learning activities (Alvermann, 1995). As a result, it becomes important to consider the language factors that effect literacy achievement in middle grades programs, with a specific look at the roles these factors play in literacy achievement: (a) pedagogic discourse and literature discussion in the classroom, (b) language differences and cultural influences on vocabulary development,

(c) language difficulties and instructional modifications in literacy activities, and (d) the language of technology and media in supporting language and literacy connections. Each of these areas is further developed as we consider the seminal role of language in the lives of young adolescents.

PEDAGOGIC DISCOURSE IN THE CLASSROOM

In many ways, students' learning in the classroom is tied to the instructional language routines that are set by the teacher and used by peers to question and respond to new information (Bernstein, 1990; Cazden, 2001; Wilkinson & Silliman, 2000). These instructional language patterns provide a context that influences learning and literacy development (Gutierrez, 1995; Hynde, 1999; Nystrand, 2006). In seminal research studies, classroom talk is equated with education as the medium of learning (e.g., Lemke, 1989, Tharp & Gallimore, 1988). Young adolescents need preparation for cooperative learning through appropriate dialoguing with peers and in small groups, modeled and guided by teachers (Garmston & Wellman, 1998). In fact, the need for more talk, the vocabulary for talking, and the nature of language interaction in the classroom requires careful learning in order to support critical questions that extend young adolescents' thinking (Santman, 2005). Therefore, students with language difficulties or language differences are at a disadvantage in classrooms where language participation is valued and used for evaluative purposes (Wells, 1999). As a result, collaborative support and development of students' language needs has gained attention (Falk-Ross, 2002; Risko & Bromley, 2002).

Expanded Forms of Classroom Dialogue

Teacher talk in classrooms is generally characterized by a familiar pattern, referred to as IRE or IRF: the teacher ***i***nitiates a question or direction to the student(s), the appointed student ***r***esponds with an answer or comment, and then the teacher provides ***e***valuation or ***f***eedback for the student's response with an acknowledgement or judgmental comment (Cazden, 2001; Wells, 1999). This flow of discourse revolves around shared knowledge about the structure of turn allocation and contingent participatory moves in classroom routines. A large percentage of these teacher initiations are in the form of questions, and are skewed in favor of a high percentage of teacher talk (Nystrand, Gamoran, Kachur, & Prendergast, 1997). For young adolescents, who are diverse in their backgrounds and often unpredictable in their compliance with structured routines, this form of interaction is not well matched. Varying traditional questioning strategies to include forms that are more expansive will motivate students to voice personal connections and draw students into literacy discussions with their class members and the teacher (Falk-Ross, 2001; Nystrand et al., 2003).

One useful example of these expanded forms is higher level questioning strategies such as intertextual associations and text-to-world connections (Close & Ramsey, 2000; Keene & Zimmerman, 1997). A second effective expansion is the use of open questions for which several responses would be appropriate to guide and scaffold instruction for young adolescents (Wilkinson & Silliman, 2000). A third approach is to use negotiated meanings such as a compilation of students' suggestions or interpretations of meaning rather than the dictionary or teacher-constructed definitions. Each of these strategies provides for an increased level of student ownership of classroom talk, which feeds into young adolescent learners' burgeoning sense of self. Teachers, however, may not be capitalizing on the specifics of communication competence (or academic language) that are necessary to engage in discussion during teaching and learning events (Collins, 1995).

Advantages of Small Group Work

Interactions between peers during classroom discourse have been shown to have positive bearing upon literacy development (Almasi, O'Flahavan, & Ayra, 1997). Research indicates that collaborative approaches, such as small group work, balanced by individual choice and personal connections are most appropriate (Jackson & Davis, 2000; NMSA, 2003). Following models to reorganize junior high program organizations to fit the new middle level models, studies have shown progress in achievement scores and behavioral issues of students in this age group (e.g., Felner, Jackson, Kasak, Mulhall, Brand, & Flowers, 1997). According to publications initiated by middle grades educators and researchers, optimal strategies for reading instruction and assessment for this age group should include creative projects, integrative learning such as inquiry or research units, and authentic service learning, each of which may be accomplished in small groups or peer/pair combinations to allow for learning consistent with a social-constructivist model (Broaddus & Ivey, 2002; Carr, 2002; Rizzo & Brown, 2006). Writing activities using graphic organizers or charts to develop vocabulary, organize information, and stimulate reflection within small groups for feedback can be used effectively, as well (Falk-Ross & L'Allier, 2006).

Conferencing for Reading and Writing

Language is an assumed component of all reading activities, and it provides an important opportunity for concept clarifications in middle level classrooms (Moje, Ciechanowski, Kramer, Ellis, Carrillo, & Collazo, 2004). In most classrooms, this activity will focus on comprehension of content material that may be unfamiliar to students with language challenges, but for which there is elaboration. Acknowledging that a balanced program also includes meaning-based strategies, Lewis (2001) explains that a careful close reading of words in text through discussion can demystify the process of comprehension. Atwell (1998) recommends that teachers go to a students' desk, meeting with them as they read or write in their space. She recommends that the questions mostly be students' as they resolve their confusions or experiment with new ideas. Almasi (2003) notes the strong advantages for literacy development using small group organizations such as literature circles, during which students take responsibility for reading, summarizing, clarifying, and questioning the author's text and perspective.

LINGUISTIC DIVERSITY AND LITERACY ACHIEVEMENT

As Rodríguez (1998) has pointed out, "the effectiveness of classroom instruction for bilingual students, especially in reading and writing, will be enhanced by the teachers' understanding of the differences that exist (cultural, lexical, in discourse forms) between the students' native and second languages" (p. 37). The problems may have stemmed from the confusions of second language learners or from those students with dialectical or cultural differences, for whom vocabulary misunderstandings may challenge reading comprehension and writing fluency.

Language Differences

As the student population in all schools becomes more diverse with time, the issue of how to integrate supportive literacy interventions into content area instruction gains importance. Students who are engaged in the lengthy process of learning to read in a language different from their native language need additional support and understanding from their teacher during this time, especially in middle grades settings where self-esteem and social connections are so important to young adolescents. In this process of acquiring an additional language and developing literacy in that language, English Language Learners (ELL) will naturally have gaps in their linguistic knowledge and, thus, may struggle with literacy achievement. For example, it is important to remember that cognitive bases of language-to-literacy development underlie reading and writing instruction (Gee, 2001; Halliday & Hasan, 1989; Rosenblatt, 2005). For most ELL students, the sounds and patterns of their second language are still being learned and consciously thought through.

Students' individual needs may be met with a more thorough understanding of the connections and disconnections between language elements in second languages (Rodríguez, 1998). The connections are that many of the phonemes are similar to those of English; the disconnections are in vocabulary cognates (such as the word *once* has different meanings in English and Spanish) and language arts (such as possessive forms and prepositions). Verbal-visual associations are recommended for word learning strategies for ELLs (Echevarria, Vogt, & Short, 2000). Because teachers are likely to use new knowledge and new strategies that build on their everyday existing practices rather than radically change their classroom instruction, the use of several well-worn strategies, such as think-alouds, personal vocabulary collection, and language experience approach, may be revisited as practical starting places for introduction to preservice and practicing teachers within teacher education and professional development activities (Falk-Ross & Carrier, 2005).

Vocabulary Needs of Students

Vocabulary knowledge is key to literacy development because it strongly influences reading comprehension. Young adolescents who struggle with vocabulary difficulties due to dialectical or cultural differences or second language acquisition will be at a disadvantage in a classroom literacy activities (Catts & Kamhi, 2004; Jimenez, Garcia, & Pearson, 1994). In general, repeated presentations of a word and its meaning are more effective than single presentations, and effective approaches are those that encompass strategies to build background experiences, develop schema representation, and support language comprehension.

Incorporating explicit and vocabulary strategies into those activities that have been shown to be most beneficial to young adolescents, such as teams, themes, voice, and choice allow for necessary repetition that serves all students well. Strategies that match these students' interests and focus on vocabulary development for students challenged by diversity include small group work for more focused learning, interdisciplinary units for overlap of concepts, expressive writing for practice and incremental vocabulary development, and self-selection of texts and resources.

LANGUAGE DIFFICULTIES AND READING INTERVENTIONS

Research studies have focused on the interconnection of all language forms in literacy development (Adger, Snow, & Christian, 2002; Catts & Kamhi, 2004; Richgels, 2002). From either a language or literacy perspective, measures of language competence are highly predictive of reading success (Ehri, Nunes, Willows, Schuster, Yaghoub, & Shanahan, 2001; Torrence & Olson, 1984), and difficulties with reading achievement may be caused by underlying disorders involving word retrieval (German, 1992) and language organization (Duchan, 1995; Snow, Griffin, & Burns, 2005). Government initiatives for accommodating students with academic achievement problems have provided the groundwork for school programs to address these challenges (e.g., U.S. Department of Education, 2004). These new programs have also increased the number of students in middle grades classrooms who struggle with literacy and widened the range of literacy competencies that teachers are responsible to teach. A challenge created by these inclusive approaches is that teachers who sense that a student is having reading difficulty are not sure if the problem is due to a language difficulty and are unsure whether to add more information for background knowledge or reduce the amount of information to eliminate confusion. Appropriate reading interventions may be proposed through teaming with grade level teachers or through collaborative consultation with reading coaches (NMSA, 2003)

Language and reading specialists may be aware of their own students' needs but due to the often-separated nature of resource delivery of departmental or discipline-based team meetings, they may not routinely share this information (Lipsky & Gartner, 1997). Change in perceptions of students' reading competencies during assessment and instructional activities can occur as a result of collaborative professional development activities, cooperative teaching experiences, and ongoing discourse with students and mentors. These discourses, as Gee (2001) refers to them, develop through conversations with close friends, written evaluations from peers, teachers, and suggestions from mentors or department members. Each may contribute to new understandings, which slowly changed the specialist's views and identity as an educator. For example, initially seeing themselves as mostly resource teachers, questions and conversations with colleagues may lead to a larger perspective of pedagogical approaches that will transfer to classroom activities (i.e., less transmission of information to more transference of information), and teaching may begin to transform to a more effective level. In short, modifications for individual literacy difficulties and needs may be more appropriately created through collaborative resource and curriculum approaches (Falk-Ross, 2002; Friend & Bursuck, 2005). Increased collaboration between the two sets of educators is a necessary extension of the present research.

One of the important roles of reading specialists as specified by the International Reading Association (IRA) (IRA, 2003) and in the research with administrators (Bean, Hamilton, & Knaub, 2003), is collaboration with other professionals to improve instruction and guide assessment in reading programs. Professional publications on this topic (e.g., Friend & Bursuck, 2005; IRA, 2005; Quatroche, Bean, & Hamilton, 2001; Risko & Bromley, 2002) consist of anecdotal narratives, suggestions, and lists of characteristics of collaborative teaching for professionals, yet both sets of educators classroom teachers still seem to find the "jump" into sharing their everyday assessment results and instructional approaches with other professionals/specialists to be a difficult step. Documentation of the number of school programs that actively use teaming and the results of such programs on the students' success are difficult to find, but the practice is not used as often as either group would prefer (Quatroche, Bean, & Hamilton).

On the other hand, reading coaches find that the transference of the reading strategies taught to struggling students in tutoring and out-of-class resource programs into classroom reading activities is difficult to achieve (Toll, 2004). Increased collaboration between the two sets of educators for classroom-based instruction is necessary for the success of struggling students' literacy achievement. Supportive approaches for students are based on modifying instruction and assessment to scaffold success in literacy achievement.

Teaming Opportunities

The process by which students' reading problems are addressed by a team of teachers, and then strategies are implemented in the classroom by one or more educators is referred to as collaborative consultation or co-teaching (Friend & Bursuck, 2005). An important first step in organizing more effective reading improvement programs is to document in-depth transitional moves in teaching methods toward collaboration between classroom teachers and the schools' reading coach(s) to modify and accommodate curriculum for struggling readers. The older model for assistance was characterized by a fragmented nature of separated resource delivery of remedial services and is no longer supportive of everyday classroom literacy activities (Lipsky & Gartner, 1997). Thus, modifications for individual literacy difficulties need to be appropriately created through classroom and curriculum-centered collaborative approaches (Falk-Ross, 2001; International Reading Association, 2005;

Vaughn, Bos, & Schuum, 1996). This negotiation process for the teaching professionals working together to strengthen the impact of literacy lessons through common foci requires a sustained and increased level of metalinguistic and metacommunicative awareness of students' performance in the classroom (Christie, 1995; Sarangi, 1998).

Each of several models for building collaborative relationships among educators includes, among other factors, (a) identification of a transdisciplinary educational plan, (b) ongoing communication among members, (c) evaluation of evolving stages of roles and responsibilities, (d) enlistment of administrative support, and (e) in-service training for all team members and professionals (Falk-Ross, 2002; Lipsky & Gartner, 1997; Prelock, Miller, & Reed, 1995). Each of the components is necessary in some measure to develop collaborative relationships in educational environments (Blosser & Kratkowski, 1997; Friend & Bursuck, 2005, Risko & Bromley, 2002) and point to the social, emotional, and academic advantages of having children with reading difficulties receive consultative help from coaches (Lipsky & Gartner). The most obvious changes that may result from this collaboration will be in students' responses or participation and in the response complexity during discourse routines, including qualitative characteristics of student engagement and increased student connections or elaborations with reading content. More inclusive modifications for individual language and literacy difficulties need to be appropriately created through curriculum-centered collaborative approaches.

Modifications and Interventions in the Classroom

Achievement challenges are most obvious in the areas of language and literacy; however, they affect all content areas because mastery of each discipline requires a modicum of language-based performance at some point. Interventions may be focused on comprehension using reading organizers in the form of charts, supportive resource sheets (e.g., with a word list for spelling help or reminders for meta-cognitive or repair strategies), and leveled reading groupings. In this way, students receive the structure that they require within the context of his or her regular classroom confines (Falk-Ross, 1997). Interventions focused on written expression may include writing frames or partially completed sentence frames to initiate a dynamic building of context.

For young adolescents, literacy centers may also be used to provide extensions of guided reading through independent practice with language arts activities and reading rehearsal (Fountas & Pinnell, 2000). Literacy centers may be used to capitalize on language challenges through interactive discussion about reading elements, strategies, and/or genre.

The tasks may focus on reading elements in the recent lessons, and reader response work can emphasize details, connections, comparisons, and critical review of the topic. Peer group discussion within literacy centers will further support language confusions.

LANGUAGE AND MEDIA LITERACY

The current expanded view of literacy in this age of global technology extends the boundaries of literacy to acknowledge that readers derive meaning from various types of text in nonprint, visual, and auditory formats (Luke, 2003). The use of media can serve as an emerging and effective method for accomplishing literacy goals considering students' fascination with media, including internet and computer-based activities. In addition, media forms often provide instructional alternatives and learning opportunities for students with special needs, (e.g., learning difficulties, second language acquisition) (Kamil, Intrator, & Kim, 2000). Use of media in literacy education allows for coding of information in two modes—verbal and visual—and as such may provide alternatives to traditional reading and writing assignments (Meyerson & Kulesza, 2002).

It becomes the teacher's responsibility to intercede and mediate, or remediate, the deeper (i.e., socially and politically charged) thinking and understanding of media texts by all students (Luke & Freebody, 1997; Moje, Young, Readence, & Moore, 2000). To this end, the integration of closer looks at the language used and implied in media become important to the vulnerable population of middle graders.

Critical Media Literacy

Critical media literacy strategies can be accomplished using several overlapping pedagogical approaches, as those suggested by the New London Group (2000): situated practice, or "immersion in experience and simulations;" overt instruction; critical framing, or "students' standing back … and viewing it critically;" and transformed practice, or "transferring the new … practice to other contexts" (p. 35).

In defining the characteristics of critical media literacy, theorists refer to the individual nature of students' assessment and understanding of everyday print and nonprint texts, and how these influence students' knowledge of the world in social, economic, and political ways (Alvermann, Moon, & Hagood, 1999; Luke & Freebody, 1997). Issues related to culture and positioning within society and of ideology, power, and gendered identities are addressed when considering media and artifacts of popular culture (Buckingham, 1998). Explanation of the deeper language of text within media, or its "design," is aligned with discussion of the elements of a new capitalism (Fairclough, 1995; Gee, 2000). The emotional engagement of the students with media is acknowledged and explored (Alvermann & Hagood, 2000; Hobbs, 1998), and students use this knowledge to build their access to resources for social discourse and literacy practices. Students need to incorporate careful readings through consideration of questions focused on target audience and persuasive advertising techniques. This deep viewing approach (Pailliotet, Semali, Rodenberg, Giles, & Macaul, 2000) can be one component in a process through which teachers may guide their students in order to become more responsible readers and more engaged citizens (Linder & Falk-Ross, 2005).

Language and Media Instruction

Hobbs and Frost (2003) have guided teachers' media instruction by providing them with fundamental questions as to (a) who is sending this message, (b) what techniques are used to attract and hold attention, (c) what lifestyles, values, and points of view are represented in the message, (d) how different people might interpret the message differently, and (e) what is omitted from the message. McLaughlin and DeVoogd (2004) provide similar questions focusing on any missing elements in the media, the representation of *voice,* the intentions of the author(s), and the use of content information for promoting equity. Kempe (2001) poses questions related to the readers' feelings, connections, and reactions to the content and differences between men and women's reactions. Provisions may be made for discussions related to student choice in textual and symbolic reading selections. Interdisciplinary units and research projects may involve students' use of the varied genres of text and media can be used for oral presentation of new knowledge. The language from podcasts and text from musical scripts can be integrated into literacy activities as Shakespeare and poetry are used to provide wide reading for young adolescents' exposure to all genres of text.

DISCUSSION AND IMPLICATIONS

Research focused on the importance of holistic views of language learning and use emphasizes the role that language plays in social interactions and literacy, especially at the middle grade levels, where personal communication and social interaction are foundations for building learning in positive learning environments (NMSA, 2003). Young adolescents need preparation for cooperative learning through appropriate dialoguing, led and guided by teachers (Garmston & Wellman, 1998). In fact, the need for more talk, the vocabulary for talking, and the nature of language in the classroom requires careful learning in order to support critical questions that extend middle-level students' thinking (Santman, 2005). Therefore, students with language difficulties or language differences are at a disadvantage in classrooms where language participation is valued and used for evaluative purposes (Wells, 1999). As a result, collaborative support and development of students' language needs has gained attention (Falk-Ross, 2002; Risko & Bromley, 2002).

Implications of the research include the suggestion that middle grade teachers promote more frequent, expanded, and higher level discourse opportunities for students in order to elicit students' own perspectives and to understand their individual needs (Nystrand, 2006). For some teachers, collaboration and group development of units of instruction, combining strategies that are appropriate for regular and at-risk students, is a new format. Many teachers may feel that they are familiar in theory with appropriate language routines to develop reading knowledge and literacy strategies for students, but are less able to use that knowledge effectively in practice without modeling, as suggested by Lampert and Clark (1990). Understanding the nature of pedagogic discourse and the effects of changes in language routines for young adolescents within educational interactions is an important endeavor for teacher educators and for preservice and practicing teachers. This practice has implications for teacher education preparation and professional development programs for middle grades educators in the form of models for future placements and matching of professionals for middle-grades program development.

REFERENCES

Adger, C. T., Snow, C. E., & Christian, D. (Eds.) (2002). *What teachers need to know about language*. McHenry, IL: Delta Systems.

Almasi, J. F. (2003). *Teaching strategic processes in reading*. New York: Guilford Press.

Almasi, J. F., O'Flahavan, J. F., & Arya, P. (1997). A comparative analysis of student and teacher development in more proficient and less proficient peer discussions of literature. *Journal of Literacy Research, 28*(1), 107-146.

Alvermann, D. E. (1995, April). *Talking is something we're pretty deprived of at school: Middle school students speak out*. Paper presented at the annual conference of the American Educational Research Association, San Francisco, CA.

Alvermann, D. E., & Hagood, M. (2000). Critical media literacy: Research, theory, and practice in 'new times.' *Journal of Educational Research, 91*(3), 193-205.

Alvermann, D. E., Moon, J. S., & Hagood, M. C. (1999). *Popular culture in the classroom: Teaching and researching critical media literacy.* Newark, DE: International Reading Association.

Atwell, N. (1998). *In the middle: New understandings about writing, reading, and learning* (2nd ed.). Portsmouth, NH: Boyton/Cook.

Bean, R. M., Hamilton, R., & Knaub, R. (2003). Reading specialists in schools with exemplary reading programs: Functional, versatile, and prepared. *The Reading Teacher, 56*(5), 446-455.

Bernstein, B. (1990) *The structure of pedagogic discourse: Vol. IV. Class, codes, and control.* London: Routledge.

Blosser, J. L., & Kratcowski, A. (1997). PAC's: A framework for determining appropriate service delivery options. *Language, Speech, and Hearing Services in Schools, 28,* 99-107.

Broaddus, K., & Ivey, G. (2002). Taking away the struggle to read in the middle grades. *Middle School Journal, 34*(2), 5-11.

Buckingham, D. (Ed.). (1998). *Teaching popular culture.* London: University College London Press.

Carr, M. S. (2002). *Inquiring minds: Learning and literacy in early adolescence.* Portland, OR: Northwest Regional Educational Laboratory.

Carroll, P. S. (2004). *Integrated literacy instruction in the middle grades: Channeling young adolescents' spontaneous overflow of energy.* Boston: Pearson/Allyn & Bacon.

Catts, H. W., & Kamhi, A. G. (2004). *Language and reading disabilities.* Boston: Allyn & Bacon.

Cazden, C. (2001). *Classroom discourse* (2nd ed.). Portsmouth, NH: Heinemann.

Christie, F. (1995). Pedagogic discourse in the primary school. *Linguistics and Education, 7,* 221-242.

Close, E., & Ramsey, K. D. (2000). *A middle mosaic: A celebration of reading, writing, and reflective practice at the middle level.* Urbana, IL: National Council of Teachers of English.

Collins, J. (1995, April). *Discourse and resistance in urban elementary classrooms: A poststructuralist perspective.* Paper presentation for the American Educational Research Association, San Francisco, CA.

Duchan, J. F. (1995). *Supporting language in everyday life.* San Diego, CA: Singular.

Echevarria, J., Vogt, M., & Short, D. (2000). *Making content comprehensible for English language learners: The SIOP model.* Boston: Allyn & Bacon.

Ehri, L. C., Nunes, S. R., Willows, D. M., Schuster, B. V., Yaghoub, Z. Z., & Shanahan, T. (2001). Phonemic awareness instruction helps children learn to read: Evidence from the National Reading Panel's meta-analysis. *Reading Research Quarterly, 36*(3), 250-287.

Fairclough, N. (1995). *Critical language awareness.* London: Longman.

Falk-Ross, F. C. (1997). Developing metalinguistic awareness in children with language difficulties, *Language Arts, 74*(3), 206-216.

Falk-Ross, F. C. (2001). Classroom discourse routines: Changing the rules. *American Reading Forum Yearbook, 21,* 243-253.

Falk-Ross, F. C. (2002). *Classroom-based language and literacy intervention: A programs and case studies approach.* Boston: Allyn & Bacon /Longman.

Falk-Ross, F. C., & Carrier, K. (2005). Transitions from Spanish to English: Supporting students' language and literacy constructions in the classroom. *Illinois Reading Council Journal, 33*(4), 9-20.

Falk-Ross, F. C., & L'Allier, S. K. (2006). Cross-cultural self-to-text connections: An examination of the diverse life experiences of middle schoolers. *Illinois Reading Council Journal, 34*(4), 3-12.

Felner, R., Jackson, A., Kasak, D., Mulhall, P., Brand, S., & Flowers, N. (1997). The impact of school reform for the middle years. *Phi Delta Kappan, 78*(7), 528-550.

Fountas, I. C., & Pinnell, G. S. (2000). *Guiding readers and writers (Grades 3-6): Teaching comprehension, genre, and content literacy.* Portsmouth, NH: Heinemann.

Friend, M., & Bursuck, W. D. (2005). *Including students with special needs: A practical guide for classroom teachers* (4th ed.). Boston: Allyn & Bacon/Longman.

Garmston, R., & Wellman, B. (1998). Teacher talk that makes a difference. *Educational Researcher, 55*(7), 30-34.

Gee, J. P. (2000). New people in new worlds: networks, the new capitalism and schools. In B. Cope & M. Kalantzis (Eds.), *Multiliteracies: Literacy learning and the design of social futures* (pp. 43-68). London: Routledge Falmer.

Gee, J. P. (2001). Reading as situated language: A sociocognitive perspective. *Journal of Adult and Adolescent Language, 44*(8), 714-725.

German, D. J. (1992). Word finding intervention for children and adolescents. *Topics in Language Disorders, 13*(1), 33-50.

Gutierrez, K. (1995). Unpackaging academic discourse. *Discourse Processes, 19*(1), 21-37.

Haig, Y., & Oliver, R. (2003). Language variation and education: Teachers' perceptions. *Language and Education, 17*(4), 266-280.

Halliday, M. A. K., & Hasan, R. (1989). *Language, context, and text: Aspects of language in a social-semiotic perspective*. Oxford University Press.

Hobbs, R. (1998). The seven great debates in the media literacy movement. *Journal of Communication, 48*(1), 16-29.

Hobbs, R., & Frost, R. (2003). Measuring the acquisition of media literacy skills. *Reading Research Quarterly, 38*(3), 330-355.

Hynde, C. (1999). Instructional considerations in middle and secondary schools. In J. Guthrie & D. Alvermann (Eds.), *Engaged reading: Processes, practices, and policy implications* (pp. 81-104). New York: Teachers College Press.

International Reading Association. (2003). *Standards for reading professionals*. Newark, DE: Author.

International Reading Association. (2005). *Standards for middle and secondary school coaches*. Newark, NJ: Author.

Jackson, A. W., & Davis, G. A. (2000). *Turning points 2000. Educating adolescents in the 21st century.* New York: Teachers College Press.

Jimenez, R. T., Garcia, G. E., & Pearson, P.D. (1994). *Case studies of bilingual and monolingual readers: Focus on strategic reading processes* (Technical Report No. 602). Champaign: University of Illinois at Urbana-Champaign, Center for the Study of Reading.

Kamil, M. L., Intrator, S. M., & Kim, H. S. (2000). The effects of other technologies on literacy and literacy learning. In M. L. Kamil, P. B. Mosenthal, P. D. Pearson, & R. Barr (Eds.), *Handbook of reading research* (Vol. III, pp. 771-788). Mahwah, NJ: Erlbaum.

Keene, E. O., & Zimmerman, S. (1997). *Mosaic of thought: Teaching comprehension in a reader's workshop*. Portsmouth, NH: Heinemann

Kempe, A. (2001). No single meaning: Empowering students to construct socially critical reading of the text. In H. Fehring & P. Green (Eds.), *Critical literacy: A collection of articles from the Australian Literacy Educators' Association* (pp. 40-57). Newark, DE: International Reading Association.

Lampert, M., & Clark, C. M. (1990). Expert knowledge and expert thinking in teaching, *Educational Researcher, 19*(5), 21-23, 42.

Lemke, J. (1989). *Using language in the classroom*. Oxford University Press.

Lewis, C. (2001). *Literary practices and acts: Power, status, and cultural norms in the classroom*. Mahwah, NJ: Erlbaum.

Linder, M., & Falk-Ross, F. C. (2005). Reading between the lines: Middle school readers uncover messages in magazine advertisements. In M. B. Sampson, P. E. Linder, J. R. Dugan, & B. Brancato (Eds.), *The twenty-sixth yearbook of the College Reading Association* (pp. 376-393). Texas A&M University: College Reading Association.

Lipsky, D. K., & Gartner, A. (1997). Inclusion, school restructuring, and the remaking of American society. *Harvard Educational Review, 66*(4), 762-796.

Luke, C. (2003). Pedagogy, connectivity, multimodality, and interdisciplinarity. *Reading Research Quarterly, 38*(3), 397-403.

Luke, A., & Freebody, P. (1997). The social practices of reading. In S. Muspratt, A. Luke, & P. Freebody (Eds.), *Constructing critical literacies* (pp. 185-225). Creskill, NJ: Hampton Press.

McLaughlin, M. & DeVoogd, G. (2004). *Critical literacy: Enhancing students' comprehension of text*. New York: Scholastic.

Meyerson, M. J., & Kulesza, D. L. (2002). *Strategies for struggling readers: Step by step*. Upper Saddle River, NJ: Merrill Prentice Hall.

Moje, E. B., Ciechanowski, K. M., Kramer, K., Ellis, L., Carrillo, R., & Collazo, T. (2004). Working toward third space in content area literacy: An examination of everyday funds of knowledge and discourse. *Reading Research Quarterly, 39*(1), 38-70.

Moje, E. B., Young, J. P., Readence, J. E., & Moore, D. W. (2000). Reinventing adolescent literacy for new times: Perennial and millennial issues. *Journal of Adolescent and Adult Literacy, 43*(5), 4-14.

National Middle School Association. (2003). *This we believe: Developmentally responsive middle level schools.* Westerville, OH: Author.

National Center for Education Statistics. (2004). *The Nation's Report Card*. Washington, DC: Author.

National Reading Panel. (2000). *Report of the National Reading Panel. Teaching children to read: An evidence-based assessment of the scientific research literature on reading and its implications for reading instruction. Reports of the subgroups.* Washington, DC: National Institutes of Health, National Institute of Child Health and Human Development.

New London Group. (2000). A pedagogy of multiliteracies: Designing social futures. In B. Cope & M. Kalantzis (Eds.), *Multiliteracies: Literacy learning and the design of social futures* (pp. 9-37). London: Routledge Falmer.

Nystrand, M. (2006). Research on the role of classroom discourse as it affects reading comprehension. *Research in the Teaching of English, 40*(4), 392-412.

Nystrand, M., Gamoran, A., Kachur, R., & Prendergast, C. (1997). *Opening dialogue: Understanding the dynamics of language and learning in the classroom.* New York: Teachers College Press.

Nystrand, M., Wu, L. L., Gamoran, A., Zeiser, S., & Long, D. A. (2003). Questions in time: Investigating the structure and dynamics of unfolding classroom discourse, *Discourse Processes, 35*(2), 135-198.

Pailliotet, A., Semali, L., Rodenberg, R., Giles, J., Macaul, S. (2000). Intermediality: Bridge to critical media literacy, *The Reading Teacher, 54*(2), 208-219.

Prelock, P. A., Miller, B. E., & Reed, N. L. (1995). *Working with the classroom curriculum: A guide for analysis and use in speech therapy.* Tucson, AZ: Communication Skill Builders.

Quatroche, D. J., Bean, F. M., & Hamilton, R. (2001). The role of the reading specialist: A review of the research. *Reading Teacher, 55*(3), 282-94.

Richgels, D. J. (2002). Sociocultural perspectives on language and literacy. *Reading Teacher, 55*(8), 730-733.

Richgels, D. J. (2004, October). Theory and research into practice: Paying attention to language. *Reading Research Quarterly, 39*(4), 470-477.

Risko, V. J., & Bromley, K. (2002) *Collaboration for diverse learners: Viewpoints and practices.* Newark, DE: International Reading Association.

Rizzo, M., & Brown, J. (2006). *Building character through community service: Strategies to implement the missing element in education.* Lanham, MD: Rowman & Littlefield Education.

Rodríguez, A., Jr. (1998). Research summary on the teaching of reading in Spanish to bilingual students. In A. Carrasquillo & P. Segan (Eds.), *The teaching of reading in Spanish to the bilingual student* (2nd ed., pp. 17-42). Mahwah, NJ: Erlbaum.

Rosenblatt, L. (2005). *Making meaning with texts: Selected essays.* Portsmouth, NH: Heinemann.

Sarangi, S. (1998). "I actually turn my back on [some] students": The metacommunicative role of talk in classroom discourse. *Language Awareness,* 7(2&3), 90-108.

Snow, C., Griffin, P. & Burns, M. S. (2005). *Knowledge to support the teaching of reading: Preparing teachers for a changing world.* San Francisco: Wiley.

Santman, D. (2005). *Shades of meaning: Comprehension and interpretation in middle school.* Portsmouth, NH: Heinemann.

Tharp, R. G., & Gallimore, R. (1988). *Rousing minds to life.* New York: Cambridge University Press.

Toll, C. A. (2004). *The literacy coach's survival guide: Essential questions and practical answers.* Newark, DE: International Reading Association.

Torrence, N., & Olson, D. (1984). Oral language competence and the acquisition of literacy. In A. D. Pelligrini & T. Yawkey (Eds.). *The development of oral and written language in social contexts* (167-181). Norwood, NJ: Ablex.

U.S. Department of Education. (2002). *No Child Left Behind Act.* Office of Elementary and Secondary Education. Washington, D.C: Author.

U.S. Department of Education. (2004). *Individuals with Disabilities Education Improvement Act.* Office of Special Education and Rehabilitative Services. Washington, D.C: Author.

Vaughn, S., Bos, C., & Schumm, J. S. (1996). *Teaching mainstreamed, diverse, and at-risk students in the general education classroom.* Boston: Allyn & Bacon.

Vukelich, C., Christie, J., & Enz, B. (2002). *Helping young children learn language and literacy.* Boston: Allyn & Bacon.

Wells, G. (1999*). Dialogic inquiry: Towards a sociocultural practice and theory of education.* New York: Cambridge University Press.

Wilkinson, E. R., & Silliman, L. C. (2000). Classroom language and literacy learning. In M. Kamil, P. D. Pearson, & R. Barr (Eds.), *Handbook of reading research* (Vol. III, pp. 337-360). Mahwah, NJ: Erlbaum.

CHAPTER 5

STUDENT PERCEPTIONS OF CURRICULUM INTEGRATION AND COMMUNITY

"Always Give Me a Chance to Shine"

Penny A. Bishop, Garet Allen-Malley, and Kathleen Brinegar

ABSTRACT

The degree to which the middle level learner and the middle level school "fit" directly impacts students' motivation, performance, and behavior (Wigfield & Eccles, 1994). Advocates have identified integrative curriculum and teaming, in particular, as cornerstones of a developmentally responsive middle school (Erb, 2005). Yet how do students on a multiage team perceive an integrative curriculum model? How can one be sure the "fit" is strong, without consulting the students themselves? This chapter presents the design and findings of a qualitative case study into student perceptions of a nationally recognized middle school team employing an integrative curriculum model. Findings include the centrality of student responsibility, community, and caring teachers.

The Young Adolescent and the Middle School
pp. 91–120

> Sometimes the teachers—what they want you to do isn't as interesting. Choosing your own questions, and figuring out what they are, makes you more into whatever you are doing, and more aware of what you are doing. (Erin, Grade 6)

INTRODUCTION

For well over a century, educators in the United States have been concerned with the education of 10- to 14-year-olds, organizing schools as far back as 1896 with the express purpose of providing "appropriate educational programming for early adolescents" (Lounsbury, 1984, p. 6). Attending to the intersection between middle schoolers' unique developmental needs and the pedagogy employed in schools is critical. The degree to which those two entities "fit"—the middle level learner and the middle level school—has the potential to directly impact students' motivation, interest, performance and behavior (Eccles et al., 1993; Wigfield & Eccles, 1994).

The middle school reform movement of the past few decades has been predicated on this need for a strong fit between learners' developmental needs and schooling practices. Advocates have identified integrative curriculum and teaming, in particular, as cornerstones of a developmentally responsive middle school (National Middle School Association, 2003). Yet what happens when learners on a multiage team engage in an integrative curriculum model? How can one be sure the "fit" is strong, without consulting the students themselves? How do students perceive the team's approach as meeting, or not meeting, their academic and social needs?

The purpose of this chapter is to present the research design and findings of qualitative research of middle school students' perceptions of a nationally renowned, multiage team employing an integrative curriculum model. In particular we examine how students perceive the following: (1) the degree of fit between their learning needs and the pedagogy employed, and (2) the attributes of the team that contribute or detract from that fit.

We begin by briefly presenting the theoretical underpinnings that informed the study. Next we outline the methodology employed, with an emphasis on the use of visual methods. We then describe the findings, noting the team's attributes and practices identified by students as critical to their academic and social engagement. We conclude by considering these students' perceptions as contributors to the context of the middle school reform movement.

THEORETICAL UNDERPINNINGS

Three bodies of theoretical literature inform this research in particular. Stage-environment fit theory, as posited by Eccles et al. (1993), provides a compelling case for the need for social and schooling environments to meet the developmental needs of young adolescents. Integrative curriculum, as conceptualized by Beane (1997), offers the context for considering what is embodied, and not embodied, by the multiage team experienced by the middle schoolers in this study. And the literature on student perceptions and voice, as explored by Cook-Sather (2002) and others, lays the foundation for understanding the historically undervalued but crucial role of the learner perspective in educational research.

Stage-Environment Fit Theory

Stage-environment fit theory emphasizes the importance of attending to the fit between young adolescents' needs and their school environment (Eccles et al., 1993; Wigfield & Eccles, 1994). The theory asserts that the fit between an individual's characteristics and the characteristics of the individual's social environment influences that person's mental health, motivation, and behavior. Given this perspective, one could predict that if the school environment during the adolescent years does not fit with the developmental needs of the adolescent, a middle schooler's motivation, behavior, and performance will be negatively affected (Eccles et al.). Typical mismatches in stage-environment fit include an increase in teacher control, ability grouping, and discipline; and a decrease in positive relationships, opportunities for decision-making, and challenging assignments (Eccles et al.).

Integrative Curriculum

Although integrative curriculum is often confused with, or applied as a misnomer for, the concepts of interdisciplinary or integrated curriculum, several distinctions are crucial to understanding the concept. Beane (1997) identified four components of curriculum integration as helpful indicators of an integrative program. First, *integration of experience* entails using past experiences to assist one in understanding and solving new problems. Second, *social integration* calls for applying new ideas to one's daily life and the lives of others. Third, the *integration of knowledge* enables students to construct the "big picture" of learning. Fourth and finally, *integration as curriculum design* encourages learners and teachers to explore material without the constraints of typical disciplinary boundaries. Curriculum integration is rooted in a foundation of democracy and a faith in the ability of students to participate in their education. "Educators in a democratic society have an obligation to help young people seek out a range of ideas and to voice their own" (Apple & Beane, 1995, p. 13).

Student Perceptions

Educational researchers long have undervalued student perception as a viable and valuable data point in understanding schooling (Shultz & Cook-Sather, 2001). Instead researchers historically have inferred the learner's experience through the responses of adult informants, via survey, interview, or observation. Erickson and Shultz (1992) asserted that some researchers consider it a distraction, a nuisance even, to think that students might inhabit and construct profoundly differing subjective worlds as they encounter a school's standardized curriculum. And indeed students report that adults in their schools do not listen to their views, nor do they invite students to become active participants in decisions affecting their lives and work (Noddings, 1992; Poplin & Weeres, 1993).

While of course exceptions exist (e.g. Cook-Sather, 2002; Mee, 1997; SooHoo, 1993), only recently have educational researchers considered student voice to be a worthwhile and substantive addition to the educational dialogue. As Cook-Sather advocated,

> Authorizing student perspectives … can improve current educational practice, re-inform existing conversations about educational reform, and point to the discussions and reform efforts yet to be undertaken. Authorizing student perspectives can directly improve educational practice because when teachers listen to and learn from students, they can begin to see the world from those students' perspectives. (2002, p. 3)

The belief that student perspectives hold great potential for informing school renewal efforts directly informed the focus and the methodology of this study.

METHODOLOGY

Case study methods are widely employed in education research (Stake, 2000; Vavrus & Bartlett, 2006) and are particularly well suited for analyzing how cultural, situational, and political forces within a given context play out in schooling. Crossley and Vulliamy (1984) referred to this as "ecological validity" (p. 198), asserting that what can be known about one context cannot be assumed to be true in another. Because case study methods situate local action and interpretation within these broader considerations, a case should be grounded in a particular site. That site within this research was the Alpha team, and the case centered on the intersections between pedagogical intentions and student experience. This study could be classified as an "intrinsic case study," because "the researcher at least temporarily subordinates other curiosities so that the stories of those living the case will be teased out" (Stake, p. 437). Crossley and Vulliamy asserted that case studies in education can "expose the gap between rhetoric and practice" (1984, p.198), a gap that is critical to understand in the improvement of sound educational practices for young adolescents.

Context

The Shelburne Community School serves students in grades K-8 in Shelburne, Vermont, a relatively affluent community with a population of approximately 7,000 people. A predominantly White town, Shelburne's median household income is $68,000, well over the state of Vermont's median of $40,800 (Center for Rural Studies, 2005). The school itself is comprised of 850 students in grades K-8, divided into 15 multiage teams of differing sizes and configurations.

The Alpha team, situated at Shelburne Community School, is staffed by three teachers who serve approximately 65 learners in Grades 6-8. Alpha was established in 1972, born out of a desire for a progressive, alternative experience within a public school setting (Kuntz, 2005). Rooted in the Deweyan principles of experience, responsibility, and democracy (Dewey, 1938/1997), Alpha's progressive tradition has continued now for over three decades, as students on the team continue to learn in a multiage context with deep involvement in directing their own education. "The underlying notion in Alpha was that students would be active in their learning, determining not only what was to be studied but also how to go about it" (Kuntz, p. 17).

Basing the curriculum development on two questions—What questions or concerns do you have about yourself?, and What questions do you have about the world?—Alpha students play a central role in determining what and how they will learn over the course of the year. Involvement in this process enables students to link their personal interests with the larger social world that surrounds them. Answers to these questions become the bases for the year's curriculum. Students then partake in their own goal-setting and responsibility for time management in order to bring the study of their "owned" curriculum to life. Alpha's commitment to democratic ideals is observed by many who have spent time on the team. "Strong communities are comprised of individuals who embrace commonly held beliefs, who function democratically, and who are bound by traditions they cherish. These principles are foundational in Alpha" (Stevenson, in Kuntz, 2005, p. vii).

Alpha's approach to the "social integration" (Beane, 1997) of curriculum, in particular, has gained the team a fair degree of notoriety in the middle school landscape over the years, as the subject of several articles (e.g., Smith, 2001), a video (Vermont Association for Middle Level Education, 1990) a book (Kuntz, 2005), and a national award (NMSA's Teams that Make a Difference). Additionally, individual teachers on the Alpha team have received their own set of accolades, including holding Vermont's Teacher of the Year and National Board Certification. Many would assume from these external indicators that the Alpha team is responding effectively to the unique nature and needs of young adolescents. Yet what do those most involved in the daily life of Alpha—the students—say about what works and what does not? What do Alpha students most value, and conversely find problematic, in this progressive approach to education?

Participants

Thirteen young adolescents comprised the participant group for this research (see Table 5.1). The 3-year design of the study—to follow entering sixth grade students annually over the course of their experience on the Grades 6-8 Alpha team—provided the rationale for inviting all entering sixth grade students to participate in the study. Of the 13 invited, all elected to participate and all chose to remain in the study for the full 3 years, with the exception of two students who moved out of district at the end of year two.

As seen in Table 5.1, the participant group was fairly evenly balanced in terms of gender, with six females and seven males. There was a range of behavior and academic achievement, including two students receiving special education services, one for giftedness and another for developmental delays. Academic status was indicated by teacher rating, based upon classroom and state level assessment data. The sample's racial and ethnic make-up (all participants are White) reflected the predominantly Caucasian population of Vermont, the state in which the school resides. Similarly, the relatively high socioeconomic status of the sample reflected the community of Shelburne overall.

We ensured confidentiality by interviewing the students individually in a private space, and by providing pseudonyms for all individuals. Students were assured that participation in the study was strictly voluntary

Table 5.1. Participant Attributes

Student	*Gender*	*SES*	*Special Education/504*	*Academic Status*
Abby	F	Middle	No	Middle
Amelia	F	High	No	Middle
Amy	F	Middle	No	Middle
Arial	F	Middle	No	Middle
Erin	F	Middle	No	Middle
Isabel	F	Middle	No	Middle
Kent	M	Middle	504*	Low
Max	M	High	No	Middle
Miles	M	Middle	No	Low
Natalie	F	High	No	Middle
Neal	M	High	No	Middle
Ned	M	Middle	No	Middle
Robert	M	High	504**	High

Note: *Student has developmental delays; **Student is a gifted learner.

and that they were free to end an interview or withdraw from the study at any time.

Data Collection

Within this study we employed three primary means of data collection annually over 3 years. We engaged students annually in interviews; we collected student drawings of Alpha experiences; and we observed the Alpha team in action over the course of 3 years.

Interview

Students were interviewed each year with a common protocol (see Appendix) that was structured, open-ended, and depth-probing (Patton, 2002). Students were invited to reflect on their time in Alpha, including describing times of engagement and disengagement, aspects that should remain the same, and aspects they would change. The choice of a common protocol enabled a cross-case analysis and also resulted in our ability to track the evolution of a participant's responses over time.

Visual Methods

Embedded within the traditionally ethnographic technique of interviewing was the less utilized approach of participant-produced drawing.

As Haney, Russell, and Bebell (2004) have asserted, "If educational researchers want to know more about what children think and feel about their school experiences and to give them more active control over their learning, a good place to begin is to take children's drawings more seriously" (p. 249). Others also have emphasized the potential of student drawings to inform schooling reform. "If we wish to know more intimately what children think and feel, we might begin by taking their drawings more seriously. Although art educators have been aware of this for decades, most educational researchers have not" (Weber & Mitchell, 1995, pp. 34-35). Drawing holds particular power in eliciting participant perceptions, as it honors graphic expression as an alternative form of knowing, a perspective that stems from the postmodern argument for deconstructing the deeply established modes of traditional research (Lather, 1991).

To that end, students were invited in the context of their interviews to draw a learning experience on the Alpha team in which they felt engaged. Conversely, the students went on to draw a picture of a learning experience on the Alpha team in which they were not engaged. In each case, we modified the use of our terms to describe engagement and lack thereof, based upon the developmental level of the participant. For each drawing, students were offered graphite or colored pencils, crayons, or markers for their drawings. Drawing offered students a nonverbal opportunity to convey their knowledge, thereby increasing the range of potential responses about an experience—schooling—that historically has honored verbal intelligence above all others (Gardner, 1991).

Participant Observation

Additionally, one member of our research team spent more than 300 hours as a participant-observer over the course of 3 years on the Alpha team. Participant observation aims to establish a many-sided and long-term relationship with individuals and groups in their natural setting, for the purposes of developing a scientific understanding of those individuals and groups (Glesne, 2005; Patton, 2002). To become part of and participate in a social context requires a degree of acceptance of the researcher. This period of gaining trust and rapport was both methodologically and personally important within this study.

Data Analysis

Interview

All interview tapes from each year were transcribed verbatim, and subsequently coded independently by all three researchers for the purposes of analysis. We began by applying an open coding process, selecting and naming categories from the data by identifying, labeling, categorizing and relating together the overall features in an outline form. We then utilized axial coding as a means to identify explicit connections between categories and sub-categories (Strauss & Corbin, 1994). At that point, we came together as a research triad to compare and refine our organizational schema.

Visual Methods

Analyzing student drawings played an important role in triangulation. We used both verbal and visual data to triangulate the students' responses, and viewed the drawings on two concurrent levels. First, we considered the degree of consistency with interview findings, looking both for ways in which the drawings supported the interview findings and for ways in which the interview data supported the drawings. We also sought negative cases, or instances where attributes in the drawings would raise questions about or negate the findings from the interviews (Bishop & Pflaum, 2005; Haney et al., 2004).

Participant Observation

In our study, the participant-observer employed a continual process of reflection on the focus of observations in accordance with analytic developments. Observations from the field served to triangulate data as they were analyzed; at times affirming and reinforcing a theme; at times calling into question the trustworthiness of the interview and drawing data; and at still other times extending our acquisition of knowledge.

Limitations

The primary limitation of this study is the lack of generalizability common to all qualitative studies, in that a qualitative approach was well suited to the descriptive and analytical purposes of this research but the findings should not be generalized to other settings or populations. Rather, the findings can be utilized to raise questions about other settings and for future research. Additionally, given that the study was conducted in a school where there is little ethnic and racial diversity, a limitation of our study was the relative ethnic homogeneity of the student population from which we drew. On the other hand, teams offering this degree of student responsibility and ownership are rare. In this manner, we chose to place the pedagogical approach over other attributes as the primary source of site selection. Finally, we conducted interviews each January, and the time of year may have influenced the characteristics and activities students chose to emphasize.

FINDINGS AND DISCUSSION

Students in this multiyear case study had much to say about the fit between their own educational and developmental needs and Alpha's pedagogical approach. Three themes, in particular, were developed from the data by the researchers. First, students resoundingly identified their own involvement in curriculum design as an essential element of the valued Alpha experience, lending credence to the theory that curriculum built upon students' interests in themselves and the world is a good developmental fit. We present these findings first, in the section entitled Empowering Students through Responsibility. We then discuss a second element of the Alpha experience identified by students as critical to meeting their needs: Building Community through Drama. Next we examine the students' perceptions of teacher roles and dispositions on Alpha in the section entitled Caring Teachers. Finally we consider the challenges inherent in Alpha's approach conveyed by students' perceptions.

Empowering Students Through Responsibility

Students perceived three aspects of Alpha's design in particular as responding to their voiced developmental needs for empowerment and responsibility. On a macro level, students valued their responsibility over curriculum development. On a micro level, students appreciated holding dual responsibility for project design and for their own time.

Responsibility for Curriculum Development

The idea that students would have input into both *what* they would learn and *how* they would learn it proved powerful for these young adolescents. Erin expressed the importance of this responsibility when asked what she would change about Alpha, if given a magic wand,

> I don't really want to change anything. 'Cause like other teams, they're just like you do this, and then this and then this. And they have a print out schedule of what they're gonna do all year. And ours is changing every single day.... It's a fun way to learn instead of like going to social studies or other things, science and stuff. And 'cause all of that is included into the theme while doing other fun stuff, to make you learn better and—yeah. We get to choose the themes. We get to choose what we want to learn about besides the ones that the state says that we have to learn. Like we get to

> choose which ones we want to do. I don't know. It's just—it's just more—like I get more engaged in what I'm doing when I know what I'm gonna learn about, and I want to learn about that specific subject.

Miles echoed the importance of being responsible for curriculum design. When asked what should always stay the same in Alpha, Miles stated in his sixth grade year,

> We get to design our theme so we get to pick what to do ... I would definitely keep that the same because I think that was really good 'cause in my old team the teachers just said, "OK, now we're doing light." And then we're studying light. And they had it all designed. But this time like we got to design like what the culminating event is. Not like what time it is at ... but what we *do* at the culminating event and how the whole theme works.

Both Miles' contrast to his former team and his distinction between designing the culminating event and simply having input into what time the event occurs are poignant reminders of how acutely aware students are of the authenticity of their responsibility.

Natalie also chose to contrast her former team with her experience on Alpha. When asked about what should always stay the same on Alpha, Natalie replied,

> They give you like a choice. It's like not as controlled as all the other teams but we still get just as much work done if not better, and it's—and they make it really easy to understand. And it's like we get more freedom on our work and I love how the students get to run—like this morning, Erin and I were—we get to run the morning meeting this week, and last week a couple other of my friends, and then the week before there were others who did it. And instead of just making the choices for us the teachers have us do like team time or community time, and we have to—we—the whole team gets to decide what we're doing. Like where we were going on our camping trips and stuff. So it's like the kids get to help choose what happens and the teachers don't make every decision that needs to be made.... Last year I loved my team... But most of the time they would make the decisions. They would ask us what we would like but they didn't really like—they would, in the end, they would do what they think was best. And here in Alpha, every—like the students definitely get to have an impact on what happens.

Natalie and Miles, like others in the study, expressed an awareness of the authenticity of their responsibility. As they described their previous experiences with great acuity, highlighting young adolescents' awareness of the genuineness of their choices and decisions, they articulated an awareness of what Kohn (1993) referred to as "pseudochoices." In lieu of pseudochoices, Kohn advocated,

> A structured opportunity for members of a class or school to meet and make decisions provides several advantages: it helps children feel respected by making it clear that their opinions matter; it builds a sense of belongingness and community; and it contributes to the development of social and cognitive skills. (1993, p. 8)

These structured opportunities in Alpha extended from the macro-level responsibility for overarching curriculum design to the micro-level responsibility for particular assignments and projects.

Responsibility for Project Design

Ariel shared a moment in her sixth grade year that exemplified the sense of empowerment she felt when imbued with real responsibility to create a project that reflected her learning.

> This is one of the projects that we did in the beginning of the year, in problem solving groups. It was called Mouse Trap.... The trap would go off and it would bump the block forward, which would hit the marble, which would go down and hit the golf ball, which would hit the car with needles on top, and pop the balloon ... and it worked every single time except for the competition, so it wasn't exactly a success but ... this was really fun because we got to design it ourselves and it ... was our idea and we were really proud of it. I really liked it because *we* built it and *we* did it and it was *our* accomplishment and no one helped us. It just makes you feel really special.

In her words and drawing of the mousetrap project (see Figure 5.1), Ariel revealed her personal indicators for success: not that it was successful in competition but rather that she took pride in having their own idea and in having the responsibility to create the project without adult assistance. Stevenson (2002) cited responsibility as essential for the healthy development of young adolescents. "Demonstrating personal responsibility is important evidence of that (sic) an individual is making the transition from the dependency of childhood toward the self-sufficiency of adulthood" (p. 86). Certainly Ariel's words, like many others in our study, embodied this need.

Responsibility for Time

Students on the Alpha team valued having responsibility for their own time management. Kent explained that he appreciated how the teachers "let us finish up our goals when we want, so that we're not pressured to get them done in a certain amount of time. We have a whole week to plan out what we're gonna do when. They let us do what we want, when we want." Kent elaborated by drawing a comparison to other teams,

Figure 5.1. Ariel's mousetrap.

> I think it's better. Like in some teams, like if you have something, like you have to—they pile up the homework on you for one night. Like they try to even it out but if you have some like activity that you're doing that night, like a basketball game or something, then you can't get that done then you get—they get mad at you because you didn't do your homework. But here, you can sort of plan it out around your schedule.

Ariel also described her positive regard for being empowered with time management. She noted the importance of planning her own time while in Alpha, recognizing, like Kent, the power of being able to plan around other aspects of her busy life.

> Something that should always stay the same is (independent work time) because it gives me time to do my work without having to take it home. Because sometimes my parents might surprise us with like taking us out to a movie or something, and there's really no time to do homework and it's not like you can come into class the next day and say, "I couldn't do my homework 'cause I went to a movie.

Responsibility for their own time, for the design of their projects, and for the year's curriculum met a felt need by these young adolescents.

Empowered by ownership, the students in Alpha expressed a match between their needs and their schooling environment. This match was also embodied by the sense of community fostered on the team.

Building Community Through Drama

Students identified a strong sense of community as a strength of the Alpha team. When probed to reveal what contributed to that sense of community, students revealed the unique role of a drama production as central. An integral part of the Alpha experience is the annual play. It unfolds over a six-week period, with the last two weeks devoted almost entirely to the play's final preparation and presentation. Like the responsibility for curriculum design that the students cherish, the structure of the Alpha play also dictated that students assume major responsibility for the design and execution of the play, with the teachers acting in a primarily advisory capacity. For the past 20 years, the students have taken charge of the process, conducting try outs; designing sets, costumes, choreography; arranging for publicity and ticket sales; and all technical aspects of the production.

When asked to recall an engaging learning experience, many of the students quickly chose to draw and talk about this event. What was it about this drama experience that loomed so large in the memories of Alpha students? How did students perceive its influence on their development and how did this experience intersect with Alpha's integrative curriculum model?

Building Personal Efficacy

The words and pictures of these young adolescents revealed that the play resonated with them as a memorable, engaging learning experience because it responded directly to their developmental need for personal efficacy. Stevenson (2002) posited the following essential components of efficacy for the middle school student: (a) competence, (b) awareness, (c) affiliation, (d) ethical sense of self, and (e) responsibility. In myriad ways, the Alpha play experience responded to all of these elements.

First, recognition by peers, family, and significant adults as competent in at least one area of their lives is critical as young adolescents begin to develop a sense of self. The structure of the play afforded students multiple opportunities to try out and become competent in a variety of different situations. Kent's sense of his newfound competence as an actor was evident in his recounting of his role in the *Alice in Wonderland* play. He explained why the play was such an important learning experience for him.

> We had to try out for the play and I got a good part. We had to rehearse a lot and I found out I was a *really* good actor. The play helped me trust in myself and helped me become a better actor.

Similarly, when asked if the Alpha program should continue to offer students the chance to produce their own play, Ned replied,

> Yes, I love to act. It's like one of the things that always give me pleasure and I would just give us as many plays as possible. Yeah … always give me more chances to shine!

Second, as young adolescents begin to develop an awareness of the world around them, they concomitantly develop the ability to understand another's perspective and to understand the impact of their actions on others. Ned's budding awareness of himself and his interactions with his peers were the result of his involvement with the play. He confided,

> You can't always win. You can't always get what you want. Sometimes you just have to take what you don't get, even though you think you have everything going towards it. Like, in music class when we had to sing, and yeah it would be graded. And the kid who got the part, who I'm not gonna name for this, he didn't sing for it but he still got the part anyways. So I was angry. But now he's one of my best friends, so I got over it.

Third, finding one's place in the world, figuring out where one belongs, developing an affiliation with a team, and having a group of friends all contribute to the young adolescent's quest to define his or her sense of self. The structure of the Alpha play provided a place for students to forge affiliations that would be unlikely within the confines of the regular classroom experience. Amelia's first Alpha play as a sixth grader helped her to find her place on the team.

> I really liked the play because it gives you—we do it at the very beginning of the year—so it gives you a chance to really meet new people. It's because you're not with your friends when you work on the play and because you all have different parts. And so it really gives you a chance to meet new people and it kind of like welcomes you into Alpha. And you have to work together as a whole team to pull off the play and stuff.

Fourth, the young adolescents' increased capacity to think more abstractly allowed them to begin considering issues from multiple perspectives. They began to ponder, what kind of person do I want to be? What is really important to me? How would I have responded to that situation? These questions are the beginning construction of the young adolescent's ethical sense of self. The supportive culture created by the play

Figure 5.2. Amelia in the Alpha play.

prompted students to think beyond their own needs and respond to their classmates in a caring and ethical manner.

Amelia's description of her interaction with her peers illustrated how this evolved during the play. When asked to draw a time of engagement in Alpha, Amelia, like many of her peers, quickly chose to depict the Alpha play. Her choice to draw lines surrounding and projecting from herself (see Figure 5.2) conveyed an energy and enthusiasm for the experience and for her role.

Amelia explained,

> And I learned like how you had to help a lot of people, especially in costumes and stuff because you need like—"oh I need a magnifying glass." And if they didn't have a magnifying glass then you have to like—you could bring it in for them. So you have to be aware of everyone else around you. And I learned how to be kind and comfort people when they didn't get the part they wanted. Yeah. And other stuff like that. I just said, "It's ok and just do your part and it will be fun."

Finally, the young adolescent's ability to move from dependency to self-sufficiency is enhanced by providing them with opportunities to assume responsibility for tasks and activities they deem important and useful.

Since the success or failure of the Alpha play rested squarely on the students' responsibility and accountability for all facets of the production, there were multiple opportunities for them to demonstrate their dependability and ability to follow through and meet expectations. Amelia aptly captured the seriousness with which students approached their part in the production.

> I liked the dedication that everyone had to have. We had three after school practices and in like those practices, almost everyone had like all their lines memorized and they had all their costumes ready and we practiced like almost every day in school. So if you work really hard to pull it off then at the end it will be really great because it was.

The sense of accomplishment fostered by participation in drama has been noted by others,

> We can showcase the talents of actors, singers, dancer, painters, builders, technical wizards, and behind-the-scene organizers.... The auditory learner with the magnificent voice, who struggles mightily with reading but learns lines ... the ordinary student who does not stand out in class, but who can operate the most sophisticated ... electronic equipment ... the shy artist can have work displayed.... Many of the students get a new sense of accomplishment that carries over into their academic work. (Lewicki, 2002, p. 44)

This new sense of accomplishment relates directly to the facets of personal efficacy that were served via participation in the play, supporting the young adolescents' ability to be productive, caring members of their classroom community.

Connecting Learners

In addition to responding to the developmental need for personal efficacy, the Alpha play was identified by students as instrumental in connecting the learners to a strong sense of community. This sense of community is a critical element in the integrated curriculum model used on the Alpha team described earlier. The validity and relevance of this curriculum methodology relies on "whether young people reveal their "true" selves in the classroom given the complexities of gender, race, class and other sources of power dynamics within a group" (Orner, cited in Beane, 1997, p. 53).

These group differences can emerge during the middle school years with newfound energy as young adolescents struggle to carve out their own place in the "group," often at the expense of those perceived as different from them. In an effort to negotiate these challenging group dynamics, Alpha teachers engaged in "genuine planning with students" (that) "counter(s) these issues by first building a sense of community and trust" (Beane, 1997, p. 53). Failure to develop an inclusive, accepting classroom culture invariably leaves some students silent and thus negates their buy-in and ownership of the curriculum building process, which could ultimately influence the quality of their learning.

> This spirit of cooperation and collaboration can be fostered by participation in drama. Drama seems to create a more cooperative learning environment that provides for the adolescent's need to have a "say" in the learning activities.... Drama initiates an interaction between the learner and the content that sparks genuine learning by integrating what they experience into their system of understanding. (Smith & Herring, 1994, p. 30)

Alpha students noted this effect repeatedly as they recalled their play experience. Ned described how the play served as a catalyst for community,

> One of the reasons teachers do it every year is it's kind of a way to welcome the new 6th graders and because we all have to learn to rely on each other. If one person messes up their lines, we have everyone else to help them, which really builds a sense of community. Without community there's no team. You need teamwork, community, that's what makes us Alpha team really.... Just everyone being interdependent, trusting each other, knowing that they can always have friends to help them.

In the Alpha play, students found a sense of responsibility similar to that embodied by the integrative curriculum model embraced by Alpha overall. They also appreciated the strong sense of community and personal efficacy that resulted from their participation in the endeavor. Ned's striking awareness that community, interdependence and trust are "what makes us Alpha team really" was a potent testimony to the power of Alpha's approach.

Caring Teachers

In accordance with this powerful sense of community felt by students, the participants in our research were quick to identify the important role of the teacher in the Alpha experience. Noddings asserted, "Good teachers do not reject what students see and feel but, rather, work with what is presently seen and felt to build a stronger position for each student. To do this effectively requires the creation and maintenance of a trusting relationship" (1992, p. 107). Indeed, the perceptions of students on Alpha resonated with Noddings' perspective; these students appreciated the trusting relationship that was built upon caring and connection. They also valued the teachers' pedagogical emphasis on active learning.

Embodying Caring and Connection

Ned was quick to answer when asked what would be important to stay the same in Alpha,

> The teachers. Definitely. The teachers are amazing. They are really smart. They always ask the right questions. They're always looking for the answer that they know you can give. They always—they never give a question that's impossible. They're always making sure that you're listening. They're kind of tough, but if they weren't tough, then we wouldn't be able to get out of here. Alpha is pretty much the best, in my opinion, because of its teachers.... Although they are tough, they also have sympathy. Like you can relate to them. Like if you have something going wrong, they'll help you with it. They're always available. You can always talk to them. Very open.... They're there to help us; they're there to help us get back on our feet when we've taken a blow.

Abby echoed the importance of the Alpha teachers' understanding and compassion, "The teachers are very nice and they're very understanding if you don't have your stuff done and they give you more time if you need it." Kent concurred, stating simply, "They're really nice and they do a really good job doing what they do."

Although Noddings noted, "Caring is a way of being in relation, not a set of specific behaviors" (1992, p. 17), the students in our study recognized their teachers' care through certain actions. For example, Ned noticed the depth of his teachers' caring during his student-led portfolio conferences, "Well, like, when we have our conferences, they're so one on one with us and our parents that you're like "Wow. They really paid attention to me all this time and I thought they weren't."

Similarly, Alpha students appreciated the fact that their teachers treated them as people, rather than children. Many commented on the freedom they possessed to use the microwave to make popcorn during their free time, a seemingly small thing to adults but a concrete action that communicated to the students that they were responsible. When asked what should stay the same in Alpha, Isabel put forth,

> The fact that we have a microwave so we can have popcorn. Like when we have free time we can make popcorn, or like if we need to heat something up for lunch we don't need to go down to the cafeteria and ask them. We can just do it here.... They don't have any microwaves on other teams. Or like if they do, then only the teachers can use it.

The words of Isabel and her peers are powerful reminders of the type of teachers we need and require in our middle grades classrooms. Beane (1997) described just such educators when he stated,

> These teachers respect the dignity of young people. They take their ideas, hopes, aspirations, and lives seriously. They listen carefully to young people, whether the message is clear or confused.... These teachers believe in democracy and see no reason why democratic values and rights should not be extended to young people in schools.... They believe that young people have not only a right to have a say in what happens in school, but an obligation to do so. (pp. 68-69)

The caring and compassion conveyed by the teachers laid the groundwork for acting upon democratic ideals. These dispositions were coupled with a commitment to active pedagogy that also met the needs of these young adolescents.

Employing Active Pedagogy

Like much of the literature emphasizing the effectiveness of experiential, hands-on approaches to teaching young adolescents (e.g., Bohnenburger & Terry, 2002; Broda, 2002), the students in our study stressed the importance of active learning as they considered the attributes that contributed to and detracted from their engagement on Alpha. Max described the picture he drew of a time of deep engagement (see Figure 5.3),

> We're doing an experiment because I think I do like hands on experiments, and with vinegar and baking powder I think ... or baking soda ... I like doing stuff like that ... it's a good way to learn because you sort of remember it. Because you think well I had fun so maybe I should remember that.

Max went on to explain why active learning is preferable to him, by distinguishing his Alpha experience from that on other teams.

> They're really good teachers. Like they actually teach you, and mostly in a fun way. It makes it easier to learn ... it's more creative and interactive with the kids. 'Cause in other teams you might just read text but in Alpha you might do like an experiment or do an activity or something.

In contrast, Max depicted a time of disengagement on Alpha. He explained his drawing (see Figure 5.4) matter-of-factly,

> Well, I'm reading and I like reading, but if we don't have work to do, we have to do that an hour, and that seems like a lot. I mean maybe like for

Figure 5.3. Max's experiment.

Figure 5.4. Max's clock watching.

that, for at least a half an hour we could do something. (The clock) is just because like you're waiting for lunch.

With these words and visuals, Max expressed the importance of active pedagogy in the Alpha experience. Robert agreed with his peers when he summarized their perspectives succinctly, "It's like fun to do experiments rather than like copying all from like direct text."

In addition to appreciating active learning approaches, students on the Alpha team also valued active ways to demonstrate their learning. When asked to draw and talk about a time of engagement in Alpha, Ariel described her opportunity to showcase her knowledge at a culminating event, the Blizzard Breakfast, as seen in Figure 5.5.

> So this is an experience of me and Anna presenting to a couple of parents about our project, which was things about Earth's evolution. Tons of parents were coming like every second so we had to start over like right in the middle of our presentation, and then when no one was around we'd go in the other room and eat and come back really quickly. And it was just really fun because I had someone to talk to and we were presenting it together instead of just me presenting it all alone. There were some adults who didn't know

Figure 5.5. Ariel's active assessment.

> some of the stuff that we were teaching so it felt kind of good to know something that adults don't know.

Erin also chose to represent her final assessment at the Blizzard Breakfast as a time of deep engagement. Again, the importance of a hands-on approach was emphasized.

> I thought that one of my favorite parts was our Blizzard Breakfast where we presented posters of what we studied, and we had this like maze type illusion where everyone came around and like looked at your poster. And I just thought that was really fun to make, and get ready for. It involved like physically like doing things instead of just writing ... I did a presentation on stars and we made a 3-D model of the evolution of the star, and it was just really fun to make.

Ariel and Erin both recognized the power of an authentic audience as they actively conveyed their learning to others. This power was also revealed by what students found disengaging. When reflecting on what he'd change in Alpha if he had a magic wand, Miles' perspective underscored the importance of active assessment described above. He stated, "OK what I'd probably do is I'd probably change that we don't have to take tests, as much at least. Or shorter ones." Active approaches to learning and assessment were at the heart of Alpha students' engagement.

Challenges to Empowerment and Community

Our young respondents illuminated many valuable aspects of the Alpha experience, aspects that responded to students' need for personal efficacy overall and for responsibility in particular. While the data revealed many strong examples of pedagogy that "fit" young adolescents' developmental needs, what challenges inherent in such an approach did the data reveal?

The Challenge of Responsibility

While students expressed great appreciation for their authentic involvement in curriculum design, these learners also revealed that they themselves did not always make the most engaging choices. The passive intake of a video series on the decades, for example, emerged again and again as a disengaged moment. Yet, Miles explained that the decision to watch the video series had been the students',

Figure 5.6. Isabel's video viewing.

> Well, we decided that we're gonna have like a bunch of guest speakers and watch this video series that went from the whole 20th century from 1900 to 2000, and so and we had to take notes on them.

Isabel was one of several students who chose to draw and talk about this experience, as seen in Figure 6.

> It's when we have to watch videos and take notes on the 1900s and it was really boring because the movies were talking about like the wars and like how—and like bad stuff and it was all old and black and white and it was really uninteresting. That's the teacher (points at standing figure) and she's mad at the people for sleeping and talking when they're supposed to be watching and taking notes but they couldn't want to because it was really boring.

The students' choice in this case ran counter to their own awareness of their need for active learning approaches. Does empowering students with real responsibility mean trusting them to make their own choices, even when the choices may not always result in engagement? The learning that results from decision making is powerful, even with both positive and negative outcomes.

The Challenge of External Standards

Our interview transcripts were peppered with asides, like Erin's earlier, that there are at times themes that "the state says we have to learn." Students were aware of the external standards that drove some of their curriculum. More often than not, when the students in our study depicted times of disengagement, they were times when students did not have as great a voice in the curriculum development, times when choice was limited and often dictated by external demands.

For example, in contrast to the deep involvement in their learning expressed earlier by Miles, Natalie and Ariel as they planned curriculum, Erin described the lack of responsibility that resulted in her lack of engagement. When asked to talk about her drawing of a time of disengagement on Alpha, Erin explained,

> You have to figure out something about a county in Vermont, and like, yeah, just give information and then we're gonna post it on the poster board and yeah ... I don't know. I think it's just not as interesting as I would want it to be. I don't really care much about, like, our counties very much 'cause I'm never gonna really visit any of them or like it's nice to find some places that we can go to if we're bored or something but I don't know. I just don't find that I'm like really interested in this subject.

The need to study the counties of Vermont stemmed from an external requirement, one that did little to interest Erin in her learning.

Similarly, Kent drew and talked about his lack of engagement when he was not an active part of the curriculum development. He was completing a project on how the moon affects the tides. He explained,

> You picked what you were gonna study out of a hat and I didn't want to study what I got.... I want to study something that I'm interested in, that I want to know about.

Kent and Erin's perspectives on disengagement are perhaps even starker in contrast to their other experiences on Alpha, which afforded them deep participation in negotiating the year's curriculum. With these perspectives the students revealed a major challenge with integrative curriculum: how to empower students with authentic responsibility for curriculum design and at the same time be beholden to external standards and expectations.

The Challenge of Idiosyncratic Needs

Strikingly, the majority of students struggled to identify things they would want changed in Alpha. Time and time again, when asked what they would change with a magic wand, these respondents asserted with confidence, "Nothing!" When probed further, the types of changes desired by students were idiosyncratic rather than thematic.

For example, Ariel spoke to her desire for more writing time.

> I think that I'd probably want more writing time 'cause it's fun writing and everything. And we get a block on Thursday to do our assessment, but I don't really like doing it at home because my printer isn't working. And so I'd have to hand write it and typing it is a lot easier.

Kent expressed his interest in more science,

> Probably science. Science is cool. I want to do it.... We're doing this theme now on matter, motion and energy, that's kind of like science but we're not—we don't really have science. Yeah. So I probably I'd like to do chemistry and yeah.

Amy articulated concern about homework,

> I would lower the homework 'cause it's sort of like there's a lot of homework. But like I like doing it 'cause I learn but it's just boring and a lot.

And Robert noted the abundance of reflections,

> There are like a lot of reflections we have to do. So like I'd like to do like a few less of those. You reflect on like practically everything.

These idiosyncratic needs are a reminder of the diversity of young adolescents' individual preferences and learning styles. They are a reminder of the challenge all classrooms and teams face to differentiate, if they desire to meet all students' needs.

CONCLUDING THOUGHTS

The young adolescents in our study had much to say about the quality of their learning experiences on Alpha. They valued the authentic opportunity to design their curriculum and to manage their own time; such chances provided them with a sense of responsibility so critical to their development of personal efficacy. They perceived their teachers as responsive and caring, contributing to the sense of community so necessary for learning to occur. And while their own curricular choices occasionally resulted in boredom (e.g., the "endless" video series so often cited by these young respondents) they deeply appreciated the active pedagogy typically employed.

The perspectives of these Alpha students are invaluable to those involved in middle grades reform. When asked to consider how well the approaches practiced on their team fit with their own learning needs, the young adolescents were clear. Responsibility and community matter. Yet too often we overlook the perspectives of the learner in the dialogue on schooling reform. In middle grades education, with its strong reform agenda and its resounding calls for student voice, the lack of student perspective is a particularly stark omission. We must continually ask, listen, and act. As noted by Kuntz (2005),

> The Alpha story is one that needs to be told widely, and its messages contemplated seriously by middle level educators. The remarkable success of this multiage, genuinely student-centered educational community, wherein the curriculum is integrated ... should give heart to those who want to make the educational of young adolescents all that it needs to be and can be. Are we willing to listen to Alpha students? Are we willing to invest in procedures students identify as crucial to their learning? The answers could shape the middle school agenda for the coming years. (p. xii)

Are we willing to listen? The Alpha students in our study held many important perspectives on how to ensure that the "fit" between middle grades learner and middle level school is strong. Imagine more students actively engaged in experiences like Alpha, in which young adolescents "have a right ... to search for meaning in their world, to be engaged with significant issues, to do authentic work, to learn the whole story, to think critically, to form values, to make judgments, and to be respected" (Beane, 1997, p. 103).

When the middle grades community invites and respects the input of young adolescents in authentic ways by inviting them to participate in lively debate about school reform, adults learn much about what should occur inside middle level schools in order to engage students. Although there are pragmatic and political challenges to embracing an integrative curriculum model, the young adolescents in our research articulated deep engagement and a strong sense of developmental "fit" when empowered by an integrative approach that offers them responsibility and embraces them with community. When asked what he would change about Alpha if given a magic wand, Kent was quick to reply,

> Oh, probably the fact that they're giving out magic wands to everybody so that they could change Alpha 'cause I don't want Alpha changed.

If more young adolescents could echo Kent's remarks about their own schooling experiences, the middle grades reform movement would be succeeding indeed.

APPENDIX: ALPHA INTERVIEW PROTOCOL

Beginning the Interview:

Ask student to state full name, date of birth, grade level and that they are on the Alpha team.

Video Interview Questions:

1. Tell me about yourself.
2. What do you like to do in your free time?
3. Tell me about things you do best in school.

Drawing Prompts:

1. Please draw a picture of a time when you were really engaged in what you were learning or doing in Alpha.
2. Please draw a picture of a time when you were not engaged in what you were learning or doing in Alpha.

Program Questions:

1. If you had a magic wand and could change anything about Alpha, what would it be?
2. What should always stay the same in Alpha?

Closing the Interview:

1. Is there anything else we should know?
2. Do you have any questions for us?

REFERENCES

Apple, M., & Beane, J. (1995). *Democratic schools*. Alexandria, VA: Association for Supervision and Curriculum Development.

Beane, J. (1997). *Curriculum integration: Designing the core of democratic education*. New York: Teachers College Press.

Bishop, P., & Pflaum, S. (2005). *Reaching and teaching middle school learners: Asking students to show us what works*. Thousand Oaks, CA: Corwin Press.

Bohnenburger, J. E., & Terry, A. W. (2002). Community problem solving works for middle level students. *Middle School Journal 34*(1), 5-12.

Broda, H. W. (2002). Learning "in" and "for" the outdoors. *Middle School Journal, 33*(3) 34-38.

Center for Rural Studies. (2005). *Vermont indicators online*. Retrieved December 11, 2006, from http://maps.vcgi.org/indicators/profiles.cfm

Cook-Sather, A. (2002). Authorizing students' perspectives: Toward trust, dialogue and change in education. *Educational Researcher, 31*(4), 3-14.

Crossley, M., & Vulliamy, G. (1984). Case study research methods and comparative education. *Comparative Education 20*(2), 193-207.

Dewey, J. (1997). *Experience and education*. New York: Macmillan. (Original work published 1938)

Eccles, J. S., Midgely, C., Wigfield, A., Miller Buchanan, C., Reuman, D., Flanagan, C., et al. (1993). Development during adolescence: The impact of stage environment fit on young adolescents' experiences in schools and in families. *American Psychologist, 48*(2), 90-101.

Erb, T. (Ed.). (2005). *This we believe ... in action*. Westerville, OH: National Middle School Association.

Erickson, F., & Schultz, J. (1992). Students' experience of the curriculum. In P. Jackson (Ed.), *Handbook of Research on Curriculum* (pp. 465-485). New York: Macmillan.

Gardner, H. (1991). *The unschooled mind: How children think and how schools should teach*. New York: Basic Books.

Glesne, C. (2005). *Becoming qualitative researchers: An introduction* (3rd ed.). New York: Allyn & Bacon.

Haney, W., Russell, M., & Bebell, D. (2004). Drawing on education: Using drawings to document schooling and support change. *Harvard Educational Review, 74*(3), 241-271.

Kohn, A. (1993). Choices for children: Why and how to let students decide. *Phi Delta Kappan*. Retrieved September 15, 2006, from http://www.alfiekohn.org/teaching/cfc.htm

Kuntz, S. (2005). *The story of Alpha: A multi-age, student-centered team—33 years and counting*. Westerville, OH: National Middle School Association.

Lather, P. (1991). *Getting smart: Feminist research and pedagogy with/in the postmodern*. New York: Routledge.

Lewicki, K. (2002). Satisfying multiple intelligences and diverse talents through musical theater. *Middle School Journal, 34*(2), 39-44.

Lounsbury, J. (1984). *Perspectives: Middle school education*. Columbus, OH: National Middle School Association.

Mee, C. (1997). *2000 voices: Young adolescents' perceptions and curriculum implications*. Columbus, OH: National Middle School Association.

National Middle School Association. (2003). *This we believe: Successful schools for young adolescents*. Westerville, OH: Author.

Noddings, N. (1992). *The challenge to care in schools*. New York: Teachers College Press.

Patton, M. Q. (2002). *Qualitative research and evaluation methods*. Thousand Oaks, CA: Sage.

Poplin, M., & Weeres, J. (1993). Listening at the learner's level. *Executive Educator, 15*(4), 14-19.

Schultz, J., & Cook-Sather, A. (2001). (Eds.). *In our own words: Students' perspectives on school*. Lanham, MD: Rowan & Littlefield.

Smith, C. (2001). Addressing standards through curriculum integration. *Middle School Journal, 33*(2), 5-6.

Smith, L. J., & Herring, D. J. (1994). Drama in the middle level classroom: Bringing content to life. *Middle School Journal, 26*(1), 30-36.

SooHoo, S. (1993). Students as partners in research and restructuring schools. *Educational Forum, 57*(4), 386-393.

Stake, R. E. (2000). Case studies. In N. K. Denzin & Y. S. Lincoln (Eds.). *Handbook of qualitative research* (pp. 435-454). Thousand Oaks, CA: Sage.

Stevenson, C. (2002). *Teaching ten to fourteen year olds* (3rd ed.). Boston: Allyn & Bacon.

Strauss, A., & Corbin, J. (1994). Grounded theory methodology: An overview. In N. K. Denzin & Y. S. Lincoln (Eds.). *Handbook of qualitative research* (pp. 1-18). Thousand Oaks, CA: Sage.

Vavrus, F., & Bartlett, L. (2006). Comparatively knowing: Making a case for the vertical case study. *Current Issues in Comparative Education, 8*(2), 1-7.

Vermont Association for Middle Level Education. (1990). *Student directed learning: The Alpha program, a middle school approach that works.* Johnson, VT: Author.

Weber, S., & Mitchell, C. (1995). *That's funny, you don't look like a teacher: Interrogating images and identity in popular culture.* London: Falmer.

Wigfield, A., & Eccles, J. S. (1994). Middle grades schooling and early adolescent development: An introduction. *Journal of Early Adolescence, 14*(2), 102-106.

CHAPTER 6

GIFTED LEARNERS IN THE MIDDLE GRADES

In Search of Equity and Excellence

Carol Ann Tomlinson and Maureen Murphy

ABSTRACT

Highly able students are part of the student population in all middle schools and share common developmental needs with other young adolescents in cognitive, social, emotional, and physical realms. Experiences with high ability can create additional challenges for very bright middle school students in areas such as achieving and belonging, uneven development, undeveloped study and organizational skills, perfectionism, and unwillingness to accept challenge. Serving bright learners in the middle school is made more complex because of the variety of students with high performance and high potential to perform. Extending challenge for these learners is a part of the middle school goal of excellence. Ensuring that high potential students from low economic and culturally diverse backgrounds are recognized and actively mentored in developing their capacity is part of the middle school goal of equity. To achieve equity and excellence simulta-

The Young Adolescent and the Middle School
pp. 121–140

neously calls for classrooms with the highest quality curriculum and pervasive differentiation. Research indicates such classrooms are in short supply.

Addressing the academic and affective needs of students identified as gifted in the middle grades is complex for a variety of reasons. First, there has been contention between proponents of middle school and of gifted education about what constitutes an effective school experience for highly able, young adolescents. Second, there is great diversity in the population of students that might appropriately be thought of as "gifted." Third, if the lives of middle schoolers are generally complex, adding the element of high ability to young adolescence only creates another layer of complexity for those students and for their teachers. In the end, however, it is possible to make useful assertions about the needs of very bright, young adolescents and about how schools and school personnel can address those needs. This chapter will briefly examine some of the issues that have existed—and persist to some degree—between the fields of middle school education and gifted education, diversity in the population of high ability and high potential middle schoolers, cognitive and affective needs of students in this group, and guidelines for addressing those needs in the context of middle school.

ISSUES IN MIDDLE LEVEL EDUCATION AND GIFTED EDUCATION

Institutions called middle schools first developed during the 1970s as it became evident that young adolescents were not "junior" high school students and that "junior" high schools were not constructed to address the academic or affective needs of this age group (Carnegie Council on Adolescent Development, 1989). Among its visions for schools responsive to young adolescents, leaders of the middle school movement envisioned and advocated schools that provided equity of opportunity for all students (Carnegie Council on Adolescent Development, 1989; Jackson & Davis, 2000). To ensure that all middle level students are taught as though they merit high quality curriculum and instruction, leaders in the middle school movement consistently advocated elimination of tracking as a practice that sorts students by teacher expectations (and often by race and economic status as well), favoring some students with curriculum and instruction born of high expectations, leaving others with curriculum that both stems from and reflects low teacher expectations (Dawson, 1987; George, 1988, 1993; Jackson & Davis, 2000; Riccio, 1985; Stevenson, 2002). Proponents of the middle school concept pointed to a long and growing body of research indicating that tracking is disadvantageous to most students (Carnegie Council on Adolescent Development, 1989; Dawson, 1987; Gamoran, Nystrand, Berends, & LePorte, 1995; Oakes, 1985; Slavin, 1987; Wheelock, 1992).

Many advocates for gifted education, by contrast, believed that the academic needs of highly able learners were seldom met in heterogeneous classroom settings (Gallagher, Coleman, & Nelson, 1995; Plucker & McIntire, 1996: Rogers, 1991; Sicola, 1990) and pointed to research indicating that homogeneous grouping results in higher achievement for bright students than does heterogeneous grouping (e.g., Allan, 1991; Kulik & Kulik, 1992). Educators with this perspective feared that excellence in the middle grades was being sacrificed in deference to equity. Related practices such as cooperative learning which were strongly advocated by middle school leaders as vehicles for achieving academic equity and attending to the diverse needs of middle level learners (Jackson & Davis, 2000; Slavin, 1980; Stephenson, 2002) were also decried by leaders in gifted education (Robinson, 1990) as similarly sacrificing the needs of advanced learners in the name of equity.

In more recent years, the fields of middle level education and gifted education have worked to find common ground that affirms both the middle level emphasis on academic equity and the gifted education emphasis on academic excellence. In 2005, the National Middle School Association and the National Association for Gifted Children created a joint position statement on teaching bright young adolescent learners. *Meeting the Needs of High-Ability and High-Potential Learners in the Middle Grades* (NAGC/NMSA Joint Task Force, 2005) emphasized shared beliefs of the two fields as well as the need for middle schools that vigorously support both equity and excellence for all of their students. Of particular importance in finding a common direction, the report notes the imperative of attending to the needs of students who already perform at high levels and students who have the potential to do so but who have not yet recognized or tapped that potential. More specifically, the joint statement made the following recommendations to address the academic and affective needs of high performing and high potential students in middle schools:

District and School Leaders Should:

1. Provide leadership in creating a school climate that vigorously supports both equity and excellence.
2. Ensure that teachers have meaningful knowledge and understanding about the needs of gifted adolescents, including training in differentiated instruction so that the needs of all students—including

those with advanced performance or potential—are appropriately addressed.

3. Develop and implement an appropriate and flexible system for identifying high-ability learners from diverse populations.
4. Use organizational structures such as teaming and advisory programs to ensure that needs of young adolescents, including high-ability young adolescents, are central in instructional planning.
5. Encourage consistent collaboration among all teachers and support personnel in the school to ensure appropriate services for high-ability learners.
6. Ensure a continuum of services including options such as differentiation, advanced classes, acceleration, short-term seminars, independent studies, mentorships and other learning opportunities matched to the varied needs of high-potential and high-ability learners.
7. Provide counseling-related services for students with advanced academic performance or potential.
8. Develop and maintain a written plan to guide educational planning for advanced learners and to inform the community of those plans.
9. Regularly evaluate the effectiveness of curriculum, instruction, resources, and other services in supporting the development of high-ability learners.

Teachers, Gifted Education Specialists, and Support Personnel Should:

1. Be knowledgeable about students with advanced academic abilities and those who have the potential to work at advanced levels.
2. Meet regularly to discuss the needs of all students, including those with high-ability.
3. Provide curriculum, instruction, and other opportunities to meet the needs of students with high-ability.
4. Use a variety of developmentally appropriate instructional practices to enable each student to experience a high degree of personal excellence.
5. Collaborate with colleagues at elementary and high school levels to ensure a smooth transition as students progress throughout the grades.

6. Keep parents informed about their children's growth and invite parent participation in educational planning for their children.

In this joint statement, the fields of gifted education and middle school education find common ground identifying two categories of students who require attention related to giftedness—those who are already performing at very high levels in the middle grades and those who have the potential to do so, but who are not yet working to their advanced potential. In this space of common ground is the opportunity to extend high-end excellence for high performers as well as to insist on equity of access to excellence for students whose considerable potential may well go unrecognized and unrealized without the keen eye and active support of teachers. Such a view of giftedness is expansive and recognizes broadening conceptions of giftedness. It asks educators to assume at least three roles in terms of developing the capacity of gifted students—the roles of talent spotter, talent developer, and talent extender.

DIVERSITY IN THE POPULATION OF GIFTED LEARNERS IN THE MIDDLE GRADES

The image of a gifted student in the minds of many educators would likely incorporate making high grades and test scores, being compliant, exhibiting maturity, and liking school. Indeed, there are very bright students in the middle grades who match that description. These high performing students clearly need to find consistent opportunities in middle school to extend their cognitive and affective reach, as well as the active investment and support of teachers in ensuring such opportunities.

There is also in middle school, however, a wide array of students who have high potential, but who do not yet exhibit high performance. Among students who might fall into this category are those with high potential who:

- come to school from low economic backgrounds;
- come to school from insecure or unsafe home settings;
- have learning disabilities, attention disorders, or emotional difficulties;
- are highly creative and do not fit the school mold;
- are from cultural groups that view education differently from a Caucasian perspective;
- feel alienated from school;
- are chronic underachievers;
- have reading and/or writing difficulties;

- are socially or emotionally immature; or
- have great strengths in areas not emphasized by school (e.g., spatial abilities, leadership, intrapersonal strengths).

History is replete with examples of young people who—to varying degrees—struggled and often failed in school, looking anything but gifted, and who subsequently made noteworthy contributions to society, typical of those individuals we *do* think of as "gifted." Among a *very* large group of such individuals are: Ben Carson, Nelson Rockefeller, Thomas Edison, F.W. Woolworth, Pablo Picasso, General George Patton, Walt Disney, Michael Jordan, Winston Churchill, Woodrow Wilson, Albert Einstein, Hans Christian Anderson, Agatha Christie, Charles Schwab, Ted Turner, Walter Dean Myers, Patricia Pollaco, Whoopi Goldberg, Ansel Adams, Bill Cosby, Robin Williams, and Frank Lloyd Wright to name only a few. There are, no doubt, legions of others whose potential was *never* realized, at least in part due to negative school experiences. High potential in young people can be difficult to detect.

In addition, of course, high performing and high potential middle schoolers—like other students their age—often find school constraining, confusing, and/or in competition with an array of changes and distractions in their rapidly evolving lives. They need to move, are physically awkward, are beset by hormones that are unpredictable at best, have evolving brains, struggle with organization, are uncertain about their relationships with adults, seem at the mercy of emotions, and are drawn magnet-like to peers (Tomlinson & Doubet, 2006). Thus like other young adolescents, high performing and high potential middle school students have a great deal to contend with and may be erratic—sometimes for the first time in their lives—in the classroom.

Middle grade teachers who play the roles of talent spotter, talent developer, and talent extender for all the full range of high performing and high potential young adolescents are: attuned to and accepting of student learning differences, alert for evidence of student strengths, and quick to capitalize on those strengths. Further, such teachers not only seek to understand the unique developmental needs of young adolescents, but also how those needs are shaped by other factors such as ability, disability, economics, ethnicity, race, gender, and so on.

COGNITIVE AND AFFECTIVE NEEDS OF BRIGHT MIDDLE SCHOOLERS

A fundamental goal of education for high achieving and high potential learners—as for other learners—is to assist them in becoming self-actualized individuals. In the simplest terms, self-actualization is reaching one's full potential. Students who have reached self-actualization according to Maslow (1943), make the most of their abilities, embrace reality, enjoy problem solving, and judge without prejudice. Research on gifted adolescents point directly to three factors that affect this particular population's self actualization: self-concept (Feldhusen, 1986), perceived challenge, and motivation (Moneta & Csikszentmihalyi, 1996). In other words, middle schools that are effective in helping bright young adolescents move toward self-actualization would support the students in developing positive identities, experiencing appropriate challenge, and motivation to learn.

Noting the variability among young adolescents, Stevenson (2002) cautioned that generalizations about the population are risky. He proposes five caveats that apply to high performing and high ability learners in this age group as well as to all others: (1) young adolescence is characterized by great growth and great variability among its members; (2) individuals develop idiosyncratically; (3) home, neighborhood, gender, race, and ethnicity impact development; (4) the effects of young adolescent experiences are powerful and long lasting; and (5) young adolescents flourish when their needs are being met.

Likewise, it is difficult to generalize about the diverse population of young adolescents we might call "gifted." They, too, change greatly but variably during young adolescence, are shaped by factors like home, gender, and ethnicity, and will benefit from environments that address their needs or be diminished by those that do not. It is useful, nonetheless, to delineate some key ability-related issues in the lives of many young, high performing or high ability young adolescents (Tomlinson & Doubet, 2006). These intersect and combine with basic developmental issues and needs of young adolescents in general and can cause a different "spin" on the general needs for students in this group who are advanced performers or have advanced potential.

Potential Issues for High-Performing and High Potential Young Adolescents

1. **The need to both achieve and belong.** In the elementary years, many students in this group received positive feedback on their achievement from both peers and teachers and advanced achievement became a part of their identities. In middle school, as young adolescents inject space between adult endeavors and peer endeavors, it may become less acceptable for a peer to invest in the essentially adult endeavor of school. High performing and high potential students may find that they sacrifice peer approval if they

continue to pursue achievement or must sacrifice achievement to be acceptable to peers (Gross, 1989; Tomlinson, 1998). Such middle level learners need environments that enable them to maintain their identities as high achievers and simultaneously to develop friendships that are of paramount importance in young adolescent development.

2. **Coping with uneven development.** It is often the case that a very able young adolescent talks more like an adult than an early teen. As a result, it's easy for teachers to conclude that these students are, in fact, adult-like. While that may be the case for some advanced middle schoolers, it is also the case that others may be mature conversationalists with teachers and have no idea how to make friends. They may be precocious verbally but immature emotionally or physically. Bright students who are very self aware can also be easily frustrated by "the pieces of themselves" that don't fit together. In any case, they need adults who understand that bright, young adolescents often experience uneven development and may need opportunities to be very mature in some areas and support for "catching up" in others.
3. **Living with heightened sensitivities.** Some—but not all—young adolescents are super sensitive to the world around them (Dabrowski, 1964). They can, for example, suffer deeply and personally when they witness injustice or inequity at school or in the broader world. They simultaneously feel the need to "fix" the problems they see and are aware that they lack the skills for doing so. Without effective adult guidance, the students can develop feelings of helplessness and hopelessness. Further, highly sensitive students can be overly attuned to the expectations of adults around them and fear disappointing those adults. Whether these young adolescents struggle with intellectual or emotional sensitivities, they need adults who respect their deep feelings and concerns, and who can help them find appropriate ways to act on issues that trouble them.
4. **Lacking effective study or organizational skills.** Very bright students may achieve success in the elementary grades with little or no studying. If these students are provided with advanced challenge in the middle grades, they may lack the coping skills necessary to achieve them. Not only may such students be deficient in study and organizational skills but may also have little experience with persisting in the face of difficulty. Experiencing, tolerating, and embracing challenge is a key developmental need for many highly able young adolescents to enable them to develop the habits of mind necessary to move toward intellectual self-actualization

(Tomlinson, 1998). They need teachers who recognize the problem and help them develop the attitudes and skills necessary to achieve challenge that is commensurate with their capacity to do so.

5. **Pursuing perfection.** Many highly able students enter middle school with the expectation that they should make straight A's as a matter of course because that is the pattern to which they became accustomed in the elementary grades. In the face of lower grades (even an A- for some students), the self-concept of such students is threatened. Lacking perspectives that maturity can offer, the students may become angry at teachers, or alternatively at themselves, when they cannot live up to the standards they expect. If this leads to behaviors associated with perfectionism, procrastination, prolonged unhappiness, depression, eating disorders, and other negative patterns can result. These students need teachers who recognize the problem and help them learn to pursue excellence rather than perfectionism.
6. **Hungering to learn more**. In the same way that a talented young musician longs to explore music deeply or a talented young athlete longs to be on the playing field, a middle schooler with high academic ability hungers to probe issues, ideas, and subject areas in depth and breadth. Their advanced thinking abilities can make grade level curriculum feel like a starvation diet. They feel constrained, restricted, restless, and perhaps rebellious. Students like this need teachers who ensure that classroom challenge is geared to the varied academic needs of students in the classes and who support advanced learners in working in increasingly more expert-like ways (Tomlinson, Kaplan, Renzulli, Percell, Leppien, & Burns, 2001).
7. **Being good in too many areas**. There are highly able middle school students who excel in many areas. While that may seem a blessing rather than a curse, having great potential in many areas can be a frustration to young adolescents who are seeking self-identity and who may feel pressure from well-meaning adults to focus their talents in a variety of endeavors. It can be difficult to begin to envision a future. Such students need teachers who help them explore possibilities without the expectation of long-term commitment to any particular domain.
8. **Feeling different**. Wanting to fit in is a descriptor of young adolescents—including those who are exceptionally bright. Some highly able students sense that their hunger to learn sets them apart from peers. They may be perceived as asking too many questions, studying too hard, being a "geek." At such points, the student's ability

feels more like a curse than an opportunity. They need teachers who overtly value the traits of all of their students, guide their students to be respectful of all their peers, and at the same time work to make sure that students have the opportunity to establish and maintain friendships with peers who share their interests and perspectives.

Potential Issues for High Potential Young Adolescents

In addition to ability-related issues that may affect both high achieving and high potential young adolescents, there are additional ability-related issues that can be troubling to students with high potential who are not high performers (Tomlinson & Doubet, 2006). They are of particular concern during the middle school years when the search for selfhood is central.

1. **Being unaware of their own possibilities**. Some bright students who do not stand out as achievers in school know they are highly able despite profiles that would indicate otherwise. There are, however, middle schoolers with great potential to achieve who have never seen themselves in that light. Their teachers do not signal them that they see advanced potential in the students. Their friends may not invest heavily in school. Their parents may not push them to do well academically. The students simply have never considered themselves in that light. The middle school years are critical for such students to develop a sense of their own potential and they need teachers who believe in them and provide them with opportunity, support, and insistence to excel intellectually.
2. **Feeling alienated from academics and school**. There are many young adolescents who get clear messages from society, neighborhood, peers, and school that academics do not belong to people like them. To be smart is to "act White," and the message is reinforced when they do not see members of their own race or economic groups represented in the pages of textbooks, and when they look at who comprises advanced classes, honor societies, and recipients of academic recognitions and do not see themselves there. Further, what these students study in school may seem very disconnected from their interests and their world. Such students have a critical need for teachers who consistently and overtly make connections between academic content and the varied worlds of the students they teach. They also need teachers who persistently provide messages and evidence that academics belong to everyone.

3. **Lacking gatekeeper knowledge and skill**. High potential students who do not have a strong affiliation with academic achievement enter middle school at a disadvantage compared with their like-potential peers who have been stellar achievers for years. Such students may lack academic vocabulary, be behind in reading, suffer from poorly developed study skills, participate in few extra curricular activities, and in general be less than savvy about how to "do school." Such deficits further exacerbate the prevailing message that academics is not the place for these students. They need teachers who help them make up gaps in past knowledge, attitudes, and skills while supporting them in working on ideas, issues, and tasks that provide advanced intellectual challenge.
4. **Feeling pulled in multiple directions**. High potential middle schoolers who have not yet seen themselves as high achievers may have parents who urge them to do well in school and peers who do the opposite. They may have teachers who talk with them about preparing for college and parents who tell them there is no way to afford college. They may be at once attracted to a world of ideas and feel out of place in school. It is still the case in some settings that bright girls are discouraged from appearing smart or planning for an advanced education. These students need teachers who understand and help the students understand how to live in multiple worlds, respect all of them, and still find one's own identity.
5. **Lacking a roadmap to the future**. Some highly able students don't believe they have a future. Some don't believe academics are a part of their future. Some believe that learning is very important, but that there is no way for them to achieve more than a high school education. The middle school years are critical ones for these students to learn not only to recognize and value their high potential but also to learn practical steps and strategies necessary to realize that potential. They need teachers who actively and wisely mentor them in both regards.
6. **Lacking a support system.** Students who are successful in school typically have numerous adults in their lives who groom them for that success. The adults teach them outside of school, read to them, have intellectual discussions with them, see that they take advantage of out-of-class learning opportunities, model the behaviors of adult achievement, and send regular messages about the students' abilities. When high potential students do not have adults in their lives playing these roles, they are at high risk of failing to develop their potential. Young adolescents who have high poten-

tial and who lack such adult advocates sorely need middle grade teachers willing to take on these roles for the students.

7. **Fearing "stereotype threat."** Students from low economic groups and/or African American, Native American, Hispanic, and other ethnic backgrounds receive a steady stream of messages from media, institutions, and individuals that people like them are not smart. Thus the students believe that significant adults do not expect as much of them as of others. Research suggests that, in fact, this belief may be the accurate (Steele, 1997). Even when it is not, however, students from these groups fear that others perceive them as less able and the fear of being stereotyped is an inhibitor for academic success. Students who experience stereotype threat need teachers who make clear their high expectations of the students and who provide them with messages and models that counter stereotype threat.

Young adolescence is a particularly complex time of life. There is likely no such thing as a middle school student who doesn't need the active partnership of teachers for the journey. Young adolescence should also be a particularly promising time of life during which the world of possibilities begins to unfold for young adolescents who increasingly see themselves in those possibilities. High performing and high potential adolescents—like all others—need educators who help them recognize, prepare for, and act on the possibilities within them. Middle level educators who effectively fill that role for highly able students are guided by a number of key principles of talent recognition, talent development, and talent extension.

KEY PRINCIPLES OF EFFECTIVE SCHOOLING FOR HIGH ABILITY YOUNG ADOLESCENTS

While it is difficult to compress the principles and practices of talent recognition, talent development, and talent extension for high achieving and high potential students into a brief space, the following principles are important.

1. **Educators must recognize advanced ability to develop and extend it.** While there are pros and cons to a formal identification system that labels students, it is the case that it's difficult for teachers to serve what they don't recognize. For that reason, there is merit to formally searching for middle level students with high ability. To ensure that such identification methods are inclusive

rather than exclusive, it is critical to use multiple measures of ability (e.g., nominations, portfolios/samples of student work, auditions, tests of aptitude, tests of achievement, nominations from parents and/or community members, teacher ratings) and to look for confirming rather than disconfirming evidence of ability (Callahan, Tomlinson, & Pizzat, 1993; Gubbins, 2006). The use of single measures of ability falls short of recognizing the multi-facetedness of intelligence and talent (Gardner, 1983; Groth-Marnat, 2003; Sternberg, 2000) and is likely to work to the disadvantage of high ability students from low economic and non-Caucasian groups, as well as high potential students with handicaps, whose first language is not English, who are highly creative, who are alienated from school, and so on (Esters, Ittenback, & Han, 1997; Joseph & Ford, 2006). It is important also to assist teachers in knowing how to look for indications of high potential in both classroom and out-of-classroom contexts in which they interact with young adolescents, to use authentic assessment tools, and to be attuned to ways in which ability is manifest in various cultures (Callahan, Tomlinson, & Pizzat, 1993).

2. **Strong, positive connections between teachers and middle level students build bridges to discovering, developing, and extending talent.** For many highly able students in the middle school years, teachers represent important issues and ideas. A teacher may well be the source of the most challenging conversation in the student's day. For other highly able students, the teacher is someone to talk with comfortably when peer relationships are uncomfortable. For still others, the voice of the teacher may be the only one in the student's life affirming the student's potential, insisting on working up to that potential, and providing support for realizing the potential. In each instance, when teachers affirm the worth of ability (as well as of humor, musical talent, helpfulness, and the like) through positive human connections, young adolescents in search of identity are strengthened and doors to growth are opened.
3. **High quality curriculum and instruction are precursors for advanced learning opportunities**. Good curriculum and instruction for advanced learners begins with rich, meaning-making, student-centered instruction (Tomlinson, 1996, 2005; Tomlinson et al., 2001). Virtually all students benefit from curriculum and instruction that ensures they understand the key concepts and principles of a discipline, learn for coherent understanding, can transfer what they learn, build on previous experiences, organize what they learn in ways that help them remember, and move per-

sistently toward expertise in the disciplines (National Research Council, 1999; Tomlinson & McTighe, 2006). Such curriculum and instruction is essential to developing the capacity of high achieving and high potential learners—as it is for the preponderance of learners (Tomlinson et al., 2001). Instructional approaches such as Student-Centered Discussion (Hale & City, 2006), Problem Based Learning (Delisle, 1997), and Complex Instruction (Cohen, Lotan, Scarloss, & Arellano, 1999) support authentic, contextualized learning.

4. **Challenge is particular to individuals**. We have long known (e.g., Vygotsky, 1978, 1986) that people learn when challenges moderately exceed their current knowledge, understanding, and skill in a particular area and when there is support from others to bridge the gap between past knowledge and the new goal. There is no such thing as a curriculum that is challenging to middle schoolers. Rather, it must be appropriately challenging to the growth needs of particular middle schoolers. In the case of highly able students, that calls on teachers to extend the complexity of content and materials, provide opportunities for study in greater depth and/or breadth, support increasing independence, necessitate more advanced thinking, create more multi-faceted tasks, adjust the pacing of work, and so on (Kaplan, 1994; Tomlinson, 1999, 2003). In the case of students with high potential but not high performance, it calls on middle level teachers to learn to teach backwards and forwards simultaneously—that is, to help students address learning deficits while still providing intellectually rich and complex learning opportunities (Tomlinson & Doubet, 2006).
5. **Passions for learning are powerful motivators**. Highly able students often bring to school with them a keen interest in or a keen desire to know about particular topics. Those may or may not be a match for a particular curriculum. However, wise middle grade teachers who connect with their students are or can become aware of such passions. They recognize the teachable moment and provide an impetus for students to explore topics of interest. That may occur through strategies such as Curriculum Compacting (Reis, Burns, & Renzulli, 1992), Independent Study (Tomlinson, 1993), Orbital Studies (Stevenson, 2002), Interest Groups (Tomlinson, 2003), Mentorships, or simply by encouraging the student to pursue the topic and share findings with the teacher and appropriate peers. Researchers (Csikszentmihalyi, Rathunde, & Whalen, 1993) suggest that when adolescents have and pursue some passion for learning, they are much more likely to survive the rigors of adolescence in a position of strength than are those who do not have or

do not pursue such avenues. The researchers note that the passion for learning need not be linked to the formal school curriculum. Effective teachers of high performing and high potential students acknowledge and support students in deepening their knowledge in areas of high interest or expertise as well as in developing new areas of interest.

6. **Flexible teaching is a precursor to and product of teaching to individual needs.** It is highly unlikely that high achieving or high potential middle schoolers will be well served in classrooms with a lockstep curriculum and one-size-fits-all instruction. To attend to the needs of academically diverse learners—including those who are highly able—requires understanding students' varied needs, accepting responsibility for addressing those needs, and teaching in a way that allows attention to individuals and small groups of learners as well as to the class as a whole (Tomlinson, 1999, 2001, Tomlinson et al., 2003). This is the case in heterogeneously grouped classes, but also in classes that are more homogeneous in nature. The skills of responsive teaching are developmental and evolve as teachers apply and hone them in practice with strong support through leadership and professional development (Tomlinson, Brimijoin, & Narvaez, in press).

A LOOK AHEAD AT TEACHING GIFTED LEARNERS IN THE MIDDLE GRADES

"Perhaps the biggest challenge stemming from the approach to middle grades education … is inherent in the very notion of a school that is equally dedicated to excellence and equity" (Jackson & Davis, 2000, p. 227). While achieving such an ideal is elusive, key literature of middle level education in the past decade and a half clearly describe a kind of school that supports both goals.

Turning Points (Carnegie Council on Adolescent Development, 1989) is a seminal document detailing the attributes of effective middle schools. It notes the need for rigorous curriculum relevant to students and based on how students learn best, for teaching young adolescents to be critical thinkers, and for using varied instructional methods to prepare a broad base of students to achieve at high levels.

A second key middle level document, *Turning Points 2000* (Jackson & Davis, 2000) examines progress made since the original *Turning Points* document in 1989 and presents a more contemporary understanding of effective middle schools. The document advocates—among other things—middle grade classrooms that: meet students where they are academically; are student centered; provide rich learning environments with access to diverse materials, opinions, and options; help students understand the key concepts of the disciplines; engage students in challenging work that causes them to stretch in order to succeed; connect curriculum and instruction with students' own interests and experiences; attend to student differences by differentiating content, process, and product based on students' varied readiness levels, interests, and learning profiles; and use on-going assessment to understand students' learning needs and adjust teaching/learning plans accordingly.

A third and still more recent key document describing high quality middle level schools is *This We Believe: Successful Schools for Young Adolescents* (National Middle School Association, 2003) counsels that successful schools for young adolescents are characterized by a school culture that includes—among other elements, environments that are inviting, supportive, and safe; an adult advocate for every student; connections with family; curriculum that is relevant and challenging to the individual learner; multiple teaching and learning approaches that respond to the cultural and academic diversity in middle grades classrooms; and multifaceted guidance and support services. In elaborating on the nature of curriculum and instruction in effective middle schools, the report calls for curriculum that is geared to a student's level of understanding, interests, and learning preferences, that allows for choice and increasing independence, and provides challenges that enable each student to grow—whatever their current level of ability. Further, the report notes, curriculum in the middle grades should focus on studying important issues centered around essential questions, the use of complex tasks, and opportunity to understand both how and why things happen.

The contents of these and other seminal descriptions of the goals and practices of middle level education written in the past 15 years sound quite compatible with the goals of gifted education. In fact, *Turning Points 2000* concludes with the assertion that middle schools should aspire to educate every middle grades student to his or her fullest potential, noting that there is no more important goal in American education.

The issue of effectively teaching both high performing and high potential students effectively in the middle grades is likely not so much a problem of dueling philosophies between the fields of middle level education and gifted education, but rather one of deficient practice.

That the goals of both arenas of education practice align seems evident. The authors of *Turning Points 2000* (Jackson & Davis, 2000) make clear that the aim of middle grades education is to promote both equity and excellence. Attention to both ideals is imperative for the social justice goals that have typified middle schools since their inception. For the field of gifted education, an emphasis on excellence—including individual excellence—is imperative to realize the potential of high achieving students, while an emphasis on both equity and excellence is a nonnegotiable for developing the capacity of high potential learners who are at risk for falling short of realizing their possibilities.

The chief barrier to addressing tensions between the fields of middle level education and gifted education, then, is not so much philosophical but practical. Research clearly suggests that the typical middle grades classroom—as has been the case for over 15 years—is less likely to focus on intellectually rigorous, student-centered, meaning-making curriculum than on a curriculum focused on practice of rote information and skills (Jackson & Davis, 2000). Further, effective attention to individual needs in the middle grades is the exception rather than the rule (Brighton, Hertberg, Moon, Tomlinson, & Callahan, 2005; Moon, Tomlinson, & Callahan, 1997; Tomlinson, 1995; Tomlinson, Moon, & Callahan, 1998). To address the ideals of educational equity and excellence necessitates implementation of both very high quality curriculum and highly personalized instruction. In the absence of either, the ideals of both are, at best, rhetorical.

The aspiration to develop heterogeneous middle grades classrooms in which equity and excellence are simultaneously the norm remains, by most practical measures, a vision more than a reality. Working collegially to ensure that the vision is not permanently deferred is the next challenge for the fields of middle level education and gifted education.

REFERENCES

Allan, S. (1991). Ability-grouping research interviews: What do they say about grouping and the gifted? *Educational Leadership, 48*(6), 60-65.

Brighton, C., Hertberg, H., Moon, T., Tomlinson, C., & Callahan, C. (2005). *The feasibility of high-end learning in a diverse middle school.* Research Monograph RM05210. Charlottesville, VA: The University of Virginia, National Research Center on the Gifted and Talented.

Callahan, C., Tomlinson, C., & Pizzat, P. (1993). *Contexts for promise: Noteworthy practices and innovations in the identification of gifted students.* Charlottesville, VA, University of Virginia: National Research Center on the Gifted and Talented.

Carnegie Council on Adolescent Development. (1989). *Turning points: Preparing American youth for the 21st Century.* New York: Carnegie Corporation of New York.

Cohen, E., Lotan, R., Scarloss, B., & Arellano, A. (1999). Complex instruction: Equity in cooperative learning classrooms. *Theory into Practice, 38*(2), 80-86.

Csikszentmihalyi, M., Rathunde, K., & Whalen, S. (1993). *Talented teenagers: The roots of success and failure.* New York: Cambridge University Press.

Dabrowski, K. (1964). *Positive disintegration.* London: Little, Brown & Co.

Dawson, M. (1987). Beyond ability grouping: A review of the effectiveness of ability grouping and its alternatives. *School Psychology Review, 16*, 348-369.

Delisle, R. (1997). *How to use problem-based learning in the classroom*. Alexandria, VA: Association for Supervision and Curriculum Development.

Esters, I., Ittenback, R., & Han, K. (1997). Today's IQ tests: Are they really better than their historical predecesors? *School Psychology Review, 26*, 211-223.

Feldhusen, J. (1986). A conception of giftedness. In K. A. Heller & J. F. Feldhusen (Eds.), *Identifying and nurturing the gifted. An international perspective* (pp. 33-38). Toronto, Ontario, Canada: Huber.

Gallagher, J., Coleman, M., & Nelson, S. (1995). Perceptions of educational reform by educators representing middle schools, cooperative learning, and gifted education. *Gifted Child Quarterly, 39*(2), 66-76.

Gamoran, A., Nystrand, M., Berends, M., & LePorte, P. (1995). An organizational analysis of the effects of ability grouping. *American Educational Research Association Journal, 32*, 687-715.

Gardner, H. (1983). *Frames of mind: The theory of multiple intelligences*. New York: Basic Books.

George, P. (1988). Tracking and ability grouping: Which way for the middle school? *Middle School Journal, 20*(1), 21-28.

George, P. (1993). Tracking and ability grouping in the middle school. Ten tentative truths. *Middle School Journal, 24*(4), 17-24.

Gross, M. (1989). The pursuit of excellence or the search for intimacy? The forced choice of gifted youth. *Roeper Review, 11*, 189-194.

Groth-Marnat, G. (2003). *Handbook of psychological assessment* (4th ed.). New York: Wiley.

Gubbins, J. (2006). Constructing identification procedures. In J. Purcell & R. Eckert (Eds.), *Designing services and programs for high ability learners: A guidebook for gifted education* (pp. 49-61). Thousand Oaks, CA: Corwin.

Hale, M., & City, E. (2006). *The teacher's guide to using student-centered discussions*. Thousand Oaks, CA: Corwin.

Jackson, A., & Davis, G. (2000). *Turning points 2000: Educating adolescents in the 21st century*. New York: Teachers College Press.

Joseph, L., & Ford, D. (2006). Nondiscriminatory assessment: Considerations for gifted education. *Gifted Child Quarterly, 50*, 42-51.

Kaplan, S. (1994). *Differentiating core curriculum and instruction to provide advanced learning opportunities*. Sacramento, CA: California Association for the Gifted.

Kulik, J., & Kulik, C. (1992). Meta-analytic findings on grouping programs. *Gifted Child Quarterly, 36*, 73-77.

Maslow, A. (1943). A theory of human motivation. *Psychological Review, 50*, 370-396.

Moneta, G. B., & Csikizentmihalyi, M. (1996). The effect of perceived challenges and skills on the quality of subjective experience. *Journal of Personality, 64*(2), 276- 310.

Moon, T., Tomlinson, C., & Callahan, C. (1997). *Academic diversity in the middle school: Results of a national survey of middle school administrators and teachers*. (Research Monograph 95124) Storrs, CT: National Research Center on the Gifted and Talented.

NAGC/NMSA Joint Task Force. (2005). *Meeting the needs of high ability and high potential learners in the middle grades: A joint position statement of the National Middle School Association and the National Association for Gifted Children*. Westerville, OH: NMSA and Washington, DC: NAGC.

National Middle School Association. (2003). *This we believe: Successful schools for young adolescents*. Westerville, OH: Author.

National Research Council. (1999). *How people learn: Brain, mind, experience, and school*. Washington, DC : National Academy Press.

Oakes, J. (1985). *Keeping track: How schools structure inequality*. New Haven, CT: Yale University Press.

Plucker, J., & McIntire, J. (1996). Academic survivability in high-potential, middle school students. *Gifted Child Quarterly, 40*(1), 7-14.

Riccio, L. (1985). Facts and issues about ability grouping. *Contemporary Education, 57*, 26-30.

Reis, S., Burns, D., & Renzulli, J. (1992). *Curriculum compacting*. Mansfield Center, CT: Creative Learning Press.

Robinson, A. (1990). Cooperation or exploitation? The argument against cooperative learning for talented students. *Journal for the Education of the Gifted, 14*(1), 9–27.

Rogers, K. (1991). *The relationship of grouping practices to the education of gifted and talented learners*. Storrs, CT: University of Connecticut, National Research Center on the Gifted and Talented.

Sicola, P. (1990). Where do gifted students fit? An examination of middle school philosophy as it relates to ability grouping and the gifted learner. *Journal for the Education of the Gifted, 14*(1), 37–49.

Slavin, R. (1980). *Using student team learning*. Baltimore, MD: Center for Research on Elementary and Middle Schools.

Slavin, R. (1987). Ability grouping and student achievement in elementary schools: A best evidence synthesis. *Review of Educational Research, 57*, 293-336.

Steele, C. (1997). A threat in the air: How stereotypes shape intellectual identity and performance. *American Psychologist, 52*, 613-29

Stevenson, C. (2002). *Teaching ten to fourteen year olds* (3rd ed.). Boston: Allyn & Bacon.

Sternberg, R. J. (2000). The concept of intelligence. In R. J. Sternberg (Ed.), *Handbook of intelligence* (pp. 3-15). Cambridge, England: Cambridge University Press.

Tomlinson, C. (1993). Independent study: A flexible tool for encouraging personal and academic growth in middle school learners. *Middle School Journal, 25*(1), 55-59.

Tomlinson, C. (1995). Deciding to differentiate instruction in middle school: One school's journey. *Gifted Child Quarterly, 39*(2) 77-87.

Tomlinson, C. (1996). Good teaching for one and all : Does gifted education have an instructional identity ? *Journal for the Education of the Gifted, 20*, 155-174.

Tomlinson, C. (1998). Curriculum and instruction for gifted learners in the middle grades: What would it take? In R. Williamson & J. Johnston (Eds.) *Able learners in the middle level school* (pp. 21-32). Reston, VA: National Association of Secondary School Principals.

Tomlinson, C. (1999). The differentiated classroom: Responding to the needs of all learners. Alexandria, VA: Association for Supervision and Curriculum Development.

Tomlinson, C. (2003). *Fulfilling the promise of the differentiated classroom: Strategies and tools for responsive teaching*. Alexandria, VA: Association for Supervision and Curriculum Development.

Tomlinson, C. (2005). Quality curriculum and instruction for highly able students. *Theory into Practice, 44*, 160-166.

Tomlinson, C., Brimijoin, K., & Narvaez, L. (in press). *Leading and learning to differentiate instruction: Changing schools and classrooms for responsive teaching*. Alexandria, VA: Association for Supervision and Curriculum Development.

Tomlinson, C., & Doubet, K. (2006). *Smart in the middle grades: Classrooms that work for bright middle schoolers*. Westerville, OH: National Middle School Association.

Tomlinson, C., Kaplan, S. Renzulli, J., Purcell, J., Leppien, J., & Burns, D. (2001). *The parallel curriculum model : A design to develop high potential and challenge high ability learners.* Thousand Oaks, CA: Corwin.

Tomlinson, C., & McTighe, J. (2006). *Integrating differentiated instruction and Understanding by Design: Connecting content and kids*. Alexandria, VA: Association for Supervision and Curriculum Development.

Tomlinson, C., Moon, T., & Callahan, C. (1998). How well are we addressing academic diversity in the Middle School? *Middle School Journal, 29*(3), 3-11.

Vygotsky, L. (1978). *Mind in society.* Cambridge, MA: Harvard University Press.

Vygotsky, L. (1986). *Thought and language* (A. Kozulin, Trans. & Ed.). Cambridge, MA: MIT Press.

Wheelock, A. (1992). *Crossing the tracks: How 'untracking' can save America's schools.* New York: The New Press.

CHAPTER 7

SOCRATIC SEMINAR AND YOUNG ADOLESCENT MOTIVATION

A Developmentally Appropriate Practice

Molly M. Mee

ABSTRACT

The middle school years are a time when young adolescents experience difficulties with motivation and a time when teachers look for instructional methods to motivate students. This case study explores three middle school students' perceptions of the influences of Socratic Seminar on their motivation for learning. Qualitative data consists of observations, individual and focus group interviews, student journals, and surveys. Data were examined according to the four characteristics of motivation (attention, relevancy, confidence, and satisfaction) as defined by Keller (1983) and according to new characteristics of motivation that presented themselves in the data (student talk, peer collaboration, control, safety, and student-teacher relationship). The research question driving the study was how and in what ways do 3 seventh-grade students perceive that Socratic Seminar influences their motivation for learning? The students indicated that Socratic Seminar is a method that captures their attention, is relevant to their lives, enhances their self-confidence, and is satisfying.

The Young Adolescent and the Middle School
pp. 141–161

INTRODUCTION

Middle school educators are concerned with adapting instruction to the unique characteristics of the young adolescent student. Physically, the young adolescent is growing at a rapid rate. Intellectually, the young adolescent, who is accustomed to the elementary school curriculum, often finds the middle school curriculum daunting. And perhaps most importantly, the young adolescent faces a variety of social issues such as making new friends, fitting in among peer groups, and communicating with peers and teachers. With all of these pressing issues and more, it is not surprising that the adolescent middle school student may find it difficult to be motivated to learn.

A growing body of data provide evidence that student motivation is a significant issue at the middle school level and that levels of motivation decrease as children transition from the elementary schools into the middle schools (Anderman & Maehr, 1994; Anderman & Midgley, 1998; Carnegie Council on Adolescent Development, 1989; Eccles, Wigfield, A., Flanagan, C. A., Miller, C., Reuman, D. A., & Yee, 1989; Eccles, Wigfield, Midgley, Reuman, Mac Iver, & Feldlaufer, 1993; Good & Brophy, 1994; Harter, 1981; Jackson & Davis, 2000; Lumsden, 1994). This decline in motivation is due, not only to physical changes in young adolescents but, also to the methods of middle school instruction (Anderman & Maehr; Eccles & Midgley, 1989; Eccles et al., 1993; Harter). Researchers (Eccles et al., 1993) maintain that "the traditional middle grades are not providing appropriate educational environments for early adolescents" (p. 554) and that it is imperative for educators of young adolescents to explore various modes of instruction and the impact of the modes on student motivation. Socratic Seminar is a child-centered instructional method that, according to researchers (Adler, 1982; Polite & Adams, 1996; Strong, 1996; Tredway, 1995), can motivate young adolescents by providing an appropriate environment for their age. Strong says that through Socratic Seminar "students become intrinsically motivated lifelong learners" (p. 131). This study explores three middle school students' perceptions of the influences of Socratic Seminar on their motivation for learning.

REVIEW OF LITERATURE

Adolescent Development

According to Erikson (1950/1993), adolescence is characterized as a time when childhood ends and youth begins. He maintained that not only does puberty and sexual maturation take place during adolescence but also, youths are faced with identity and role confusion issues. *Turning Points 2000* (Jackon & Davis, 2000) says, "too often, though, the main educational institution serving young adolescents—the middle grades school—falls short of meeting the educational and social needs of millions of students" (p. 2). Adolescence can also be a time when students become disinterested and problems such as school drop-out begin to occur (Eccles et al., 1993; Eccles, Lord, & Midgley, 1991; Hamburg & Takanishi, 1989). Researchers (Hamburg & Takanishi; Harnett, 1991; Jackson & Davis; Jackson & Hornbeck, 1989; National Middle School Association, 2003) agree that because young adolescence is a time of significant change, vulnerability and rapid growth, it is deserving of the attention of middle level educators. Erikson's theory of psychosocial development provides a framework for the development of humans within the context of society and maintains that individuals enter stages as they travel through life. He suggested that at each stage conflicts arise, and the manner in which individuals resolve these conflicts determines how they approach the next stage. According to this model, the middle school student borders between stage four, industry versus inferiority, and stage five, identity versus role confusion.

Stage four is what we generally refer to as the prepubescent years. This is "socially a most decisive stage" (Erikson, 1950/1993, p. 260) when issues of motivation are affected and when methods of learning are critical to the development of the adolescent (Anderman & Maehr, 1994; Eccles et al., 1993; Good & Brophy, 1994). Stage five occurs when "childhood proper comes to an end" (Erikson, p. 261) and marks the time in a teenager's life when peer pressure and self-esteem are issues of major concern. It is at this time that children transition from the child-centered, holistic environment of the elementary school to a larger, more abstract, and compartmentalized middle school. "Amid the stresses of early adolescence, entry into middle school itself can be troubling" (Jackson & Davis, 2000, p. 7).

Motivation and the Young Adolescent

There tends to be a disconnect between how young adolescents want to learn and how middle grades educators teach. Researchers (Anderman & Maehr, 1994; Eccles et al., 1993; Eccles & Midgley, 1989; Harter, 1981) maintain that the decline in motivation is due, not simply to physical changes in young adolescents but, also to environmental and structural conditions of the middle school and methods of middle school instruction. *Turning Points 2000* (Jackson & Davis, 2000) echoed this sentiment and said "although many young people reach late adolescence healthy and ready for the challenge of high school and adult life early adolescence for many others is the beginning of a downward spiral" (p. 8). A vast body of literature suggests the position that motivation for learning decreases as children grow older and transition into the middle school years (Anderman & Maehr; Anderman & Midgley, 1998; Eccles et al., 1989; Eccles et al., 1991; Eccles et al.; Good & Brophy, 1994; Haladyna & Thomas, 1979; Harter; Lumsden, 1994). With this in mind, it is imperative that middle school educators design and implement age-appropriate instructional methodologies that motivate the young adolescent. If we ignore this disconnect and the potential dangers it may cause, we could lose our students at a developmentally crucial time that can be an academically rewarding and enlightening period in a young adolescent's life.

Stage Environment Fit Theory

The stage-environment fit theory (Eccles et al., 1993) suggested that in order for students to be motivated, their learning environment must be appropriate to their current stage of development. There is a mismatch between the middle school environment and the unique needs of the developing young adolescent and "the traditional middle grade schools are not providing appropriate educational environments for early adolescents" (Eccles et al., p. 554). Researchers (Anderman & Maehr, 1994; Eccles et al.; Good & Brophy, 1994; Hamburg & Takanishi, 1989; Harter, 1981; Jackson & Hornbeck, 1989) suggested that changes in school structure at this stage in a child's psychosocial development can be detrimental to the child in various ways; one of which is motivation. Many (Clark & Clark, 1993; Eccles et al.; Jackson & Davis, 2000; Mac Iver & Epstein, 1993; National Middle School Association, 2003) claim that middle school instruction should facilitate a child-centered style of learning; fulfill the instinctual need of the students to focus on themselves; and, allow for development of personal identity, ideals, and values. Mac Iver and Epstein maintain that "most middle grades classes emphasize passive learning and drill and practice" (p. 525). Claiming that "an emphasis on passive, drill-oriented instruction is significantly associated with students' greater boredom at school, lower rates of homework completion, and less confidence that schoolwork will be useful in the future" (p. 526), they call for middle schools to focus more on the student and implement "active and interactive, and discovery instructional approaches" (p. 526).

The ARCS Model of Motivational Design

A review of the literature on motivation reveals a significant number of motivational instructional models for middle school students (Armstrong

& Savage, 1998; Eccles et al., 1991; Good & Brophy, 1994; Keller, 1983; Strong, 1996). One model of motivation of particular relevance to this study is the ARCS Model of Motivational Design (Keller). Keller noted:

> The ARCS model is a system for improving the motivational appeal of instructional materials, of instructor behavior, and of the way in which lessons (or modules) and courses are designed. It provides strategies that a course designer can use to make instruction responsive to the interests and needs of learners. (p. 1)

Keller examined literature on student motivation, looked for common themes and elements in the literature, and constructed the model according to four overarching characteristics of student motivation. The four characteristics are (a) attention (A), (b) relevance (R), (c) confidence (C), and (d) satisfaction (S). The purpose of the ARCS Model is to help educators to design motivating lessons and educational strategies and to determine how these methods influence motivation. The model can be simply applied to any age or grade level, including middle school (J. Keller, personal communication, October 20, 1999).

Attention

According to Keller (1983), in order for a student to be motivated, the lesson must grab his or her attention. He referred to attention as a prerequisite for learning and describes attention-getting tactics as unexpected events, mentally stimulating problems, and variation. He says that "ultimately, the best way to fight boredom and indifference is to stimulate their curiosities so the instructor can spend more time directing attention than in getting it" (p. 1).

Relevance

Another requirement to create motivation is to make instructional content relevant to student lives. Keller (1983) defined relevance as perceived value to the learner and as connecting content of a lesson to goals, interests, and learning styles of the learner. He says that, "relevance can come from the way something is taught; it does not have to come from the content itself" (p. 2).

Confidence

Keller (1983) suggests that confidence is established when students understand what is expected in order to succeed and when they know to what they can attribute success or lack there of. For example, if a student can attribute his or her success to his or her own efforts then confidence increases, but if the student views success as out of his or her control then confidence decreases.

Satisfaction

In order to sustain motivation, satisfaction is necessary (Keller, 1983). He defines satisfaction as positive feelings about one's accomplishments and learning experiences, and feelings that one has been treated fairly.

Socratic Seminar as a Motivating Method of Instruction

In order to promote and nurture student motivation, learning activities must foster active group learning that allows for students to interact with their peers. According to a study of seventh and eighth grade students, reasons for alienation from school and lack of motivation included students' feelings of alienation from the learning process and from their peers (Fontes, 1988). According to Maehr (1991), schools can foster student motivation by creating positive psychological environments and suggests group learning and problem solving activities to promote this type of environment. Turner and Meyer (1995) posited that the teacher relinquish some control of the students and encourage students to interact with each other via discussion. They said that when control of learning is shared among teacher and students, students become more interested in the learning process and take more responsibility for their own learning. In his article summarizing literature on motivation, Brophy (1987) identified ways to "capitalize on intrinsic motivation" (p. 44) by implementing activities that the majority of students will find interesting and rewarding. He suggested providing opportunities for students to respond actively and to interact with peers.

Socratic Seminar is one instructional method that makes connections between the curriculum and the lives of students; helps to build confidence, self-esteem and motivation (Strong, 1996); incorporates active learning (Chalupa & Sormunen, 1995; Lambright, 1995; Strong); and meets the unique needs of the adolescent student. Unfortunately, the method is all too uncommon in our nation's middle schools. The pressures of standardized tests and intensive curricula make it difficult for teachers to integrate Socratic Seminar in their classes, even though the young adolescent craves it.

Defining Socratic Seminar

Socratic Seminar is discourse or dialogue about ideas, centered on a text and an opening question where students are encouraged to discuss many possible answers (Gray, 1989; Lambright, 1995; Strong, 1996; Tredway, 1995). "Seminars encourage students to plumb the world deeply" (Parker, 2006, p. 12). Strong maintained that "society is constructed through social interactions" (p. 18) and that Socratic practice provides a forum in which students participate in authentic, intellectual, and social interactions. Rather than knowledge simply being transmitted from the teacher, students learn by engaging in dialogue with their peers.

The purpose of Socratic Seminar is to enlarge understanding of ideas, issues, and values (Gray, 1989; Lambright, 1995), and to make meaning through intensive conversation (Gray) doubt and systematic questioning (Tredway, 1995). "The task involves a rich and challenging text, a central question, the multiple interpretations that are brought to bear by discussants, and the relations among them" (Parker, 2006, p. 12).) "[Its] primary academic function is to develop reading and thinking skills to the point where students can understand academic materials" (Strong, 1996, p. 3). The goal is not to lead students to the *right* answer or to have them master information. Rather, Socratic Seminar is meant to be a rigorous thinking activity that requires students to explore many ideas, opinions, and thoughts. "Through doubt and systematic questioning of another person, one gets to ultimate truth" (Tredway, p. 26).

There are five primary elements of a Socratic Seminar. They are (a) the text, (b) the opening question, (c) the leader, (d) the participants, and (e) the Socratic circle. The Socratic Seminar begins with the reading of a common text either prior to or during the seminar. The text for a Seminar may include a poem, play, painting, novel, essay, and sermon. "Almost any text will work if it is rich in ideas that challenge and engage the participant" (Lambright, 1995, p. 30). Strong (1996) said that the text should be "incomprehensible to students" (p. 21) and "must contain an abstract idea" (p. 59). If the students understand the text immediately then there is nothing to discuss. Once the text has been read, the group begins its discussion with an opening question. Generally asked by the teacher or the assigned leader, the question should be open-ended and should "require students to evaluate options and make decisions" (Tredway, 1995, p. 26). The best questions, according to Lambright are those that develop out of natural curiosity. One basic characteristic that distinguishes Socratic Seminar from a didactic approach to teaching is the role of the teacher. There is a shift in power of the teacher from that of someone who dominates to one who interacts on the same level as the students (Letts, 1994; Strong). Strong described the teacher as a learner and says that the best leader is one with an "open, honest, and inquiring mind" (p. 43). The role of the teacher is to select a challenging text, construct an open-ended provocative opening question, and to guide the students to a deeper understanding of the text. The true sign of a successful seminar is when the participants leave the discussion with more questions than answers. Any person of any age, ability, or demographic can participate in a Socratic Seminar. "The younger the participants are, the more readily they catch on to the main purpose of seminars and master basic techniques" (Gray, 1989, p. 6). A basic premise of a Socratic Seminar is the promotion of equality of all members. Thus, the most appropriate arrangement is the circle or the semi-circle, known as the Socratic circle. This arrangement allows for the need for all participants to see each other as they engage in dialogue.

Constructivism

For several thousand years, philosophers have argued over the notions of knowledge and truth and how humans obtain them. "Constructivism is a form of pragmatism" (Von Glasersfeld, 1988, p. 3) that suggests that "much of learning originates from inside the child" (Kamii & Ewing, 1996, p. 260) and in which the child comes to know things through experiences, activities, discourse, and interaction with others. Early in the twentieth century, Dewey (1916/1966) called for a shift in the focus of education away from the teacher and toward the student. He emphasized the importance of linking subject matter to the student's life, and recognized and treated learning as an interactive, social process. He believed that the ideal society is one where education "gives individuals a personal interest in social relationships and control" (p. 99). Dewey also believed that education and democracy should be supportive of each other. He maintained that education is a process of living, not a preparation for living, and that democracy is a way of life, not a form of government. According to Dewey, education is essential to the progress of democracy and that democracy is in turn essential so that all may be educated.

Vygotsky's (1962, 1978) thinking echoes Dewey's (1902/1990, 1916/1966) in that he suggested that the child and the culture must work together in the cognitive development of the child. His work emphasizes the importance of language and interaction with others in the development of the child, affirming that language creates a forum for conversation and questioning, which guides thinking and learning. Much of his research and writing derive from the thought of Piaget who maintained that "cognitive development arises out of the activity of the child. Thus, the best methods of education for development are those that foster the activity or learning of the child" (as cited in Wadsworth, 1978, p. 102).

Linking Adolescent and Constructivist Theory to Socratic Seminar

Socratic Seminar is one instructional method that fits within the constructivist paradigms of Dewey (1902/1990, 1916/1966) and of Vygotsky (1962, 1978), and within the psychosocial development theory of Erikson (1950/1993). Strong (1996) suggested that Socratic Seminar "serves as a bridge between those issues which are compelling to a student and the academic issues which lie at the foundation of most curricula" (p. 135). He also maintained that Socratic Seminars facilitate a child-centered style of learning; fulfill the instinctual need of the students to focus on themselves; and allow for development of personal identity, ideals, and values. Students are able to discuss critical issues that affect the manner in which they view themselves and the ways they interact with their peers.

METHODOLOGY

This study followed a qualitative, multicase design. The intent was to explore, in-depth, the phenomenon of motivation from the perspective of three seventh-grade students within their classroom setting. Creswell (1998) said "a case study is an exploration of a 'bounded system' or a case (or multiple cases) over time through detailed, in-depth data collection involving multiple sources of information rich in context" (p. 61). Educators are interested in students' views on their education. However, "rarely is the perspective of the student herself explored" (Erikson & Shultz, 1992, p. 467). The research question driving the study was "in what ways do three middle school students perceive that class discussion influences their motivation for learning?" Four subquestions aligned with the ARCS Model's themes of attention, relevance, confidence, and satisfaction (Keller, 1983) were (a) in what ways do three middle school students perceive that Socratic Seminar influences their attention?; (b) in what ways do three middle school students perceive that the content of Socratic Seminar topics is relevant to their own lives?; (c) in what ways do three middle school students perceive that Socratic Seminar influence their confidence?; and (d) in what do three middle school students perceive that Socratic Seminar influence their satisfaction with learning? A fifth sub question was (e) what other ways do three middle school students perceive that Socratic Seminar influences their motivation for learning? This sub question was formulated by the researcher to address any other ways that middle school students may perceive that Socratic Seminar influences their motivation that were not associated with the four themes as addressed in the ARCS Model.

Site and Sample

The study took place in one seventh-grade language arts classroom, in a 6-8 school configuration, where the teacher conducted Socratic Seminar on a weekly basis. The small public school is located in a working class rural/suburban town located within a 1-hour drive of three mid-Atlantic cities. The class of 30 students was predominantly Caucasian with one female teacher. The class was considered "multiability" in that there was a combination of on-level and special education students.

The researcher employed a purposeful sampling strategy known as site selection (McMillan & Schumacher, 1997) to locate the middle school classroom for the study. This strategy is used "when one wants to understand something about those cases without needing or desiring to generalize to all such cases ... to yield many insights about the topic ... and to locate people involved in a particular event" (p. 397). After the researcher located the middle school classroom (site) where a teacher conducted Socratic Seminar on a weekly basis, a maximum variation sampling strategy was used to select the three students within the school site. McMillan and Schumacher explain that this strategy is used when one wants to obtain maximum differences of perceptions on a particular subject. Together the classroom teacher and the researcher selected the three students according to varying levels of motivation (high, medium, low) as determined by observations, standardized test scores compared to class grades, attendance records, attitude, behavior, and the Course Interest Survey (CIS) (Keller & Subhiyah, 1993). The CIS is a "situational measure of students' motivation to learn in a specific classroom setting ... designed with a theoretical foundation represented by the ARCS Model" (p. 1).

Data Collection

The multiple data sources for this study consisted of nine Socratic Seminar observations, six individual and one focus group interview, 18 student journals, and the Course Interest (CIS) survey for the three students occurring over a 10-week time frame. The researcher observed nine Socratic Seminars for a total of 10.5 hours of discussion. She acted as a participant observer, took handwritten field notes, and created vivid illustrations of the classroom, the students, and the seminars. With each subsequent observation, the researcher developed new themes of motivation as they became present in the data. The new themes are (a) student talk, (b) peer collaboration, (c) control, (d) safety, and (e) student-teacher relationship.

In addition to observations, the researcher conducted two individual interviews with each of the three cases and a focus group interview with all three cases, resulting in over 8 hours of interview data. An iterative (Rubin & Rubin, 1995) data collection process began broadly and narrowed with each successive interview. The first group of individual interviews was open-ended and conversational and depicts the students' overall perceptions of Socratic Seminar. The researcher conducted a second group of interviews with a more narrowed focus. Lastly, she conducted a focus group interview with all three students. The focus group questions more closely examined data from the individual interviews.

Student journals provided another forum for students to reflect on their seminar experiences. The classroom teacher provided writing prompts in the form of thought-provoking questions specifically related to the research questions. The students were provided ten minutes at the end of every Seminar to reflect on and answer the journal questions in writing. All students in the class wrote in journals and all journal entries were collected. However, only the journals of the three cases were read and analyzed.

Finally, the Course Interest Survey (CIS) (Keller & Subhiyah, 1993) examined the three students' perceptions of their motivation for Socratic Seminar. The wording on the survey was altered so that the words *this course* were replaced with *Socratic Seminar*. For example, one survey item read, *I feel that the Socratic Seminar gives me a lot of satisfaction* instead of *I feel that this course gives me a lot of satisfaction*. The classroom teacher administered the survey to the students at the end of the study.

Data Analysis

Miles and Huberman (1994) suggested conducting early analysis as "it helps the field-worker cycle back and forth between thinking about the existing data and generating strategies for collecting new, often better, data and makes analysis on ongoing, lively enterprise that contributes to the energizing process of fieldwork" (p. 50). Also referred to as the empirico-inductive approach by McMillan and Schumacher (1997), early analysis is the process of examining data as it is collected and constructing a picture of the cases early on in the study. The researcher in this study conducted early and ongoing analysis beginning with the first observation and continuing through the writing of the case narratives.

Data coding occurred in two stages using open and axial coding processes. "Open coding is where the researcher examines the text (e.g., transcripts, field notes, documents) for salient categories of information supported by the text" (Creswell, 1998, p. 150). Axial coding compares and analyzes the interconnectedness of these categories. The researcher coded the data according to the themes of attention, relevance, confidence, satisfaction as illustrated in the research questions. Additionally, the researcher developed new themes including (a) student talk, (b) peer collaboration, (c) control, (d) safety, and (e) student-teacher relationship, and coded them accordingly.

The researcher created a vivid written illustration of the various themes, their interconnectedness, and influence on each of the students' perceptions of their motivation. Then, she identified the primary themes of motivation for each case. Primary themes of motivation are those characteristics of motivation that, according to the student, have the greatest impact on the students' motivation for learning. Greatest impact is determined by the amount of emphasis the students place on that particular theme. The researcher reviewed the data again and used direct quotes from the students to illustrate the themes.

RESULTS

The Case of Larry

Larry is a 13-year-old boy with a history of academic and social difficulties in school. Although he possesses above-average ability, he receives low grades. In addition, he has a history of discipline problems and has spent numerous days in the principal's office or in the in-school-suspension room. Larry describes himself as a student who dislikes school and his teachers but who likes to learn new things.

All four themes of motivation (attention, relevance, confidence, and satisfaction) according to the ARCS Model of Motivational Design (Keller, 1983) are evident in the data on Larry. In addition to the existing four themes, Larry presents two new themes of peer collaboration and student talk. Larry's primary themes of motivation are (1) peer collaboration, (2) student talk, and (3) relevance.

Peer Collaboration

Larry maintains that he enjoys working in groups and prefers group work to individual work, and that when given the opportunity to do so, he is more motivated to learn. He indicates that if school incorporated more group-learning activities he would be more motivated to learn and most importantly he would make a conscious effort to stay out of the in-school-suspension room so that he would be able to participate in the group activities. In relation to peer collaboration, Larry says:

- Some kids know some things about certain parts and some kids know about other parts and we are all together and we put all our parts together and we all know the same amount about that.
- It is not that hard because you are working with the whole class so you understand it better and ... when you have the whole class doing it usually you get it.

- It is something that you have fun at. We're getting to do stuff and move around and we are working with partners and we get to do hands-on stuff

Student Talk

According to Larry, engaging in student talk increases his satisfaction and his attention, thus increasing his motivation for learning. More specifically he claims that talking to his peers captures his attention and is more satisfying than listening to his teachers or than engaging in written work. Interview data reveal that Larry finds classes where the majority of time is spent on individual written work or listening to the teacher talk boring and difficult. Conversely, he refers to Socratic Seminar as an activity that is fun and easy. He says, "I don't like school when we don't get to discuss what we think on something or when we have to write it all down.... Some classes are boring because they [the teachers] just talk a lot." About the importance of student talk, Larry continues:

- You read about it, you learn something. You talk about it, you learn more.
- I think it is a good way for us to learn because we are not by ourselves. We have other kids giving opinions and working with the whole class helps you understand it better and it makes you feel good.
- You learn more when you get to give your opinions and hear others' opinions.
- I like group work activities because that is what I am best at.

Relevance

Dewey (1916/1966) emphasized the importance of connecting what is learned to the lives of the students, saying that "isolation of subject matter from a social context is the chief obstruction in current practice to securing a general training of mind" (p. 67). According to the National Middle School Association (2003), a developmentally responsive middle school provides curriculum that is relevant, challenging, integrative, and exploratory.

Larry's claim that Socratic Seminar is a motivating method of instruction because it is relevant supports researchers (Adler, 1982; Polite & Adams, 1996; Strong, 1996; Tredway, 1995) who maintain that stimulating class discussions can motivate students by bridging the gap between the child and the curriculum. About Socratic Seminar and its relevance to his life, Larry says:

- Usually it is interesting when we know a lot about it ... and when it is boring we don't know everything about it ... and when we don't know anything about it we don't understand it.
- The first one was cool because we had a lot of knowledge about it because we had just got done learning about Mt. Everest and all the mountains.
- I had a lot to say about that because it does have a lot to do with my life.

The Case of Helen

Thirteen-year-old Helen describes herself as an intellectual student who loves school and loves learning. She receives straight A's and prides herself on her intellectual qualities. She has never been in trouble of any kind, has a perfect attendance record, and participates in many extracurricular activities. Helen perceives Socratic Seminar to be a satisfying student-controlled learning activity in which students are free to speak their minds in an environment that is safe from peer criticism. She states, "it is powerful and intense and I always look forward to the next discussion." All four themes of motivation (attention, relevance, confidence, satisfaction) according to the ARCS Model of Motivation Design (Keller, 1983) are evident in the data on Helen. In addition to the existing four themes, Helen presents two new themes of safety and control. Helen's primary motivational themes are (1) satisfaction, (2) control, and (3) safety.

Satisfaction

According to Keller (1983), in order to sustain motivation one must be satisfied. Helen says that participating in Socratic Seminar is satisfying because she "learns a great amount from it and because it is an intense learning experience." Helen receives a great amount of satisfaction from the intensity of the discussions and attributes much of this intensity to collaboration with her peers. She mentioned many times that listening and talking to her friends taught her something new, changed her perspective, or confirmed her previous thoughts. About the impact of class discussion on her satisfaction, Helen suggests:

- I like talking to other people and interacting with other students.
- Having a Socratic Seminar really makes you want to come to class. You are like "oh yeah, I get to talk and say things I want to say."
- In a Socratic Seminar we get to use every bit of our brain like memory, thinking, connecting, cooperation, listening, speaking, and opinionating. Every bit.

- Last year we would sit down and read like pages 159 to 162. And then you would have to sit there and have to answer questions about what you read and that is really, really downright boring. You learn much better when you are doing something and you are up and moving. Where as when you read a textbook, you're not interested in it and you forget it as soon as you walk out the door. If you are sitting there with a textbook, it is like nothing. Nothing strikes you. But if you are in a group you learn better. And then all of a sudden there is an explosion in your head. In a group, you are more likely to work together and come up with a great answer then if you are reading out of a book.

Control

Helen defines control in learning as a situation where the learning is directed in part by the students, one in which learning is active, and one in which students are involved in the process. Regarding control she maintains, "There is no real teacher involvement like the teacher is not ruling the class. That is why I like it a lot because the teacher is not saying blah blah blah do this and how do you feel about this subject. You kind of say what you feel at the moment. And I like it a lot." She continues:

- The kids are the ones that control the conversation. They are the ones who make meaning out of the whole conversation.
- It makes me feel very powerful because I think that is the only place that you can be where you're in control. Every where else there's somebody higher than you. Like in the regular classroom the teacher is in control. At home your parents are in control. On the bus the bus driver is in control. That is the only place where the kids can rule what they are doing.
- You know that you have some power so that makes you strive for more. It makes you strive for the best that you possibly can be.

Safety

"Positive intergroup relations are essential to a safe and healthy school" (Jackson & Davis, 2000, p. 24). Helen defines safety as freedom to say, think, and feel what she wants without fearing criticism from her peers. When she feels safe from judgment or criticism of her peers she is more motivated to learn, and because of this sense of safety she is more motivated to learn. About the issue of safety, Helen says,

- I think some discussions and topics are hard to understand but some people bring it to an easier level because you can talk about what you feel ... and nobody is there to criticize you. There is no real difficulty in that ... and when there is a group of people there are more people to help you understand.

- You are more likely to go out on a limb if you feel safe. If you do not feel safe you are going to crawl back in your shell and you are going to stay home until it is safe to come out ... like a turtle ... but if you know that other people are like you, then you are gonna reach out and say something that if you were not safe you would not go out for.
- You can say anything you want to say. There is not some boundary. You can stretch out and go far beyond normal.

The Case of Andy

Andy is a 13-year-old boy who expresses satisfaction with his grades, his performance, and his academic ability. He is described, however, by his teachers as a student who possesses above-average ability and below-average performance. All four themes of motivation (attention, relevance, confidence, and satisfaction) according to the ARCS Model of Motivational Design (Keller 1983) were evident in the data on Andy. In addition to the existing four themes, Andy presents the theme of student-teacher relationship. Andy's primary themes of motivation are (1) student-teacher relationship and (2) confidence.

Student-Teacher Relationship

Andy describes Socratic Seminar as a method of learning where there is a unique student-teacher relationship. He says that in order for him to be motivated for school he must have a friendly relationship with his teachers in a positive school environment. In situations where he does not have a good relationship with his teachers he can rely on his classmates to provide support. The Socratic circle is a place where he and his peers take on the guiding role of the teacher and this helps him through the learning process. Collaborating with his peers makes learning easier and therefore satisfying because he is able to receive help and guidance from many people rather than just one. About the impact of student-teacher relationship and Socratic Seminar, Andy maintains:

- After a good class discussion, I feel better about myself so then I do better in school.
- If a teacher doesn't like me then there is tension and it is hard to do my work. But if a teacher likes me and always says hello then it is easier to do my work.

Confidence

It is important to Andy to feel good about himself and to help others to feel good about themselves. He describes himself as a kind and religious boy who believes in being kind and respectful to others. According to Andy, one of the greatest benefits of participating in a Socratic Seminar is the feeling he receives from the experience. He maintains that feeling good about himself is a result of being recognized for saying something good during a discussion. This positive feeling makes him more motivated for school. In addition, when he feels good he enjoys spreading his happiness to make others feel good as well. The following quotes illustrate his feelings on the relationship between confidence and Socratic Seminar. He says:

- A reward of participating in class discussion is that you could say something good and like five people say that they agree with you and the reward is that you have a good feeling about yourself. When the teacher takes one of your quotes that you said during the discussion and says it out loud that makes you feel good too.
- When I leave class I feel good about myself so then I do better in school. Like if I am really bummed out and feeling blue then you don't really want to do schoolwork and you just want to sit there. And when you feel good you are all cheery and you say hi to everyone and maybe if you say hi to someone who is feeling bummed out it will make them feel better too.
- It makes me feel good to talk and when I am talking I hope someone is listening and like they hear what I am trying to say and that they can understand it.
- It makes me feel good if they are listening. When someone is learning something from me at the age I am it makes me feel really good.

CONCLUSION

This qualitative study contributes to our current understanding of motivation, adolescent development, and Socratic Seminar, and sheds light on how the three are interrelated. Rich data add credence to the literature that suggests that motivation is a significant issue at the middle grades; contribute to the literature on methods to motivate middle grade students; suggest that Socratic Seminar is a method of instruction that enhances student motivation; and add five possible new themes of student talk, peer collaboration, safety, control, and student-teacher relationship to the ARCS Model of Motivation Design (Keller, 1983). For middle level educators more research is needed that further examines the impact that Socratic Seminar has on motivation of the young adolescent. It is important to examine how we can close the existing gap between how middle level students want to learn and how middle level teachers instruct using this method. It is equally important that educators take an active role in exploring ways to motivate the unmotivated young adolescent. This study can act as a springboard for educators who want to further explore the interconnectivity of motivation, adolescent development, and Socratic Seminar.

Although the sample size of the study was small and representative of only one middle school, the findings are deep and meaningful. The intentional focus on depth of data rather than breadth of data allowed the researcher to delve into the whys and hows of the impact of Socratic Seminar on young adolescent motivation that would not have been possible with a wider and shallower sample. Conversely, in examining the perceptions of only three students, the study does not offer a wide range of views. This can be examined in future studies but was not the intent of this study. It was the researcher's intent that the study pique the interest of middle level teachers who want to explore Socratic Seminar in their classroom and see for themselves the ways in which this interactive method of instruction can and may transform their classroom.

Examining Socratic Seminar and its impact on student motivation from the perspective of the students themselves, this study provides insight into the developmental needs of the middle school student. The voices of the students reveal that Socratic Seminar is an instructional method that allows the student to talk (student talk theme), collaborate with peers (peer collaboration theme), be in control (control theme), feel safe (safety theme), have a positive relationship with their teachers (student-teacher relationship theme), feel confident (confidence theme), and relate school to their lives (relevance theme), which in turn helps them to feel satisfied (satisfaction theme), attentive (attention theme), and ultimately motivated for learning.

A Socratic Seminar in a middle school classroom can be an invigorating experience for all participants. The young adolescent becomes actively engaged in a student-centered activity that all too often is so out of the norm that, while not knowing what to expect or how to act, motivates the students in unexpected and unanticipated ways. To understand the impact of Socratic Seminar on young adolescent motivation for learning one simply needs to listen to the word of the students themselves:

Andy: Having Socratic Seminars is my favorite things to do in class and it is really fun.

Larry: You read about it, you learn something. You talk about it, you learn more.

Helen: A good Socratic Seminar motivates you because it really makes you want to come to class. It brings out a whole different person. You know, like those ugly caterpillars that turn into beautiful butterflies.

REFERENCES

Adler, M. J. (1982). *The Paideia proposal: An educational manifesto.* New York: MacMillan.

Anderman, E. M., & Maehr, M. L. (1994). Motivation and schooling in the middle grades. *Review of Educational Research, 64*(2), 287-309.

Anderman, L. H. M., & Midgley, C. (1998). *Motivation and middle school students* (Report No. EDO-PS-98-5). Champaign, IL: ERIC Clearinghouse on Elementary and Early Education. (Eric Document Reproduction Service No. ED421281)

Armstrong, D. G., & Savage, T. V. (1998). *Teaching in the secondary school: An introduction* (4th ed.). Upper Saddle River, NJ: Simon & Schuster.

Brophy, J. (1987). Synthesis of research on strategies for motivating students to learn. *Educational Leadership, 45*(2), 40-48.

Carnegie Council on Adolescent Development. (1989). *Turning points: Preparing American youth for the 21st century.* New York: Carnegie Corporation of New York.

Chalupa, M. R., & Sormunen, C. (1995). Strategies for developing critical thinking: You make the difference in the classroom. *Business Education Forum, 49*(3), 41-43.

Clark, S. N., & Clark, D. C. (1993). Middle level school reform: The rhetoric and the reality. *The Elementary School Journal, 93*(5), 447-458.

Creswell, J. W. (1998). *Qualitative inquiry and research design: Choosing among the five traditions*. Thousand Oaks, CA: Sage.

Dewey, J. (1990). *The child and the curriculum.* Chicago: The University of Chicago Press. (Original work published 1902)

Dewey, J. (1966). *Democracy and education.* New York: The Free Press. (Original work published 1916)

Eccles, J. S., Lord, S., & Midgley, C. (1991). What are we doing to early adolescents? The impact of educational contexts on early adolescents. *American Journal of Education, 99*(4), 521-542.

Eccles, J. S., & Midgley, C. (1989). Stage environment fit: Developmentally appropriate classrooms for early adolescents. In R. E. Ames & C. Ames (Eds.), *Research on motivation in education* (Vol. 3, pp. 139-186). New York: Academic Press.

Eccles, J. S., Wigfield, A., Flanagan, C. A., Miller, C., Reuman, D. A., & Yee, D. (1989). Self concepts, domain values, and self-esteem: Relations and changes at early adolescence. *Journal of Personality, 57*(2), 283-310.

Eccles, J. S., Wigfield, A., Midgley, C., Reuman, D., Mac Iver, D., & Feldlaufer, H. (1993). Negative effects of traditional middle school students' motivation. *The Elementary School Journal, 93*(5), 553-574.

Erickson, F., & Shultz, J. (1992). *Handbook of research on curriculum.* New York: MacMillan.

Erikson, E. H. (1950/1993). *Childhood and society.* New York: W.W. Norton.

Fontes, C. O. (1988). A qualitative study of middle school students' perceptions regarding school alienation: Causes and remedies for improved motivation (Doctoral Dissertation, Boston University, 1988). *Dissertation Abstracts International, 49,* AAT 8806761.

Good, T. L., & Brophy, J. E. (1994). *Looking in classrooms* (6th ed.). New York: Harper Collins.

Gray, D. (1989, Fall). Putting minds to work: How to use the seminar approach in the classroom. *American Educator,* 17-23.

Haladyna, T., & Thomas, G. (1979). The attitudes of elementary school children toward school and subject matters. *Journal of Experimental Education, 48*(1), 18-23.

Hamburg, D. A., & Takanishi, R. (1989). Preparing for life: The critical transition of adolescence. *American Psychologist, 44*(5), 825-827.

Harnett, A. M. (1991). *Preparation of middle school teachers* (Report No. EDO-SP-90-1). Washington, DC: ERIC Clearinghouse on Teacher Education. (ERIC Document Reproduction Service No. ED335356)

Harter, S. (1981). The new self-report scale of intrinsic versus extrinsic orientation in the classroom: Motivational and informational components. *Developmental Psychology, 17*(3), 300-312.

Kamii, C., & Ewing, J. K. (1996). Basing teaching on Piaget's constructivism. *Childhood Education, 72*(5), 260-264.

Keller, J. M. (1983). *Development and use of the ARCS Model of Motivational Design.* (Tech. Rep. No.143). Enschede, Netherlands: Twente University, Technische Hogeschool Twente.

Keller, J., & Subhiyah (1993). Course interest survey (survey). Tallahassee, FL: Florida State University.

Jackson, A. W., & Davis, G. A. (2000). *Turning points 2000: Educating adolescents in the 21st century.* New York: Carnegie Corporation of New York.

Jackson, A. W., & Hornbeck, D. W. (1989). Educating young adolescents: Why we must restructure our middle grade schools. *American Psychologist, 44*(5), 831-836.

Lambright, L. L. (1995). Creating a dialogue: Socratic seminars and educational reform. *Community College Journal, 65*(4), 30-34.

Letts, N. (1994). Socrates in your classroom. *Teaching K-8, 24,* 48-49.

Lumsden, L. S. (1994). *Student motivation to learn* (Report No. EDO-EA-94-7). Eugene, OR: ERIC Clearinghouse on Educational Management. (ERIC Document Reproduction Service No. ED370200)

Maehr, M. L. (1991, April). *Changing the schools: A word to school leaders about enhancing student investment in learning.* Paper presented at the meeting of the American Educational Research Association, Chicago, IL.

Mac Iver, D. J., & Epstein, J. L. (1993). Middle grades research: Not yet mature, but no longer a child. *The Elementary School Journal, 93*(5), 519-531.

McMillan, J. H.,& Schumacher, S. (1997). *Research in education: A conceptual introduction* (4th ed.). New York: Addison-Wesley.

Miles, M. B., & Huberman, A. M. (1994). *Qualitative data analysis.* Thousand Oaks, CA: Sage.

National Middle School Association. (2003). *This we believe: Successful schools for young adolescents.* Westerville, OH: Author.

Parker, W. (2006). Public discourse in schools: Purposes, problems, possibilities. *Educational Researcher, 36*(8), 11-18.

Polite, V. C. & Adams, A. H. (1996). Improving critical thinking through Socratic seminars. *Spotlight on student success, No. 110.* Philadelphia, PA: Mid-Atlantic Laboratory for Student Success.

Rubin, H. J., & Rubin, I. S. (1995). *Qualitative interviewing: The art of hearing data.* Thousand Oaks, CA: Sage.

Strong, M. (1996). *The habit of thought: From Socratic seminars to Socratic practice.* Chapel Hill, NC: New View.

Tredway, L. (1995). Socratic seminars: Engaging students in intellectual discourse. *Educational Leadership, 53*(1), 26-29.

Turner, J. C., & Meyer, D. K. (1995). Motivating students to learn: Lesson form a fifth grade math class. *Middle School Journal, 9*(1), 18-25.

Von Glasersfeld, E. (1988). *Cognition, construction of knowledge, and teaching.* Washington, DC: National Science Foundation. (ERIC Document Reproduction Service No. ED294754)

Vygotsky, L. S. (Ed.). (1962). *Thought and language* (E. Hanfmann & G. Vakar, Trans.). Cambridge, MA: MIT Press.

Vygotsky, L. S. (Ed.). (1978). *Mind in society: The development of higher psychological processes* (M. Cole, V. John-Steiner, S. Scribner, & E. Souberman, Trans.). Cambridge, MA: Harvard University Press.

Wadsworth, B. J. (1978). *Piaget for the classroom.* New York: Longman.

CHAPTER 8

THE INTERFACE OF SCHOOL AND FAMILY IN MEETING THE BELONGING NEEDS OF YOUNG ADOLESCENTS

Lynley H. Anderman and Valerie S. Leake

ABSTRACT

The need to belong to a social group and to feel a sense of connectedness to others is a fundamental human characteristic. For young adolescents, this need is often met in school and family settings. This chapter reviews empirical research that has examined middle school students' sense of belonging in both settings, in terms of potential outcomes of a secure sense of belonging and individual and group characteristics that have been associated with the sense of belonging. The characteristics of school and family settings that are likely to promote a sense of belonging are described and the chapter concludes with a discussion of future research needs.

The Young Adolescent and the Middle School
pp. 163–182

INTRODUCTION

The notion that individuals have an innate need to feel a sense of connectedness to others and belonging to a larger social group is hardly a new one (e.g., Maslow, 1962, 1987; McClelland, 1985). Both educational and counseling theories of motivation, particularly self-determination (Deci, Vallerand, Pelletier, & Ryan, 1991) and choice theories (Glasser, 1998), have included the need for belonging as a central concept in explaining human behavior. In a comprehensive review, Baumeister and Leary (1995) described the human need to belong as "a pervasive drive to form and maintain at least a minimum quantity of lasting, positive, and significant interpersonal relationships" (p. 497).

In terms of young adolescents, the primary contexts within which the need for a sense of belonging is most likely to be met are the school and the home. These global perceptions of belonging undoubtedly are influenced by a number of factors within the setting. Influences on the sense of belonging in school, for example, include variables related to peers, teachers, and more general structures and policies of the school as a whole (Anderman & Freeman, 2004). To date, it is not clear how these various influences interact with and, perhaps, compensate for one another. What is more clear, however, it that the degree to which young adolescents feel a sense of belonging in these contexts, and an understanding of the ways in which the sense of belonging can be fostered, may be important areas of study for promoting young adolescents' adaptive development and academic success. In reviewing the status of research on student motivation in 1990, Weiner stated "achievement behavior influences and affects others ... school motivation requires the development and incorporation of the values of others. Hence, we have to consider frameworks larger than the self and older motivational constructs, such as 'belongingness' must be brought into play when examining school motivation" (p. 621). As research interest in the study of belonging has increased over recent years, the majority of empirical studies have focused on adolescent, and often specifically middle school, populations. Undoubtedly, this focus reflects the developmental importance of peer relationships and influence (Berndt, 1982, 1999; Csikszentmihalyi & Larson, 1984; Furman & Buhrmester, 1992; Hartup, 1993) and relationships with nonparental adults (e.g., Chen, Greenberger, Farruggia, Bush, & Dong, 2003), as well as young adolescents' vulnerability to feeling self-conscious (Elkind, 1967). In addition, increased interest in young adolescents' perceptions of belonging probably reflects concern over rates of risky behaviors and delinquency at this time (Carnegie Council on Adolescent Development, 1989; Resnick et al., 1997). Nevertheless, the study of students' subjective sense of belonging has tended to be neglected in empirical studies of students' motivation and learning, which have focused instead on the need for achievement and self-perceptions (e.g., Eccles, Wigfield, Flanagan, Miller, Reuman & Yee, 1989; Harter, 1999; Marsh, 1990), and on other constructs particular to young adolescents in their family context, such as family functioning (e.g., Pedersen & Revenson, 2005) and parental interactions (e.g., Ream & Savin-Williams, 2005).

In the early 1990s, Carol Goodenow began a program of research focused on the importance of the social context of schooling as influences on individual learning and motivation. Goodenow (1992) argued that "the interpersonal relationships, interactions, and group dynamics that occur in schools and classes influence education significantly" (pp. 178-179). In particular, she called for greater research attention to the provision of social support within schools, as demonstrated through both student-teacher and student-student relationships. This focus on social support included the subjective sense of belonging to a reciprocal social network in which students experienced feeling "included, accepted, and valued." (p. 185). A more detailed description of Goodenow's findings will be provided later in the chapter.

The rise in interest in the sense of belonging for young adolescent students, however, was probably most influenced by the publication of a highly visible study conducted by Resnick et al. (1997). This study utilized data from the National Longitudinal Study of Adolescent Health (ADD Health), a comprehensive school-based study of health-related behaviors of adolescents in the United States. Resnick and his colleagues reported that two constructs, perceived parent-family connectedness and school connectedness, were protective factors against adolescents' engagement in risky behaviors. The sense of connectedness, or belonging, predicted a range of outcomes including lower emotional distress, lower suicidal ideation, and lower levels of involvement in violence, substance abuse, and early sexual activity. This first study, although cross-sectional in nature, greatly increased research attention on the potential importance of perceived belonging within family and school for adolescents' general well-being.

Since the publication of Resnick et al. (1997), a large number of researchers have started to explore potential relationships between perceived belonging and a range of positive outcomes. Although the focus in the Resnick study was on health-related outcomes, much of the recent research has picked up on Goodenow's (1993a, 1993b) early focus on school belonging specifically and on academic outcomes. A few studies since Resnick's have concentrated on family belonging as a protective factor (Annunziata, Hogue, Faw, & Liddle, 2006, Hogue, Liddle, Becker, & Johnson-Leckrone, 2002, Kliewer et al., 2006, Lagana, 2004) though far fewer than those related to school belonging.

Because empirical research in this area has been conducted utilizing several different theoretical frameworks, some differences in terminology are apparent across studies. Goodenow (1993b) defined students' sense of belonging in school settings as the sense of "psychological membership in the school or classroom, that is, the extent to which students feel personally accepted, respected, included and supported by others in the school environment" (p. 80). Similar constructs examined by other researchers have utilized the terms "school connectedness" (e.g., McNeely, Nonnemaker, & Blum, 2002; Resnick et al., 1997) and "bonding to school" (Kester, 1994). Finn's (1989) model of school identification and participation includes the sense of belonging as one component of identification with school (see also Voelkl, 1996, 1997). Similarly, researchers who have examined students' sense of community in their classes and schools have included the sense of belonging as one dimension of that broader concept (e.g., Battistich, Solomon, Watson, & Schaps, 1997; Solomon, Battistich, Kim, & Watson, 1997). Nevertheless, the term "belonging" generally seems to be the most commonly used (e.g., Anderman, 2002; Anderman, 2003; Baumeister & Leary, 1995; Goodenow, 1993a, 1993b; Ryan, 1995) in the school domain and will be used in this chapter.

Similar to research in school-related belonging, studies related to belonging in the family realm have differed in the terminology used due to various theoretical underpinnings. However, an additional factor in the variety of terms used in the family domain, including connectedness, attachment, and cohesion, as well as belonging, is that there appear to be some differences in how these constructs are defined. Resnick et al. (1997) and King, Vidourek, Davis, and McClellan (2002) use the term "connectedness," when discussing affective feelings of being cared for and supported by parents and family. Attachment, a concept originated by Bowlby (1983), is defined by current theorists as an experienced and learned approach to relationships between two individuals (Perry, 2002) rooted in past familial patterns. Other researchers using "cohesion" define this construct as the emotional bond each family member feels for other family members (Olson, Russell & Sprenkle, 1983) or the level of commitment and support family members supply one another (Fuhr, Moos & Dishotsky, 1981). In contrast, "family belonging" refers not only to affection, support, and an emotional bond, but also to feeling valued and accepted, and feeling that one fits with the group or environment (Anant, 1966; Hagerty, Lynch-Sauer, Patusky, Bouwsema, & Collier, 1992). Therefore, the term "belonging" appears to be the most comprehensive, yet parsimonious, term with regard to the family domain, and will be used throughout this chapter as well.

The purpose of the current chapter is to review empirical research examining the sense of belonging in school and family contexts that has focused on students in the middle grades. The chapter will be organized in terms of what is known about outcomes and correlates of the sense of belonging in school and family settings, followed by a discussion of individual and group characteristics that tend to be associated with higher levels of belonging. Next, what is known about contextual variables, in the school and the family, which may promote a sense of belonging will be described. The chapter concludes with a discussion of directions for future research.

MIDDLE SCHOOL STUDENTS' SENSE OF BELONGING IN SCHOOL

As noted earlier, a number of empirical studies have been conducted in the past decade to examine the potential of students' subjective sense of belonging at either the school or classroom level for explaining variation in school-related outcomes. Generally, these studies have found the sense of belonging to be associated with a range of adaptive motivational variables, general academic achievement, and positive school-related affect. Much of the renewed interest in students' sense of school belonging was triggered by the research of Carol Goodenow (1993a, 1993b; Goodenow & Grady, 1993). In this body of work, Goodenow focused primarily on young adolescent students' subjective sense of belonging or relatedness in association with their academic motivation and achievement. Middle school students' self-reported sense of positive peer relationships in school, teacher support and general sense of belonging in school were found to be associated with their academic expectancies for success. In addition, perceived teacher support and sense of belonging were associated with perceived task values (Goodenow, 1993a). Goodenow and Grady examined similar associations among an ethnically diverse sample of young adolescent students and found that students' sense of belonging was moderately associated with their expectancy for success in school, valuing of academic work, and general motivation for school.

Despite the importance of those early studies, they were limited somewhat by their cross-sectional design. This concern was addressed to some extent by Anderman and Anderman (1999) who examined changes in students' personal achievement goals as they transitioned from elementary school to middle school. Students' perceptions of the goal structures of their sixth grade (middle school) classes were included in the analyses as potential predictors of change in personal goal orientations. Even with other predictors taken into account, the students' sense of school belonging in their new middle school was associated with an increase in personal task goal orientation and was a modest predictor of decreased performance goal orientation, over time. Even stronger evidence of the association between school belonging and academic motivation comes from the Child Development Project (CDP; Battistich, Solomon, Kim, Watson, & Schaps, 1995) which was designed to intervene with schools to enhance students' sense of community. The intervention included several elements, including cooperative learning approaches, an emphasis on prosocial values and activities, and developmental discipline. In evaluations of the CDP, young adolescent students' sense of community was found to be associated with their general academic motivation, intrinsic motivation, and task orientation. The sense of community also was found to be somewhat negatively associated with an ego orientation and work avoidance (Battistich et al.; Solomon, Watson, Battistich, Schaps, & Delucchi, 1996).

Although much of the interest in students' sense of belonging has been generated by motivational researchers, a small number of researchers have reported associations between students' sense of school belonging and various measures of academic achievement. In most studies, achievement has been operationalized in terms of students' GPA or teacher-assigned grades, which have been found to be modestly to moderately positively associated with the sense of belonging (e.g., E. M. Anderman, 2002; Anderman, 1999, 2003; Goodenow, 1993a; McNeely et al., 2002; Nichols, 2006). This positive association appears to be quite robust across samples, regardless of whether belonging is conceptualized as an outcome or a predictor of academic achievement.

In addition to strictly academic outcomes, a smaller number of researchers have examined associations between young adolescents' sense of school belonging and their school-related affect and sense of well-being. Currently there is no generally accepted theoretical model that captures the interplay of affective and academic outcomes in relation to the sense of belonging (see Anderman & Freeman, 2004, for a discussion). Nevertheless, the empirical evidence that is available is quite consistent regarding the association between perceived belonging and positive affective outcomes. As noted earlier, Resnick et al. (1997), reported associations between sense of school connectedness and lower rates of emotional distress. E. M. Anderman (2002) also found that sense of belonging was associated with greater general optimism and lower levels of depression in students drawn from 7th through 12th grades. Specifically in terms of middle school students, Roeser, Midgley, and Urdan (1996) reported that eighth-graders' sense of school belonging mediated the relationship between perceived teacher-student relationships and positive school-related affect. Similarly, in a longitudinal study, Anderman (1999) examined change in students' positive and negative school-related affect as they transitioned from elementary to middle school. Although students' positive school-related affect, such as feelings of contentment, happiness and excitement, generally declined across the transition to middle school, students' sense of belonging in their new school was associated with an increase in positive affect and a decrease in negative affect (such as anger, frustration and anxiety in school), over time.

In their evaluations of CDP classes, Battistich and his colleagues (Battistich et al., 1995; Solomon et al., 1996) also have documented associations between students' sense of community in school or in a classroom and various affective outcomes. Indeed, the associations between the sense of community and affective outcomes, including variables such as students' liking and enjoyment of school, empathy, self-esteem, and quality of relationships with teachers, have tended to be stronger than findings related to more academic variables.

MIDDLE SCHOOL STUDENTS' SENSE OF BELONGING IN THE FAMILY

As discussed previously, Resnick et al.'s (1997) large-scale study of adolescent well-being highlighted the protective nature of both school and family belonging for young adolescents. Other researchers have also reported that higher levels of family belonging may be protective against a variety of poorer outcomes for adolescents, including suicide (Borowsky, Ireland, & Resnick, 2001). The sense of feeling close to, of being understood by, of feeling satisfied with, and of feeling cared about in their familial relationships appears to be a factor in protecting young adolescents from tobacco use (Scal, Ireland, & Borowsky, 2003). Sale, Sambrano, Springer, and Turner (2003) found that family belonging was a strong mediator for adolescent use of cigarettes, alcohol, and marijuana in a study of 10,473 youth. These findings reinforce the longitudinal findings of Bray, Adams, Getz, and Baer (2001) who noted a decrease in the use of alcohol during the middle school years for those young adolescents with a greater sense of family belonging. Additionally, Pilgrim, Abbey, and Kershaw (2004) noted continued protective effects of family belonging in their study of 225 middle school adolescents where greater family belonging was related to negative attitudes toward substance a year later. Huffine (2004), in a statement on youth violence by the American Society for Adolescent Psychiatry, partially blamed the fragmentation of familial ties in today's society, as a factor related to youth violence, particularly school shootings. These and the previous findings would indicate the importance of a sense of family and school belonging for middle-school age adolescents. However, other research suggests that belonging for young adolescents may be more complex than previously believed.

INDIVIDUAL AND GROUP CHARACTERISTICS ASSOCIATED WITH BELONGING

To date, the literature on young adolescents' sense of belonging, both in school and at home, has tended to focus on variables that have been conceptualized as outcomes rather than predictors of the sense of belonging. That is, although many of the studies in question actually are based on cross-sectional data, they reflect an assumed causal direction in which the sense of belonging precedes other academic and affective responses (see Anderman & Freeman, 2004, for a discussion). Much less is known about individual and context-level variables that might increase the probability of any young adolescent reporting a sense of belonging. Nevertheless, a small number of studies have begun to document both individual and group level characteristics associated with the sense of belonging in school settings. In addition, there is some evidence of particular social contextual variables in schools and classrooms that are more likely to foster a sense of belonging in students. To date, similar research on family belonging is not available.

Individual and Group Characteristics

As noted earlier, one of the most robust findings in terms of young adolescents' likelihood of reporting a sense of belonging in school is related to their academic achievement. Several researchers have found that GPA is positively associated with the sense of belonging in middle school students. This pattern has been replicated in both multilevel analyses of cross-sectional data (e.g., E. M. Anderman, 2002; McNeely et al., 2002) and longitudinal studies (Anderman, 2003). A number of researchers also have reported that middle school girls are more likely to report a sense of belonging in school or in the classroom, than are their male classmates (e.g., E. M. Anderman, 2002; Freeman, Anderman, & Jensen, in press; Goodenow & Grady, 1993; Nichols, 2006; Voelkl, 1997). Similarly, several researchers have suggested that students' ethnic and cultural backgrounds may be associated with their sense of school belonging (E. M. Anderman, 2002; Freeman, Jackson, Strand, Matthews, McNally, & Brown-Wright, 2003; Goodenow & Grady; McNeely et al.; Nichols; Voelkl). The findings of these studies are mixed. Some studies have found that European American students report higher levels of school belonging than those identifying as African American (McNeely et al.) or Native American (E. M. Anderman, 2002), whereas others have found no significant differences between ethnic groups (e.g., Goodenow & Grady) or higher levels of belonging among African American students (Voelkl).

These mixed findings suggest that examining simple associations between students' ethnic or cultural background and their sense of school belonging may be of limited utility. Instead, it is important to consider the characteristics of the school context to which they are responding. In particular, students' sense of belonging may well be influenced by the extent to which the student body of a school is racially integrated (E. M. Anderman, 2002; McNeely et al.) and by the diversity of the teaching faculty (Freeman et al., 2003). In other words, the experience of being a minority within one's school, rather than within the larger society, may be more important in terms of feeling a sense of belonging there. For example, Nichols found that when Hispanic students represented the majority culture of a particular school, they reported a higher sense of belonging than their White, African American, or Native American peers.

With regard to young adolescents and belonging within their families, some individual and group characteristics have surfaced in the literature. Common wisdom would dictate that young adolescents' sense of belonging should decrease as they grow older and embark on the quest for individuation from the original family unit commonly known as launching, and indeed, some research backs this view, specifically that conducted by Conger and Ge (1999) who found increased conflict and lower cohesion between parents and young adolescents beginning during the middle school years. However, recent studies indicate that family belonging may not necessarily decrease with age, particularly in those families that exhibit an appropriate "stage-environment" fit as discussed by Eccles et al. (1993). Eccles and colleagues noted continued positive relationships between young adolescents and their families, when the family environment allows the young adolescent to display age-appropriate increases in autonomous behavior. Family structure also appears to be associated with differing levels of family belonging experienced by young adolescents. Leake (2004) found not only that adolescents residing in stepfamilies reported lower levels of family belonging than those residing in other family structures, but also that adolescent girls in stepfamilies espoused less of a sense of family belonging than did adolescent boys who lived in stepfamilies (Leake, 2007), findings that echo those of Bray and Berger (1993). Bray (1995) suggested that the well-documented difficulties reported by stepfamily adolescents may be attributable in part to the divergence between the developmental level of the adolescent and the developmental level of the emerging stepfamily.

In terms of family belonging, young adolescents who are members of stepfamilies appear to feel less of a sense of family belonging than do young adolescents from other family structures (Leake, 2004). Bray and Berger (1993) found that adolescents have greater difficulty adapting to stepfamily living than children of other ages and that even long-term residence in a loving and stable stepfamily does not prevent an increased likelihood of behavior problems from stepchildren entering adolescence.

Contextual Influences on the Sense of Belonging

Given the accumulating importance of young adolescents' perceptions of belonging in both the theoretical and empirical literature, understanding the ways in which the sense of belonging might be fostered becomes similarly important. In terms of the literature on school and classroom belonging, however, much less attention has been paid to potential contextual influences on the sense of belonging than on individual-level correlates of that perception (see also Anderman & Freeman, 2004). Some studies have examined objective characteristics of schools, such as school (E. M. Anderman, 2002; McNeely et al., 2002) and class size (Anderman; Freeman, Anderman & Jensen, in press) however the results of these analyses have been either mixed or nonsignificant. Studies of school type (e.g., public, private, Catholic, other parochial) also have found no differences, although there is limited evidence that students in rural schools may report higher levels of belonging, on average, than do those in urban schools (Anderman; Freeman & Anderman, 2005). There also is some evidence that grade configuration may affect students' sense of school belonging, with K-8 and K-12 configurations having an advantage over more traditional middle and high schools (Anderman). Another more objective characteristic related to school configuration is the use of a "Small House," multi-age organization of classes. Kester (1994) reported that both students and parents in her African American middle school sample saw an increased sense of school belonging associated with the implementation of a "school within a school" model. Caution should be exercised in generalizing from the findings of that study, which displays several methodological limitations. Nevertheless, the findings are suggestive and emphasize the need for further study.

Beyond the role of structural characteristics of educational contexts, there is growing evidence that students' experiences and perceptions within those settings probably are more important in terms of their sense of belonging. Several researchers have begun to describe a range of instructional and inter-personal characteristics of classes and schools that tend to foster a greater sense of belonging among students. Although not all of these studies have been conducted with middle school populations the findings with older (e.g., Freeman et al., 2003) populations are strikingly similar to those that have focused on young adolescents (e.g., Anderman, 2003; Freeman & Anderman, 2003; Solomon et al., 1997). These studies have shown that variables reflecting several different dimensions of classroom experiences may foster the sense of belonging in individual students. These include instructional practices, such as emphasizing the understanding and improvement as the purpose for academic work (i.e., a mastery goal class structure), assigning tasks that students perceive as interesting and relevant, elicitation of student thinking, and encouragement of cooperative approaches to learning. In addition, characteristics of the teacher-student relationship, such as students' perceptions of pedagogical caring (see Wentzel, 1997); commitment, warmth and supportiveness seem to increase students' sense of belonging. Finally, dimensions of the overall tone of class interactions among peers also appear to be important. For example, explicitly teaching pro-social values (Solomon et al.) or communicating an expectation that students should treat one another respectfully (Anderman), along with developmental discipline strategies and avoiding extrinsic behavioral controls (Solomon et al.) also appear to promote the sense of belonging.

Though significantly less researched than the school setting, contextual influences also have an impact on level of family belonging. Two contextual factors seem particularly worthy of mention, the strength of individual parent-child relationship, and appropriate developmental fit between the young adolescent and the family. In the Resnick et al. (1997) study, the strongest single factor within the Parent-Child Connectedness Scale was that of strength the individual relationships between each parent and the young adolescent, a finding echoed by Leake (2006) who found in a study of stepfamily adolescents that the relationship strength between the biological parent and the adolescent made the greatest contribution to the adolescent's level of family belonging. With regard to developmental fit between the young adolescent and family, Eccles et al. (1993), as discussed previously, used a stage-environment fit perspective to predict a negative impact on familial relationships when a "poor fit between the child's desire for increasing autonomy and the opportunities for independence and autonomy provided by the child's parents" (p. 97) occurs. Worden (1991) also suggested that, because an adequate fit between adolescents and their families is requisite to optimal development, improvement of the fit between adolescents and their families may be the ultimate treatment plan for therapists working with these young adolescents. Additional research and new interventions for both parents and family level may help strengthen parent-adolescent relationships and support family changes to allow for appropriate adolescent autonomy and independence, thereby increasing the likelihood that young adolescents will feel a stronger sense of belonging within their families.

A Caveat: Potential Negative Outcomes of Belonging

While most of the research available to date tends to portray the sense belonging as both necessary and always positive, this view has been challenged recently by research noting that belonging, especially for young adolescents, may lead to either positive or negative outcomes, depending on the characteristics of the context to which one belongs. For example, in a longitudinal study of middle school students' goal orientations, Anderman and Hughes (2003) found that students' sense of school belonging moderated the association between their perceptions of a performance avoidance structure in their classes (i.e., an emphasis on avoiding looking incompetent and hiding lack of knowledge) and their personal endorsement of a performance avoidance orientation. In that study, students with a higher sense of belonging were more likely than their peers to adopt an avoidance orientation towards their academic work; a motivational profile well-established as maladaptive (e.g., Harackiewicz, Barron, Tauer, Carter, & Elliot, 2000). Similarly, in a study of self-reported academic dishonesty and cheating in undergraduate college students, Mueller, Anderman, Freeman and Wright (2006) found that students' sense of university belonging was associated with higher levels of cheating and dishonesty. These seemingly unexpected findings can be understood in terms of the theoretical functioning of the sense of belonging as described in self-determination theory (e.g., Deci et al., 1991). This theory proposes that individuals are more likely to internalize the values of settings in which their need for belonging is at least partially satisfied. Similarly, Finn's (1989) identification-participation model proposes that the sense of belonging in school and identification with the values of that setting go hand-in-hand. This process is well illustrated in Anderman and Hughes' findings, in that students with a high sense of belonging were more likely to internalize and adopt a maladaptive motivational orientation, when they perceived that orientation being emphasized in their classes. Similarly, in the Mueller et al. study, the authors interpreted their results as illustrating the internalization of an undergraduate college culture that includes widespread acceptance of cheating and other forms of academic dishonesty as acceptable (see Anderman & Murdock, 2007).

This premise is echoed in the family context as well. In the family realm, parents and siblings who form the family belonging context for young adolescents also provide a template for adolescents' behavior, either for good or for ill. Alltucker (2004) found that youth who had a parent or sibling convicted of a felony were more than twice as likely to become "early start" delinquents as those without felons in the family. Though limited by a small sample size, Arraiga and Foshee's (2004) study of adolescent dating violence found that the risk of experiencing or perpetrating dating violence was greater for those adolescents whose parents were violent towards one another. Pomery, Gibbons, Gerrard, Cleveland, Brody, & Wills (2005) noted that older siblings' willingness to use substances predicted adolescents' substance use 2 years later, both positively and negatively. When viewed collectively, these findings suggest that feeling a strong sense of belonging to a troubled family may be even more problematic than not experiencing any sense of family belonging for young adolescents.

Also worth noting is the idea that young adolescents who do not experience a sense of belonging at home or at school may seek to fill that need in settings that may prove less beneficial to their development over the long run. Clark (1992) noted an increased tendency of adolescents who lack a sense of belonging in other contexts, such as at school or at home, to embrace deviant subcultures such as Satanism, neo-Nazism, and violent gang membership. Curtis and Curtis (1993) noted the increased susceptibility of adolescents with to recruitment by religious cults, similar to findings by Turpin-Petrosino (2002) with regard to recruitment of disaffiliated youth by hate groups. Affiliation with deviant peers is highly correlated with the initiation and increase of adolescent substance use (Wills, Cleary, S., Filer, M., Shinar, O., Mariani, J., & Spera, 2001; Wills & Yaeger, 2003). Taken as a whole, these findings suggest that when healthy family and social relationships are not present, the thwarted need for belonging may steer youth into associations with groups like cults, gangs and hate groups with negative implications for themselves and society.

Taken together, these findings raise an important caveat in terms of our understanding of young adolescents' sense of belonging. Simplistic assumptions that the sense of belonging, in any context, will always have positive developmental and educational outcomes are misleading. The point here is to understand that the perception of belonging in a particular setting is not inherently positive or negative but, rather, that the values being promoted within that setting are critically important.

DIRECTIONS FOR FUTURE RESEARCH

Despite the recent growth in interest and empirical research in students' sense of belonging in both school and family contexts, it is clear that there are many questions that remain to be addressed. First, although the need to belong is conceptualized as a universal human need (e.g., Baumeister & Leary, 1995), it is not clear that the sense of belonging in school is equally important for the school adjustment and success of all students. That is, it may be particular cultural groups may place a higher importance on belonging as necessary for academic engagement, than do others. For example, Phelan, Davidson, and Yu (1998) suggested that the subjective sense of acceptance and belonging in school may be more influential for Latino students than for those from other ethnic groups. In contrast, Battisitch et al. (1995) noted that sense of belonging may be more important for ethnic minority students in general than White students. Equally importantly, members of different cultural groups may define school belonging differently (see Nichols, 2006) and these definitional differences are important in determining the role of belonging in school adjustment. Similar questions exist on the importance of potential gender differences in the role of perceived school belonging. Although several researchers have reported mean level differences in adolescent boys' and girls' school belonging, these findings do not tell us whether the sense of belonging is equally important for both groups. In a sample of middle school students, Goodenow (1993) found that belonging, particularly in terms of teacher support, was more important in predicting females' expectancies for academic success, than males'. To date, however, it is not clear how generalizable this pattern might be or, indeed, whether school belonging is defined similarly by male and female students.

Beyond group-level differences, there also may be important individual differences in terms of the relative importance of the sense of belonging for successful performance in school. As noted earlier, one of the most robust findings in the empirical research to date is the positive association between academic achievement and perceived belonging. While this association is not surprising, it does suggest that fostering a sense of belonging may be particularly important for those students who have not experienced high levels of success. In particular, the potential role of perceived belonging in preventing truancy and early school leaving (as proposed by Finn, 1989) remains understudied. All of these questions suggest that the field needs to move beyond examining general associations among belonging and various motivational and educational variables in the full population, toward a more focused approach.

A second major direction for future research is to examine the interplay between home and school contexts, specifically in relation to students' belongingness needs. As noted throughout this chapter, research on family belonging is sparse. Research that spans both the family and school contexts is even more rare. Despite growing interest in the challenges of negotiating the different contexts of home and school (e.g., Arunkumar, Midgley, & Urdan, 1999; Phelan, Davidson, & Yu, 1998), this focus has yet to be brought to bear in the research on perceived belonging in a systematic way. In one study, Gutman and Midgley (2000) examined the effects of several psychological, family, and school factors on changes in the academic grades in a sample of African American middle school students living in poverty. As students managed the transition from elementary to middle schools, their perceived school belonging in their new schools predicted an increase in GPA. Of particular interest, however, is that the authors also reported a significant interaction which showed that the positive effect of parental involvement was stronger in students who reported higher levels of school belonging. In contrast, parental involvement in school showed little effect on the GPA of students with low school belonging. In a similar study, Annunziata, Hogue, Faw, and Liddle (2006) found that family belonging and parental monitoring were predictors of level of engagement in school for at-risk middle school students, though not of GPA. These initial findings are suggestive and point out the importance of a greater research focus on the interplay between family and school contexts in understanding and supporting the developmental and educational needs of young adolescents.

Finally, the recent literature on belonging, particularly in terms of school belonging, has tended to focus on the definition and measurement of perceived belonging, as well as on establishing the importance of this perception in relation to a range of adaptive outcomes. Much less attention has been paid to understanding the precursors of the sense of belonging, in school or family settings, and to the implications of this work for practice (for exceptions see Anderman & Leake, 2005; Visher & Visher, 2000). Nevertheless, many of the dimensions of schools and families that seem to promote a positive sense of belonging are open to intervention. Thus, the time seems right for researchers to focus on specific policy and practice changes that have the potential to increase students' sense of belonging in both school and home environments.

REFERENCES

Alltucker, K. W. (2004). Factors influencing the development of juvenile delinquency: Differences between early and late starters. Dissertation-Abstracts-International-Section A:-Humanities-and-Social-Sciences. *Vol 65(6-A) 2004,* 2369.

Anant, S. (1966). The need to belong. *Canadian Mental Health, 14,* 21-27.

Anderman, E. M. (2002). School effects on psychological outcomes during adolescence. *Journal of Educational Psychology, 94,* 795-809.

Anderman, E. M., & T. B. Murdock (Eds.) (2007). *Psychological perspectives on academic cheating*. New York: Academic Press.

Anderman, L. H. (1999). Classroom goal orientation, school belonging and social goals as predictors of students' positive and negative affect following the transition to middle school. *Journal of Research and Development in Education, 32,* 89-103.

Anderman, L. H. (2003). Perceived classroom characteristics and change in middle school students' school belonging. *Journal of Experimental Education, 72,* 5-22.

Anderman, L. H., & Anderman, E. M. (1999). Social predictors of changes in students' achievement goal orientations. *Contemporary Educational Psychology, 25*, 21-37.

Anderman, L. H., & Freeman, T. (2004). Students' sense of belonging in school. In P. R. Pintrich & M. L. Maehr (Eds.), *Motivating students, improving schools: The Legacy of Carol Midgley. Advances in motivation and achievement* (Vol. 13, pp. 27-63). New York: Elsevier.

Anderman, L. H., & Hughes, H. K. (2003, April). *The role of school belonging in students' adoption of classroom goal orientations*. Poster presented at the annual meeting of the American Educational Research Association, Chicago, IL.

Anderman, L. H., & Leake, V. S. (2005). The ABC's of motivation: An alternative framework for teaching preservice teachers about motivation. *The Clearing House, 78*, 192-196.

Annunziata, D., Hogue, A., Faw, L., & Liddle, H. (2006). Family functioning and school success in at-risk, inner-city adolescents. *Journal of Youth and Adolescence, 35*, 105-113.

Arriage, X. B., & Foshee, V. A. (2004). Adolescent dating violence: Do adolescents follow in their friends', or their parents', footsteps? *Journal of Interpersonal Violence, 19*, 162-184.

Arunkumar, R., Midgley, C., & Urdan, T. C. (1999). Perceiving high or low home-school dissonance: Longitudinal effects on adolescent emotional and academic well-being. *Journal of Research on Adolescence, 9*, 441-466.

Battistich, C., Solomon, D., Kim, D., Watson, M., & Schaps, E. (1995). Schools as communities, poverty levels of student populations, and students' attitudes, motives, and performance: A multilevel analysis. *American Educational Research Journal, 32*, 627-658.

Battistich, V., Solomon, D., Watson, M., & Schaps, E. (1997). Caring school communities. *Educational Psychologist, 32*, 137-151.

Baumeister, R., & Leary, M. (1995). The need to belong: Desire for interpersonal attachments as a fundamental human motivation. *Psychological Bulletin, 117*, 497-529.

Berndt, T. J. (1982). The features and effects of friendship in early adolescence. *Child Development, 53*, 1447-1460.

Berndt, T. J. (1999). Friends' influence on students' adjustment to school. *Educational Psychologist, 34*, 15-28.

Borowsky, I., Ireland, M., & Resnick, M. (2001). Adolescent suicide attempts: Risk and protectors. *Pediatrics, 107*(3), 485-494.

Bowlby, J. (1983). Attachment and loss: Retrospect and prospect. *Annual Progress in Child Psychiatry & Child Development*, 29-47.

Bray, J. (1995). Systems-oriented therapy with stepfamilies. In R. H. Mikesell, D. Lusterman, & S. H. McDaniel (Eds.), *Integrating family therapy: Handbook of family psychology and systems theory* (pp. 125-140). Washington, DC: American Psychological Association.

Bray, J., Adams, G., Getz, J., & Baer, P. (2001). Developmental, family, and ethnic influences on adolescent alcohol usage: A growth curve approach. *Journal of Family Psychology, 15*, 301-314.

Bray, J., & Berger, S. (1993). Developmental issues in StepFamilies Research Project: Family relationships and parent-child interactions. *Journal of Family Psychology, 7,* 76-90.

Carnegie Council on Adolescent Development. (1989). *Turning points: Preparing American youth for the 21st century.* Washington, DC: Carnegie Corporation of New York.

Chen, C., Greenberger, E., Farruggia, S., Bush, K., & Dong, Q. (2003). Beyond parents and peers: The role of important non-parental adults (VIPS) in adolescent development in China and the United States. *Psychology in the Schools, 40,* 35-50.

Clark, C. (1992). Deviant adolescent subcultures: Assessment strategies and clinical interventions. *Adolescence, 27,* 283-293.

Conger, R., & Ge, X. (1999). Conflict and cohesion in parent-adolescent relations: Changes in emotional expression from early to midadolescence. In M. J. Cox & J. Brooks-Gunn (Eds.), *Conflict and cohesion in families: Causes and consequences* (pp. 185-206). Mahwah, NJ: Erlbaum.

Curtis, J., & Curtis, M. (1993). Factors related to susceptibility and recruitment by cults. *Psychological Reports, 73,* 451-460.

Csikszentmihalyi, M., & Larson, R. (1984). *Being adolescent.* New York: Basic Books.

Deci, E., Vallerand, R., Pelletier, L., & Ryan, R. (1991). Motivation and education: The self-determination perspective. *Educational Psychologist, 26*(3/4), 325-346.

Eccles, J., Midgley, C., Wigfield, A., Buchanan, C., Reuman, D., Flanagan, C., et al. (1993). Development during adolescence: The impact of stage-environment fit on young adolescents' experiences in schools and in families. *American Psychologist, 48,* 90-101.

Eccles, J., Wigfield, A., Flanagan, C., Miller, C., Reuman, D., & Yee, D. (1989). Self-concepts, domain values, and self-esteem: Relations and changes at early adolescence. *Journal of Personality, 57,* 283-310.

Elkind, D. (1967). Egocentrism in adolescence. *Child Development, 38,* 1025-1034.

Finn, J. D. (1989). Withdrawing from school. *Review of Educational Research, 59,* 117-142.

Freeman, T. M., & Anderman, L. H. (2005). Changes in mastery goals in urban and rural middle school students. *Journal of Research in Rural Education, 20*(1). Retrieved November 15, 2006, from http://www.umaine.edu/jrre/articles/vol20.htm

Freeman, T. M., Anderman, L. H., & Jensen, J. M. (in press). The psychological sense of belonging in college freshmen: Relations to motivation and instructor practices. *Journal of Experimental Education*

Freeman, T. M., Jackson, C. H., Strand, K. H., Matthews, K. E., McNally, J. L., & Brown-Wright, L. (2003, August). *Role model influence in predicting belongingness among African American students.* Poster presented at the annual conference of the American Psychological Association, Toronto, Canada.

Fuhr, R., Moos, R., & Dishotsky, N. (1981). The use of family assessment and feedback in ongoing family therapy. *The American Journal of Family Therapy, 9*(1), 24-36.

Furman, W., & Buhrmester, D. (1992). Age and sex differences in perceptions of networks of personal relationships. *Child Development, 63,* 103-115.

Glasser, W. (1998). *Choice theory: A new psychology of personal freedom.* New York: Harper Collins.

Goodenow, C. (1992). Strengthening the links between educational psychology and the study of social contexts. *Educational Psychologist, 27,* 177-196.

Goodenow, C. (1993a). Classroom belonging among early adolescent students: relationships to motivation and achievement. *Journal of Early Adolescence, 13,* 21-43.

Goodenow, C. (1993b). The psychological sense of school membership among adolescents: Scale development and educational correlates. *Psychology in the Schools, 30,* 79-90.

Goodenow, C. & Grady, K. E. (1993). The relationship of school belonging and friends' values to academic motivation among urban adolescent students. *Journal of Experimental Education, 62,* 60-71.

Gutman, L. M., & Midgley, C. (2000). The role of protective factors in supporting the academic achievement of poor African American students during the middle school transition. *Journal of Youth and Adolescence, 29,* 223-248.

Hagerty, B., Lynch-Sauer, J., Patusky, K., Bouwsema, M., & Collier, P. (1992). Sense of belonging: A vital mental health concept. *Archives of Psychiatric Nursing, 6,* 172-177.

Harackiewicz, J., Barron, K., Tauer, J., Carter, S., & Elliot, A. (2000). Short-term and long-term consequences of achievement goals: Predicting interest and performance over time. *Journal of Educational Psychology, 92,* 316-330.

Harter, S. (1999). *The construction of the self: A developmental perspective.* New York: Guilford Press.

Hartup, W. W. (1993). Adolescents and their friends. In B. Laursen (Ed.), *Close friendships in adolescence* (pp. 3-22). San Francisco: Jossey Bass.

Hogue, A., Liddle, H., Becker, D., & Johnson-Leckrone, J. (2002). Family-based prevention counseling for high-risk young adolescents: Immediate outcomes. *Journal of Community Psychology, 30,* 1-22.

Huffine, C. (2004). Youth violence: Its meanings to society in the 21st century. *Adolescent Psychiatry, 27,* 361-374.

Kester, V. M. (1994). Factors that affect African-American students' bonding to middle school. *The Elementary School Journal, 95,* 63–73.

King, K., Vidourek, R., Davis, B., & McClellan, W. (2002). Increasing self-esteem and school connectedness through a multidimensional mentoring program. *Journal of School Health, 72*(7), 294-299.

Kliewer, W., Murrell, L., Prom, E., Ramirez, M., Obando, P., Sandi, L., et al. (2006). Violence exposure and drug use in Central American youth: Family cohesion and parental monitoring as protective factors. *Journal of Research on Adolescence, 16,* 455-478.

Lagana, M. (2004). Protective factors for inner-city adolescent at risk of school dropout: Family factors and social support. *Children and Schools, 26,* 211-220.

Leake, V. (2004, July). *Protecting stepfamily adolescents from harm: Is increased family belonging a true protective factor from risky behaviors?* Paper presented at the biannual meeting of the National Longitudinal Adolescent Health Survey Users, Washington, DC.

Leake, V. (2007). Personal, familial, and systemic factors associated with family belonging for stepfamily adolescents. *Journal of Divorce and Remarriage, 47*(1/2).

Marsh, H. (1990). The structure of academic self-concept: The Marsh/Shavelson model. *Journal of Educational Psychology, 82*, 623-636.

Maslow, A. (1962). *Toward a psychology of being*. Princeton, NJ: Van Nostrand.

Maslow, A. (1987). *Motivation and personality* (3rd ed.). New York: Harper & Row.

McClelland, D. C. (1985). *Human motivation*. Glenview, IL: Scott, Foresman.

McNeely, C. A., Nonnemaker, J. M., & Blum, R. W. (2002). Promoting school connectedness: Evidence from the national longitudinal study of adolescent health. *Journal of School Health, 72*, 138-146.

Mueller, C., E., Anderman, L. H., Freeman, T. M., & Wright, K. M. (2006, April). *Sense of belonging and academic identity: Some surprising associations with academic dishonesty.* Poster presented at the annual American Educational Research Association annual conference, San Francisco, CA.

Nichols, S. L. (2006). Teachers' and students' beliefs about student belonging in one middle school. *The Elementary School Journal, 106*, 255-270.

Olson, D., Russell, C., & Sprenkle, D. (1983). Circumplex Model of marital and family systems: VI. Theoretical update. *Family Process, 22*, 69-83.

Pedersen, S, & Revenson, T. A. (2005). Parental illness, family functioning, and adolescent well-being: A family ecology framework to guide research. *Journal of Family Psychology, 19*, 404-419.

Perry, B. (2002). Affiliation,the third core strength. *Early Childhood Today, 16*(4), 30- 32.

Phelan, P., Davidson, A. L., & Yu, H. C. (1998). *Adolescents' worlds: Negotiating family, peers, and school.* New York: Teachers College Press.

Pilgrim, C., Abbey, A., & Kershaw, T. (2004). The direct and indirect effects of mothers' and adolescents' family cohesion on young adolescents' attitudes toward substance use. *Journal of Primary Prevention, 24*, 263-283.

Pomery, E., Gibbons, F, Gerrard, M., Cleveland, M., Brody, G., & Wills, T. (2005). Families and risk: Prospective analyses of familial and social influences on adolescent substance use. *Journal of Family Psychology, 19*, 560-570.

Ream, G. L., & Savin-Williams, R. C. (2005). Reciprocal associations between adolescent sexual activity and quality of youth-parent interactions. *Journal of Family Psychology, 19*, 171-179.

Resnick, M., Bearman, P. S., Blum, R. W. Bauman, K. E., Harris, K. M., Jones, J., et al., (1997). Protecting adolescents from harm. *Journal of the American Medical Association, 278*(10), 823-832.

Roeser, R. W., Midgley, C., & Urdan, T. C. (1996). Perceptions of the school psychological environment and early adolescents' psychological and behavioral functioning in school: The mediating role of goals and belonging. *Journal of Educational Psychology, 88*, 408-422.

Ryan, R. M. (1995). Psychological needs and the facilitation of integrative processes. *Journal of Personality, 63*, 397-427.

Sale, E., Sambrano, S., Springer, J., & Turner, C. (2003). Risk, protection, and substance use in adolescents: A multi-site model. *Journal of Drug Education, 33*(1), 91-105.

Scal, P., Ireland, M., & Borowsky, I. (2003). Smoking among American adolescents: A risk and protective factor analysis. *Journal of Community Health, 28*(1), 79-98.

Solomon, D., Battistich, V., Kim, D., & Watson, M. (1997). Teacher practices associated with students' sense of the classroom as a community. *Social Psychology of Education, 1,* 235-267.

Solomon, D., Watson, M., Battistich, V., Schaps, E., & Delucchi, K. (1996). Creating classrooms that students experience as communities. *American Journal of Community Psychology, 24,* 719-748.

Turpin-Petrosino, C. (2002). Hateful sirens … Who hears their song? An examination of student attitudes toward hate groups and affiliation potential. *Journal of Social Issues, 58*, 281-301.

Visher, E., & Visher, J. (2000). Tasks for stepfamilies. In Stepfamily Association of America, *Stepfamilies stepping ahead: An eight-step program for successful family living*. Lincoln, NE: Stepfamily Association of America.

Voelkl, K. E. (1996). Measuring students' identification with school. *Educational and Psychological Measurement, 56,* 760-770.

Voelkl, K. E. (1997). Identification with school. *American Journal of Education, 105,* 294-316.

Weiner, B. (1990). The history of motivation research in education. *Journal of Educational Psychology, 82,* 616-622.

Wentzel, K. R. (1997). Student motivation in middle school: The role of perceived pedagogical caring. *Journal of Educational Psychology, 89*, 411-419.

Wills, T., Cleary, S., Filer, M., Shinar, O., Mariani, J., & Spera, K. (2001). Temperament related to early-onset substance use: Test of a developmental model. *Prevention Science, 2,* 145-163.

Wills, T., & Yaeger, A. (2003). Family factors and adolescent substance use: Models and mechanisms. *Current Directions in Psychological Science, 12*, 222-226.

Worden, M. (1991). *Adolescents and their families: An introduction to assessment and intervention.* New York: Haworth.

CHAPTER 9

THE UNIQUE NATURE OF MIDDLE SCHOOL COUNSELING

Patrick Akos

ABSTRACT

While all levels of school counseling share similarities, the development of young adolescents and the ecology of the middle school require a distinctive role for middle school counselors. This chapter explores the implications of development and the middle school philosophy on the application of middle school counselor practice and the application of the American School Counselor Association (2003) National Model. Specifically, developmental themes such as puberty and identity development, and the broader middle school phenomena like school transitions and advisory programs require middle school counselors to be developmentally and contextually responsive.

Over the last century, the American education system has seen two major shifts related to young adolescents. Initiated in the first few decades of the twentieth century, the junior high school became a fixture in America's

The Young Adolescent and the Middle School
pp. 183–200

school districts in 1940 replacing the K-8, 9-12 models with K-6, 7-9, 10-12 versions (Lounsbury & Vars, 2003). The junior high was created based on the recognition of the developmental differences of young adolescents. Junior high schools were typically subject-centered, required a six-period day, organized teachers in departments, and emphasized primarily the academic development of students. Most of the research on junior high schools (e.g., Cuban, 1992) noted that these schools evolved into miniature versions of traditional high schools.

The middle school movement, initiated in the 1960s, became the centerpiece of the K-5, 6-8, 9-12 model of education (Lounsbury & Vars, 2003). Studies have documented an increase in schools organized around the 6-7-8 grade configuration from 15% in 1981 to 59% in the most recent count (Valentine, Clark, Hackmann, & Petzo, 2003). The expansion of the middle school model has changed the way in which educators work with young adolescents. In contrast to junior highs, middle schools are characterized as striving to be more student-centered, focus on creative exploration, allow for flexible scheduling, organize teachers into interdisciplinary teams, and emphasize affective and cognitive development of students. The middle school model not only recognized young adolescence as a unique developmental phase, but also that the educational structure, teaching, and learning needed to be congruent to students' developmental needs (National Middle School Association, 2003).

As attention to the developmental needs of young adolescents and the middle school philosophy gained prominence, a focus on accountability in education has also impacted middle school counselor practice. The No Child Left Behind Act of 2001 (U.S. Department of Education, 2001) imposed a system of accountability that narrowed the mission of learning in schools to an almost singular focus on academic achievement as measured by test results. Partly in response to accountability demands, the school counselor role was redefined and more fully developed through the emergence of the American School Counselor Association (2003) National Model. In the ASCA National Model, emphasis is placed upon comprehensive counseling programs that foundationally are congruent with school missions (e.g., academic focus) and suggests school counselor leadership, advocacy, and systemic intervention are recommended to help students achieve.

As a result, middle school counselors find themselves adapting their practice to vast changes in priorities of policymakers and leadership (e.g., NCLB), structural and philosophical considerations in the building (e.g., the middle school model), emerging school counseling reform (e.g., National Model), and young adolescents in the midst of considerable developmental change. As a result, the ability of middle school counselors to be developmental advocates (Galassi & Akos, 2004) for rapidly developing students within a developmentally responsive environment is required. Embracing this culture of change provides opportunity for middle school counselors to promote optimal development and academic achievement of young adolescents.

The purpose of this article is to delineate aspects of young adolescent development and the middle school philosophy, and demonstrate how both impact middle school counseling practice and the American School Counselor Association (ASCA) National Model. The implications of puberty, identity formation, and expanding choices are considered. Further, the National Middle School Association's (2003) vision of the middle school is explored in the context of school counselor practice. Finally, the uniqueness of middle school counseling is further illustrated within the foundation and delivery system of the ASCA National Model, as well as with issues for future consideration.

YOUNG ADOLESCENT DEVELOPMENT: CHANGING STUDENTS

Aside from infancy, no other phase of life is characterized by greater, more rapid, and diverse development than early adolescence (Pruitt, 2000). While there is no formal rite of passage into adulthood in the United States, young adolescence (approximately 10-14) is often recognized as the starting point. Traditionally, this phase of development has been characterized as "storm and stress" (Freud, 1969). In fact, this author believes that there are some parallels to the toddler stage in child development in terms of taking risks and pushing boundaries, although more severe consequences exist for some of the risks (e.g., drugs, alcohol, smoking, sex) middle school students take.

While there are many challenges for young adolescents, this coming of age transition is actually a complex interaction between internal changes (e.g., self exploration, intellectual expansion) and interaction with a new and changing environment (e.g., elementary to middle to high school transitions, peer interactions). These changes also provide exciting opportunities. Middle school students tend to become planful and idealistic, able to examine grey areas in moral discussions, and build important and complex social structures. While a complete review of young adolescent development is beyond the scope of this chapter (see Scales, 2005), the understanding of developmental phenomena is critical to effective middle school counseling practice. Three developmental forces in early adolescence (puberty, identity development, and an increase in autonomous choices) are presented to illustrate the unique impact on middle school counseling practice.

Puberty

During puberty, young adolescents undergo a number of hormonal and physical changes. An imbalance between their maturity level and what their bodies start to feel often causes confusion. Puberty brings a growth spurt that includes reproductive systems, increased weight and height, and various other novel physical changes (e.g., pubic hair, voice change) (Pruitt, 2000). Since no two individuals develop at the same rate or pattern, middle school counselors are challenged to understand that normal development varies. In fact, setting outcome expectations based on the National Standards for School Counseling Programs (Campbell & Dahir, 1997) or other competencies becomes more of a challenge due to this variance and the developmental transitions students are making. This challenge also impacts interventions. For example, individual counseling sessions require learning how a student's cognitive, moral, and emotional development impacts her or his ability to communicate. Although some students may be responsive to cognitive behavioral strategies in examining metacognition (e.g., thinking about and regulating their own thinking), others may require more concrete behavioral rehearsal when resolving a conflict.

In general, females begin puberty 1 to 2 years before boys and in some cultures (e.g., African Americans) puberty tends to begin earlier (Davis & Thompson, 2005). Research has shown that boys who develop at a faster rate have more of an advantage in the area of sports and social recognition, whereas girls developing at a quicker pace often experience scrutiny from peers (Eccles, 1999). Any deviation from the perceived norm, whether developing much quicker or slower than peers, may lead to the risk of psychosocial maladaption (Wiesner & Ittel, 2002). Therefore, middle school counselors should understand the salience of culture and timing in development. Middle school counselors can purposefully target students with early or late onset of puberty to explore the psychological and psychosocial impacts. Growing-up groups or collaborative classroom guidance with health and physical education instructors provide vehicles for psychoeducation and can help young adolescents understand how puberty impacts daily functioning, peer groups, intimacy, and identity formation. According to Akos and Levitt (2002), "promoting a healthy body image is a relevant outcome goal for middle school counseling programs" (p. 139) and can serve as a protective factor in young adolescent development. Middle school counselors should also be vigilant to how these physical developments and changes can be expressed in positive (e.g., competence in sports) and negative ways (e.g., sexual harassment).

Identity Formation

During puberty, an emerging identity becomes a focal point for young adolescents. Classic Ericksonian psychosocial theory described early adolescence as a drive toward industry and identity (versus inferiority and role confusion) (Cobb, 2001). Industry or developing competence is determined daily in middle school when students actively learn by exploring and identifying talents and capabilities. Middle school counselors should be engaged in conversations with school administration and staff about maximizing students' abilities to discover competency in exploratory curriculum such as music, art, technology, and career development classes. Similarly, involvement in extracurricular activities has correlated positively to a host of important developmental (e.g., feelings of belonging and connectedness) and academic (e.g., increased grade point average) outcomes (Akos, 2006; Eccles & Templeton, 2002; Mahoney, Cairns, & Farmer, 2003) and are developmentally ideal for building competence in interest areas. Industry and identity are also promoted in interaction with other aspects of school ecology (e.g., peer groups).

Adolescents are trying to discover their own identity, and yet realize that they are a part of a social group (Cobb, 2001). Youth now contend with increased peer competition, and fear being left behind or judged as substandard. In the same way, peers can help develop feelings of intimacy or connection and social competence. Middle school counselors may take advantage of the developmental importance of peers by utilizing mentors to help shape positive identities. Research has demonstrated that young adolescents perform better academically, have more achievement oriented goals, and think more about their future when they have access to mentors (Zirkel, 2002). Peer programming (e.g., peer mediation, peer tutoring, peer ambassadors for transition programs) may be particularly potent for middle school counselors as it could capitalize on the positive use of peer pressure and potentially influence identity.

According to Fenzel (1991), middle school students often experience strain in terms of role ambiguity, role conflict, and role overload or underload. Young adolescents attempt to determine who they are with new found cognitive abilities (e.g., metacognition, abstract thinking, future orientation). As an example, one often overlooked aspect of identity formation is ethnic or racial identity. These feelings of commitment and belonging to a group differ among students, but research (Holcomb-McCoy, 2005) has made linkages to achievement and competence for an explored or achieved racial and ethnic identity (serves as a protective mechanism). As exploration and role demands increase, middle school counselors can educate parents on the various roles and competing identities of students. It is also incumbent on middle school counselors to find ways to explore with students how these experiences and choices impact feelings of competence and questions about who they will become.

New and Important Choices

While not a biological or psychosocial force, part of this quest for competence and identity involves making choices. Students at all levels make choices, but middle school students are often, for the first time, making independent and autonomous choices that may significantly shape developmental paths. The desire for independent choices and increased responsibility is developmental, as young adolescents seek differentiation from parents and must respond to the choices required in the new middle school environment. Middle school counselors should promote decision making skills and help students identify resources that can help with making choices.

For the first time, middle school students are able to choose classes they will take. They are offered multiple electives to choose from that ideally are based on students' interests. These choices serve as an early career decision point and are significant in forming early career identities (Akos, Konold, & Niles, 2004). Beyond academic choices, the middle school requires independent choices during class changes, negotiating multiple teachers and new peer groups, and determining how to be successful in a more complex environment.

THE RESPONSIVE MIDDLE SCHOOL PHILOSOPHY

Based in part on the challenging nature of young adolescent development and the need for an environment that supported this uniqueness, the National Middle School Association (NMSA) was established in 1973 and articulated a new philosophy in *This We Believe* (NMSA, 1982). This vision was revised in 1995 and the most recent, *This We Believe: Successful Schools for Young Adolescents,* was published in 2003. Table 9.1 presents the major tenants of the philosophy. These tenants include cultural beliefs and programmatic structures that respond to the developmental needs of young adolescents. Similar recommendations about educating young adolescents have come from the seminal report *Turning Points: Preparing American Youth for the 21st Century* (Carnegie Council on Adolescent Development, 1989) and the most recent revision, *Turning Points 2000* (Jackson & Davis, 2000). *The Turning Points*'s recommendations include a rigorous curriculum relevant to how young adolescents learn, staffing schools with teachers who are experts at teaching to this age group, providing a safe and healthy school environment, involving parents in student learning

Table 9.1. National Middle School Association's Vision for a Successful Middle School

National Middle School Association believes ...

Successful schools for young adolescents are characterized by a culture that includes

- Educators who value working with this age group and are prepared to do so
- Courageous, collaborative leadership
- A shared vision that guides decisions
- An inviting, supportive, and safe ecology
- High expectations for every member of the learning community
- Students and teachers engaged in active learning
- An adult advocate for every student
- School-initiated family and community partnerships.

Therefore, successful schools for young adolescents provide

- Curriculum that is relevant, challenging, integrative, and exploratory
- Multiple learning and teaching approaches that respond to their diversity
- Assessment and evaluation programs that promote quality learning
- Organizational structures that support meaningful relationship and learning
- Schoolwide efforts and policies that foster health, wellness, and safety
- **Multifaceted guidance and support services** (bold added)

and healthy development, and organizing relationships for learning and a caring community.

"For middle schools to be successful, their students must be successful; for students to be successful, the schools' organization, curriculum, pedagogy, and programs must be based upon the developmental readiness, needs, and interests of young adolescents" (NMSA, 2003, p.1). Although young adolescence is demanding, the developmentally responsive ecology put forth in middle school reform can be utilized by middle school counselors to address students' developmental needs. Most school counselors have learned about individual human development, but ecological development (Bronfrenbrenner, 1979) or the interaction and interdependence of self and various microsystems (e.g., peer groups, classrooms, schools, families) is equally salient for middle school counselors. In fact, Keys and Lockhart (1999) made a case for ecological assessment and multisystemic intervention plans for school counselors that use indirect intervention to manipulate the environment to help students. This is particularly useful in light of the middle school reform efforts at a developmentally responsive environment.

Both *This We Believe* (2003) and *Turning Points* (2000) have important implications for the way middle school counselors practice. One of the most notable tenants for school counselors endorsed by NMSA (2003) is multifaceted guidance and support services. Classroom guidance (including supporting advisory programs), one-on-one and small group guidance, peer mediation and peer tutoring, consulting with teachers and parents, and facilitating transition programs are essential to their multifaceted guidance and support services section (NMSA, 2003). In fact, NMSA advocates for school counselors as leaders with the following: "school counselors coordinate the support services provided by the school system, ensuring the most effective use of specialists such as school psychologists, social workers, and speech therapists" (p. 34). NMSA also discourages noncounseling functions noting that "counselors are important specialists with people-oriented skills and should not be burdened with administrative or report-related responsibilities" (p. 34). In fact, Bergmann (2001) noted that middle school writings documented a need for advocacy and guidance for almost 100 years.

Although NMSA (2003) language on support services resonates most with middle school counselors, school counselors need to engage other aspects of the middle school philosophy and Turning Points' recommendations in order to promote students' optimal development and achievement. In particular, an inviting, supportive, and safe environment and organizing relationships for learning and caring (Jackson & Davis, 2000) are utilized to demonstrate the congruence to school counseling and the uniqueness of middle school counseling.

An inviting environment starts with students' transition from elementary to middle school. NMSA (2003) highlighted transition programs that include comprehensive career and educational planning as being integrated and collaboratively planned to connect students to the middle school and prepare students for the rigor of high school. Middle school counselors should serve as advocates and leaders of transition programs (Akos, 2003; Akos & Galassi, 2004), as this particular role is both unique to middle school and critical in building an inviting middle school environment. Middle school counselors can collaborate with elementary school counselors to prepare students and parents for the transition, and coordinate orientation programs in the middle school to help connect and engage students. The organizational, academic, and social concerns highlighted by research (Akos, 2002; Akos & Galassi, 2004; Schumacher, 1998) on the transition to middle school parallel the National Standards (Campbell & Dahir, 1997). Wigfield, Lutz, and Wagner (2005) examine the middle school counselor role in enhancing student motivation and promoting positive adult relationships in the transition to middle school.

In addition, advisory programs and teaming are used in middle schools to promote positive adult relationships and a supportive environment. Advisory programs, where teachers and other adults in the school serve as advocates to a limited number of assigned students (12-18), vary by focus and definition. Advisory programs seek to improve teacher-student relationships, promote social and emotional development, and build feelings of belonging and caring (Galassi, Gulludge, & Cox, 1998). Murdock and Miller (2003) found that higher quality teacher-student relationships predict stronger motivation for eighth grade students. They even suggested that a perceived positive relationship with one's teacher might help compensate for lack of educational support from friends and family (although support from all is obviously most desirable). Due to the variety of advisory programs in practice, generalized conclusions about their effectiveness are limited; however, there seems to be consensus on the importance of building adult-student relationships.

Galassi et al. (1998) suggested that middle school counselors can serve as advisors, consultants, trainers, supervisors, or leaders of the advisory program. Each role has advantages and disadvantages, but middle school counselors can clearly advocate for advisory programs. They also can help middle schools initiate and maintain advisory programs by assisting advisors in understanding the developmental nature of students and by creating or sharing developmentally appropriate curriculum or activities. Examples of advisory activities include "discussing problems with individual students, giving career information and guidance, developing student self-confidence and leadership, and discussing academic issues" (Mac Iver, 1990, p. 459). "Advisory is not a time for intensive personal counseling" (Jackson & Davis, 2000, p. 144), but instead may be an effective tool to deliver guidance curriculum and may serve as a referral source for middle school counselors. A typology of advisory purposes and additional information is available in Galassi et al. (1998).

Like advisory, teaming has the potential to provide more opportunity to build meaningful relationships between students and teachers. Teaching teams in middle school typically consist of two or four teachers who teach all of the core subjects to a small group of students. By clustering teachers and students into teams, middle schools have the ability to create smaller learning communities, which have been associated with positive outcomes (e.g., increased achievement, increased feelings of belonging) (Farber, 1998). Jackson and Davis (2000) suggested teams can provide students a psychological home to reduce anonymity, help build peer group affiliation, and provide teachers a structure for professional development centered on effective instruction. Teaming has implications for how middle school counselors work and consult with teachers, and school counselors may be able facilitate more effective team leadership by sharing knowledge of group process and leadership techniques.

Middle school counselors can benefit from multiple perspectives teams may provide on student referrals or ongoing individual counseling cases. During common planning time—shared planning time for team members in addition to their individual planning time—behavioral contracts can be created with students and a team of teachers that impact multiple classes, provide multiple reinforcement strategies, and are consistently monitored across classes. Ideally, effective teacher teams can facilitate the flow of information and increase counselors' ability to schedule and deliver classroom guidance or conduct groups. Even so, as with any group structure, not all teaching teams are effective. Erb and Doda (1989) suggested that teaming in middle school has suffered from a limited vision on what teams could be. Dickson and Erb (1997) and Rottier (2000) suggested improving team process by improving team leadership and dealing with group conflict effectively. Middle school counselors can work with administrators in determining optimal composition of teams (both teachers and students) and advocating for appropriate planning time for teachers. They may also serve as consultants to team leaders to build more effective task groups and team leadership skills. As Pounder (1998) noted, teams typically need professional development on relationship building and management prior to moving to collaborative teaching and curriculum integration.

There are additional concepts in the middle school philosophy that are unique or must be uniquely applied by middle school counselors to promote young adolescent development. Active learning and exploratory curriculum, as noted earlier, are ideal ways to help students negotiate competency and identity development. Both allow for students to make choices, experience hands-on learning, and have "potential career value" (NMSA, 2003, p. 24). Middle school counselors may lead or collaboratively teach career development as part of the exploratory curriculum. Even parent engagement, while desirable at all levels of schooling, is more salient in middle school due to the typical drop off in parent involvement (Davis & Lambie, 2005). In sum, middle school counselors can advocate for middle school reform concepts (e.g., teams, advisory, active learning) that are developmentally responsive and complement a comprehensive school counseling program. This aligns middle school counselor practice with broader educational reform, and positions school counseling as an "integral part of the total educational program" (ASCA, 2003, p. 15).

RESPONSIVE PRACTICE: THE ASCA NATIONAL MODEL APPLIED TO MIDDLE SCHOOL

Several implications of young adolescent development and the middle school philosophy for middle school counselors have been noted, but these also need to be considered when developing and implementing comprehensive school counseling program in middle school. The ASCA

(2003) National Model components of foundation and delivery system are utilized to provide examples of how unique and specific applications for middle school are needed.

Foundation

The key elements of the foundation from the ASCA (2003) National Model include a set of beliefs and philosophy, a mission statement, and the ASCA National Standards (Campbell & Dahir, 1997). Principles and beliefs that guide a middle school counseling program should align to the school and district's mission. Both the middle school philosophy (see Table 9.1) and the *Turning Points'* recommendations (Jackson & Davis, 2000) outline developmentally responsive principles relevant to a shared foundation for a middle school counseling program. These system level principles should then be combined with beliefs and philosophy about young adolescent development (e.g., the heterogeneity of development, the relevance of competence and identity, and support for student autonomy needs).

Flowing from these beliefs and guiding principles, a mission that describes the program's purpose and goals is needed. To be sure, middle school counselors' efforts are most accepted and become more valuable when harmonious to the focus on academic achievement. This is particularly true as middle schools have come under fire for the declines in achievement during the middle school years (Yecke, 2003). Middle school counselors do not directly deliver core academic curriculum, but it is necessary to address outcomes that are particularly relevant for young adolescent learning in the mission. For example, academic motivation (Wigfield et al., 2005) and self-regulated learning (Lapan, Kardash, & Turner, 2002; Sink, 2005) are very salient and can be impacted by school counselor practice.

While academic achievement has been the mantra for NCLB reform, the middle school, unlike other levels, has included affective development as core to its mission. Therefore, middle school counselors are also in accord with school missions when constructing a program to promote students competencies in personal/social or affective realms. Middle school counseling programs must also construct outcome goals for young adolescents that are flexible to the heterogeneity of student development. The National Standards (Campbell & Dahir, 1997) are one useful guide, but they may not be developmentally responsive to school levels or particular stages of development. Due to the developmental variance in young adolescence and the holistic mission of middle schools, it may be more useful to center a middle school counseling program on individual assets

(Benson, 2003) or ecological conditions that research has correlated to positive youth development (Lerner et al., 2005).

"Thriving ... is representative of an active individual who is functioning across time and place to interact with active context in manners that enhance both person and setting" (Theokas et al., 2005, p. 117). The competencies within the foundation of a middle school program can utilize positive youth development (Lerner et al., 2005), with a focus on systems and building positive behavior (e.g., competence, confidence, connection, character, caring, and contribution). Galassi and Akos (2004) proposed Developmental Advocacy as a framework for school counselors to integrate emerging research on developmental assets, resilience, positive psychology, and competence. With this focus on positive developmental conditions, rather than particular developmental markers, the delivery system for middle school counselors corresponds to the developmentally responsive foundation.

Delivery System

A foundation built on promoting optimal development dictates a unique structure for the activities and methods for middle school counselor practice. Although the ASCA (2003) National Model recommends a distribution of time for middle school counselors as 25-35% for guidance curriculum, 15-25% for individual student planning, 30-40% for responsive services, and 10-15% for system support, these may vary dramatically in order to be responsive to young adolescent development and middle school pedagogy. For example, although middle school counselors will contribute and help develop a guidance curriculum, it may be entirely delivered by other school staff through advisory programming. The guidance curriculum might also be delivered to teams rather than classrooms or integrated into the core curriculum in interdisciplinary units. Middle school counselors may also deliver guidance curriculum in an exploratory class on career development. In fact, guidance curriculum may be where much of the student educational and career planning (Trusty, Niles, & Carney, 2005) occurs due to the common educational choices (e.g., exploratory choices, high school academic paths) that essentially serve as early career choices for middle school students.

The developmental phenomena of young adolescence have implications for relevant topics and how middle school counselors conceptualize responsive services. Exploring new found physical and cognitive abilities and the expanding meaning of relationships lead to the expected need for topics such as anger management, decision making and conflict resolution. While, responsive services will always be required (e.g., family change, grief), it is important that middle school counselors do not pathologize young adolescent development. A delivery system for middle school counselors should balance time proportionally to promoting positive youth development, prevention, and responsive services based on school and students' needs. Individual, group, or systemic interventions should also be selected that are most meaningful for young adolescents and that capitalize on systems (e.g., team structure) or components (e.g., advisory) present in the middle school.

FUTURE ISSUES IN MIDDLE SCHOOL COUNSELING

Although a foundation and delivery system may be unique in middle school, the ASCA (2003) National Model also includes components (i.e., management systems, accountability) that are not necessarily unique or lack evidence to warrant strong recommendations. For example, part of the ASCA (2003) National Model management system includes counselor assignment. Often counselors work as a team (2-3 counselors) in middle school. Unfortunately, there is no existing research that suggests the most effective system of assignment. ASCA (2003) provides several options including alphabet type assignment, grade level assignment (with or without looping with students or teachers), specialty area foci, or even rotating foci. While the advantage to spend multiple years with the same students (alphabet or looping) seems obvious, perhaps grade level assignment would permit more cohesive counselor-teacher relationships and more consistent transition programming.

Similarly, ASCA (2003) recommends 80% of all counselors' time be devoted to direct contact to students in order to meet students' needs and protect counselors from non-counseling activities (e.g., testing coordination, classroom coverage). It seems relevant to young adolescent development that peer programming takes on additional salience in middle school dictating an increase in indirect service through coordination of peer-related programs. The *Turning Points*'s recommendations, in fact, advocate for peer mediation and peer support groups as optimal means for a safe and healthy school environment (Jackson & Davis, 2000). It seems that developmentally responsive practice is yet undefined in the design and implementation of ASCA (2003) National Model and will need to be more precisely defined by developmental age and school setting.

Finally, the cumulative focus of the ASCA (2003) National Model on accountability will be relevant to all school counselors. Determining results is by no means easy. Young adolescents are going to be different over time due to developmental change, so pinpointing the specific effect school counselor interventions will require more than actions plans and the examination of data. Evaluation of action plans is an important initial step, and outcome research (i.e., experimental design, control groups, random assignments, large scales studies) needs to inform practices. Both Whiston and Sexton (1998) and St. Clair (1989) noted more research activity on counseling in the elementary and high school levels as compared to middle school, and limited evidence to make decisive conclusions for middle school counseling.

In sum, middle school counseling requires a unique design and implementation for a developmentally responsive comprehensive school counseling program. It will also require ongoing research to determine effective or optimal delivery systems, management systems, and practices for young adolescents.

FINAL THOUGHTS

It would be naive to assume that all middle schools are developmentally responsive and have implemented the middle school philosophy well. Although some research (Felner, Jackson, Kasak, Mulhull, Brand, & Flowers, 1997) demonstrated better student outcomes (e.g., achievement) for schools implementing middle school practices, other research (Brown, Roney, & Anfara, 2003) attributed better outcomes to different organizational factors. Additionally, a variety of configurations (e.g., K-8, 4-5, 5-6, 6-12) still exist for young adolescent education. Even so, the importance of school as a context for young adolescent development is clear (Roeser, Eccles, & Sameroff, 2000). School counselors that serve young adolescents have the opportunity to utilize systems in the school (e.g., teaching teams) and have the responsibility to create developmentally responsive practices to promote optimal student development and achievement.

As young adolescence presents many developmental challenges, it also tends to challenge their families and those school professionals who work with them. Middle school counselors have the unique opportunity to implement comprehensive counseling programs with a focus on young adolescent development within a responsive ecology.

ACKNOWLEDGMENT

An earlier version of this chapter appeared in the journal of *Professional School Counseling*, *9*(2), 95-103. *PSC* has granted permission to reprint this chapter with minor modifications.

REFERENCES

Akos, P. (2002). Student perceptions of the transition from elementary to middle school. *Professional School Counseling, 5*, 339-345.

Akos, P. (2003, March/April). Facilitating successful transitions to middle school: Comprehensive programming for school counselors. *ASCA School Counselor, 40*(4), 14-18.

Akos, P. (2006). Extracurricular participation and the transition to middle school. *Research in Middle Level Education*, 29(9), http://www.nmsa.org/Publications/RMLEOnline/Articles/Vol29No9/tabid/804/Default.aspx.

Akos, P., & Galassi, J. (2004). Middle and high school transitions as viewed by students, parents, and teachers. *Professional School Counseling*, 7, 212-221.

Akos, P., Konold, T., & Niles, S. (2004). A career readiness typology and typal membership in middle school. *The Career Development Quarterly, 53*, 53-66.

Akos, P., & Levitt, D. (2002) Promoting healthy body image in middle school. *Professional School Counseling, 6*, 138-144.

American School Counselor Association. (2003). *The ASCA national model: A framework for school counseling programs.* Alexandria, VA: Author.

Benson, P. (2003). Developmental assets and asset-building community: Conceptual and empirical foundations. In R. Lerner & P. Benson (Eds.), *Developmental assets and asst building communities: Implications for research, policy, and practice* (pp. 19-43). Norwell, MA: Kluwer.

Bergmann, S. (2001). Comprehensive guidance and support. In T. Erb (Ed.), *This we believe ... and now we must act* (pp. 108-115).Westerville, OH: National Middle School Association.

Bronfrenbrenner, U. (1979). *The ecology of human development: Experiments by nature and design*. Cambridge, MA: Harvard University Press.

Brown, K., Roney, K., & Anfara, V. A., Jr. (2003). Organizational health directly influences student performance at the middle level. *Middle School Journal, 34*(5), 5-15.

Campbell, C., & Dahir, C. (1997). *Sharing the vision: The national standards for school counseling programs.* Alexandria, VA: American School Counselor Association.

Carnegie Council on Adolescent Development. (1989). *Turning points: Preparing American youth for the 21st century: The report of the Task Force on Education of Young Adolescents.* Washington, DC: Author.

Cobb, N. (2001). *Adolescence: Continuity, change, and diversity* (4th ed.). Mountain View, CA: Mayfield.

Cuban, L. (1992). What happens to reforms that last? The case of the junior high school. *American Educational Research Journal, 29*, 227-251.

Davis, K., & Lambie, G. (2005). Family engagement: A collaborative systemic approach for middle school counselors. *Professional School Counseling, 9*(2), 144-151.

Davis, D., & Thompson, S. (2005). Creating high-performing middle schools in segregated settings: 50 years after Brown. *Middle School Journal, 36*(2), 4-12.

Dickinson, T., & Erb, T. (1997). *Teaming in middle schools: We gain more that we give*. Columbus, OH: National Middle School Association.

Eccles, J. (1999). The development of children ages 6 to 14. *The Future of Children, 9*, 30-44.

Eccles, J., & Templeton, J. (2002). Extracurricular and other after-school activities for youth. *Review of Research in Education, 26*, 113-180.

Erb, T., & Doda, N. (1989). *Team organization: Promise—Practices and possibilities*. Washington, DC: National Education Association.

Farber, P. (1998, March/April). Small schools work best for disadvantaged students. *The Harvard Education Letter*, 6-8.

Felner, R., Jackson, A., Kasak, D., Mulhull, P., Brand, S., & Flowers, N. (1997). The impact of school reform for the middle years: Longitudinal study of a network engaged in Turning Points-based comprehensive school transition. *Phi Delta Kappan, 78*, 528-532.

Fenzel, M. (1991, April). *A prospective study of the relationships among role strain, self-esteem, competence and social support in early adolescence.* Paper presented at the biennial meeting of the Society for Research in Child Development. Seattle, WA.

Freud, A. (1969). Adolescence as a developmental disturbance. In G. Caplan & S. Lebovici (Eds.), *Adolescence* (pp. 5-10). New York: Basic Books.

Galassi, J., & Akos, P. (2004). Developmental advocacy: Twenty-first century school counseling. *Journal of Counseling & Development, 82,* 146-157.

Galassi, J., Gulledge, S., & Cox, N. (1998). *Advisory: Definitions, descriptions, decisions, directions.* Westerville, OH: NMSA.

Holcomb-McCoy, C. (2005). Ethnic identity development in early adolescence: Implications and recommendations for middle school counselors. *Professional School Counseling, 9*(2), 120-127.

Jackson, A., & Davis, G. (2000). *Turning points 2000: Educating adolescents in the 21st century.* New York: Teachers College Press.

Keys, S., & Lockhart, E. (1999). The school counselor's role in facilitating multisystemic change. *Professional School Counseling, 3*, 101-107.

Lapan, R., Kardash, C., & Turner, S. (2002). Empowering students to become self-regulated learners. *Professional School Counseling, 5*, 257-265.

Lerner, R., Lerner, J., Almerigi, J., Theokas, C., Phelps, E., Gestsdottir, S., et al. (2005). Positive youth development, participation in community youth development programs, and community contributions of fifth-grade adolescents: Findings from the first wave of the 4-H study of positive youth development. *Journal of Early Adolescence, 25*, 17-71.

Lounsbury, J., & Vars, G. (2003). The future of middle level education: Optimistic and pessimistic views. *Middle School Journal, 35*(2), 20-38.

Mac Iver, D. (1990). Meeting the needs of young adolescents: Advisory groups, interdisciplinary teaching teams, and school transition programs. *Phi Delta Kappan, 71*, 458-464.

Mahoney, J., Cairns, B., & Farmer, T. (2003). Promoting interpersonal competence and educational success through extracurricular participation. *Journal of Educational Psychology, 95*, 409-418.

Murdock, T., & Miller, A. (2003). Teachers as sources of middle school students' motivational identity: Variable-centered and person-centered analytic approaches. *The Elementary School Journal, 103*(4), 383-399.

National Middle School Association. (1982). *This we believe.* Columbus, OH: Author.

National Middle School Association. (1995). *This we believe: Developmentally response middle schools.* Columbus, OH: Author.

National Middle School Association. (2003). *This we believe: Successful schools for young adolescents.* Westerville, OH: Author.

Pounder, D. (1998). *Restructuring schools for collaboration: Promises and pitfalls.* Albany: State University of New York Press.

Pruitt, D. (2000). *Your adolescent: Emotional, behavioral, and cognitive development from early adolescence through the teen years.* Washington, DC: American Academy of Child and Adolescent Psychiatry.

Roeser, R., Eccles, J., & Sameroff, A. (2000). School as a context of early adolescents' academic and social-emotional development: A summary of the research findings. *The Elementary School Journal, 100*, 443-471.

Rottier, J. (2000). Teaming in middle school: Improve it or lose it. *Clearing House, 73*, 214-216.

Schumacher, D. (1998). *The transition to middle school.* Office of Educational Research and Improvement (ED). Washington, DC. (Eric Document Reproduction Service No. ED422119)

Scales, P. (2005). Developmental assets and the middle school counselor. *Professional School Counseling, 9*(2), 104-111.

Sink, C. (2005). Fostering academic development and learning: Implications and recommendations for middle school counselors. *Professional School Counseling, 9*(2), 128-135.

St. Clair, K. (1989). Middle school counseling research: A resource for school counselors. *Elementary School Guidance & Counseling, 23*, 219-225.

Theokas, C., Almerigi, J., Lerner, R., Dowling, E., Benson, P., Scales, P., et al. (2005). Conceptualizing and modeling individual and ecological asset components of thriving in early adolescence. *Journal of Early Adolescence, 25*, 113-143.

Trusty, J., Niles, S., & Carney, J. (2005). Education-career planning and middle school counselors. *Professional School Counseling, 9*(2), 136-144.

U.S. Department of Education. (2001). No Child Left Behind Act (Pub. L. No. 107-110). Retrieved June 6, 2004, from http://www.ed.gov/nclb/overview/intro/index.html

Valentine, J., Clark, D., Hackmann, D., & Petzo. (2003). *A national study of leadership in middle level schools: Vol. I. A national study of middle level leaders and school programs.* Reston, VA: National Association of Secondary School Principals.

Whiston, S., & Sexton, T. (1998). A review of school counseling outcome research: Implications for practice. *Journal of Counseling & Development, 76*, 412-426.

Wiesner, M., & Ittle, A. (2002). Relations of pubertal timing and depressive symptoms to substance use in early adolescence. *Journal of Early Adolescence,* 22, 5-23.

Wigfield, A., Lutz, S., & Wagner, A. (2005). Early adolescents' development across the middle school years: Implications for school counselors. *Professional School Counseling, 9*(2), 112-119.

Yecke, C. (2003). *The war on excellence: The rising tide of mediocrity in America's middle schools*. Westport, CT: Praeger.

Zirkel, S. (2002). Is there a place for me? Role models and academic identity among White students and students of color. *Teachers College Record, 104*, 357-376.

CHAPTER 10

ALIGNING STUDENT SELF AND IDENTITY CONCERNS WITH MIDDLE SCHOOL PRACTICES

Thomas M. Brinthaupt, Richard P. Lipka, and Monica A. Wallace

ABSTRACT

There are good arguments to be made that middle level schooling is an especially important time for aligning student self and identity characteristics with school practices. In this chapter, we review and critically analyze the research literature relevant to this issue. We first define the self and identity issues that are most salient to young adolescents. Then, we summarize current middle level practices and how they relate to these issues. We also examine the extent to which developmentally appropriate practices, in-school and out-of-school programs, and characteristics and qualities of teachers, administrators, and support staff align with the self and identity needs of young adolescents.

At every level of education, there is a need to match the characteristics of students with the practices of their teachers and schools. Of course, students are faced with increasingly complex learning materials as they move through their schooling. From preschool, to elementary school, to middle

The Young Adolescent and the Middle School
pp. 201–218

school, to high school and college, they also need to learn new routines, study skills, and how to best manage their time and behavior. At the same time, social, cognitive, and developmental changes require that school practices at all levels must adapt to keep pace with students. There are good arguments to be made that, when it comes to self and identity issues, middle level schooling is the most important, volatile and difficult time for matching student characteristics with school practices.

In this chapter, we review those arguments by examining what research says about how the most prominent self and identity concerns of middle school students are aligned with the practices of their schools. We first provide a concise overview of the major definitional, conceptual, and developmental issues pertaining to self and identity among young adolescents. Next, we summarize current middle level practices and how they facilitate and inhibit these issues.

In the third section of the chapter, we highlight developmentally appropriate practices that are sensitive to and build upon the self and identity issues of middle school students. Next, we present an overview of research on successful in-school and out-of-school programs that attend to self and identity issues with this age group. Finally, the characteristics and qualities of teachers, administrators, and support staff that are essential for working effectively with young adolescents are described. As complicated as the alignment of student concerns with middle school practices is, we hope to demonstrate the value for educators in focusing on this process.

YOUNG ADOLESCENT SELF AND IDENTITY: AN OVERVIEW

As many reviewers have noted, young adolescence is a time of frequent biological, social, and cognitive changes (e.g., American Psychological Association, 2002; Brinthaupt & Lipka, 2002; Graber, Brooks-Gunn, & Petersen, 1996; Montemayor, Adams, & Gullotta, 1990). The impact of these changes on young adolescent self and identity has also been well-documented (e.g., DuBois & Hirsch, 2000; Harter, 1999; Rosenberg, 1986). In this section of the chapter, we will highlight these changes and their potential effects on the young adolescent's emerging sense of self and identity.

First, it is necessary to define briefly what we mean by "self" and "identity." These terms are frequently used synonymously. However, there are important distinctions to be made between them. Part of the difference between self and identity can be seen by examining specific disciplinary emphases. For example, the identity concept is used more often by developmental psychologists and sociologists. This reflects a greater interest in the overall coherence of one's self-views or in the acquisition of specific roles that constitute identity. Alternatively, self and the various self-related processes are used more by social and personality psychologists as well as by educational researchers. This emphasis reflects a greater interest in the specific processes associated with self-conception and self-evaluation.

As the psychologist Baumeister (1998) noted, "self is not really a single topic at all, but rather an aggregate of loosely related subtopics" (p. 681). There are several dozen distinct self-related topics that psychological and educational researchers have studied (Leary & Tangney, 2003). A few of these topics that are relevant to the young adolescent include the ideal self, self-awareness, self-esteem, and self-concept. In an effort to capture this definitional complexity, Hoyle, Kernis, Leary, and Baldwin (1999) defined the self as "an interactive, self-regulating *system* of self-referent thoughts, feelings, and motives" (p. 11).

A useful way to consider the self and self-related processes is the distinction proposed by Beane and Lipka (1980) between self-concept and self-esteem. Self-concept typically refers to how people conceive of or describe themselves. Self-esteem, on the other hand, typically refers to the evaluation of one's self-attributes or self-descriptions. For example, middle school students can feel positively or negatively about themselves regardless of how they conceive of or describe their major self-attributes (see also Calhoun & Morse, 1977). This distinction implies that one of the goals of middle level educators might be to help students achieve self-concept clarity (i.e., understand who they are) and develop positive self-esteem (i.e., feel good or better about who they are).

Identity is frequently defined in terms of people's subjective experiences of themselves or the specific ways that they select, define, and think about themselves (Hoyle et al., 1999). Individuals' overall identity is likely to consist of a variety of social identities, such as those based on gender, race, ethnicity, culture, or country of origin (e.g., Crain, 1996). In addition, overall identity consists of a variety of personal identities, such as those based on values, traits, and unique characteristics. Researchers have shown that the incongruity between middle school students' identity characteristics and the social and economic characteristics of their schools plays an important role in affecting self-esteem levels (Rhodes, Roffman, Reddy, & Fredriksen, 2004).

The formation of a coherent sense of identity generally does not occur until older adolescence or young adulthood (Erikson, 1959, 1968). However, self-related processes appear quite early in life (Lewis, 1990), and they play an important role in directing identity formation in young and older adolescence. The young adolescents who populate our middle schools can thus be thought of as discovering and learning to use self-related processes at the same time that they are starting to define their unique identities (e.g., Carlson, Uppal, & Prosser, 2000). Parents, peers, and teachers all serve as significant others who guide these children during this vulnerable period. Because of that interplay of self and identity, we will focus on both concepts in this chapter.

As we noted earlier, there is a broad range of self-related changes that apply to the young adolescent (Brinthaupt & Lipka, 2002). The physical changes that occur at this time mean that the body unavoidably intrudes into the child's self and identity. Research shows that global self-esteem is most strongly related to self-evaluations of physical appearance regardless of age (Harter, 1993). Physical development can therefore affect young adolescents' levels of comfort with their bodies. The fact that there are large individual differences in the timing of puberty compounds the effects of these physical changes on self and identity (e.g., Brooks-Gunn & Graber, 1999; Simmons & Blyth, 1987).

With regard to cognitive changes, young adolescence is a period when greater real and ideal self-discrepancies emerge (Shirk & Renouf, 1992). In part, these discrepancies arise because children develop a more differentiated self-view, and they are able to be more realistic in their self-assessments. This developmental period is also characterized by a greater internalization of self-related components (Rosenberg, 1986). In particular, young adolescents come to realize that there are private parts of their selves (such as traits and attitudes) that others cannot see and potentially cannot know. At the same time, the development of self-esteem can take several possible trajectories as students pass through adolescence, with some showing consistently high, consistently low, or progressively rising or falling levels of self-esteem (Hirsch & DuBois, 1991; Zimmerman, Copeland, Shope, & Dielman, 1997).

As children enter young adolescence, the social and interpersonal domains also become increasingly important. There is greater independence from parents, and peer relations take on greater importance and intensity, especially in terms of how children determine their personal competence and self-worth (Harter, 1999). Combined with their increasing introspection and other newly developed cognitive capacities, young adolescents begin to think about and interact with peers and adults in new, tentative, and often risky ways (American Psychological Association, 2002).

As these various self-components develop, young adolescents must learn to understand them and to integrate them into a more cohesive sense of identity. As we noted earlier, by older adolescence and young adulthood, identity tends to stabilize. The developmental sequence of growth, change, and general lack of stability among young adolescents illustrates why middle level educators and institutions can have a particularly significant impact on their students. To what extent do middle level practices acknowledge and address that impact?

CURRENT MIDDLE LEVEL PRACTICES

In terms of clear self-concept and positive self-esteem, the issue is not middle school practices; rather it is fidelity of implementation of middle school practices (see Beane & Lipka, 2006). In large measure, current middle level practices are doing a disservice to our middle school students, their teachers, their parents, and the community at large. Many middle school students find themselves in very large classes nested in very large schools. For more than 30 years (e.g., Finn & Achilles, 1990; Glass & Smith, 1979), we have known that classes that exceed 15-17 students for every one teacher risk having an environment of increasing alienation and decreasing achievement.

For about half as long (e.g., Cotton, 1996), we have been aware of the curvilinear relationship between school size and positive outcomes in both the cognitive and affective domains. Evidence suggests that middle schools of about 400 students seem to maximize student outcomes. However, this seems to be the case only to the extent that middle school teachers concentrate on task mastery as opposed to the normative approach of comparing a students' growth to that of other students. As so aptly stated by Roeser, Eccles, and Sameroff (2000), "when adolescents perceived an emphasis on comparison, competition, and differentiated treatment by teachers based on gender or race, they were more likely to withdraw or act out in school" (p. 464).

Another current practice (or at least a stance of tacit approval on the part of middle level educators) is allowing parents to drift out of the equation. For as yet unexplained reasons, the transition from elementary school to middle school seems to coincide with decreasing parental involvement in the lives of their children as students. Epstein (2001) has spent much of her professional life empirically demonstrating the power of parental and community involvement in the lives of successful students and effective schools. While not politically popular in some quarters, it does indeed take a village to raise a child.

One should not leave the discussion of current practices without addressing the issue of "high stakes" testing (Lipka, 2005). Our middle school students, teachers, and "ideal" middle level practices are being sacrificed upon the altar of high stakes testing. Developmental psychologists in general, and Paris, Lawton, Turner, and Roth (1991) in particular, have addressed the impact of high stakes testing upon the developmental stage of young adolescence. Young children believe their own personal efforts count for the success they have in school. However, as young children grow and develop in a school environment characterized by high stakes testing, they become young adolescents who feel that when "external forces such as test scores rather than their own efforts control success, they show less interest in academic work, demonstrate less persistence, and are more inclined to take shortcuts or adopt maladaptive strategies" (Paris et al., 1991, p.14).

In short, there is a large gap between current practices and the sets of principles and practices that are best for our middle level students and educators, exemplified by such thoughtful works as *Turning Points: Preparing American Youth for the 21st Century* (Carnegie Council on Adolescent Development, 1989) and *This We Believe: Successful Schools for Young Adolescents* (National Middle School Association, 2003).

DEVELOPMENTALLY APPROPRIATE PRACTICES

Developmentally appropriate, academically rigorous, integrated, and appropriate assessments are among the components of "reformed" middle level curricula described in the literature (e.g., Beane, 1991; Carnegie Council on Adolescent Development, 1989; National Middle School Association, 2003; Williams-Boyd, 2005). A developmentally appropriate curriculum capitalizes on the unique developmental period of young adolescence rather than ignoring, fearing, or utilizing stereotypes (e.g., a period of "raging hormones") to initiate demeaning or restrictive practices (Beane, 1991). For example, schools might promote a focus away from physical appearance and onto other domains that can contribute to positive self-esteem, such as academic or athletic successes (Striegel-Moore & Cachelin, 1999).

An academically rigorous curriculum includes both core classes (e.g., math, literature, science) and extended curricular activities that are relevant both to the adolescent's emerging self and cultural context (National Middle School Association, 2003). An integrated curriculum captures student interest and motivation by using themes that evolve from student questions as a connecting point for developing and using skills from various subject areas (Beane, 1991, Williams-Boyd, 2005). Appropriate assessments are conceptualized as tools for learning that include both formative and summative evaluations (National Middle School Association).

Developmentally appropriate middle level practices that support the needs and emerging competencies of young adolescents initiate such practices as student advisory programs, cooperative learning opportunities, positive school climate, curriculum relevance, and student choice (Lee, 2002). Developmentally appropriate practices are sensitive to the adolescent's view that fitting in with the peer group and valuing and working toward academic achievement are incongruent. For example, young adolescents tend to value ability more than effort (Paris et al., 1991). This way of thinking coupled with the ever expanding arena of high stakes testing in Grades 5-8 can lead to unintended consequences. If standardized test scores are interpreted as being representative of inherent ability, this can undermine the motivation to work hard (Wheelock, 1998). If test scores are used to group students according to ability, this type of separation and labeling can negatively impact achievement motivation and identity formation. If the self at school becomes reduced to a standing on a test, students may internalize an inflexible, static view regarding their status as a learner. Not only does this set the stage for an unproductive self-fulfilling prophecy, it reinforces the belief that effort and persistence do not matter. These unproductive values may transcend the classroom if they become incorporated into the young adolescent's self-concept.

Of great importance to young adolescents are questions of identity. Questions about physical changes, relationships with peers and adults, one's place in the world, and global issues (e.g., poverty, racism, and wealth distribution) help shape what adolescents are interested in and how they see the world. According to Beane (1991), connecting young adolescents' self concerns with larger scale world issues allows for the possibility of a truly integrated curriculum. This combination of self and world concerns provides the foundation for rich themes to emerge that have relevance to young and older adolescents instead of curriculum being structured around isolated subject areas that have little inherent meaning.

When students make their own connections in a concept-oriented, skills-based, curriculum, necessary problem solving, critical thinking and application skills develop further (Williams-Boyd, 2005). These skills are useful beyond the classroom and provide a link between schooling and life. Making this link becomes especially important when trying to convince an ever-growing number of young adolescents that have decided whether they will drop out of school by the eighth grade that schooling has meaning for them (Jackson & Davis, 2000).

Service learning is a specific teaching methodology that can bridge the gap between classroom learning, issues of concern to the middle level student, and the outside world. As Hope (1999) notes, service learning supports civic responsibility, personal development and academic achievement through such activities as volunteering, tutoring, and cleanup projects. A richer knowledge base is developed through authentic learning experiences. A deeper understanding of self as a community member becomes a possibility. Consistent with a constructivist approach, service learning provides an even broader landscape for students to make observations, test hypotheses and develop conclusions about the world and themselves.

Service learning also provides the community an opportunity to relate positively to middle level youth. This may lead to a breaking down of stereotypes when students have the opportunity to have genuine interactions with people who are often different from themselves. Community members may gain a better understanding of the schools' efforts to offer students an education that will lead to responsible citizenship. In this way, a student's sense of self and possibility can be enhanced by experiencing a broader world than the classroom or home environment might allow.

A developmentally appropriate, integrated curriculum can exist within a culture of rigorous academic standards and appropriate assessments. Wheelock (1998) suggests that in creating a culture of high standards, we need to rethink how we define being smart. Smart does not mean a student earned a certain grade or scored at a particular percentile rank on a standardized test. Smart does not mean that a student answered correctly or quickly the first time. It means that students take risks, make mistakes, and ask for help. Implementing high standards means helping students improve their work quality on a daily basis. The view of one's self as a student is therefore evolving rather that a static state tied to grades or test scores.

Unfortunately, high standards are usually defined as every student being able to meet a common set of minimum standards irrespective of individual differences. As Vars (2001) argues, we communicate to students that diversity should be valued, yet our one-size-fits-all expectations ignore individual learning differences. For those students who do not meet the cut scores on standardized tests, the impact on self-concept and self-esteem may initiate a spiral of continued academic failure. If children get the message that they do not have the basic skills after having ample years of schooling, this may be internalized as "why bother?" and thus impede academic motivation.

A more equitable alternative would be to develop a culture of student engagement (Vars, 2001). Rather than focusing on the products of student work, the process of learning should be more highly valued than the results. Students who are engaged, contribute to and add meaning to their own learning and function as a partner in the broader educational system. This supports the development of self-efficacy.

Formative assessment is consistent with the idea that the process of learning should be valued. Assessment for learning or formative assessment results in higher student achievement (National Middle School Association, 2003). The fear of not making the grade or feeling stupid is replaced with an atmosphere of comfortable, meaningful feedback that is informative to both students and teachers. The potential negative impact of assessment on the student's self-esteem and motivation is replaced with information that guides continued progress.

Vars (2001) acknowledged the right of educational stakeholders to have a voice in what students should know. Goals are not considered unimportant; however, students should have the opportunity to suggest creative and multiple ways that goals could be met. Vars also notes that it is possible for students and teachers to cooperatively plan meaningful learning activities that address and monitor mandated goals. Thus, summative assessments, while important, should not be the singular criterion whereby students' achievement is measured or their academic progress labeled.

IN-SCHOOL AND OUT-OF-SCHOOL INTERVENTION PROGRAMS

There is a long history of efforts to address self and identity issues in public education. As Beane (1994) documented, this history is characterized by shifting priorities and frequent controversies. Because young adolescence is a time of multiple changes in self and identity, in-school and out-of-school interventions have been developed to facilitate positive outcomes among middle school students. Researchers and practitioners have proposed and studied a large number of self- and identity-related programs targeting young adolescents.

There is a good deal of evidence that participation in school- and community-based activities is associated with greater academic achievement, self-esteem, health, and resilience (for a review, see American Youth Policy Forum, 2003). As Barber, Stone, and Eccles (2005) noted, participation in organized extracurricular activities gives students the chance to clarify their self-conceptions and develop their identities. Such activities also can increase student understanding of and commitment to the goals and values of their schools. Dow Velarde, Starling, and Wallerstein (2002) described a young adolescent social action program for high-risk students that reduces alcohol and drug use while fostering their development as social change agents. An essential feature of this program is the opportunity for participants to develop and clarify their own identities by reducing internal conflicts and insecurities and increasing self-efficacy.

Youth development programs for adolescents tend to be community-based and focus on increasing students' knowledge, competencies, and self-efficacy across multiple domains, typically including but not restricted to self and identity issues. Roth and Brooks-Gunn (2003) noted that prototypical youth development programs have both approach and avoidance components. On the approach side are efforts that build student skills, abilities, and competencies through supportive environments and role modeling. On the avoidance side are efforts to teach students what kinds of behaviors are bad for their health and how to decrease the frequency of such behaviors. In their review, Roth, Brooks-Gunn, Murray, and Foster (1998) found that the most effective programs were more comprehensive, fostered positive relationships with peers and adult significant others, and engaged students throughout their adolescence.

In a comprehensive review of young adolescent self-esteem enhancement interventions, DuBois, Burk-Braxton, and Tevendale (2002) acknowledged that such efforts have been met with a good deal of controversy and skepticism. They note, however, that there are significant subgroups of children who develop low self-esteem or who are in other ways at risk. According to DuBois et al., programs that directly target these at-risk groups have been successful at increasing self-esteem. Interestingly, young adolescents report desiring esteem-enhancing programs that possess the kinds of positive characteristics we discussed earlier (DuBois, Lockerd, Reach, & Parra, 2003). Another review of the effects of esteem-enhancement programs (Baumeister, Campbell, Krueger, & Vohs, 2003) questioned the effectiveness of such approaches as well as raised several theoretical and methodological concerns about their design and implementation.

Of course, there are many differences between in-school or out-of-school esteem-enhancement programs and how well the self and identity concerns of young adolescents are aligned with the general and specific practices of their teachers and schools. Whether it is better to devote effort, time, and expense to implementing esteem-enhancement programs or to develop school-wide practices that recognize and acknowledge the self and identity concerns of young adolescents is still an open question. However, logically, if schools already addressed not only self-esteem but also other self-concept and identity issues, then enhancement programs would be less necessary. In the next section of the chapter, we examine what characteristics and qualities are best suited to accomplishing this alignment.

CHARACTERISTICS AND QUALITIES OF TEACHERS, ADMINISTRATORS, AND SUPPORT STAFF

In an earlier time and venue, when our country had a sense of humor and saw good in the world, Beane and Lipka (1987/2000) referred to effective middle school administrators as "con artists for kids." They were referring to administrators who realized that the educational system was not necessarily geared for the developmental needs/characteristics of the young adolescent and thus did what they could to neutralize the negative effects of the system. Furthermore, these administrators were fully cognizant of the fact that the primary reward system for middle school teachers resides in their relationships with their students. To that end, these administrators expend their energy to secure the resources (including much needed time) that will assist teachers in strengthening these relationships.

Given our present political climate, we would add a new label to our middle school administrators—that of practitioner-scholar. In addition to a solid knowledge base regarding young adolescents, these individuals must also value and be skilled at the collection, analysis, and interpretation of empirical data. Doing what's best for the students (and teachers) will require solid evidence to counter the inflammatory rhetoric such as *Mayhem in the Middle* (Yecke & Finn, 2005) that populates the media and serves as the drumbeat for those individuals intent on destroying confidence in public education. In our view, Anfara (2005) was wise to cite Daresh and Playko (1992) who stated "it takes hard work to learn the art, science, and craft of educational administration, and it takes a similar amount of hard work to keep the needed leadership skills well tuned over time" (p. ix).

Of all the personnel in schools, teachers are in the best position to encourage clear self-concept and positive self-esteem. They have the persistent, day-to-day contact that makes it possible for them to become a "significant other" in the lives of the young adolescent. Research shows that a strong, positive attachment to an adult, such as a teacher, is associated with more favorable development, self-esteem, and greater resilience among adolescents (Ryan, Stiller, & Lynch, 1994; Roth et al., 1998).

In addressing effective teachers, Hamachek (1999) made a strong case for the concept of "emotional intelligence." That is to say, teachers must make every effort to develop and hone self-awareness, mood management, self-motivation, empathy, and relationship skills. Teachers who focus upon their emotional development and who have a clear sense of their professional self will be characterized by the following behavioral descriptions (Lipka, 1997, pp. 36-37):

1. They are inclined to combine a warm and friendly attitude with firm, but reasonable, expectations.
2. They project an enthusiasm for their work that lends excitement to their teaching.
3. They are by no means perfect, in the sense of doing and saying just the right thing at all times. (This has less to do with something that teachers consciously do, and more to do, perhaps, with the wide latitude of teacher imperfections which students can live with as long as the core person is basically fair and decent.)

4. Intellectually, they are thoroughly grounded in their subject area, which, by virtue of a broad base of interests, they are able to connect to related areas of knowledge.
5. They are ready to assume responsibility for student outcomes, which they reflect in their efforts to make sure that all students have a chance to learn.
6. They make a point to know their students as individuals and to respond to them as individuals; they go beyond simply seeing them as "students."
7. They provide definite study guidelines; they are as interested in getting their students prepared to know as they are in evaluating what they know.
8. They are able to challenge without being offensive and to encourage without being condescending; more importantly, they challenge when that is appropriate and they encourage when that is needed. Neither behavior is indiscriminately practiced.
9. They give feedback that is personalized, an effect that makes the feedback more believable and powerful.
10. They take time to reflect about their work, their students, and themselves as teachers; they are, in a word, thoughtful.
11. They work on developing a positive rapport that serves as the interpersonal medium within which high, but reasonable, expectations and constructive, critical feedback can be transmitted.
12. They are able to be flexibly adaptive in terms of using direct or indirect methods of teaching to meet various students' abilities and needs.

As Roeser and Lau (2002) noted, teachers with these characteristics create the classroom contexts that encourage young adolescents to fulfill their psychological needs in healthy, growth-oriented ways. Agne (1999) pulled a number of these characteristics into a construct called: "Caring: The Leavening Agent." She argued that even a small amount of caring on the part of an effective teacher can cause the expansion of caring in the students who are exposed to it. When the caring beliefs and resultant behaviors are modeled by teachers in a persistent way, they have the ability to be absorbed by the students. The students in turn adopt caring beliefs and the resultant behaviors, and they model these to all those with which they have contact in school (and hopefully outside the school as well!). Perhaps the most powerful metaphor here is that our middle level students are the actors in the play and not the audience. Our job as teachers is to actively engage the students, thus lending credence to the constructivist view of learning and the need for hands-on activities across the curriculum. Research shows that to the extent students see their schools as a source of safety and security and to the extent that students perceive their teachers as fair, more positive self and identity development is likely (Resnick et al., 1997).

As we stated earlier, it does indeed take a village to raise a child. Within the school setting, this points to the importance of those individuals fulfilling the roles of school counselor and school social worker. Lipka, Beane, and Ludewig (1980) found that young adolescents never mentioned guidance counselors as "significant others" in their lives. Reasons for this ranged from having no counselors in their school setting to counselors who had quasi-administrative roles (e.g., functioning as attendance officers).

Counselors should be important for a number of reasons. First, most counselors know how to gather and interpret self-perception data and how to recognize self-image problems as they arise in students. These are skills not generally found in middle level teacher education programs. Secondly, counselors could work directly with students in at least two ways. They could initiate group sessions on the personal needs shared by this age group. They could and should also have a larger voice in the advisory programs found in middle schools. Advisory time is not a free time period; rather it is an opportunity for young adolescents to express their views regarding their personal and social needs inside and outside the school setting.

School social workers could well serve as the narrow part of the hourglass between the in-school services and the myriad of out-of-school services whose mission is to improve the well-being of students and their families. Most teachers have their social worker experience limited to public law 94-142 involving educational planning for special needs students. It is not unusual for the lack of understanding of the profession's responsibilities to lead to an adversarial relationship and create less than productive cooperation between the educational and social service systems. Yet there is abundant evidence (e.g., Brabeck, Walsh, & Latta, 2003; Calfee, Wittwer, & Meredith, 1998; Dryfoos, 1994; Dryfoos & Maguire, 2002) that the concept of the full service school pays attention to the multiple variables that are related to school success. And, in many instances, it is the school social worker who integrates the educational, medical, and social services necessary to meet the needs of adolescents and their families.

CONCLUSION

We began this chapter by arguing that aligning young adolescent self and identity concerns with middle level practices is an important and worthwhile goal for teachers and administrators. At each level of consideration, we have tried to demonstrate why such a goal is beneficial for students. Unfortunately, current middle level practices often come up short in meeting this goal. As we have shown, there is no shortage of developmentally appropriate practices, in-school and out-of-school programs, and facilitative school characteristics that can address young adolescent self and identity concerns. The issue remains how best to utilize these positive practices.

Perhaps we are indeed rowing against a swift current. But we are firmly convinced that a boat that has its oars held by motivated students, effective teachers, skilled administrators, counselors, social workers, and concerned helpful parents has a chance to successfully navigate the rapids of inequity and poverty we find in the river called America today.

Cognitive learning is hard won by someone whose life is in affective disarray. To ignore affective development (including the aspects of self and identity that are associated with this development) in the name of academic achievement leaves us with young people who are unsure of themselves and their futures. They will lack the strength of self and the morally-centered identity to guide their decision-making and behavior. Simply put, if we do not address the lower-order needs of young adolescents, we cannot be successful at meeting their higher-order needs.

REFERENCES

Agne, K. J. (1999). Caring: The way of a master teacher. In R. P. Lipka & T. M. Brinthaupt (Eds.), *The role of self in teacher development* (pp. 165-188). Albany: State University of New York Press.

American Psychological Association. (2002). *Developing adolescents: A reference for professionals.* Washington, DC: Author.

American Youth Policy Forum. (2003). *Finding fortune in thirteen out-of-school time programs.* Washington, DC: Author.

Anfara, V. A., Jr. (2005). Administrators: Middle level principals. In V. A. Anfara, Jr., G. Andrews, & S. B. Mertens (Eds.), *The encyclopedia of middle grades education* (pp. 103-106). Greenwich, CT: Information Age Publishing.

Barber, B. L., Stone, M. R., & Eccles, J. S. (2005). Adolescent participation in organized activities. In K. A. Moore & L. H. Lippman (Eds.), *What do children need to flourish: Conceptualizing and measuring indicators of positive development* (pp. 133-146). New York: Springer.

Baumeister, R. F. (1998). The self. In D. T. Gilbert, S. T. Fiske, & G. Lindsey (Eds.), *The handbook of social psychology* (pp. 680-740). New York: Oxford University Press.

Baumeister, R. F., Campbell, J. D., Krueger, J. I., & Vohs, K. D. (2003). Does high self-esteem cause better performance, interpersonal success, happiness, or healthier lifestyles? *Psychological Science in the Public Interest, 4*(1), 1-44.

Beane, J. A. (1991). Integrated curriculum in the middle school. *Educational Leadership, 49*(2), 9-13.

Beane, J. A. (1994). Cluttered terrain: The schools' interest in the self. In T. M. Brinthaupt & R. P. Lipka (Eds.), *Changing the self: Philosophies, techniques, and experiences* (pp. 69-87). Albany: State University of New York Press.

Beane, J. A., & Lipka, R. P. (1980). Self-concept and self-esteem: A construct differentiation. *Child Study Journal, 10*(1), 1-6.

Beane J. A., & Lipka, R. P. (1987, 2000). *When the kids come first: Enhancing self-esteem*. Troy, NY: Educators' International Press.

Beane, J. A., & Lipka, R. P. (2006). Guess again: Will changing the grades save middle school education? *Educational Leadership, 63*(7), 26-30.

Brabeck, M. M., Walsh, M. E., & Latta, R. E. (Eds.). (2003). *Meeting at the hyphen: Schools-universities-communities-professions in collaboration for student achievement and well being*. The 102nd yearbook of the National Society for the Study of Education. Chicago: National Society for the Study of Education.

Brinthaupt, T. M., & Lipka, R. P. (2002). Understanding early adolescent self and identity: An introduction. In T. M. Brinthaupt & R. P. Lipka (Eds.), *Understanding early adolescent self and identity: Applications and interventions* (pp. 1-21). Albany: State University of New York Press.

Brooks-Gunn, J., & Graber, J. A. (1999). What's sex got to do with it? The development of sexual identities during adolescent. In R. J. Contrada & R. D. Ashmore (Eds.), *Self, social identity, and physical health: Interdisciplinary explorations* (pp. 155-182). New York: Oxford University Press.

Calfee, C., Wittwer, F., & Meredith, M. C. (1998). *Building a full-service school: A step by step guide*. San Francisco: Jossey-Bass.

Calhoon, G., & Morse, W. C. (1977). Self-concept and self-esteem: Another perspective. *Psychology in the Schools, 14*(3), 318-322.

Carlson, C., Uppal, S., & Prosser, E. C. (2000). Ethnic differences in processes contributing to the self-esteem of early adolescent girls. *Journal of Early Adolescence, 20*(1), 44-67.

Carnegie Council on Adolescent Development. (1989). *Turning points: Preparing American youth for the 21st century.* New York: Carnegie Corporation of New York.

Cotton, K. (1996). *School size, school climate, and student performance.* (School Improvement Research Series, close-up #2) Portland, OR: Northwest Educational Regional Lab.

Crain, R. M. (1996). The influence of age, race, and gender on child and adolescent multidimensional self-concept. In B. A. Bracken (Ed.), *Handbook of self-concept: Developmental, social, and clinical considerations* (pp. 395-420). New York: Wiley.

Daresh, J., & Playko, M. (1992). *The professional development of school administrators: Preservice induction, and inservice applications*. Boston, MA: Allyn & Bacon.

Dow Velarde, L., Starling, R. G., & Wallerstein, N. B. (2002). Identity in early adolescence via social change activities: Experience of the Adolescent Social Action Program. In T. M. Brinthaupt & R. P. Lipka (Eds.), *Understanding early adolescent self and identity: Applications and interventions* (pp. 267-291). Albany: State University of New York Press.

Dryfoos, J. (1994). *Full-service schools: A revolution in health and social services for children, youth, and families*. San Francisco: Jossey-Bass.

Dryfoos, J., & Maguire, S. (2002). *Inside full-service community schools*. Thousand Oaks, CA: Corwin.

DuBois, D. L., Burk-Braxton, C., & Tevendale, H. D. (2002). Esteem-enhancement interventions during early adolescence. In T. M. Brinthaupt & R. P. Lipka (Eds.), *Understanding early adolescent self and identity: Applications and interventions* (pp. 321-371). Albany: State University of New York Press.

DuBois, D. L., & Hirsch, B. J. (2000). Self-esteem in early adolescence: From stock character to marquee attraction. *Journal of Early Adolescence, 20*(1), 5-11.

DuBois, D. L., Lockerd, E. M., Reach, K., & Parra, G. R. (2003). Effective strategies for esteem-enhancement: What do young adolescents have to say? *Journal of Early Adolescence, 23*(4), 405-434.

Epstein, J. L. (2001). *School, family and community partnerships: Preparing educators and improving schools*. Boulder, CO: Westview.

Erikson, E. H. (1959). *Identity and the life cycle*. New York: International Universities Press.

Erikson, E. H. (1968). *Identity: Youth and crisis*. New York: W. W. Norton.

Finn, J. D., & Achilles, C. M. (1990) Answers and questions about class size: A statewide experiment. *American Educational Research Journal, 27*(3), 557-577.

Glass, G. V., & Smith, M. L. (1979) Meta-analysis of research in class size and achievement. *Educational Evaluation and Policy Analysis, 1*(1), 2-16.

Graber, J. A., Brooks-Gunn, J., & Petersen, A. C. (Eds.). (1996). *Transitions through adolescence: Interpersonal domains and context*. Mahwah, NJ: Erlbaum.

Hamachek, D. (1999) Effective teachers: What they do, how they do it, and the importance of self-knowledge. In R. P. Lipka & T. M. Brinthaupt (Eds.), *The role of self in teacher development* (pp. 189-224). Albany.: State University of New York Press.

Harter. S. (1993). Causes and consequences of low self-esteem in children and adolescents. In R. F. Baumeister (Ed.), *Self-esteem: The puzzle of low self-regard* (pp. 87-116). New York: Plenum Press.

Harter, S. (1999). *The construction of the self: A developmental perspective*. New York: Guilford Press.

Hirsch, B. J., & DuBois, D. L. (1991). Self-esteem in early adolescence: The identification and prediction of contrasting longitudinal trajectories. *Journal of Youth and Adolescence, 20*(1), 53-72.

Hope, W. C. (1999). Service learning: A reform initiative for middle-level curriculum. *Clearing House,* 72(2), 236-238.

Hoyle, R. H., Kernis, M. H., Leary, M. R., & Baldwin, M. W. (1999). *Selfhood: Identity, esteem, regulation*. Boulder, CO: Westview Press.

Jackson, A. W., & Davis, G. A. (2000). *Turning points 2000: Educating adolescents in the 21st century*. New York & Westerville, OH: Teachers College Press & National Middle School Association.

Leary, M. R., & Tangney, J. P. (2003). The self as an organizing construct in the behavioral and social sciences. In M. R. Leary & J. P. Tangney (Eds.), *Handbook of self and identity* (pp. 3-14). New York: The Guilford Press.

Lee, M. M. (2002). Revisiting developmentally appropriate middle schools. *Educational Leadership, 78*(4), 225-27.

Lewis, M. (1990). Self-knowledge and social development in early life. In L. A. Pervin (Ed.), *Handbook of personality: Theory and research* (pp. 277-300). New York: The Guildford Press.

Lipka, R. P. (1997). Enhancing self-concept/self-esteem in young adolescents. In J. L. Irvin (Ed.), *What current research says to the middle level practitioner* (pp. 31-39). Columbus, OH: National Middle School Association.

Lipka, R. P. (2005). Testing: High stakes. In V. A. Anfara, Jr., G. Andrews, & S. B. Mertens (Eds.), *The encyclopedia of middle grade education* (pp. 370-372). Greenwich, CT: Information Age Publishing.

Lipka, R. P., Beane, J. A., & Ludewig, J. W. (1980, March). *Self concept/self-esteem and the curriculum.* Paper presented at the Annual Conference on the Association for Supervision and Curriculum Development, Atlanta, GA.

Montemayor, R., Adams, G. R., & Gullotta, T. P. (Eds.). (1990). *From childhood to adolescence: A transitional period?* Thousand Oaks, CA: Sage.

National Middle School Association. (2003). *This we believe: Successful schools for young adolescents*. Westerville, OH: Author.

Paris, S. G., Lawton, T. A., Turner, J. C., & Roth, J. L. (1991). A developmental perspective on standardized achievement testing. *Educational Researcher, 20*(5), 15-20.

Resnick, M. D., Bearman, P. S., Blum, W., Bauman, K. E., Harris, K. M., Jones, J., et al. (1997). Protecting adolescents from harm: Finding from the National Longitudinal Study on Adolescent Health. *Journal of the American Medical Association, 278*(10), 828-832.

Rhodes, J., Roffman, J., Reddy, R., & Fredriksen, K. (2004). Changes in self-esteem during the middle school years: A latent growth curve study of individual and contextual influences. *Journal of School Psychology, 42*(3), 243-261.

Roeser, R. W., Eccles, J. S., & Sameroff, A. J. (2000). School as a context of early adolescents' academic and social-emotional development: A summary of research findings. *The Elementary School Journal, 100*(5), 443-471.

Roeser, R. W., & Lau, S. (2002). On academic identity formation in middle school setting during early adolescence: A motivational-contextual perspective. In T. M. Brinthaupt & R. P. Lipka (Eds.), *Understanding early adolescent self and identity: Applications and interventions* (pp. 91-131). Albany: State University of New York Press.

Rosenberg, M. (1986). Self-concept from middle childhood through adolescence. In J. Suls & A. G. Greenwald (Eds.), *Psychological perspectives on the self* (Vol. 3, pp. 107-135). Hillsdale, NJ: Erlbaum.

Roth, J. L., & Brooks-Gunn, J. (2003). What exactly is a youth development program? Answers from research and practice. *Applied Developmental Science*, 7(2), 94-111.

Roth, J., Brooks-Gunn, J., Murray, L., & Foster, W. (1998). Promoting healthy adolescents: Synthesis of youth development program evaluations. *Journal of Research on Adolescence, 8*(4), 423-459.

Ryan, R. M., Stiller, J. D., & Lynch, J. H. (1994). Representations of relationships to teachers, parents, and friends as predictors of academic achievement and self-esteem. *Journal of Early Adolescence, 14*(2), 226-249.

Shirk, S. R., & Renouf, A. G. (1992). The tasks of self-development in middle childhood and early adolescence. In R. P. Lipka & T. M. Brinthaupt (Eds.), *Self-perspectives across the lifespan* (pp. 53-90). Albany: State University of New York Press.

Simmons, R. J., & Blyth, D. A. (1987). *Moving into adolescence: The impact of pubertal change and school context.* Hawthorne, NY: Aldine de Gruyter.

Striegel-Moore, R. H., & Cachelin, F. M. (1999). Body image concerns and disordered eating in adolescent girls: Risk and protective factors. In N. G. Johnson, M. C. Roberts, & J. Worrell (Eds.), *Beyond appearance: A new look at adolescent girls* (pp. 85-108). Washington, DC: American Psychological Association.

Vars, G. F. (2001). On standards, standardization, and student engagement. *Focus on middle school (ages 11-13): A quarterly newsletter for the education community.* (ERIC Document Reproduction Service No. ED456296).

Wheelock, A. (1998). *Safe to be smart: Building a culture for standards-based reform in the middle grades.* Westerville, OH: National Middle School Association.

Williams-Boyd, P. (2005). Middle schools that make a difference. *Childhood Education, 81*(5), 278-280.

Yecke, C. P., & Finn, C. E., Jr. (2005). *Mayhem in the middle: How middle schools have failed America—and how to make them work.* Washington, DC: Thomas B. Fordham Institute.

Zimmerman, M. A., Copeland, L. A., Shope, J. T., & Dielman, T. E. (1997). A longitudinal study of self-esteem: Implications for adolescent development. *Journal of Youth and Adolescence, 26*(2), 117-141.

CHAPTER 11

RECOGNIZING AND RESPONDING TO YOUNG ADOLESCENTS' ETHNIC IDENTITY DEVELOPMENT

Dave F. Brown and Heather L. Leaman

ABSTRACT

In this chapter, the authors present theories and research that describe how ethnically diverse adolescents' search for identity is influenced by the majority culture, school experiences, and their own ethnic backgrounds. The authors also provide a rationale for and strategies that middle level educators can use to help ethnically diverse adolescents develop a healthy identity. Three models of ethnic identity development exist that students of color and immigrant students may experience during adolescence. Diverse adolescents' ability to develop a healthy identity may be particularly affected by circumstances within their schools as they often experience prejudice and racism of which teachers may be unaware. Teachers must develop an awareness of the challenges that ethnically diverse students face, use strategies to recognize and honor their diverse students' ethnic heritage, and address prejudice and racism that occur in school.

The Young Adolescent and the Middle School
pp. 219–235

> Generations of children are disenfranchised because the relationship between their ethnic background, cultural histories, and knowledge of their human developmental process has not been adequately addressed. (Sheets, 2005, p. 52)

The middle school years are a time when young adolescents experience many developmental changes including noticeable physical changes and the hidden, less explicit social, emotional, and cognitive changes. Among the many changes they experience, young adolescents frequently struggle with choosing who they want to be, how they want to act, and what persona they want to project to those around them—collectively known as components of *identity development*. Developing an identity involves a series of decision-making opportunities that young adolescents find themselves constantly analyzing (Rice & Dolgin, 2005). Cognitive growth during young adolescence provides students with a heightened sensitivity of self and realization of the opportunity to choose new personality traits (Erikson, 1968). Adolescents have choices in their identity development in several areas; choosing an ethnic identity, however, is rarely, if ever, an opportunity—especially for students of color.

Ethnically diverse adolescents experience entirely different identity challenges of which majority Whites, including middle level educators, may be unaware. The entire identity development process creates many dilemmas for ethnically diverse youth throughout adolescence that Whites never experience. Students of color and immigrant youth frequently experience prejudice and racism in and out of school. Opportunities to discuss these sensitive issues can be beneficial to their healthy identity development. Middle level educators are responsible for recognizing their ethnically diverse students' identity needs through personal awareness, attention to, and cultivation of a positive personal ethnic identity.

CULTURAL AND ETHNIC STAGES OF IDENTITY DEVELOPMENT

> The process of identity formation is a particularly complex one for immigrant youth who must navigate various and often competing messages regarding identity. (Lee, 2005, p. 1)

The development of a healthy ethnic identity is an inherent need for humans. Many African, Native, and Hispanic American as well as various Asian American students struggle with their identity development during middle school years because they must develop a personal identity that recognizes that they are not White, European Americans (Gay, 1994; Howard, 1999; Ogbu, 1991). During the middle school years, ethnic minorities and immigrant students often realize a conflict between their family ethnic culture and the values of those other families from the communities in which they live (Rice & Dolgin, 2005). Young adolescents' responses to these differences in values define the stages of ethnic identity development they may be experiencing. Ethnically diverse adolescents who do not become comfortable with their ethnic identity have lower self-esteem (Phinney, 1992).

Ethnic Identity Development Stages

Gay (1994) presented the following stages of ethnic identity development for students of color:

- *Identity diffusion*—described as minimal exploration of ethnicity.
- *Foreclosure*—no exploration of ethnic identity. Ethnicity is instead defined by others.
- *Moratorium*—a time when students actively explore their ethnicity.
- *Achievement*—the development of an ethnic identity.

Gay's stage theory mirrors that of Marcia's (1980) general theory of identity development in which he proposed four stages for all youth: identity diffusion, identity foreclosure, moratorium, and identity achievement. Gay emphasized (1994) that students of color must experience a dual process of self-identification that Marcia described and a separate cultural identification. Culturally and ethnically different students may experience feelings of frustration during the moratorium (active exploration) period based on the discrepancies they note between their lives and those of the majority White European American culture.

Racial Identity Development Stages

> Non-White immigrant youth discover that they must negotiate their identities within a racial hierarchy where Whites are positioned at the top. Furthermore, they learn that there is a stigma attached to being non-White and immigrant (Lee, 2005, p. 2).

Cross (1991) established a five-stage theory of Black racial identity development that includes: (1) preencounter, (2) encounter, (3) immersion/emersion, (4) internalization, and (5) internalization/commitment. The *preencounter* stage is "an attempt by African Americans to distance themselves from their own racial identity" (Howard,1999, p. 86). This stage mirrors the foreclosure stage mentioned by Gay (1994).

Once an African American experiences racist comments or notices being treated differently due to color, she/he may be moving into the encounter stage—a phase in which students of color begin to notice that race, alone, can lead to negative treatment. Cross's final three stages represent African Americans' personal examination of their ethnicity, a realization of how their ethnicity and skin color impacts their lives, followed by the final stage of accepting their ethnicity and demonstrating ethnic pride. Students of color may not experience the final stages of ethnic identity development until well into their 20s.

Cross's immersion and internalization stages are similar to Gay's (1994) moratorium period, as African, Native, Asian, and Hispanic Americans begin to process their place in society based on their ethnicity and culture. The extent of young adolescents' ethnic identification development is based on their personal experiences which include developing cognitive awareness, daily social circumstances, and diversity of their home/school cultural environment.

General Ethnic Identity Development Stages

Tse (1999), in studying the ethnic identities of Asian American youth, described a general model of ethnic identity development for all culturally and ethnically diverse youth who progress through four general stages:

1. Ethnic unawareness—little, if any, awareness of ethnic differences during early childhood.
2. Ethnic ambivalence—occurs during late childhood and young adolescence characterized by an avoidance of recognition of personal ethnic differences.
3. Ethnic emergence—students begin to experiment with other ethnic identities, and also begin to accept their ethnicity.
4. Ethnic identity incorporation—diverse youth accept their differences and seek additional information about their ethnicity.

Cross's (1991) cultural identification preencounter stage and Tse's (1999) ethnic ambivalence stage are likely to occur during middle school due to the heightened social awareness that young adolescents experience. Quintana (1998) noted that middle level students begin to develop a social perspective of identity in which they begin to realize that their ethnicity affects social relations and begin to recognize discrimination and prejudice.

FACTORS AFFECTING ETHNIC IDENTITY DEVELOPMENT

Messages that students of color receive about their identity may originate via institutions like schools through tracking students by ability or busing students to schools in other neighborhoods. Young adolescents are likely to identify racism through social events that occur such as reactions by teachers or parents of interracial dating or racist remarks from other students. Media images, both positive and negative, may have the greatest influence on ethnically diverse young adolescents' perceptions about others' attitudes concerning them.

Additionally, students' communities and school demographics may also influence their attitudes concerning their identity. For instance, students of color who attend schools in which most share their ethnicity are likely to experience a smoother transition in moving through the acceptance stages of their ethnicity (Brown, 2005; Comer, 1993; Dreyer, Jennings, Johnson, & Evans, 1994). Brown discovered that immigrant eighth graders who attended a middle school with a majority of students who were also immigrant youth held more favorable beliefs about their ethnicity than immigrant students from a majority White school.

When ethnically diverse youth choose to identify with only the culture of the dominant group, the result is called *assimilation* in which students ignore their ethnic culture. *Separation* occurs when youth choose to ignore the majority culture and focus only on the values of their ethnic group. Ethnically diverse youth who are able to establish positive connections to both their families' cultural expectations and the White European American majority culture establish *integration*, that is, strong identification and comfort with both groups (Rice & Dolgin, 2005).

Phinney and Devich-Navarro (1997) revised the description of *integrated* ethnically diverse youth and chose the term, *blended biculturalism* to describe students who are able to identify commonalities between their ethnic culture and the dominant culture and act congruently with both cultures. African and Mexican American students who successfully navigated blended biculturalism were comfortable with their families' cultural heritage and had positive regard for people of other ethnic groups (Phinney & Devich-Navarro).

Educators can explicitly address the challenges that ethnically diverse youth experience at school in their efforts to reach integration. Adams and Palijan (2004) described the significance of focusing on ethnic identity development issues at school: "Numerous researchers have reported that among minority youth, ethnic identity is associated with improvement in self-esteem, academic achievement, and psychosocial adjustment" (p. 241). Those students who find that they are not comfortable fitting in with the majority group have the potential to develop *oppositional* identity.

The Development of Oppositional Identity

The behaviors of African, Hispanic, and Asian American students during the immersion/emersion stage may lead to what Ogbu (1991) described as *oppositional identity*. Students who experience oppositional identity develop unique social behaviors that ignore traditional and popular European American behaviors and attitudes. Finn (1999) further described oppositional identity: "Members of the oppressed group come to regard certain beliefs, skills, tastes, values, attitudes, and behaviors as not appropriate for them because they are associated with the dominant culture" (p. 42). Students who develop oppositional identity do not believe that schooling or any other social organization or governmental assistance will alter their economically deficient life circumstances due to their belief that they are being oppressed by the majority culture (Finn). If middle school students are aware of their families' negative concerns regarding the value of education, these young adolescents will develop identities and attitudes that reject the vision of educational success as defined by the structure of American schooling.

The identity development of culturally and ethnically different students, particularly during the middle school years, is fraught with the possibility of students acquiring negative attitudes toward schooling and teachers—particularly if their caregivers reinforce negative attitudes toward the dominant culture. Many times, school policies, teachers, and fellow students create an atmosphere of racism that further hinders the possibility of healthy identity development and blended biculturalism for ethnically diverse students.

The Inadequacy of Racial and Ethnic Labels

> I am the product of two great cultures—one African American and the other Asian. On my father's side I am African American. On my mother's side I am Thai. Truthfully, I feel very fortunate, and *equally proud*, to be both African American and Asian! (Tiger Woods, cited in Singleton & Linton, 2006, p. 168)

What label do Americans use to describe Tiger Woods's ethnicity? Think of the outdated use of the term *race* and its danger in describing many of our students. Race is a socially constructed term not based on biology, but on the hope for some to preserve the higher status frequently associated with being light skinned (Lee, 2005; Waters, 1999). The continued use of *race* is damaging for all societies for many reasons; but particularly destructive for educators. For instance, what labels would one use to describe children of these parents: a White European American mother and a Puerto Rican father; how about a Peruvian father and a Cuban mother; an African American mother and Native American father; or a Mexican mother with a Irish father (Brown & Knowles, 2007)?

Schools are often the most guilty of using racial categories which occurs when students scratch their heads trying to determine just what they are as they pencil-in the racial label allegedly describing them at the top of standardized tests. Categorizing students by race for testing purposes is required by the policies associated with the No Child Left Behind legislation (U.S. Department of Education, 2001), but those ethnic and racial designations do nothing to help students or teachers.

Teachers must recognize that labels such as *Hispanic*, *Latino*, or *Chicano*; *Native American* or *First Nation Peoples*; and *Asian American* are much too broad and inaccurate to define the different characteristics and needs of the many ethnically diverse young adolescents who have been entering America's schools in large numbers since the 1980s (Brown, 2002). Does Hispanic mean that this young adolescent's family is from Mexico, Puerto Rico, Spain, the Dominican Republic, Bolivia, or Guatemala? There are significant differences in behaviors, attitudes, culture, and customs of families from each of these countries. As well, ethnically diverse immigrant students bring with them a multitude of academic backgrounds based on the schooling they received in their native land.

Asian immigrants include students from China, Vietnam, Laos, India, Pakistan, Russia, or South Korea. Perhaps a student who has the appearance of an Asian immigrant is actually a fifth generation American whose family has lived in the school district for over 100 years. Consider this student's academic capabilities compared to her recent immigrant peers. A teacher cannot know where her students are from or understand their ethnic as well as cultural backgrounds based only on students' appearances. Yet, some teachers may make assumptions based on students' skin color or perceived socioeconomic levels.

Tuan (1998), for instance, discovered in interviews with multiple generation Asian Americans that they were identified as perpetual foreigners without being recognized solely as Americans. Rong and Preissle (1998) reported, "Despite the academic success of some, many Asian American students continue to experience feelings of inferiority, alienation, and social isolation in school" (p. 146). Lee (2005) noted that Hmong immigrant students were treated differently by teachers than other Asian Americans (Japanese or Chinese) due to their darker skin. As well, Lee asserted that the way students are treated by their teachers is often dependent on their socioeconomic status in the community noting that higher middle class immigrants generally receive more recognition, respect, and attention than working class immigrants or students of color. These levels of acceptance can also exist for Hispanic immigrants based on skin color and socioeconomic level. Many teachers may make generalizations about their students based on their students' physical traits—generalizations that prevent them from developing caring relationships that are essential for meaningful learning experiences to occur (Goodman, Sutton, & Harkevy, 1995). Many teachers believe that their primary responsibility with ethnically diverse youth is to "Americanize" immigrant students so that they become just like White European American students (Olneck, 2004).

TEACHERS' RESPONSIBILITIES FOR STUDENTS' HEALTHY ETHNIC IDENTITY DEVELOPMENT

Teachers' Understanding of Cultural Responsiveness

Much of the research concerning White teachers' attitudes and efforts to understand their ethnically diverse students' needs reflects that they know little about the cultural or ethnic histories of their students of color. As well, teachers often attribute students' academic difficulties to their own backgrounds (Goodwin, 2002; Kailin, 1999; Lee, 2005; Nieto, 2000). A principal in a Wisconsin school asserted that many teachers in the building didn't know how to work with diverse populations of students and were disinterested in learning about their needs (Lee). This particular school has a considerable population of Hmong and African American students who began entering the school district only over the past 8-10 years, and were looked on by teachers as lowering the school's academic standards.

Brown (2005) conducted interviews with 15 students who immigrated from nine separate countries to two mid-Atlantic middle schools. These students admitted that the only recognition of their ethnic identity in three years of attending middle school occurred once when one of the schools held a multicultural day to honor their cultures during their sixth grade year. All of the students stated that most teachers never asked about or recognized their ethnic backgrounds. Students in a rural mid-Atlantic middle school reported teachers' similar disregard for cultural and ethnic diversity (Leaman, Bullock, Freedman, & Wilt, 2005). In a survey of 231 seventh graders, students stated that teachers rarely discussed issues of diversity and often dismissed prejudiced remarks overheard between students. Several students from the Leaman et al. study also revealed that many of their peers were struggling with racism. Other students noted that teachers were unaware of racial conflicts among students.

The Significance of Recognizing Students' Ethnicity

It is not uncommon for some teachers to proclaim, "I treat all students the same regardless of their backgrounds or skin color." This statement reveals educators' ignorance about ethnically diverse students' need for recognition, the personal challenges they may experience due to their differences, potential difficulties they experience with other students in the school, as well as the importance of responding to their learning profiles affected by their ethnicity and culture. White European American teachers comprise approximately 88 percent of all teachers in America; therefore, the majority of educators may have serious information deficits concerning their students' ethnic and cultural experiences (Ladson-Billings, 2001). White teachers, as well, are often unaware of their own ethnic and cultural perspectives that influence their instructional processes, expectations for behavior, and relationships with students. These unintended cultural biases must be identified and addressed before teachers can hope to assist their ethnically diverse students. Ethnic and racial issues are almost always sensitive issues; but an avoidance of them by teachers sustains the status quo for many diverse young adolescents at school who experience confusion and frustration from faculty unwilling to address students' daily concerns.

School faculties who are committed to addressing the needs of their diverse students begin by reserving time for discussions among themselves about their attitudes toward ethnically diverse students and the teaching practices that result from these possible unrecognized behaviors. Singleton and Linton (2006) explained the challenges associated with initiating honest dialogue among faculty about racial and ethnic concerns: "Educators typically have not examined and discussed race in their schools because they have feared not knowing how to go about this process correctly" (p. 21). Face-to-face conversations and a reading of current literature on cultural responsiveness have the potential to encourage faculty to recognize how their perspectives on learning are also influenced by a cultural bias that may ignore their diverse students' needs. Once faculty have the opportunity to address their attitudes and admit possible biases, specific action plans must be developed that provide teachers with strategies for seeking more information about their diverse students.

Opportunities to Recognize and Honor Students' Ethnicity

Educators can better understand ethnically diverse students by initiating processes to learn more about their lives. Outreach actions should occur in which faculty visit students' neighborhoods, meet students' caregivers in their communities, and engage in conversations with diverse community members. Through these visitations, teachers can determine caregivers' perspectives on how the school can address their children's needs.

One-on-one friendly conversations with students are needed to gain information from them about their families and about their specific learning needs. Middle level teachers who genuinely care about their students take the time to observe, listen to conversations, and specifically inquire about students' academic needs and their social situations at school.

Middle school faculty might find it beneficial to develop a survey instrument for students that provides them with an opportunity to describe how they are treated by peers, teachers, and others in the school. Results from the survey can be used to alter specific policies, enforce school expectations for tolerance, and create opportunities for ethnically diverse students to share their cultural heritage with others in the school. The emphasis of these actions should be on recognition and honoring students' diverse backgrounds.

Sheets (1999) reported that a group of at-risk ninth graders from a variety of ethnic backgrounds showed higher levels of competence in their academics and social skills following the completion of a program to promote ethnic identity development (cited in Adams & Palijan, 2004). Other researchers (Davalos, Chavez, & Guardiola, 1999) discovered that "Mexican American students who reported high ethnic identity levels were more likely to stay in school and to have more positive perceptions of school than were students with lower ethnic identity levels" (cited in Adams & Palijan, p. 245).

Exploratory Studies

Middle schools can enhance student identity development through the implementation of exploratory studies. Stevenson (1998) described *exploratory studies* as "projects in which pairs or small groups of students actually 'explore' a topic that interests them and embodies legitimate intellectual substance" (p. 191). Two intended purposes of exploratories are to provide students with opportunities to develop socially and to pursue a variety of personal cognitive interests that may coincide with traditional curricula or stretch beyond the boundaries of required curricula. Some middle schools offer exploratories as separately designed mini-classes, service clubs, special interest activities, or as learning experiences which may occur outside of school (Forte & Schuurr, 2002). Teachers guide students through exploratory studies by helping them locate resources, analyze data, and reflect on the significance of their learning through frequent student conferences.

Stevenson (1998) believes that much of the curriculum for middle level students should be exploratory rather than dominated by traditional direct instructional processes. Exploratories can be specifically designed to give students a chance to examine issues of ethnicity and diversity personally, among the student body, and throughout the community. Middle schools can offer a diversity club for students interesting in studying their own and others' ethnicity.

Students can also engage in service learning as a part of exploratory activities with the surrounding community to identify issues of concern to local residents. Service learning experiences can be used to explore personal questions of ethnic history through student designed surveys and interviews conducted with local residents. These positive connections to the community may help students see ethnically diverse adults in different roles. Students may also invite diverse community members into the classroom to address oppositional identity issues among students who demonstrate frustration with schooling with similar ethnic backgrounds. These same community members can become teacher aids who provide assistance and encouragement to frustrated students.

Advisory Programs

Advisory programs provide a comfortable environment for middle school teachers to assist ethnically diverse students in facing identity development challenges. Sessions are organized into 15-to-45 minute time periods offered one-to-three times a week. Middle school teachers are assigned approximately 15 students as their advisory group. Because of the limited number of students, teachers are able to develop a close relationship with each student and provide individualized attention when a student needs it. Advisories provide students with opportunities to ask questions about personal issues such as peer pressure, bullying, developing friendships, prejudice, racism, and other personal interest topics that affect their identity development (Galassi, Gulledge, & Cox, 1998). These sessions allow teachers to develop genuine relationships with students in which they learn about students' nonacademic interests and ethnic backgrounds through informal conversations.

Advisories provide an appropriate forum to discuss how ethnically diverse students are being treated by others and to address the challenges they may experience. Students can initiate discussions about diversity during advisory periods that may otherwise be avoided by teachers who may feel uncomfortable talking about cultures other than their own. Advisories also provide additional time and opportunities to discuss these sensitive issues for those teachers who may think that the school's content standards aren't designed to cover issues of racism and prejudice. Finally, the small number of students in each advisor's classroom may create a more comfortable environment for students to express their views on these possible controversial issues.

Curricular Connections to Ethnic Identity Issues

> The curriculum lets students know whether the knowledge they and their communities value has prestige within the educational establishment. (Nieto, 2000, p. 96)

Perhaps the most powerful method of insuring that students engage in conversations about issues of ethnic identity development is the inclusion of identity issues in schools' curricula. Beane (1993) suggested that the development of the middle school curriculum should always be based on students' questions about themselves and the world around them. Called *curriculum integration*, this student-driven study insures that the developmental concerns of students will be an integral aspect of their studies throughout the year. Middle level students who choose the topics they want to study frequently ask questions about how they fit into the world around them (Brown & Knowles, 2007).

Many of the topics that occur naturally in middle schools' social studies and literature curricula address issues of cultural diversity. Issues of prejudice and racism are common themes throughout history and are also reflected in daily national and international events. Teachers who take the time to address these issues with young adolescents provide them with the opportunity to reflect on and demonstrate their own concerns about how they are treated by others in school and in the community. Teachers are ultimately responsible for engaging students in meaningful learning experiences. Educators are then responsible for initiating frequent conversations about ethnicity and culture since ethnic development is such an integral aspect of young adolescent development.

Classroom teachers should also identify opportunities within the existing curricula to connect learning in all subject areas to the ethnic lives of their students. Lee (2005) noted that at a high school where many

Hmong immigrant students were attending, "the largely Eurocentric curriculum tells Hmong American students that they are not important, and it also tells them that Whiteness is central to being American" (p. 35). Teachers can use curriculum to help students understand how other people from different cultures and ethnicities throughout history have been oppressed, how these circumstances may mirror their lives, and how groups can gain authority and respect.

Students should be invited to evaluate curricular materials for their inclusion and accurate portrayal of ethnic diversity in both images and text. Teachers can display and use text and media images of ethnically diverse people, incorporate stories of diverse people in the traditional curriculum, and encourage discussion of how media images and traditional school curricula portray ethnic diversity.

With an awareness of the needs of ethnically diverse adolescents, teachers can learn to be cognizant of the messages they are sending students either by inclusion or omission of their cultural heritage in their teaching and interaction with students. Teachers can also assist students who are displaying oppositional identity. They can find other students who share similar ethnic and cultural backgrounds to become role models and mentors for their peers, and they can invite community members from similar cultural and ethnic backgrounds to become class assistants. Such adjustments to classroom interaction with students and an attention to including the multiple perspectives of diverse people can help ethnically diverse adolescents develop healthy identities.

Research on Effective Teacher Intervention Strategies

Stephan (1999) provided a summary of the research on ethnic awareness instructional strategies that appear to positively impact students' attitudes and beliefs on ethnic diversity. Effective activities used include the following:

- stressing positive similarities among groups;
- learning about the norms, roles, and values of other groups;
- dividing students into arbitrary groups and having them experience discrimination on the basis of this arbitrary distinction;
- writing essays supporting increased opportunities for minority groups;
- acting out cases of discrimination that can occur in school settings;
- role playing being a member of another group; and

- keeping journals related to intergroup relations (adapted from p. 60).

Students placed in mixed ethnic cooperative learning groups also develop positive attitudes toward each other as a result of interacting with one another in academic situations. Davidson and Davidson (1994) noted the following as valuable activities for encouraging moral growth among students on the issues surrounding cultural differences:

- describing social practices in different groups and noting the similar values underlying them;
- creating booklets of family history or maps of family origins;
- arranging visits to the class by representatives of the various groups; and
- role playing or brief dramas using racial or ethnic themes (cited in Stephan, 1999, p. 66).

Some secondary schools begin by teaching the Holocaust experiences to students as a strategy for sensitizing students to the mistreatment of Jews during World War II, and to connect students to the central issues related to protection of all citizens and their civil liberties (Fine, 1993).

Learning experiences are affected by students' emotions, and young adolescents' emotional behaviors are connected to the way they are treated by both peers and teachers. Finding and implementing both affective and academic strategies to genuinely connect to ethnically diverse students is a primary responsibility for middle level teachers.

CONCLUSION

The National Middle School Association (2003) in its most recently revised edition of *This We Believe* noted that "successful schools for young adolescents provide multiple learning and teaching approaches that respond to their diversity" (p. 7). This proclamation places the responsibility for the healthy ethnic identity development of young adolescents squarely on the shoulders of middle school teachers. Successfully meeting the affective needs of ethnically diverse young adolescents is an ever present need of many schools with the recent onset of an increase in the immigrant population in American schools (Brown, 2002). Young adolescent intellectual growth leads to middle school students asking insightful and meaningful questions through their own curiosity about how their lives are affected by their ethnicity.

Middle level principals must insist on encouraging teachers to design experiences and school structures that provide young adolescents with opportunities they need to examine their own ethnic and cultural experiences. Middle level teachers must be knowledgeable of and willing to implement activities that engage students in the necessary experiences to explore, question, discuss, and identify healthy components of ethnic identity.

REFERENCES

Adams, G. R., & Palijan, S. (2004). The "identity-education" link: Six themes in an educational setting that influence adolescent identity development and well-being. In T. Urdan & F. Pajares (Eds.), *Educating adolescents: Challenges and strategies: A volume in adolescence and education* (pp. 237-254). Greenwich, CT: Information Age Publishing.

Beane, J. A. (1993). *A middle school curriculum: From rhetoric to reality* (2nd ed.). Columbus, OH: National Middle School Association.

Brown, D. F. (2002). *Becoming a successful urban teacher.* Portsmouth, NH & Westerville, OH: Heinemann & National Middle School Association.

Brown, D. F. (2005). Interviews with immigrant eighth graders on school recognition of their ethnicity. Unpublished raw data.

Brown, D. F., & Knowles, T. (2007). *What every middle school teacher should know* (2nd ed.). Portsmouth, NH & Westerville, OH: Heinemann & National Middle School Association.

Comer, J. (1993, March). *African American parents and child development: An agenda for school success.* Paper presented at the biannual meeting for the Society for Research in Child Development, New Orleans, LA.

Cross, W. E., Jr. (1991). *Shades of black: Diversity in African-American identity.* Philadelphia: Temple University Press.

Davalos, D. B., Chavez, E. L., & Guardiola, R. J. (1999). The effects of extracurricular activity, ethnic identification, and perception of school on student dropout rates. *Hispanic Journal of Behavioral Sciences, 21*(1), 61-77.

Davidson, F. H., & Davidson, M. M. (1994). *Changing childhood prejudice: The caring work of the schools.* Westport, CT: Greenwood Press.

Dreyer, T. H., Jennings, C., Johnson, F., & Evans, D. (1994, April). *Culture and personality in urban schools: Identity status, self-concepts, and loss of control among high school students and monolingual and bilingual homes.* Paper presented at the meeting of the Society for Research on Adolescents, San Diego, CA.

Erikson, E. H. (1968). *Identity: Youth and crisis.* New York: W. W. Norton.

Fine, M. (1993). Collaborative innovations: Documentation of the Facing History and Ourselves program at an essential school. *Teachers College Record, 94*(4), 771-789.

Finn, P. J. (1999). *Literacy with an attitude: Educating working-class children in their own self-interest.* Albany: State University of New York Press.

Forte, I., & Schurr, S. (2002). *The definitive middle school guide* (Rev. ed.). Nashville, TN: Incentive Publications.

Galassi, J. P., Gulledge, S. A., & Cox, N. D. (1998). *Advisory: Definitions, descriptions, decisions, directions.* Columbus, OH: National Middle School Association.

Gay, G. (1994). Coming of age ethnically: Teaching young adolescents of color. *Theory into Practice, 33*(3), 149-155.

Goodman, J. F., Sutton, V., & Harkevy, I. (1995). The effectiveness of family workshops in a middle school setting: Respect and caring make a difference. *Phi Delta Kappan, 76*(9), 694-700.

Goodwin, A. L. (2002). Teacher education and the education of immigrant children. *Education in Urban Society, 34*(2), 156-172.

Howard, G. R. (1999). *We can't teach what we don't know: White teachers, multiracial schools*. New York: Teachers College Press.

Kailin, J. (1999). How White teachers perceive the problem of racism in their schools: A case study in "liberal" Lakeview. *Teachers College Record, 100*(4), 724-750.

Ladson-Billings, G. (2001). *Crossing over to Canaan: The journey of new teachers in diverse classrooms*. San Francisco: Jossey-Bass.

Leaman, H. L., Bullock, P., Freedman, D., & Wilt, B. (2005, November). *Kids should be punished for saying the "N" word: Conversations about race and prejudice in a rural middle school*. Paper presented at the annual conference of the National Middle School Association, Philadelphia, PA.

Lee, S. J. (2005). *Up against Whiteness: Race, school, and immigrant youth*. New York: Teachers College Press.

Marcia, J. (1980). Ego identity development. In J. Adelson (Ed.), *The handbook of adolescent psychology* (pp. 159-187). New York: Wiley.

National Middle School Association. (2003). *This we believe: Successful schools for young adolescents*. Westerville, OH: Author.

Nieto, S. (2000). *Affirming diversity: The sociopolitical context of multicultural education* (3rd ed.). New York: Longman.

Ogbu, J. U. (1991). Cultural diversity and school experience. In C. E. Walsh (Ed.), *Literacy as praxis: Culture, language, and pedagogy* (pp. 25-50). Norwood, NJ: Ablex Publishing.

Olneck, M. (2004). Immigrants and education in the United States. In J. A. Banks & C. A. M. Banks (Eds.), *Handbook of research on multicultural education* (pp. 381-403). New York: Macmillan.

Phinney, J. S. (1992). The multigroup ethnic identity measure. A new scale for use with diverse groups. *Journal of Adolescent Research*, 7(2), 156-172.

Phinney, J. S., & Devich-Navarro, M. (1997). Variations in bicultural identification among African American and Mexican American Adolescents. *Journal of Research on Adolescence*, 7(1), 3-32.

Quintana, S. M. (1998). Children's developmental understanding of ethnicity and race. *Applied and Preventative Psychology*, 7(1), 27-45.

Rice, F. P., & Dolgin, K. G. (2005). *The adolescent: Development, relationships, and culture* (11th ed.). Boston: Pearson, Allyn & Bacon.

Rong, X. L., & Preissle, J. (1998). *Educating immigrant students*. Thousand Oaks, CA: Corwin.

Sheets, R. H. (1999). Racial and ethnic identity in school practices: Aspects of human development. In R. H. Sheets & E. R. Hollins (Eds.), *Relating competence in an urban classroom to ethnic identity development* (pp. 157-178). Mahwah, NJ: Erlbaum.

Sheets, R. H. (2005). *Diversity pedagogy: Examining the role of culture in the teaching-learning process*. Boston: Pearson, Allyn, & Bacon.

Singleton, G. E., & Linton, C. (2006). *Courageous conversations about race*. Thousand Oaks, CA: Corwin.

Stephan, W. (1999). *Reducing prejudice and stereotyping in schools*. New York: Teachers College Press.

Stevenson, C. (1998). *Teaching ten to fourteen year olds* (2nd ed.). New York: Longman.

Tse, L. (1999). Finding a place to be: Ethnic identity exploration of Asian Americans. *Adolescence*, *34* (133), 121-138.

Tuan, M. (1998). *Forever foreigners or honorary Whites? The Asian ethnic experience today*. New Brunswick, NJ: Rutgers University Press.

U.S. Departmentof Education. (2001). *No Child Left Behind Act of 2001*. Retrieved September 10, 2006, from www.ed.gov/policy/elsec/leg/esea02/index.html

Waters, M. (1999). *Black identities: West Indian immigrant dreams and American realities*. Cambridge, MA: Harvard University Press.

CHAPTER 12

A GLIMPSE INTO THE SCHOOL LIVES OF YOUNG ADOLESCENT IMMIGRANT AND REFUGEE STUDENTS

Implications for the Middle Level

David C. Virtue

ABSTRACT

The transitions of young adolescence may be especially difficult for immigrant and refugee students who often learn a new language while they are simultaneously learning academic content and navigating new social and cultural contexts each day in school. This chapter reviews 4 research studies that focus on immigrant and refugee students in middle school settings, and it reframes the discussion of the findings of these studies around implications for middle level schooling. The review calls attention to the diversity that exists across and within immigrant and refugee student groups; it highlights the ways middle school organizational structures and cultural characteristics impact the processes of acculturation and student identity

The Young Adolescent and the Middle School
pp. 237–254

development; and it affirms the importance of strong interpersonal relationships among immigrant students, their families, and their teachers.

> There is no way to keep the old self intact when migrating to a new land. The process of conversion—part acculturation, part maturation—begins in the school these children join upon arrival. Dreams of youth, fashioned in another culture and another time, must be both abandoned and rebuilt as the new American persona emerges. (Llanes, 1997, p. vii)

INTRODUCTION

Middle level educators are called on to create learning environments, curricula, and instructional programs that are responsive to the cultural backgrounds, social contexts, and developmental needs of every young adolescent they serve (Jackson & Davis, 2000; National Middle School Association, 2003). This is a formidable challenge, for young adolescence is a period of great emotional, physical, and intellectual transitions for all young people (Dryfoos, 1990; Santrock, 2005). As one middle school principal stated:

> It's like trying to change a tire on a car that's moving.... We're trying to educate them and prepare them for a lot of things. At the same time they're changing so much. Their personalities and ideas about parents and teachers are going 100 mph. (Patterson, 1995)

While young adolescence is a time of intense and rapid transitions for all middle school students, these transitions may be especially difficult for immigrant and refugee students who are learning a new language and culture (Miller & Endo, 2004; Olsen, 1997; Pryor, 2001). These students are learning to speak and read the English language while they are simultaneously expected to learn social studies, math, and science content and demonstrate progress on state assessments as required by the federal No Child Left Behind Act. In addition to the academic learning that is required, these students must also learn "how to be American middle school students" (Valdés, 1998, p. 5). Valdés captured the totality of the adjustment newcomers make in middle school when she described the experiences of two Latina immigrants.

> They knew little about school spirit. They were not sure why being in a band or in chorus or in the computer club might be important. They frequently confused teachers' friendly demeanor with permissiveness, and they quickly found themselves in trouble. They understood little of what went on around them and they often became discouraged and disinterested. (p. 5)

To what extent are middle schools responsive to the needs of immigrant and refugee students? How well has the middle school community—a community of teachers, researchers, counselors, and other education professionals—responded to the needs of this rapidly growing segment of the school-age population? In 1995, Ada (1995) made the following observation:

> The paucity of literature on the difficulties experienced by immigrant children and the lack of counseling services specifically designed to deal with the traumas of immigration suggest that the general public is either not aware or has little concern for the difficulties of the transition immigrant families experience. (p. vii)

Did Ada's criticisms more than a decade ago hold true for the middle level community, and do they hold true today?

For decades, researchers have focused their attention on immigrant and refugee students. Studies have focused on the processes of acculturation and identity development and the psychological issues associated with these issues, such as acculturative stress (Dana, 1996; Kuo & Roysircar, 2004; Mena, 1987; Miranda & Methany, 2000; Polo, 2002; Roysircar, 2004; Smart & Smart, 1995a, 1995b; Williams & Berry, 1991). However, immigrant and refugee students have only recently begun to gain attention in the practitioner-oriented middle school literature. For example, the authors of *Turning Points: Preparing American Youth for the 21st Century* addressed the issue of "diversity," yet they treated this concept almost exclusively in terms of minority status or race (e.g., Black and White) and not in terms of native language or immigrant status (Carnegie Council on Adolescent Development, 1989, pp. 25-27, 50). In contrast, the authors of *Turning Points 2000* (Jackson & Davis, 2000, pp. 86-87, 92-93, 174-177, 208-209) make frequent references to limited English proficient (LEP) students and they suggest specific interventions to help meet their needs.

An ERIC search of *Middle School Journal* indicated little attention to LEP students or English language learners (ELLs) before the late 1990s. Two articles describing programs for language minority students in middle schools were published in 1997 and 1998 (Borden, 1998; Van Ness & Irvin, 1997), and since then a continuous stream of work featuring effective instructional strategies and special programs for ELLs has been disseminated through *Middle School Journal*.

While the recent attention given to young adolescent ELLs in the middle level literature is much needed and long overdue, the emphasis of this body of work is on second language acquisition and associated implications for instructional design and implementation. This narrow view of immigrant and refugee students tends to reduce the complex processes of acculturation and identity development to English language learning. In reality, positive, productive middle school experiences for immigrant and refugee middle school students involve much more than English language acquisition. They must also address the social and psychological development of the student, while affirming and respecting his or her cultural background.

This chapter attempts to go beyond the narrow view of immigrant and refugee students as "English language learners" by providing a glimpse into the lives of immigrant and refugee students in middle school settings. I focus on four ethnographic accounts of daily life in schools for immigrant and refugee students in the middle grades (Costello-Herrera, 2004; Custodio, 2001; Igoa, 1988, 1995; Meador, 2000; 2005), and I reframe the discussion of the findings of these studies around implications for middle level schooling. Three assumptions drove the selection of studies for the review and, to some extent, my analysis of them.

First, many immigrant and refugee students are at risk of school failure. Drawing on extensive U.S. Department of Education data, Garcia (2001) identified numerous factors that place certain immigrant youth at risk of school failure. He groups these factors into three broad categories. Category I factors relate to personal characteristics of youth, such as language use and proficiency, immigrant status, physical or medical conditions, peer relations, and prior school experiences. Category II factors are conditions in the non-academic environments of home, neighborhood, and community. These factors include poverty level, family structure, parent and sibling educational backgrounds, crime rates, and access to healthcare. Factors related to the conditions that facilitate student learning are Category III factors. These are the institutional and systemic factors that provide "opportunities to learn," such as teacher preparation and working conditions, the curriculum and instructional program in the school, and the physical and organizational structure of the school (Garcia, p. 322). Garcia's list served as a useful framework for this review, as I sought to include studies which illustrate multiple categories of risk factors.

The second assumption is that school-based interventions addressing the psychological and social development of students can help to improve the lives of immigrant youth. While the four studies included in the following review describe the middle school experiences of students who are learning English, the researchers look beyond the process of language acquisition and turn a critical eye toward the complex and multilayered processes of acculturation and identity development. Middle level educators must understand how these processes operate and, importantly, how existing organizational structures, cultural norms, and power relations impact these processes if they are to develop and implement successful interventions.

The third assumption is that context is important. The middle school experiences described in the studies represent the intersection of diverse personalities, communities, cultures, and institutions. As a result, I sought studies that focused on students from a range of backgrounds (e.g., Mexican, Somali, Cambodian, Salvadorian) and that were set in both urban and rural middle schools.

A LOOK INTO THE DAILY LIVES OF IMMIGRANT AND REFUGEE STUDENTS IN MIDDLE SCHOOL

Barriers to Success

Custodio (2001) conducted a qualitative action research study focusing on factors affecting the academic achievement of young adolescent immigrants (n = 90) in an urban middle school in Ohio. The dominant groups represented in her study were Somali (52%) and Cambodian (33%) immigrants. The Somali students came to the United States as refugees. Most of them escaped their war-torn country via Kenya, where it was against the law for them to attend public school. As Custodio recalled, "some of these students came to secondary school in the U. S. having never held a pencil or written their own name" (p. 24). In contrast, most of the Cambodian students were second-generation immigrants who had near native oral English language proficiency, but who had difficulty with reading and/or writing. The other students in her sample came from Latin America, Southeast Asia, and former Yugoslavia, and they possessed varying levels of proficiency in English.

Custodio (2001) reported that instructional decisions in the English as a second language (ESL) program were greatly influenced by two factors: the length of time a student had been in the United States and a students' prior level of and experience with education. While the students in the ESL program varied considerably along these two dimensions, 83% of the Somali students arrived in the United States with less than two years of formal education experience. Custodio described some of the challenges that often overwhelmed teachers in all subject areas during her study.

> Many of the students in this classroom had never spent time in a formal educational setting and needed practice with common school tasks such as using scissors, calculators, rulers, dictionaries, and computers. Classroom behaviors which most children learn in kindergarten such as turn taking and sharing had to be modeled and practiced. Even the practice of needing a hall pass for the drinking fountain or restroom had to be explained and reinforced. (p. 29)

In addition to the difficulties described above, Custodio (2001) noted that many of the ESL students in her study needed the support of special education services. While some of the students were placed in special education programs, many others did not receive services because of parental resistance or because their limited proficiency in English made it very difficult for school psychologists to assess them. Even when students did get access to the special education services they needed, the teachers were often not properly prepared to support English language acquisition or to provide cultural understanding for immigrant and refugee students.

Custodio (2001) is primarily concerned with issues that impacted the academic achievement of students in the ESL program, which she groups into four broad categories: academic, social, physical, and emotional. Academic difficulties were evidenced by low academic achievement, high rates of retention, and poor performance on standardized tests. The daily frustrations experienced by the students as they struggled to learn sometimes led to withdrawal from class activities or socially unacceptable behaviors.

Custodio (2001) described several social factors that had an adverse impact on the academic achievement of the students in her study. Difficulties with cultural adjustments were a persistent problem, and the ESL staff and other school personnel worked hard to help overcome these issues. The magnitude of the cultural adjustments in school was often exacerbated by cultural misunderstandings between home and school. Family background factors were influential, such as parental level of education and the value placed on formal schooling. Many students had to assume adult roles in the household, frequently serving as translators for parents and other family members, a phenomenon known as *language brokering* (see e.g., Tse, 1996; Weisskirch, 2005; Weisskirch & Alva, 2002). In addition, the immigrant students rarely had access to academic support outside of school, as parents often lacked the time and resources to help in significant ways.

Physical health-related issues were found to impact student attendance and time on task. Some immigrant and refugee students arrived in the United States with health-related issues that impacted their academic performance, while other problems resulted from interactions between the students and their families and the health care system. Custodio (2001) summarized the health issues reported by the school nurse:

> Poor family follow-up to referrals for hearing, vision, and dental care … non-compliance to medical treatment for tuberculosis, recurrent cases of head lice, incomplete immunizations, and time-consuming referrals and follow-ups to outside healthcare or social agencies. (p. 221)

Many of the immigrant students had great mental health and emotional needs. Their family lives were often unstable and interrupted by frequent moves and, in some cases, brief stays at homeless shelters. Other conditions included the loss of family members due to war, economics, or social pressures; and the widening generational and cultural gaps between students and their parents and grandparents.

Custodio (2001) also documented and described the design, implementation, and effectiveness of a literature-based curriculum that used historical fiction novels. This program was specially designed to provide students with practical information about American culture and to help ESL students develop reading, writing, and study skills.

QUEST FOR A BETTER LIFE

Costello-Herrera (2004) presented a collective case study of the educational experiences of six Salvadorian immigrant middle school students. The study relied upon a series of semi-structured interviews with each student as well as teacher interviews, informal observations, and analysis of student academic folders.

Costello-Herrera's (2004) analysis was framed by Ogbu's cultural-ecological framework, which posits that the attitudes and behaviors of minority children toward school are shaped by the attitudes and beliefs that the minority community holds about the culture and institutions of the dominant society (Ogbu, 1981; Ogbu & Simons, 1998). Ogbu contended that *involuntary minorities*, such as the descendants of slaves and conquered peoples, possess ambivalence about the value of education as a vehicle of social and economic opportunity, and distrust of the institutions of the dominant society. In contrast, he argued that immigrant minorities who came to the United States voluntarily tended to display a "pragmatic attitude toward school" and that parents tended to hold high academic expectations for their children (Ogbu & Simons, 1998, p. 182).

A concept that is well-illustrated in Costello-Herrera's (2004) analysis is Ogbu's (1981) notion of "folk theory of making it," which he defined as "how one performs cultural tasks in order to succeed in the status system" (p. 420). Costello-Herrera found that all of the participants in the study possessed individual folk theories of success which helped them to make their way through the school system. These folk theories were based on their own cultural frames of reference, their family experiences and expectations for them, and the opportunities to learn provided by the school.

The Salvadorian immigrant students were eager to learn English and to adopt the cultural norms of the United States in order to fulfill their folk theories of making it. However, in some respects they remained caught between two worlds. As Ms. Marin, an ESL teacher in Costello-Herrera's (2004) study, described the situation:

> Because they're in the middle. They're in the middle between parents who are still trying to run their homes like they are in the old country and then here where they have to understand how Americans do it here ... I think in their own way they're trying to soak up as much as they can about how it's done here. (p. 123)

While it was important to learn English and succeed in school, each of the Salvadorian students retained his or her Hispanic cultural identity primarily through peer associations.Trust is an important theme in Costello-Herrera's (2004) study. The Salvadorian students and their parents placed a great deal of trust in the school system. They believed that school provided opportunities that would allow them to fulfill their folk theories of success. In addition, all of the students had a strong, trusting relationship with their ESL teacher, a relationship to which Costello-Herrera attributes much of the students' success.

One of Costello-Herrera's (2004) key conclusions relates to the distinctiveness of the young adolescent Salvadorians she studied. She calls for a particular focus by school personnel on the unique needs of Salvadorian students, and she stresses the importance of facilitating cultural adaptation through programs that respect Hispanic cultural heritage.

The Inner Worlds of Immigrant and Refugee Students

Igoa's (1988, 1995) research attempts to access the thoughts and feelings—the inner worlds—of some of the students she taught in a special program for young adolescent immigrant and refugee students in a California school. Her research methodology was dual dialogic retrospection in which both she and her former students reflected dialogically upon their experiences eight years prior in the language intervention program (Igoa, 1988). Writing about her own experience as an immigrant student, she recalls:

> Each time I encountered an unexplained cultural difference ... I would feel awkward, confused, ashamed, or inadequate. The innumerable differences had nothing to do with language, because I was raised bilingually. I was more affected by the sense of cultural difference; loss of cultural identity and feelings of inadequacy would well up inside me as I sat in class. I felt an unexplained void, an emptiness inside. I read well. I could illustrate. But these were mere skills. What I needed was a cultural connection. I was con-

> stantly adapting to the system. I needed the system to meet me halfway, to collaborate, to include my thoughts and feelings. (Igoa, 1995, p. 16)

Igoa (1988, 1995) found that the inner worlds of immigrant children may be characterized by isolation, exhaustion, loneliness, cultural differences, and a struggle to succeed in school. She recognizes the emotional and social issues that arise as immigrant children adjust to a new home and school, and she attributes student performance in school settings to "the complex interaction of his or her cultural background, individual nature, and length of time that student has been in the host country" (Igoa, 1995, p. 17).

A salient concept in Igoa's (1988, 1995) work is the notion of *uprootedness*. Igoa conceptualizes the phenomenon of uprooting as occurring in six stages. First, a child experiences mixed emotions—both excitement and apprehension—when he or she first learns about the decision to leave the homeland. The second stage is characterized by the sense of adventure that is associated with the long and sometimes arduous journey to the new country. In the third stage, the child expresses a sense of curiosity about the new country. Often a child experiences culture shock as he or she tries to make sense of the vastly different realities in the new homeland. At this point, the child has entered the fourth stage, which is marked by a spiral of depression and confusion. In the fifth stage, the child is actively engaged in the process of assimilation or acculturation. In the sixth and final stage, the child is immersed in the mainstream culture.

Igoa (1988, 1995) proposed that school districts develop newcomer programs that will serve as transitional places in which caring teachers can intervene into the persistent patterns of loneliness, anxiety, and helplessness that characterize the school experiences of immigrant and refugee students. Such programs must address the cultural, academic, and psychological (CAP) dimensions of adjustment and acculturation. Moreover, programs must be driven by a vision that embraces and values the immigrant and refugee students' languages, cultures, and personal voices.

Becoming a Student in Middle School

Meador (2000) offered an ethnographic account of how two newly immigrated Mexican girls constructed student identities within the context of rural Colorado middle schools. The central concept in the study is "student identity," which is defined as "the presentation of self in the school setting in relation to the work of the school" (p. 142). The author looked closely at ways the social organization of the school shapes and constrains the process of identity construction. Meador employed a framework through which she examined student identity in terms of motivation towards, engagement with, and conformity to the work of school.

According to Meador (2000), "a narrow set of categories and labels that are made available in the social organization of the school contributes to the ways Mexican girls orient themselves toward the work of school" (p. 175). Student identities available to Mexican girls are limited by aspects of the social organization of the school, including scheduling, instructional grouping, grading practices, and academic norms.

Meador (2000) described a pervasive, White, middle class norm within the school culture that characterizes the ideal student as popular, athletic, and academically high achieving. She points out that:

> Conforming to a cultural ideal is nearly impossible in a setting that so privileges the American girls. Conformity then becomes an obstacle in many ways to Mexicanas who have their own culture, language, and personal orientation to school to express. (p. 120)

The girls in Meador's study constructed their student identities in relation to the American girls and a cultural ideal that was unattainable. As a result, some girls appropriated the negative labels available to them, and some girls actively resisted these labels. Still other girls withdrew into passive silence.

Meador (2000) described certain coping strategies employed by the students, including a "cycle of non-participation" whereby Mexican girls pass through school virtually unnoticed.

> The girls were largely ignored by teachers and American students, and formed their own strategies for staying in school. Some girls found "brains" to help them out, other girls perfected ways to go unnoticed. And a few girls, like Mary, persisted each day determined to succeed in a setting that gave little back to reward their efforts. (p. 155)

Of interest to this review is the way the students in Meador's (2000) study compared their elementary and middle school experiences.

> Most of the students related a feeling of value to their elementary school years when they felt they were treated as individuals and not as members of a group. They talked about teachers who were their friends, who cared about their lives and their academic progress as teachers who elicited positive behavior from them.... All of the girls felt that elementary school had been a place where someone had cared about them and that middle school was less than that. (p. 156).

While the elementary teachers valued the Mexican girls as individuals, the middle school teachers in the study stereotyped the girls and knew or understood little of the backgrounds or home lives. This stark contrast between student perceptions of elementary and middle school caused Meador to raise the question: "What happens in middle school that changes the climate from one of affection to one of estrangement?" (p. 157).

Meador (2000) identified three conditions that may have engendered these perceptions. First, in the middle school relationships become bureaucratized because the teachers are responsible for five times more students than elementary teachers. Second, middle school teachers are held to higher expectations for teaching academic content which becomes increasingly abstract and, therefore, far more difficult to teach to ELLs because their academic English has not developed. Finally, the middle schools sorted students in groups based on ethnicity, and these groupings afforded students few opportunities to define themselves as individuals.

LESSONS LEARNED

One of the key assumptions of this chapter is that school-based interventions can make a difference in the education of young adolescent immigrant and refugee students. As Llanes (1997) contended:

> The school is the social institution where the first steps in articulating a new view of self are taken, and it plays a major role in defining that self. The school 'tells' the newcomer how he or she is perceived by the host society, mainly through its hidden curriculum, which begins during matriculation and continues through graduation. This image of the newcomer's self that the school reflects is imprinted on the newcomer forever. (p. viii)

Too often, the images that schools impress upon immigrant and refugee students are negative and damaging. Yet, there are numerous programs in schools and districts throughout the United States that are having a positive impact on the educational trajectories of immigrant youth (Dentler & Hafner, 1997; Fashola, Slavin, Calderon, & Duran, 2001; Lockwood, 2001). The ethnographic accounts of immigrant and refugee students yield three essential understandings that can be instructive for middle school practitioners and researchers as they seek to improve the educational experiences of these unique students.

1. Immigrant and refugee student groups are not monolithic.

2. Middle school organization and culture shape the educational experiences of immigrant and refugee students.
3. Interpersonal relationships matter.

First, *immigrant and refugee student groups are not monolithic*. The ethnographies (Costello-Herrera, 2004; Custodio, 2001; Igoa, 1988, 1995; Meador, 2000, 2005) revealed great variation within the broad categories of ethnic identification commonly used (e.g., Hispanic, Asian, Pacific Islander) as well as variance among individuals within subcategories. Costello-Herrera (2004) highlighted the uniqueness of the Salvadorian immigrants in her study, and she challenges the sweeping generalizations that are often made about students from Latin America. Custodio (2001) urged educators to consider the uniqueness and individuality of each class of immigrant and refugee students. "It is only by looking at each class individually and discovering those needs and personality that the students will have their needs met" (p. 234).

How can middle schools effectively address the wide-ranging needs of all students, especially in communities characterized by great cultural and linguistic diversity? Jackson and Davis (2000) recommend that middle school leadership teams form inquiry groups to solve problems and address school-wide issues collaboratively. By taking an ethnographic approach, middle school inquiry groups can learn to transcend borders of language and culture and tap into the *funds of knowledge* in the homes and communities of the youth they serve (see González, Moll, & Amanti, 2005; Moll, Amanti, Neff, & González, 1992; Vélez-Ibáñez, & Greenberg, 1992).

Garcia (2001) recommended four steps that can help middle school inquiry groups make well-informed decisions about immigrant and refugee students.

1. Identify the full compliment of factors that define these students, especially those who are at risk of educational failure.
2. Understand how the factors bundle within individual Latino students and across groups of students so as not to over generalize across particular student subgroups
3. Determine what the factors imply for the typical array of educational and related social/health services provided and for professional development.
4. Design appropriate educational and management responses for Latino students that stem from the identification of these factors. (pp. 328-329)

While he is primarily concerned with Latino students, Garcia's (2001) recommendations are applicable to immigrant and refugee students of any background.

A second lesson from the ethnographies is that *middle school organization and culture shape the school experiences of immigrant and refugee students*. These factors are determinants in all developmental processes, including identity development, acculturation, and intellectual growth. Meador (2000) and Costello-Herrera (2004) illustrated how the cultural norms and instructional program in a school impact student identity development and how structural arrangements in schools may isolate and further silence marginalized immigrant students (see also Hu & Fell-Eisenkraft, 2003). Both Meador and Custodio (2001) revealed the sad irony that ESL programs may actually work against the acquisition of standard academic English (see also Schmida, 2004), while Igoa (1995) provided an example of a program model that may work very effectively with the proper support. Middle school leaders must carefully consider grouping arrangements, scheduling, the curriculum, and norms and policies for language use as they design academic program (Benjamin, 1998).

The education of immigrant and refugee students must be a whole-school effort and not the responsibility of a single ESL instructor (Custodio, 2001). Classroom teachers cannot be expected to know everything about the psychology of acculturation and identity construction, nor can they attain expert knowledge about the cultural backgrounds of every child and family. Successful work with young adolescents, and especially immigrant and refugee middle school students, requires a community approach. The middle school concept calls for schools to be structured in ways that allow teachers to get to know their students well and that facilitate connections among all of the professionals in the school, including psychologists, school social workers, and counselors.

The third lesson is that *interpersonal relationships matter.* All of the ethnographies illustrate the centrality of interpersonal relationships among students, school personnel, and parents to the success of immigrant students (Cline, 2003). Ideally, middle school counselors are positioned to establish such relationships; however typical caseloads of one hundred or more students make it very difficult for this to occur (Benjamin, 1998). Immigrant students need to establish strong, positive relationships with adults in a middle school, as was the case with the ESL teacher in some of the studies (Costello-Herrera, 2004; Igoa, 1995). Meador (2000) observed that "when students felt valued by teachers they participated in the work of the school" (p. 170).

Advisory programs in which a teacher works closely with ten to fifteen students through the year hold some promise, especially "when teachers/advisors know and understand the developmental needs of their students" (Benjamin, 1998, p. 252). With regards to Latino students, Benjamin added:

> It also requires that advisors learn about the Latino cultures and the particular communities their students represent. It is also necessary that teachers understand their students' need for developing an ethnic identity and the difficulties their students can face in this process, particularly with existing racist attitudes. This can often be a difficult issue for teachers, especially when they have not resolved these issues for themselves. (p. 252)

Implied in Benjamin's recommendation is the need for focused, high-quality staff development for teachers, administrators, and other middle school personnel who work with immigrant and refugee students.

Middle level educators should strive to extend the web of relationships beyond school and into the immigrant community. Benjamin (1998) pointed out the importance of parent and family involvement in Latino children's education, particularly during the middle school years. She cautions, however, that schools should look beyond traditional notions of involvement and seek to access the funds of knowledge embedded in the immigrant community (see González, Moll, & Amanti, 2005; Moll, Amanti, Neff, & González, 1992; Vélez-Ibáñez, & Greenberg, 1992).

Middle level educators also need to consider instructional strategies that may help to promote interaction between native English speakers and ELLs, such as small group instruction (Brown, 2002). The social support that these strategies offer can help mediate transition stress in young adolescent students, however teachers should note that the quality of relationships is more important than the mere frequency of interactions. Ultimately, having friends who help one cope with problems is more important than superficial contact and interaction with peers, no matter how frequent (Kurita & Janzen, 1996).

CONCLUSION

While young adolescence is a dynamic period in the development of all students, it may be an especially difficult time for newly arrived immigrant and refugee students who are learning a new language and culture while also developing a new sense of identity. The purpose of this chapter was to call attention to the complexity of immigrant and refugee education in middle schools. The review of four studies that focus on immigrant and refugee students in middle school settings called attention to the diversity that exists across and within immigrant and refugee student groups; it highlighted the ways middle school organizational structures and cultural characteristics impact the processes of acculturation and student identity development; and it affirmed the importance of strong interpersonal relationships among immigrant students, their families, and their teachers. Unfortunately, the review does not do justice to the richness of these studies, nor does it attend to the full importance of the findings.

As Manning (1993) suggested, research highlighting the salience of cultural differences "provides a more powerful rationale for basing educational experiences on individual needs and characteristics" of students (p. 17). While an influx of immigrant and refugee students may signal a need for an ESL program in a middle school, it may also be viewed as a call to build small learning communities within the school and to strengthen or implement teaming, advisory programs, and other aspects of the middle school concept.

REFERENCES

Ada, A. F. (1995). Foreword. In C. Igoa, *The inner world of the immigrant child*, (pp. vii-ix). New York: St. Martin's Press.

Benjamin, R. (1998). Middle schools for Latinos: A framework for success. In M. L. Gonzalez, A. Huerta-Macias, & J. V. Tinajero (Eds.), *Educating Latino students: A guide to successful practice* (pp. 239-267). Lancaster, PA: Technomic.

Borden, J. F. (1998). The pitfalls and possibilities for organizing quality ESL Brown, D. F. (2002). Culturally responsive instructional processes. In V. A. Anfara, Jr. & S. Stacki, (Eds.), *Middle school curriculum, instruction, and assessment* (pp. 57-73). Greenwich, CT: Information Age.

Carnegie Council on Adolescent Development. (1989). *Turning points: Preparing American youth for the 21st century.* Washington, DC: Carnegie Corporation of New York.

Cline, Z. (2003). Buscando la voz que siempre tenia—In search of the voice I always had. *Middle School Journal, 34*(3), 28-31.

Costello-Herrera, L. A. (2004). Quest for a better life: The educational experiences of Salvadorian immigrant middle school students in the United States School. *Dissertation Abstracts International, 65(*05), 1602. (UMI No. 3132916).

Custodio, B. K. (2001). Barriers to success: A study of the academic, social, physical, and emotional challenges faced by the ESL students in one urban middle school. *Dissertation Abstracts International, 62*(4), 1304. (UMI No. 3011040).

Dana, R. H. (1996). Assessment of acculturation in Hispanic populations. *Hispanic Journal of Behavioral Sciences, 18*(3), 317-328.

Dentler, R. A., & Hafner, A. L. (1997). *Hosting newcomers: Structuring educational opportunities for immigrant children.* New York: Teachers College Press.

Dryfoos, J. G. (1990). *Adolescents at risk: Prevalence and prevention.* New York: Oxford University Press.

Fashola, O. S., Slavin, R. E., Calderón, M., & Duran, R. (2001). Effective programs for Latino students in elementary and middle schools. In R. E. Slavin & M.

Calderón (Eds.), *Effective programs for Latino students* (pp. 1-66). Mahwah, NJ: Erlbaum.

Garcia, G. N. (2001). The factors that place Latino children and youth at risk of educational failure. In R. E. Slavin & M. Calderón (Eds.), *Effective programs for Latino students* (pp. 307-329). Mahwah, NJ: Erlbaum.

González, N., Moll, L. C., & Amanti, C. (Eds.). (2005). *Funds of knowledge: Theorizing practices in households, communities, and classrooms*. Mahwah, NJ: Erlbaum.

Hu, Y., & Fell-Eisenkraft, S. (2003). Immigrant Chinese students' use of silence in the language arts classroom: Perceptions, reflections, and actions. *Teaching & Learning, 17*(2), 55-65.

Igoa, C. (1988). Toward a psychology and education of the uprooted: A study of the inner world of immigrant children. *Dissertation Abstracts International, 51*(03), (UMI No. AAT 9021136).

Igoa, C. (1995). *The inner world of the immigrant child*. New York: St. Martin's Press.

Jackson A. W., & Davis, G. A. (2000). *Turning points 2000: Preparing American youth for the 21st century*. New York: Teachers College Press.

Kuo, B. C. H., & Roysircar, G. (2004). Predictors of acculturation for Chinese adolescents in Canada: Age of arrival, length of stay, social class, and English reading ability. *Journal of Multicultural Counseling and Development, 32*(3), 143-154.

Kurita, J. A., & Janzen, H. L. (1996, August). *The role of social support in mediating school transition stress*. Paper presented at the biennial meeting of the American Psychological Association, Toronto, Ontario, Canada. (ERIC Document Reproduction Service No. ED 407 636)

Llanes, J. R. (1997). Foreword. In R. A. Dentler & A. L. Hafner, *Hosting newcomers: Structuring educational opportunities for immigrant children,* (pp. vii-ix). New York: Teachers College Press.

Lockwood, A. T. (2001). Effective elementary, middle, and high school programs for Latino youth. In R. E. Slavin & M. Calderón (Eds.), *Effective programs for Latino students* (pp. 101-124). Mahwah, NJ: Erlbaum.

Manning, M. L. (1993). Cultural and gender differences in young adolescents. *Middle School Journal 25*(1), 13-17.

Meador, E. A. (2000). The social organization of schools and student identity construction: The practice of becoming a student in middle school among newly immigrated Mexican girls. *Dissertation Abstracts International, 61*(12), (UMI No. 9995747).

Meador, E. A. (2005). The making of marginality schooling for Mexican immigrant girls in the rural southwest. *Anthropology & Education Quarterly 36*(2), 149-164.

Mena, F. (1987). Acculturative stress and specific coping strategies among immigrant and later generation college students. *Hispanic Journal of Behavioral Science,s 9*(2), 207-225.

Miller, P. C., & Endo, H. (2004). Understanding and meeting the needs of ESL students. *Phi Delta Kappan 85*(10), 786-791.

Miranda, A. O., & Matheny, K. B. (2000). Socio-psychological predictors of acculturative stress among Latino adults. *Journal of Mental Health CounselingJournal 22*(4), 306-317.

Moll, L. C., Amanti, C., Neff, D., & Gonzalez, N. (1992). Funds of knowledge for teaching: Using a qualitative approach to connect homes to classrooms. *Theory into Practice, 31*, 132-141.

National Middle School Association. (2003). *This we believe: Successful schools for young adolescents*. Westerville, OH: Author.

Ogbu, J. G. (1981). Origins of human competence: A cultural-ecological perspective. *Child Development, 52*, 413-429.

Ogbu, J., & Simons, H. D. (1998). Voluntary and involuntary minorities: A cultural ecological theory of school performance with some implications for education. *Anthropology & Education Quarterly, 29*(2), 155-188.

Olsen, L. (1997). *Made in America: Immigrant students in our public schools*. New York: The New Press.

Patterson, L. (1995, March 20). Middle schools, major changes—State's teachers race to keep up with kids' growing minds, bodies. *The State*. p. A1.

Polo, A. J. (2002). Mexican American youth: An examination of the role of cultural, social, and family correlates of their mental health. *Dissertation Abstracts International, 63*(5), UMI No. 3052437).

Pryor, C. B. (2001). New immigrants and refugees in American schools. *Childhood Education*, 77(5), 275-283.

Roysircar, G. (2004). Child survivor of war: A case study. *Journal of Multicultural Counseling and Development 32*(3), 168.

Santrock, J. W. (2005). *Adolescence* (10th ed.). New York: McGraw-Hill.

Schmida, M. K. (2004). Language acquisition through linguistic affiliation: The influence of ESL pedagogy, educational constraints, and urban sub-culture on students' linguistic abilities and perceptions of self. *Dissertation Abstracts International, 66*(02), (UMI No. AAT 3165553).

Smart, J. F.,& Smart, D. W. (1995a). Acculturative stress of Hispanics: Loss and challenge. *Journal of Counseling & Development*, *73*(4), 390-396.

Smart, J. F., & Smart, D. W. (1995b). Acculturative stress: The experience of the Hispanic immigrant. *Counseling Psychologist, 23*(1), 25-42.

Tse, L. (1996). Language brokering in linguistic minority communities: The case of Chinese- and Vietnamese-American students. *Bilingual Research Journal, 20* (3-4), 485-498.

Valdés, G. (1998). The world outside and inside schools: Language and immigrant children. *Educational Researcher, 27*(6), 4-18.

Van Ness, J., & Irvin, J. L. (1997). Linguistic minority students in middle schools. What research says. *Middle School Journal, 29*(1), 57-58.

Vélez-Ibáñez, C., & Greenberg, J. (1992). Formation and transformation of funds of knowledge among U.S. Mexican households. *Anthropology and Education Quarterly, 23*(4), 313-335.

Weisskirch, R. S. (2005). The relationship of language brokering to ethnic identity for Latino early adolescents. *Hispanic Journal of Behavioral Sciences, 27*(3), 286-299.

Weisskirch, R. S., & Alva, S. A. (2002). Language brokering and the acculturation of Latino children. *Hispanic Journal of Behavioral Sciences*, *24*(3), 369-378.

Williams, C. L., & Berry, J. W. (1991). Primary prevention of acculturative stress among refugees: application of psychological theory and practice. *American Psychologist*, *46*(6), 632-641.

CHAPTER 13

CONSIDERING SINGLE-SEX ACADEMIC CLASSES FOR YOUNG ADOLESCENTS

Time Flies When You're Having Fun

Frances R. Spielhagen

ABSTRACT

As more schools experiment with single-sex class arrangements, close scrutiny of one middle school is warranted because it has successfully implemented this organizational reform since 2002. This 3-year study employed a mixed methods design to explore single-sex academic classes in a small ($N = 600$) middle school through two lenses: first, to examine the perceptions of the stakeholders in this organizational reform (students, parents, and teachers); and second, to explore the extent to which the reform affected student achievement, as measured by standardized test scores. Age, gender, and social development were evident as important considerations in the organization of single-sex classes in public middle schools.

The Young Adolescent and the Middle School
pp. 255–276

"Have you ever heard of that saying, 'Time flies when you're having fun?' All-boy classes are fun!" James, age 11 and in the sixth grade, cheerfully offered his opinion of the single-sex academic classes at his public middle school. However, he quickly and quietly added a cautionary note, "Please write down that I will probably want to be with girls when I am in high school." With equal enthusiasm, Melissa, age 13 and in the eighth grade, responded from her more adolescent point of view, "You can say what you want and not be afraid of being teased in all-girl classes ... but sometimes we just want to be with the guys." Despite her satisfaction with the academic benefits of the single-sex arrangement, she clearly reinforced the developmental need of the adolescent for social interaction in the opposite sex.

These divergent statements (Spielhagen, 2006) captured the essence of the student view of single-sex classes, a somewhat controversial paradigm that has gained popularity in public schools over the last few years. As more schools experiment with single-sex class arrangements (Vu, 2006), close scrutiny of one middle school is warranted because the school has successfully implemented the organizational reform since 2002. Therefore, this study, conducted from 2002 to 2005, employed a mixed methods design to examine single-sex academic classes in a small (N = 600) middle school. The purpose of this two-phase study was first to examine the phenomenon of single-sex classes through the perceptions of participants drawn from all the stakeholders in this organizational reform (i.e., students, parents, and teachers). The second phase set out to explore the extent to which single-sex classes affected student achievement, as measured by standardized test scores. An additional quantitative component was derived from surveys administered to members of the three stakeholder groups.

Historical Context

During the Progressive Era of the early twentieth century, education policymakers struggled with the massive influx of students, both boys and girls into high schools. Coeducation became a staple of American high schools at that time, a significant change from common practice during the nineteenth century when single-sex schools were the usual organizational pattern. In these single-sex schools and classes, women were most often enrolled only in basic skills courses and did not often study academic subjects that would lead to higher education. Therefore, early feminists urged access for all students to the entire academic curriculum, particularly the precollegiate academic subjects, like math and science.

This resulted in substantial increases in the enrollment of girls in colleges across the nation throughout the twentieth century.

However, in the latter half of the twentieth century, second-wave feminists decried the inequities within coeducational settings, particularly in athletics. Secondary schools had organized separate single-sex physical education classes and teams but the girls' facilities and arrangements routinely lacked the same resources as the boys. In the early 1970s, litigation surrounding these inequities coincided with other civil rights legislation. Ultimately, in 1972, the federal government responded to these lawsuits by establishing Title IX (Tyack & Hansot, 2002), which specifically forbade separate single-sex physical education classes. School districts construed this prohibition to extend to academic classes. However, Salomone (2003) pointed out that the various statutory exemptions to Title IX "suggest that Congress did not intend to impose a sweeping ban on all single-sex education" (p. 184).

Over the last 2 decades, education policymakers have targeted declines in achievement among students of both genders. Sadker and Sadker (1995) claimed that schools were shortchanging girls, gaining the support of the American Association of University Women (AAUW), which endorsed single-sex arrangements as a means of promoting female achievement, particularly in mathematics and science. However, within a few years, the AAUW (1998) concluded that single-sex classes were potentially harmful for girls. Meanwhile, Sommers (2002) stated that single-sex arrangements were advantageous for boys who were found to be lagging in academic areas, particularly reading and writing. In general, however, advocates on both sides of the gender argument agree that the middle school years are the most critical time for the formation of habits that promote academic achievement (Clewell, 2002).

In 2002, an amendment to No Child Left Behind (NCLB) legislation opened the door for schools to experiment with single-sex classes as a means of improving educational outcomes for their students. Such arrangements began to increase throughout the nation, reaching at least 241 schools in 2006 (Vu, 2006) according to Stateline, an organization that tracks educational changes across the nation. In 2003, the Office of Civil Rights immediately began reviewing arguments about the legality of single-sex classes. In October, 2006, the United States Department of Education confirmed the legality of single-sex arrangements.

From 2002 to 2006, while the legality of single-sex classes remained in question, some schools took advantage of the language of NCLB and experimented with single-sex class arrangements. School administrators found that after an initial flurry of controversy, the classes became an established option among their student population. Students and teachers settled into the routines of schooling, while parents who had opted for these arrangements for their children seemed comfortable with their choice. However, analysis of value and effectiveness of these arrangements provides fertile ground for research and discussion.

Jackson and Davis (2000) recommended that middle schools organize learning climates that promote intellectual development and shared educational purpose. Moreover, they further recommended that effective middle schools provide a safe and healthy school environment and, at the same time, involve parents in supporting student learning and healthy development. The results of this study show that single-sex class options in public middle schools can support these goals.

One School's Experience

Since Fall 2002, Forest Valley Middle School (a pseudonym), a public middle school (N = 600 students) in rural New York State has provided a somewhat unique organizational arrangement that involves single-sex classes. The arrangement itself was a composite model that provided for maximum flexibility for the students. The district has offered voluntary single-sex classes to all students in Grades 6, 7, and 8 in the four core academic subjects: language arts, math, science, and social studies. All students in those grades remain in mixed groups for all nonacademic classes and at lunchtime. Therefore, the students are not completely isolated from the peers of the opposite sex, but have ample time within the normal school day (approximately 50% of the day) to interact and socialize. The critical component of this arrangement has been the element of choice within the routine structure of an established middle school with minimal disruption for the students. In the first year of the reform, approximately 75% of the students chose the single-sex academic classes. Over the next 2 years, the majority of those students remained in single-sex classes.

RESEARCH DESIGN

Any reform must be examined from multiple points of view in order to capture "the essence of the experience" (Creswell, 1998) for all the stakeholders. Therefore, the complete study of this district's reform employed a sequential, exploratory, mixed-methods design (Creswell, 2003), involving both qualitative and quantitative analyses. The first phase consisted of the qualitative component, which included classroom observations in both single-sex and mixed-gender classes and interviews with teachers (n = 12), students (n =24), and parents (n = 7). These data were analyzed and ultimately used to construct the questions for the surveys that were administered in the second semester of that first year.

Convenience sampling of members of all three groups of participants, i.e., teachers, students, and parents, resulted in the final interview pool. A letter was sent to all teachers of both mixed and single-sex classes, inviting them to participate in the interviews. Their involvement was voluntary and varied according to their availability at the time of the interviews. Approximately one third of the teachers (n=12) participated in the interviews, which were held during and after the school day.

Parents of all students received letters requesting permission to interview their children and inviting the parents to come to the school for interviews. The return rate on the letters was low (approximately 8% of the available population), but from those returns, interviews were scheduled for 29 students, of which 24 finally participated. The remaining five were not available on the days the interviews were being conducted or decided not to participate when they were called for the interviews. All parents (n = 7) who agreed to be interviewed were included in the study.

The interviews, lasting approximately one class period (40 minutes), were conducted in a conference room attached to the main office of the school. The door was left open at all times, and a secretary was seated directly outside the door to the room. All adult participants signed releases agreeing to their voluntary participation. In addition to the release forms signed by their parents, students were asked personally if they wanted to be involved in the interview. Two students decided not to be involved before the questioning began. All participants were advised that they could discontinue the interviews at any time, but all opted to continue once the interviews began.

The interviews were structured around ten basic questions; with one open-ended question at the end (Is there anything else you would like to say about single-sex classes?) Interview data were recorded, transcribed, and explored for common themes. These themes were then converted into questions for the surveys that were later administered to all three data populations. Two years later, follow-up interviews were conducted with a purposeful sample of teachers (n = 6) and eighth grade students (n = 12) who had been interviewed in the sixth grade. The second phase of interviews employed the same questions that were used in phase 1.

Classroom observations, lasting 40-minutes each, were conducted throughout the three years of the study. A balanced selection of single-sex and mixed classes were derived from among the sixth, seventh, and eighth grades. Initially, the role of the observer was not stated to the students, who were accustomed to the presence of visitors to their classes. As the study progressed, however, the observer became recognized by the students, so that her role switched from complete observer to participant observer. From the onset of the study, the teachers were informed of the observer's purpose. As a result, they frequently engaged the observer in conversation after the classes had taken place. The teachers were reassured that the observations were not evaluative but for research purposes only. One first-year, nontenured, teacher expressed the fear that the observation might in some way be used as an evaluation tool, and she ultimately refused to allow the observer into her class. All the other teachers willing allowed the observer into their classes.

In this sequential design, the quantitative component was conducted after the initial interviews. Three surveys were created using the key ideas and statements derived from the interviews. These surveys were administered to all three stakeholder groups at the end of the third year of the study. Survey responses were analyzed for frequencies of the responses according to a Likert scale of 1 to 5. For the purposes of reporting, this scale was collapsed into three categories: agree, neutral, and disagree.

The students responded to the survey in their homeroom classes and were advised that their response was voluntary. The return rate for the students' surveys was approximately 98% of the population, with the 2% attrition due to attendance the day the survey was administered. A small number of surveys were discarded because the students' responses were invalid. A few students responded to all questions in the same way, "disagree strongly," even though the questions could not possibly have the same positive or negative response. Teachers received surveys in their interoffice mailboxes and were informed that their return of the surveys was voluntary. This yielded a return rate of 54% within a week after the surveys were distributed. Parents were invited to complete a voluntary survey at an evening event, the annual middle school science fair. This imposed a limitation on the survey sample, restricting it to parents (n = 78) who happened to attend the science fair.

The quantitative component also included analysis of the students' scores on TerraNova achievement tests in 2002, 2003, and 2004, and employed both descriptive and comparative statistics. These test scores were examined at the request of school administrators, who were interested in determining the efficacy of the reform in terms of the academic performance of the students. For the purposes of this study, the analysis of test scores promised to provide another means of examining the potential effects of single-sex classes. However, other reforms, enacted simultaneously to the single-sex configuration, prevented clear interpretation of the changes in test scores.

RESULTS

Student Interviews

In general, the younger the student the more likely there were positive reactions to the single-sex classes. Sixth grade students routinely reported that they found students of the opposite sex "distracting" and "noisy" (a common response among both boys and girls) and that they preferred to be with their same-sex friends. Observations in the mixed academic classes and other mixed environments during the day, i.e., lunch, art and music classes, physical education classes, supported this preference for same-sex interaction in the sixth grade. Sixth graders naturally and without prompting routinely chose to be with same sex peers.

One slightly built 11-year-old boy in sixth grade, responded energetically to questions about his reaction to being in all-boy classes. He noted that he did not pay much attention to the girls in the universally mixed gym classes because he and his friends (all boys) liked to be on teams together. He said that he felt "more challenged" in his all-boy classes because he enjoyed the competition with the boys in his classes, "I want to try to beat them. I didn't try to beat the girls (when he was in mixed classes) because I didn't think I could beat the top girls, so why bother?"

A sixth grade girl emphasized that she was happy she chose all-girl classes because "you don't have to worry about boys picking on you or making fun of you." Another sixth grade girl, age 12, reported that she had asked her mother to enroll her in the all-girl classes because "the boys picked on me because I am smarter than them." She asserted that in all-girl classes the teachers "word things better and say them differently. In mixed classes they say things more simply for the boys." She felt that girls have the same ideas and can work well together, because the boys think of "disgusting things," especially in science. She added that all-girl classes are more fun and get more accomplished, even though the girls "get loud and ask too many questions."

The preference for single-sex classes began to change in the seventh grade, as these young adolescents progressed through puberty and began to express their developmental need to socialize with the opposite sex. By the eighth grade, most students said they preferred mixed environments, even if they had opted to stay in the single-sex classes. The boys were more vocal than the girls in their dislike of the single-sex arrangement, particularly those boys who were less physically developed and more likely to be bullied by their more aggressive peers. One boy in the seventh grade noted that he had been curious about all-boy classes, but now that he was in them, he planned to choose mixed-gender classes for eighth grade. He conceded that in the all-boy classes he could talk more about sports with his friends and "just hang out," but that in the single-sex environment, "Boys try to act tougher."

One eighth grade boy stated that the school had organized all-boy classes "because of fights and stuff." He admitted that he had been picked on by other boys in seventh grade, but that it was worse in the all-boy classes. He explained, "The guys who pick on us would be more interested in impressing the girls" in mixed classes. He added that he missed his friends who are girls, because he cannot rely on their friendship in the all-boy classes. Another eighth grade boy agreed that there was bullying in mixed-gender classes, but that there seemed to be more of it in the all-boy environment.

Both boys and girls noted that they could concentrate more in single-sex classes and decided that they were getting better grades in the single-sex classes than they might in the mixed classes. Observations in the single-sex suggested that the students appeared to be livelier than their peers in mixed classes, as well as more focused and more on-task.

Two years later, the students offered more seasoned perspectives on the arrangement. One eighth-grade girl reported that she thought at first that she would try all-girl classes for just a year but had decided to stay with the arrangement because "I can concentrate better." She noted that she has seen a definite improvement in her grades because "I am not afraid to raise my hand. The boys picked on you (in mixed classes) and laughed at you if you got an answer wrong." Other girls also reported that they felt they had gotten better grades "because we pay attention more and don't get distracted." She decided to stay in all-girl classes in eighth grade because she could not think of any reason to change. However, another girl reported that cliques and cattiness seemed to intensify in the all-girl seventh grade classes, but she later said that this had improved by the time they were in eighth grade.

One eighth grade boy said that he enjoyed the all-boy classes because "I can concentrate more. The girls make too much noise." However, he suggested that the choice for single-sex classes should be for individual subjects and not all the academic classes, as had been organized by the school. He also offered his opinion that bullying had become a problem in seventh and eighth grade single-sex classes.

Polling the Population: Student Survey Responses

Surveys developed from responses during student interviews were administered to all students in single-sex classes in Grades 6, 7, and 8. Table 13.1 contains the array of all the responses to selected questions

Table 13.1. Student Survey: Selected Survey Responses in Grades 6, 7, 8 Combined (*N* = 263)

Survey Statement	*Agree*	*Neutral*	*Disagree*
You can concentrate more in single-sex classes.	51%	21%	30%
You don't have to be afraid of being wrong in a single-sex class.	42%	35%	23%
Single-sex classes are quieter than mixed classes.	33%	14%	53%
You can act more like yourself in single-sex classes.	45%	27%	28%
Single-sex classes are fun because you can see your friends.	46%	27%	27%
Students should have a choice between single and mixed classes.	86%	11%	3%

Table 13.2. Comparison of Responses by Grade and Gender

	Grade 6			*Grade 7*			*Grade 8*		
Survey Statement	*All*	*Boys*	*Girls*	*All*	*Boys*	*Girls*	*All*	*Boys*	*Girls*
I wanted to experience single-sex classes.	40%	29%	51%	24%	9%	35%	21%	8%	30%
You can concentrate more in single-sex classes.	60%	36%	84%	46%	43%	49%	50%	22%	70%
My grades have improved in single-sex classes.	53%	45%	67%	31%	23%	37%	33%	22%	41%
Single-sex classes are fun because you get to see your friends.	57%	52%	54%	48%	51%	46%	38%	46%	32%
I would choose single-sex classes again.	40%	21%	58%	30%	23%	35%	19%	10%	25%

from the student survey, which was administered to students in all single-sex classes at the end of the third year of the arrangement.

Closer scrutiny of the survey responses revealed that positive reactions to single-sex classes were greatest in the sixth grade, dipped in the seventh grade, and increased dramatically in the eighth grade. Table 13.2 records student responses according to their gender and grade.

Sixth grade students gave more positive responses on all key questions than their older peers, with the girls sounding a positive note across the board on all points. An astounding 84% of the sixth grade girls stated they could concentrate more in all-girl classes, compared to 60% of the boys in those classes. According to their responses on the surveys, the ability to concentrate regained importance among the oldest girls in the study.

Boys, on the other hand, provided the most negative responses on the survey. When asked whether they had wanted to experience single-sex classes, only 9% of the seventh grade boys agreed, followed by a low of 8% among the eighth grade boys. Overall, 19% of all eighth grade students said they would choose single-sex classes again, but only ten per cent of the boys agreed to the statement. Among the girls, 25% of the eighth grade girls would choose single-sex classes again, compared to 58% of the sixth grade girls.

Teacher Interviews

Teachers who worked with both single-sex and mixed classes volunteered to be interviewed about their perceptions of their students in each environment. Two rounds of interviews were conducted. The first took place during the first year of the reform, and follow-up interviews were conducted 2 years later, at the close of the third year of the reform. In the first year, the teachers were generally favorably disposed to the single-sex classes. They reported differences in the responses of boys and girls to their work in class when in the single-sex configuration. The teachers in the first year were very conscious of the change from the usual order of business in which all students were in typical mixed classes. However, the teachers also stated that the single-sex classes allowed them to teach the students more effectively. One teacher objected to the arrangement in the interest of promoting diversity among the students, noting, "We don't live in a world segregated by sex, so why should they go to school in that world?" Another expressed concern about the long-term effectiveness of such an arrangement. Overall, however, most teachers interviewed in the first year were comfortable with the single-sex classes. They were curious about how the reform would work out over time and open to trying to address student needs in this arrangement.

Two years later, teachers had become more polarized and more vocal either in their support or in their disapproval of the single-sex classes. One teacher approached the interviewer in the hall and stated, "I hope you found it didn't work. I hate those classes." However, another related in her interview that she still believed strongly that single-sex classes provided the safest learning environment for her students, especially for the girls. "They are more engaged and less social in the all-girl classes." Clearly lines were drawn, and the teachers had taken sides in the reform.

During both series of interviews, several teachers noted the need for specialized training to teach in single-sex classes. At the end of the first year, basic training on student styles was provided on a voluntary basis during the summer months. Most teachers did not attend this training. By the third year, several teachers expressed strong concerns about dealing with the negative dynamics among the students, particularly the boys. They suggested that administrators who are scheduling boys into single-sex classes should take into account the previous aggressive behaviors exhibited by some of the boys and break up combinations that prove to be negative. They also explained that other organizational concerns, specifically the teaming paradigm that was the basis for the school's organization and the segregation of honors math students, also affected the composition of the single-sex classes. While several teachers stated that they would choose to teach single-sex classes again, they were adamant that they should be given the choice of teaching single-sex classes, rather than simply being assigned to those classes by the dictates of the schedule or discretion of the school administration. The teachers stated empathically that no teacher should be required to teach single-sex classes.

Polling the Teachers: Teacher Survey Responses

At the end of the third year of the reform, the middle school teachers responded to a survey containing 30 statements regarding their experiences with single-sex classes and their opinions about the effectiveness of the arrangement for students. In general, the teachers felt both boys and girls were comfortable being with friends of the same sex and participated more in single-sex classes. Several teachers reported continued positive effects for girls in single-sex classes, but corroborated their colleagues' concerns about behavior problems and immaturity among the boys in single-sex classes. While the teachers acknowledged differences in learning styles between the girls and the boys, they also said they had changed their own teaching styles to accommodate each group. They generally agreed that they needed in-service training to teach single-sex classes.

However, on the survey, the teachers were split on whether the single-sex classes should continue: 44% agreed, 19% were neutral, and 37% disagreed that the school should keep the reform. Half of the teachers said they would teach single-sex classes again and one fourth said they were neutral about the possibility. Another 25% said they would not want to teach single-sex classes again. Table 13.3 contains selected items from the teachers' survey with their responses.

Interviews With Parents

Parents who had selected the single-sex option for their children were overwhelmingly pleased with the arrangement and satisfied with their children's behavior and academic achievement. Many of these parents

Table 13.3. Teacher Responses to Selected Survey Items at the End of Year 3

Statement	*Agree*	*Neutral*	*Disagree*
Girls are more social than boys in single-sex classes.	56%	33%	11%
Girls respond more in single-sex classes.	61%	22%	17%
Boys in single-sex classes act less maturely than they do in mixed-gender classes.	53%	5%	42%
Students are more focused and on-task in single-sex classes.	53%	5%	42%
Girls have shown sustained, positive growth in single-sex classes.	60%	33%	7%
Both genders seem comfortable with single-sex classes.	75%	13%	12%
There is greater participation by both genders in single-sex classes.	56%	6%	38%
Girls and boys process information differently.	69%	31%	0%
I focus on different aspects of the content with each single-sex class.	19%	25%	56%
I change my style to accommodate the gender I am teaching.	50%	25%	25%
Teachers need in-service training to teach single-sex classes.	44%	44%	12%
Single-sex classes should continue to be an option for students and parents.	44%	19%	37%
I would choose to teach single-sex classes again.	50%	25%	25%

had experienced single-sex classes in their own (parochial) high schools. Most of them considered the arrangement to be beneficial both academically and socially for their children as they entered puberty.

The parents cited the social nature of the middle school years and pressures on their children, particularly the girls, to act older than they were. Several parents expressed concerns about the sexual precocity of their children and the pressures on young adolescents to be socially engaged with the opposite sex. One parent stated that the single-sex classes "seemed to be working in the beginning of the school year" but wondered how her daughter would react when she matured and became more social. Another mother, with twin daughters, chose single-sex classes for one child and mixed classes for the other because each child "needs different environments." She had conferred with both girls and based her decision on their preferences.

Another parent, who had opted not to put her son in a single-sex arrangement, objected to the program on philosophical grounds. She felt that he "needed to be with girls in order to learn how to live with women when he grows up." On the other hand, some parents of boys said that they felt that the single-sex classes afforded their sons the opportunity to concentrate and flourish. Mothers were the most vocal about this.

All parents interviewed emphasized their right to choose single-sex arrangements. They did not want the school to make that decision for them. They also wanted to be able to make that decision each school year, according to the development of their children. However, very few parents reported that they had changed their children's classes over the three years of the study. An overwhelming majority of the parents who had selected the single-sex option for their children in the first year continued with that option in the second and third school year.

Polling the Parents

At the end of the third year, the parents were surveyed about their reactions to the single-sex classes that had been offered to their children. Not surprisingly, their responses reflected their concerns over the social pressures their children experience as young adolescents and their desire to stabilize the learning environment for their children. Most parents (63%) felt they were adequately informed about the single-sex arrangement. This is important since the informed consent of parents is critical in instituting this type of reform. A large number (49%) felt that single-sex classes help students learn better, but they were not decisive about whether single-sex classes provide a safer learning environment for children. An even larger number of parents (61%) felt that mixed classes create more social pressure than single-sex classes, but many (51%) also felt that mixed classes help children learn how to function in the real world. A large number of parents (59%) also felt that single-sex classes should continue to be an option at this school, and many (46%) would choose single-sex classes again for their children. Table 13.4 contains responses to selected survey questions.

Quantitative Analysis: Achievement Tests

Questions of social and emotional safety of students aside, the current educational environment (i.e., NCLB) mandates accountability through evidence-based practice that enhances student achievement. As a result, the potential of single-sex class arrangements has entered the discussion among educators striving to address declines in student performance, especially in the middle school years. Therefore, an examination of this

Table 13.4. Parent Responses at the End of Year 3

Statement	*Agree*	*Neutral*	*Disagree*
I was adequately informed about the option of single gender classes for my children.	63%	16%	20%
I have had experience with single-sex classes myself as a student.	17%	18%	65%
I wanted my child to be in single-sex classes.	51%	24%	25%
My spouse/partner agreed with my decision about single-sex classes.	56%	32%	12%
My child agreed with the decision we made about single-sex class placement.	60%	21%	19%
Single-sex classes help students learn better.	49%	26%	25%
Single-sex classes provide a safer environment for children.	38%	38%	24%
I have seen an improvement in my child's school achievement because of single gender classes.	29%	43%	28%
My child has enjoyed single-sex classes.	36%	42%	22%
Mixed-gender classes create more social pressure than single-sex classes.	61%	18%	21%
There is more bullying in single-sex classes than in mixed classes.	31%	42%	27%
Single-sex classes allowed my child to stay younger longer.	22%	56%	22%
Mixed-gender classes help children learn how to function in the real world.	51%	30%	19%
I would choose single-sex classes again.	46%	22%	32%
Single-sex classes should continue to be an option at Forest Valley Middle School.	59%	25%	16%

school's experience through the lens of achievement tests scores might inform policymakers about the efficacy of this arrangement.

Standardized testing is an annual event in this school. Since TerraNova tests were being used to predict student performance on the state's eighth grade proficiency test, school officials were eager to examine these tests to assess the effectiveness of the single-sex classes. Therefore, after the first year of the reform, a comparison was made of that year's TerraNova scores of students with the scores of the previous school year when all students were in mixed classes. This analysis revealed small gains in achievement throughout the dataset, for students in both single and mixed classes. Interestingly, these gains in achievement test scores were more pronounced in the sixth grade. However, it is important to note that t

Table 13.5. Grade 6 in Year 1: Total Population (N = 114)

Content Area Tested	*Grade 5: 2001-2002 Mean (SD)*	*Grade 6: 2002-2003 Mean (SD)*	*Change? (+, –, =)*	*t*	*Sig. (2-tailed)*
Reading	47.8 (28.7)	49.1 (28.3)	+	–.324	.747
Vocabulary	42.7 (28.9)	44.0 (25.8)	+	–.846	.399
Reading comprehension	45.2 (29.7)	46.6 (28.1)	+	–.951	.344
Language	46.4 (28.9)	46.5 (28.6)	=	–.076	.939
Language mechanics	39.1 (25.2)	42.2 (23.5)	+	–1.225	.223
Language composite	42.2 (28.1)	44.4 (26.7)	+	–.968	.335
Mathematics	46.5 (26.5)	47.6 (28.1)	+	–.275	.783
Math computation	45.3 (25.0)	47.6 (24.4)	+	–.829	.409
Math concepts	45.9 (26.4)	48.1 (26.3)	+	–.786	.434
Total battery	46.6 (27.6)	46.7 (29.3)	=	–.224	.823
Science	44.5 (28.8)	50.6 (25.2)	+	–1.524	.130
Social studies	45.9 (27.7)	49.0 (27.4)	+	–.571	.569
Spelling	46.6 (29.1)	52.3 (28.9	+	–2.057	.042

tests for independent samples revealed no statistically significant differences among the scores in both grades, except in the area of spelling.

Overall, in the first year of the study, the mean scores for *all* students in Grade 6 showed improvement on the TerraNova tests over their performance in Grade 5. The results were not as positive for seventh grade students. Interviews with the seventh grade students had already revealed greater resistance to the single-sex arrangements in the first year of the reform. Therefore, not surprisingly, in the analysis of the first year's test scores, although mean scores for Grade 7 students showed improvement in some areas of study over their performance in Grade 6, they did not exhibit the same global gains as their younger peers. Table 13.5 contains the analysis of test scores for all sixth grade students. Table 13.6 contains the overall analysis of all students in Grade 7 who had been in the total population for both Grade 6 (when all classes were mixed) and Grade 7.

Two years later, after the single-sex classes had been established for 3 years, comparison of the TerraNova test scores from Year 1 and Year 3 revealed specific and perhaps more interesting results, with some limitations. Because the student population had changed over time due to normal attrition and change within the community, students not in school for all three years were eliminated from the sample. This reduced the dataset

Table 13.6. Grade 7 in Year 1: Total Population (n = 133)

Content area tested	*Grade 6: 2001 - 2002 Mean (SD)*	*Grade 7: 2002 - 2003 Mean (SD)*	*Change? (+, –, =)*	*t*	*Sig. (2-tailed)*
Reading	57.8 (22.7)	56.6 (25.5)	–	.805	.422
Vocabulary	49.8 (23.8)	49.2 (24.5)	=	.302	.763
Reading comprehension	54.0 (23.8)	52.8 (25.0)	–	.443	.658
Language	55.9 (26.8)	56.8 (26.2)	+	–.208	.836
Language mechanics	55.9 (26.8)	44.4 (26.8)	–	1.067	.288
Language composite	47.4 (26.0)	50.0 (26.9)	+	.702	.484
Mathematics	52.3 (26.9)	54.5 (27.6)	+	.540	.590
Math computation	55.7 (27.7)	55.9 (26.8)	=	–.166	.868
Math concepts	55.1 (27.5)	56.0 (27.6)	=	.283	.777
Total battery	57.2 (25.1)	56.6 (26.7)	–	.346	.730
Science	57.1 (25.0)	54.3 (26.4)	–	.305	.761
Social studies	55.6 (25.9)	54.1 (26.9)	–	.263	.793
Spelling	57.8 (25.5)	49.9 (26.2)	–	2.757	.007

but made it possible examine the performance of the students over the three years of the reform.

However, an important change in the data sample occurred because the school placed students with higher academic grades into mixed honors mathematics classes. Because of staffing concerns, the school had not created three separate honors level math classes, one each for boys and girls and one mixed class. This organizational change caused students to switch from single-sex to mixed arrangements for academic reasons that precluded the choice to remain in single-sex classes. This was a clear example of how other organizational reforms within the school environment make it difficult to attribute any changes in achievement solely to single-sex classes.

Despite this important limitation, several interesting insights emerged about the performance of students in each of the arrangements. In reading, there were gains across the board for all students regardless of whether they were in mixed or single-sex classes. In math, scores declined in single sex-classes, but increased for all students in mixed classes, with a notably large increase among girls in the mixed classes. This finding seems to contradict conventional wisdom about the achievement of girls in mathematics classes. However, the gains in mathematics scores in the

Table 13.7. Percentile Changes on TerraNova Tests in Year 3

	Reading	*Math*	*Language Arts*	*Total Battery*
Whole school	+1.7	−.85	+3.6	+1.4
Total boys	+1.1	−1.2	+3.2	+.95
Total girls	+2.3	−.49	+3.9	+1.8
All students in single-sex classes	+1.4	−1.6	+6.1	+2.0
All students in mixed classes	+3.5	+5.6	−10.8	−1.5
Single-sex boys	+.80	−1.9	+6.0	+1.8
Single-sex girls	+2.0	−1.4	+6.3	+2.3
Mixed boys	+2.9	+2.3	−11.1	−3.3
Mixed girls	+4.1	+9.0	−10.4	+.28

mixed classes quite logically derived from the sample of honors students in those mixed classes and the rigor of the curriculum. Students in the mixed mathematics classes started with higher scores and gained more over the year.

Students in the single-sex classes showed the greatest gains on the Language subtest. On the other hand, students in mixed classes declined sharply (10 percentile points) in the language section of the test, with the sharpest decline among boys in the mixed classes. These findings merit further exploration. There were also gains on the Total Battery of the TerraNova test, except among boys in the mixed classes and among all mixed students taken as a group. Although the scores among the girls in mixed classes virtually stayed the same from Grade 5 to 7 on the Total Battery of the test, there were large gains in reading and mathematics. Table 13.7 contains the percentile changes for all academic courses over the 3 years of the single-sex arrangement.

DISCUSSION

This study set out to explore the phenomenon of newly implemented single-sex classes in a public middle school. Standard qualitative protocols, i.e., interviews and observations, were supplemented by quantitative explorations, through the surveys derived from the interviews. Other quantitative analyses of standardized test scores were also conducted to provide additional information that might further illuminate the phenomenon.

Age, gender, and social development are evident as important considerations in the organization of single-sex classes in this public middle school. According to the students interviewed and surveyed, the majority of students in all grades stated that they could focus more in single-sex classes. However, students in the sixth grade reported greater satisfaction with single-sex classes than the older students. Seventh grade students felt the most negatively about the arrangement, verbalizing the importance of social concerns. On the other hand, eighth grade students were more positive about the arrangement than the seventh graders. These generalizations suggest that single-sex classes are not a panacea for the conventional stresses and discontent experienced by adolescents in seventh grade. Not surprisingly, all students overwhelmingly agreed that they should have the power to decide whether they would be in single-sex classes and how long they would remain in those classes. The right to choose the organizational format of their classes was perceived as beneficial by both students and their parents.

The adults in this study, the teachers and the parents, gave mixed reviews to the reform. Most of the parents regarded the single-sex arrangements as both socially and academically safe. The teachers were divided in their assessment of the reform. Many of them attested to the cognitive benefits of the reform, but several others also decried the behavioral dynamics of students in the seventh and eighth grade. The placement of the students with higher academic grades into mixed mathematics classes in seventh and eighth grade may have affected those dynamics among those students left in the single-sex classes.

The analysis of achievement test scores provide limited support for the conclusion that can be drawn from the qualitative component of this study. Single-sex class arrangements seem to have worked for some students. Tests of statistical significance failed to reveal strong quantifiable results, but those analyses were ancillary to the qualitative explorations. The quantitative analyses of test scores after the first year of single-sex classes suggest that other factors might well have been working together that year to produce these results among the sixth grade students. First, changes in curriculum delivery and/or awareness of curriculum delivery might have impacted the ways in which teachers presented that information to the students. Second, the opportunity to select the type of class arrangement might well have affected the way in which students approached their studies. In other words, because students had more control over how they were arranged, they might have interacted more readily and more eagerly with their course work. Moreover, the age and development of the students may also have affected the outcomes.

In the third year, test score gains revealed minimally positive patterns of achievement in reading and language arts, especially in the single-sex classes. On the other hand, gains in mathematics in the mixed classes may have been related to the curriculum and rigor of instruction in the honors level class. Gains in language arts were the greatest, but the decline in language scores in mixed classes deserves further scrutiny. Therefore, no definitive statement can be made about the effectiveness of this school's single-sex classes in raising test scores across the entire population.

CONCLUSION

Two key conclusions emerged from this study. First, single-sex class arrangements seem to be most effective when related to the developmental needs of the students: that is the younger the student, the more likely that being in a single-sex class will be a positive experience. Second, in a public school environment, single-sex classes should be presented as optional to parents and students, with flexibility within the school day and over the student's middle school years.

This study suggests that single-sex class arrangements seem to have merit for those students who are positively disposed to being involved in them, as long as they are given the choice to participate and the opportunity to opt out. Moreover, it seemed that the younger the student, the more likely that student responded favorably to single-sex classes. Both in the interviews and the surveys that followed, students in the sixth grade reported more positive responses than the older students in the study. Teachers corroborated the benefits for the youngest students in the population. Therefore, this study further suggests that providing single-sex classes for students in fifth and sixth grade might be the most effective organizational design.

Students of all grades reinforced the importance of emotional, intellectual, and physical safety in single-sex classes. These are perennial concerns in the middle grades. However, the problem of bullying emerged among the seventh and eighth grade boys in single-sex classes, but the students who were interviewed did not agree on which arrangement might be less bully-prone. The teachers, on the other hand, cited negative behaviors, like bullying, as a problem they associated with the single-sex classes in seventh and eighth grade.

Therefore, caution dictates that further analysis might reveal a pattern of bullying developing over time, especially in the all-male environment. The school must take measures to assure that a "Lord of the Flies" scenario does not emerge from a policy that keeps students in the same single-sex classes over the 3 years of middle school. Sorting students into different all-male configurations in each of the three grades might address this problem. On the other hand, the predominantly positive responses among the girls in this study seem to suggest that single-sex classes might be effective for girls in the middle school grades. Teachers and parents alike regarded the single-sex classes as positive environments for the girls, providing both social and academic benefits.

TAKING THE LONG VIEW: IMPLICATIONS FOR PRACTICE

In the middle school years, choice and ownership are critical to the development of young adolescents into autonomous learners. Jackson and Davis (2000) strongly recommended the involvement of the students and their parents in decision-making involving school arrangements for students. When schools implement single-sex classes, they should also offer that choice equitably to both girls and boys, and there must be no distinction about the types of courses afforded to students of either sex. By providing the option of single-sex environments within the existing school framework for students in the early middle years (Grades 5 and 6), middle schools can also provide cost-effective school choice for parents, and thereby involve them as stakeholders in the education of their children. The responses of the parents in this survey corroborate the recommendations of *Turning Points 2000* (Jackson & Davis, 2000) regarding the rights and responsibilities of parents in helping the school to structure the learning experiences of their children.

Much of the rhetoric surrounding the school choice debate centers on the monolithic structure of the typical public school. Other issues, particularly those that involve staffing and facilities, often create obstacles for choice in a typical public middle school, particularly in suburban and rural schools where there is only one school to serve all students. Creating single-sex classes for academic areas allows students to experience the benefits of single-sex classes, to interact with other genders throughout the day, and to remain within the confines of one school building. However, a recent study of single-sex classes in California concluded that, while providing choice for parents and students, single-sex public schooling "is not necessarily a panacea for the problems of gender equity in public education" (Datnow, Hubbard, & Conchas, 2001, p. 203).

Teacher buy-in is also important, as is the professional development of teachers for this reform. Recent studies (Gurian, 2000) on the ways in which boys and girls learn can inform teachers about the ways in which they might best serve their students, whether they are in single-sex or mixed classes. Teachers should also have the choice of whether they will teach in single-sex classes. This study did not explore the assignment of teachers to single-sex classes according to their sex, an arrangement that has recently gained attention (Dee, 2006).

Survey and interview responses from all stakeholder groups strongly suggest that single-sex scheduling should be flexible within the school environment, allowing for variations in the organization of teams. This district displayed innovative programming by restricting single-sex classes to only the academic core courses and providing for coeducational interaction throughout the rest of the school day. Offering subject specific single-sex classes in each grade would provide even more flexibility within the existing school walls. Although this would stretch the limits of the traditional teaming concept, when two equally good goals are at issue, creative and collaborative school administrators can and should design innovative educational environments that are not prescriptive while meeting the needs of the particular student population.

The teachers who taught both single-sex and mixed classes in this study attested to their belief that cognitive benefits derived from the single-sex arrangement for those students who had selected that option. Parents also corroborated the teachers' perspectives, but it was the students' themselves who offered the most salient observations of this phenomenon that has been regarded as new among public schools but actually has had a long history in American education. In this school, single-sex classes provided opportunities for success among the students involved in them. For these young adolescents, single-sex classes fostered a situation in which time flies, because the students were having fun, while learning with their same-sex peers.

REFERENCES

American Association of University Women. (1998). *Separated by sex: A critical look at single-sex education for girls*. Washington, DC: Author.

Clewell, B. (2002). Breaking the barriers: The critical middle school years. In E. Rassen, L. Iura, & P. Berkman (Eds.), *Gender in education* (pp. 301-313). San Francisco: Jossey-Bass.

Creswell, J. W. (1998). *Qualitative inquiry and research design: Choosing among five traditions*. Thousand Oaks, CA: Sage.

Creswell, J. W. (2003). *Research design: Qualitative, quantitative, and mixed method approaches* (2nd ed.) Thousand Oaks, CA: Sage.

Datnow, A., Hubbard, L., & Conchas, G. (2001). How context mediates policy: The implementation of single gender public schooling in California. *Teachers College Record, 103(2)*, 184-206.

Dee, T. S. (2006). *The why chromosome: How a teacher's gender affects boys and girls*. (Hoover Institution, Education Next, 2006: No. 4). Stanford, CA: Stanford University.

Gurian, M. (2000). *Boys and girls learn differently*. San Francisco: Jossey-Bass.

Jackson, A., & Davis, G. (2000). *Turning points 2000: Educating adolescents in the 21st century.* New York: Teachers College Press.

Sadker, M., & Sadker, D. (1995). *Failing at fairness: How our schools cheat girls.* New York: Simon & Schuster.

Salomone, R. (2003). *Same, different, equal: Rethinking single-sex schooling.* New Haven, CT: Yale University Press.

Sommers, C. (2002). Why Johnny can't, like, read and write. In E. Rassen, L. Iura, & P. Berkman (Eds.), *Gender in education* (pp. 700-721). San Francisco: Jossey-Bass.

Spielhagen, F. (2006). How 'tweens view single-sex classes: Students talk about some benefits—and some drawbacks—of single-sex classes. *Educational Leadership, 63*(7), 69-75.

Tyack, D., & Hansot, E. (2002). Feminists discover the hidden injuries of coeducation. In E. Rassen, L. Iura, & P. Berkman (Eds.), *Gender in education* (pp. 12-50). San Francisco: Jossey-Bass.

Vu, P. (2006). *Single-gender schools on the rise*. Retrieved September 21, 2006, from www.stateline.org

CHAPTER 14

EXAMINING THE TRANSITION FROM MIDDLE SCHOOL TO HIGH SCHOOL

Translating Research Into Practice

Joshua S. Smith and Sungtaek Lim

ABSTRACT

This chapter introduces a transformative research process to the study of the transition from middle school to high school. The author worked closely with a large school district in the Midwest to conduct a comprehensive multiple method study examining perceptions of the transition. Students completed a pretransition and posttransition survey about their expectations and experiences in the academic, social, organization, and school support aspects of high school. Focus groups and interviews with eighth grade teachers, guidance counselors, and principals were conducted to understand the context in which the student perceptions were reported. Four repeated measures 2 × 2 analyses of variance (ANOVA) with time and gender as variables revealed no significant difference between students' pre- and postperceptions of academic or social areas. A pattern of change on the social subscale

The Young Adolescent and the Middle School
pp. 277–296

shows girls growing increasingly more confident, while boys report a slight decrease in social confidence as they transitioned to high school. Significant changes on the organization subscale for girls suggest that their pretransition concerns were alleviated in the ninth grade. Eighth grade school personnel expressed concern that both boys and girls would experience academic and behavioral challenges because the high school operates distinctly different from the middle school. This chapter has implications for university and school collaborative research and provides a transferable process for examining schoolwide phenomena such as educational transitions.

The transition from middle school to high school is receiving increased attention from researchers, practitioners, and policymakers. Reasons for the interest can be tied to the fact that ninth grade course failures, expulsions and suspensions, and high school dropout rates exceed that of all other secondary school grades (Hertzog & Morgan, 1998; National Center for Education Statistics, 2002; Roderick & Camburn, 1999). For students and parents, the transition from middle school to high school equates with feelings of anticipation and anxiety (Mizelle & Irvin, 2000; Morgan & Hertzog, 2001; Zeedyk, Gallacher, Henderson, Hope, Husband, & Lindsay, 2003). A rite of passage aura exists with regard to moving to high school. Increased social and academic opportunities and the requisite responsibilities that go along with them are often not uniformly defined in the minds of students, families, and teachers (Akos & Galassi, 2004a).

Schiller (1999) defined academic transition as "a *process* during which institutional and social factors influence which students' educational careers are positively or negatively affected by this movement between organizations" (pp. 216-217). The process Schiller speaks of echoes Hertzog and Morgan's (1999) reminder that transition is not an event, but rather an extended period of time that influences student attitudes and behaviors across two distinct organizations. Middle schools following the major tenets of the middle school philosophy (e.g., student-centered instruction, building a community of learners, teaming, experiential learning, alternative scheduling) operate quite differently from the traditional junior high and high school setting (Kienholz, 2001). The many differences in organizational structure, pedagogical approaches, and systems of support have implications for how students experience the transition to high school. There is nothing magical about the summer between eighth and ninth grade that prepares students to be successful in traditional high school settings. Middle school and high school personnel offer programs and experiences to help familiarize students with the similarities and differences in the academic, social, and organizational structures of the schools (Mizelle, 1999). Unfortunately the programs often occur in isolation rather than as a coherent, comprehensive series of programs (Mizelle, 2005). For example, some transition program are purely informational settings where the focus is course selection and others are school visits designed to show students the physical layout of the high school building and grounds. There is little evidence of coordination or consistency in the program goals across the middle school and high school divide. The transition from middle school to high school has not received much scholarly attention (Akos & Galassi, 2004a; Mizelle, 1999). One way for school districts to better understand transition is to systematically collect information about how students, families, and school personnel view the transition period and use the data to develop materials and programs that assist students in making a successful transition from middle school to high school.

In this chapter, we suggest that there is a positive relationship between the extent to which stakeholders in middle schools and high schools: (a) understand discrepancies in their perspectives, (b) consistently and accurately describe the similarities and differences between middle school and high school, (c) collaboratively articulate curriculum, and (d) describe the transition from middle school to high school. This chapter provides an example of how university researchers partnered with school personnel to collect data, interpret findings, and act on those findings to improve student and school personnel communication around the transition from middle school to high school. The process reflects a transformative, participatory research approach to studying schoolwide issues (Kemmis & McTaggart, 2005; Sanders, 1981).

Research on the Transition From Middle School to High School

Large-scale quantitative studies of the impact of transition on academic achievement show that students experience a "normative" decrease in grades from middle school to high school (Alspaugh, 1998a, 1998b; Isakson & Jarvis, 1999). Alspaugh (1998a) suggested that the relationship between transition and achievement is not consistent across school configurations and the number of school-to-school transitions was related to achievement loss. In an ex post facto study of 48 school districts, Alspaugh (1998a) found that students who attended school districts with transitions at Grade 6 and Grade 9 experienced greater achievement loss than students attending schools with K-8 and 9-12 configurations. Seidman, Allen, Aber, Mitchell, and Feinman (1994) coined the term *double-jeopardy* to describe the negative impact of multiple transitions on students' academic and social development.

The advent of freshmen centers and ninth grade wings within high school buildings adds another dimension to the school configuration debate around transition. Many freshmen centers operate more closely to the middle school philosophy than a high school approach. The centers attempt to build a learning community and often include teaming and advisory programs. In one of the few published works on the impact of freshmen centers or wings on student outcomes, McIntosh and White (2006) showed a progressive reduction in ninth grade course failures and suspensions and expulsions in the years since the freshmen wing was opened. More research is needed regarding the impact of freshmen centers on students' outcomes.

Akos and Galassi (2004a) compared students', caregivers', and teachers' retrospective perceptions of the transitional aspects that they "looked forward to" or "worried about." Although students and caregivers had similar perceptions of the positive aspects of the transition, teachers and school staff perceived different concerns for students. For example, the top concerns for students included the amount of homework and classes being more difficult. Parents also mentioned the amount of homework and pressure to do well in school. Teachers' top concerns were about social issues such as the students' difficulty fitting in or making new friends. Another study examined middle school students' perceptions of "making it" or being successful in secondary school (Zeedyk et al., 2003). Prior to entering high school, students cited academic ability as the most important characteristic. After entering high school, students added issues such as time management, ability to stay on task, social skills, and behavior as essential elements in being successful. Students' social concerns such as bullying, getting lost, and establishing peer relationships at secondary school overshadowed the middle-level concerns that focused on the academic and ability aspects of being successful in school. Smith, Feldwisch, and Abell's (2006) study of parent and student perceptions of the transition to high school revealed that eighth graders expressed greater concern than parents about academic issues such as having difficult teachers and classes in high school. However, students reported less concern than parents about social issues such as being bullied and experiencing peer pressure. The general patterns indicate that students look forward to the positive social dimensions of high school, whereas their parents are concerned about potential social problems. The study presented in this chapter expands on the research by involving school personnel and comparing ninth graders' experiences with their eighth grade perceptions of high school.

Students do not experience transition uniformly, and research shows that the effects of transition differ for boys and girls. Girls tend to experience greater difficulties adjusting to high school with respect to social aspects, whereas boys are more likely than girls to struggle academically (Eccles et al., 1993). For example, Alspaugh (2000) showed that irrespective of school configuration and the timing of transition, boys had higher dropout rates than girls. Linking this finding with the research on achievement loss in his previous studies highlights the importance of addressing transition issues regardless of school configuration. Akos and Galassi (2004b) examined gender differences in the transition to high school. In a study of 320 ninth graders, they reported no significant differences in boys' and girls' perceptions of school difficulty. However, boys reported feeling more connected to the school and felt a greater level of support from family other than parents and students. Weinstein, Mermelstein, Hedeker, Hankin, and Flay's (2006) study of peer and family support and its impact on mood during the transition to high school showed that girls reported higher levels of support from peers, but boys reported higher levels of support from their family. A noteworthy finding is that peer support was a predictor of girls' negative mood and family support was a strong predictor of positive mood for boys. These studies point to the importance of a comprehensive examination of the transition from middle school to high school that includes an attention to similarities and difference by gender.

Transition Programs

Transitional programming must involve intentional collaboration between eighth and ninth grade buildings and personnel (Mizelle, 2005). Stakeholders in both buildings must systematically identify what Gibson (1969) called the *distinctive features* of academic, social, and organization logistics and philosophies in middle school and high school. The idea is not to say that middle schools and high schools should operate or function the same, but rather that they intentionally identify what makes each unique and determine the ways in which those differences are explained to students and families. Transition programs and messages about transition that encourage students and families to reflect on and experience the complexities and nuances of the distinctive features of high school are likely to have a greater impact than isolated information sessions (Mizelle & Irvin, 2000). High school dropout rates are significantly lower in school districts that have explicit middle school to high school transition programs (Morgan & Hertzog, 2001; Smith, 1997). The same is true for high schools that have programs to identify students who are failing courses early in the ninth grade (Roderick & Camburn, 1999).

Patterns of effective transition programs include such things as expanding the number and duration of visits between schools, allowing students to spend a day with secondary school students, inviting secondary school students and teachers to speak at the feeder schools, and providing mentoring to middle school students by secondary school students. Academic aspects of effective transition supports include curriculum articulation and clearly articulating academic expectations (e.g., academic rigor of courses). Effective transition programs also include organization issues such as exposing students to various facilities (e.g., location of classrooms and restrooms), and sharing information about issues safety and how discipline is handled (e.g., rules and discipline code; Mizelle, 2005; Zeedyk et al., 2003). Beyond having aspects of transition programs, schools should consider how each program or events inform other programs and they should collect and analyze data to see if individual programs and their overall approach to transition meet their intended goals.

Translational Research in Middle-Level Education

Issues such as understanding academic transition and assessing the effectiveness of transition programs are best investigated using the translational research model. Educational research, including research in middle level education, is generally university focused and rarely intentionally includes schools and school personnel as partners in the research. Over 20 years ago Sanders (1981) cautioned university professors and researchers about languishing in the ivory towers, stating:

> Research tends to be an activity conducted by an elite class of professionals; practitioners are generally expected to depend on the results of research "disseminated" to them. The consequence is that scientific studies tend to be reported to the specialized subgroup with which the investigator identifies. Researchers identify with, and publish for, communities that do not include practitioners and vice versa. (p. 10)

Researchers employing participatory research, community action research, and action research frameworks attempt to counter the traditional university, research-centered model (Greenwood & Levin, 2005). Combining ideas from participatory action research (Kemmis & McTaggart, 2005) and the scholarship of teaching frameworks in higher education (Shulman, 2000), this section presents the framework that guided the study.

Partly in response to the lack of research on instruction, as well as the time it takes for research to inform practice, Shulman (2000) challenged faculty in higher education to engage in the scholarship of teaching and learning. He pointed to three important reasons, including professionalism, pragmatism, and policy. In middle-level education terms, professionalism refers to teachers' and administrators' obligations to understand their students, pedagogy, and programs and to share what they glean in public and professional organizations. Pragmatism is the need to constantly reflect on what one is doing and to modify what is not working. For example, looking critically at practice and sharing it publicly (e.g., *Middle School Journal, Middle Ground*) informs the field and encourages other practitioners to engage in scholarship. Finally, Schulman noted the policy implications associated with the scholarship of teaching and learning. Systematic investigation of the impact on pedagogy and programming is needed to make decisions regarding efficacy, investments, and evidence to external stakeholders (e.g., school board, families, teachers, and students) regarding the value of the education provided to citizens.

Translational research can be applied to schoolwide issues (e.g., transition, character education, citizenship, community service, and dropout prevention) since they represent specific forms of teaching and learning. The framework is not new; however, revisiting the importance of university researcher-school collaborative research is timely. Teachers and administrators are increasingly being asked to collect and analyze achievement, behavioral referral, and year-to-year school retention data (Darling-Hammond, 2004). Policy decisions and interventions to reduce negative indicators and improve teaching and learning are often not intentionally implemented, studied, or disseminated into the public for critique. This process often excludes teachers in any meaningful way, alienating them, and often resulting in teacher resistance to change. Approaching the study from a translational framework addresses these limitations by building on the shared ideas and expertise of practitioners and researchers.

RESEARCH DESIGN

The purpose of this chapter is to describe how the translational research process is being used to study the transition from middle school to high school. The research follows a previous study that looked at the similarities and differences between students' and parents' perceptions prior to the transition to high school (Smith, Feldwisch, & Abell, 2006). Based on feedback from eighth grade principals and teachers, the study was expanded to include qualitative data from focus group discussions with eighth grade teachers and interviews with eighth grade counselors and principals. In addition, the quantitative analyses moved from focusing on students perceptions in the eighth grade to include a short-term longitudinal study of the extent to which boys' and girls' expectations (pretransition) were similar or different from their experiences (posttransition).

Setting

The school district includes three middle schools that feed into a large high school. The district is located in between a large urban area and the outer suburbs. The district is committed to the middle school philosophy and the schools offer a number of programs based on the best practices literature on educational transitions. In terms of academic orientation, for example, the high school offers a curriculum night where students and families are informed about the various academic programs offered in the high school. During January of their eighth grade year, the high school director of counseling meets with students and families to describe the program offerings at the high school. Throughout the spring, students meet with middle school counselors to schedule their programs of study for the ninth grade year. Socially, the ninth graders host a dance party for the eighth graders that is held at the high school and the school band/choir perform in joint concerts with high school musicians. To address organizational barriers, middle school students visit the high school for a day. In addition, the majority of students participate in the district's long-standing transition program, PantherQuest, an all day orientation program offered in the summer prior to ninth grade. Upperclass students facilitate various workshops on academic, social, and organizational components in the high school.

Participants

At the end of eighth grade, 141 students completed a survey regarding their perceptions of the transition to ninth grade in a large township in the Midwest. Eighty-one (57%) of the students were female and 60 (43%) were male. Eighty-one (58%) of the students were White, 44 (32%) were African American, 8 (5%) were Latino, 1 (1%) was American Indian, 1 (1%) was Asian, and 4 (3%) identified themselves as multiracial. Of the 141 respondents, 43 (30%) received a free or reduced-price lunch. The mean eighth grade GPA for the participants was 2.85 of out 4.0. Ninety-four students who completed the eighth grade survey completed the post-transition survey in the ninth grade. Demographic indicators of ninth grade participants were consistent with the eighth grade sample. Four eighth grade guidance counselors and the three middle school principals participated in one-on-one interviews. Twenty teachers participated in focus group discussions regarding their perceptions of how students feel and experience the transition from middle school to high school.

Measures

Survey

Students completed the *Perceptions of Transition Survey* at the end of eighth grade and again during the middle of their ninth grade year. The survey was adapted from Akos and Galassi (2004a) and measures students' feelings about academic, social, and organization aspects of high school. Each item is scored on a 4-point, Likert-response format ranging from 1 (*strongly disagree*) to 4 (*strongly agree*). Approximately half of the items ask about issues that students are "looking forward to" and the other half ask students to reflect on areas of concern or areas that they are "worried about." The areas of concern items were reversed scored and overall subscales averages were created. Higher subscale scores reflect positive expectations and experiences in the areas of academic, social, and organization, respectively. The final subscale of the survey (Helper) asked students to rate how helpful their eighth grade counselor, eighth grade teachers, and their parents were in assisting them prior to and after the transition to high school. The three helpers were rated on a 4-point scale ranging from 1 (*not at all helpful*) to 4 (*very helpful*).

Interviews and Focus Groups

Qualitative data were gathered from interviews and focus groups with school personnel. Interviews with eighth grade guidance counselors and principals and focus group discussions with eighth grade teams of teachers focused on their expectations of the academic, social, and organizational changes that occur in high school. The questions, adopted from Letrello and Miles (2003), includes: (a) Describe the major differences between eighth grade and ninth grade, and (b) Describe the most challenging aspects students face when moving from middle school to the high school. Follow-up prompts were used to clarify and extend participants' responses and to elicit specific examples to support the participants' perspectives.

Data Analysis

Quantitative

Descriptive statistics were calculated to examine the overall trends prior to and after transitions. Gender and time were the independent variables in each analysis and the dependent variables were perceptions of academic, social, organization, and helper, respectively. To examine the presence of gender differences in pretransition and posttransition perceptions, four separate repeated measures 2 × 2 (Gender × Time) analysis of variance (ANOVA) were conducted. Examination of the main effects for gender, time, and a gender and time interaction determined the extent to which boys' and girls' expectations of high school (pretransition) differed from their experiences in ninth grade (posttransition).

Qualitative

A content analysis was performed on the interview and focus group transcripts using the consensual qualitative research (CQR) method (Hill, Thompson, & Nutt Williams, 1997). A team of graduate and undergraduate students independently reviewed the transcripts for codes. At this stage of the analysis, the goal was to label the areas of opportunities and concern within each transcript. Analysis discrepancies between the researchers were resolved via consensus. The final aspect of examining the analysis involved a cross-case analysis (Miles & Huberman, 1994). The first author of this chapter served as the auditor during each step, independently identifying codes and meeting with the research team to discuss, debate, and eventually arrive at consensus on the codes.

RESULTS

Table 14.1 presents the means and standard deviations for student perceptions of the academic, social, organization, and helper subscales prior to and after the transition to high school. Data are presented for all students and then separated by gender. Students in the sample reported generally positive perceptions of their expectations and experiences with the transition to high school. Perceptions of high school academic issues increased slightly, but not significantly from middle school ($M = 2.95$, $SD = .40$) to high school ($M = 3.05$, $SD = .50$), $F(1, 91) = 3.17$, $p = .08$. In terms of the social aspects, students remained generally optimistic before ($M = 3.21$, $SD = .41$) and after the transition ($M = 3.23$, $SD = .31$), $F(1, 91) = .01$, $p > .05$. The main effect for time was significant in the area of organization. Prior to the transition, students scores on the subscale were significantly lower ($M = 2.87$, $SD = .53$) in middle school than in high school ($M = 3.10$, $SD = .38$), $F(1, 91) = 10.67$, $p < .01$, suggesting that their concerns in eighth grade were alleviated. Students' retrospective reports of support from eighth grade counselors, eighth grade teachers, and their parents ($M = 2.68$, $SD = .73$) decreased significantly from their perceptions of support while in eighth grade ($M = 3.09$, $SD = .58$), $F(1, 91) = 29.34$, $p < .01$.

Gender Differences in Transition

There were no significant gender differences in boys' and girls' perceptions of academic issues prior to and after the transition to high school, $F(1, 92) = 1.70$, $p > .05$. Both boys' and girls' scores on the academic sub-

Table 14.1. Subscale Descriptive Statistics for Full Sample and by Gender and Time (*N* = 94)

	Pretest		*Posttest*	
Subscales	*M*	*SD*	*M*	*SD*
Academic	2.95	.40	3.05	.50
Social	3.21	.41	3.23	.31
Organization	2.87	.53	3.10	.38
Helpers	3.09	.58	2.68	.73
		Males (n = 41)		
Academic	2.99	0.40	3.12	0.64
Social	3.28	0.41	3.21	0.35
Organization	3.07	0.51	3.11	0.46
Helpers	3.07	0.60	2.75	0.82
		Females (n = 53)		
Academic	2.92	0.40	3.00	0.35
Social	3.16	0.41	3.25	0.27
Organizational	2.72	0.50	3.09	0.31
Helpers	3.11	0.57	2.62	0.70

scale scores increased (e.g., middle school perceptions for girls, $M = 2.92$, $SD = .40$; high school perceptions for girls, $M = 3.00$, $SD = .35$; middle school perceptions for boys, $M = 2.99$, SD = .40; high school perceptions for boys, $M = 3.12$, $SD = .64$), indicating that they felt slightly, but not significantly, more positive about academic issues in ninth grade compared to eighth grade. In addition, there were no significant differences in the social aspects of transition, $F(1, 92) = .40, p > .05$. However, according to the interaction pattern shown in Figure 14.1, girls' perceptions of social aspects increased slightly; whereas, boys' perceptions decreased in high school.

There was a significant main effect for time and gender on the organization subscale. Girls' scores in the eighth grade were significantly lower than the boys (middle school perceptions for girls, $M = 2.72$, $SD = .50$; middle school perceptions for boys, $M = 3.07$, $SD = .51$), but the scores were approximately the same in ninth grade (high school perceptions for girls, $M = 3.09$, $SD = .31$; high school perceptions for boys, $M = 3.11$, $SD = .46$). The interaction parameter (Gender × Time) was significant, $F(1, 91) = 7.00, p < .05$.

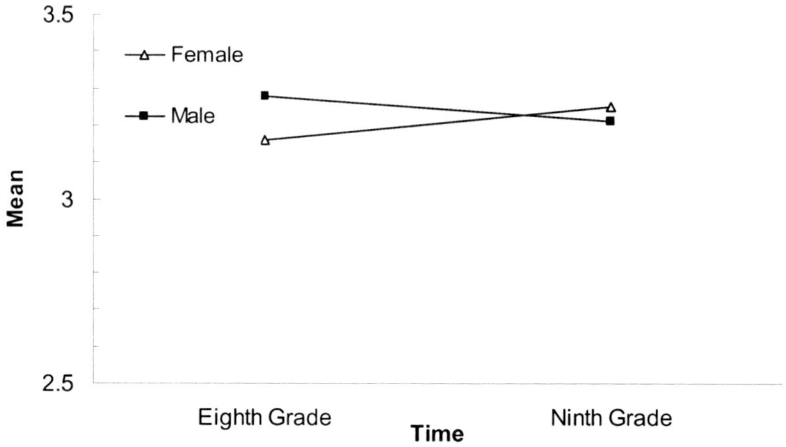

Figure 14.1. Social subscale means by time and gender.

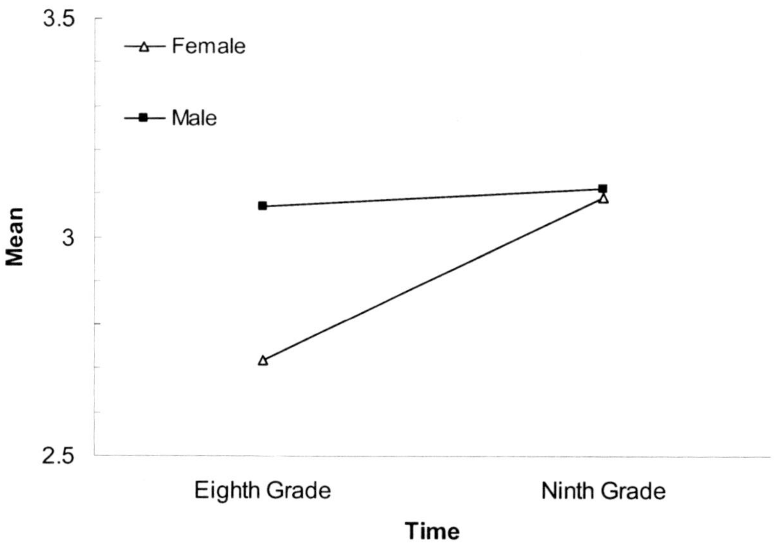

Figure 14.2. Organization subscale means by time and gender.

There were no significant gender differences on the helper subscale. Both boys and girls reported significantly lower levels of support (middle school perceptions for girls, $M = 3.11$, $SD = .57$; high school perceptions for girls, $M = 2.62$, $SD = .70$; middle school perceptions for boys, $M = 3.07$, $SD = .60$; high school perceptions for boys, $M = 2.75$, $SD = .82$.

Standard deviations were larger on the posttransition helper subscale for boys and girls, indicating greater variance in the subscale scores.

School Personnel Perceptions of Transition

Interviews and focus group discussions with school staff provided a context for the student perception data. School staff described several academic challenges that they thought would be difficult for most of their students, and they noted a lack of communication with their high school colleagues. Through the consensual qualitative research process, three major themes were developed including differences in grading, differences in disciplinary expectations and consequences, and the need for better communication between middle school and high school. Participants described the high school grading system as one that operates on a semester system similar to college. They described the system as radically different from the quarterly grade system in the middle school. Teachers and counselors were particularly concerned that students did not understand that if they failed a class they have to retake it and pass the course in order to get credit. One teacher described it this way,

> The difference between middle school and high school is that in middle school you fail the whole year. In high school, if you fail one class, you're going to take that class over again if you want to graduate. (Eighth grade teacher)

A counselor pointed to another difference in the way assessment is conducted and reported. She stated, "Grading is different. It is based on weighted grades, with honors classes weighted more heavily. Also, kids don't understand the meaning of transcripts." One principal reflected on the role of the middle school in helping to bridge these gaps. She described an advisement process that was being used to help to inform students of these academic logistical changes. She was not certain how many students truly understood what they were told and noted the importance of making sure teachers and counselors had accurate information from the high school teachers.

In terms of discipline, school personnel talked about differences in how discipline is handled at the high school. Middle school teachers and principals indicated that they believed that they had more discretion on meting out consequences for infractions than high school staff. One teacher stated that some students would be in for a "rude awakening next year," adding that students would not be able to get away with some of the verbal jarring and foul language they currently hear in the classrooms and hallways. Counselors echoed this concern by saying that there was "definitely less leniency" in academic and disciplinary situations. Principals' perspectives differed slightly from the other staff on this issue. Although principals agreed that there was less tolerance in the high school, they looked beyond the students toward the high school organization itself. Principals stated that there was less support to help "at-risk" students. They noted that some of the disciplinary consequences were not designed to help students get back on track, but rather to exclude students from the building. They noted the high expulsion and suspension rates in the ninth grade as evidence of their claim. Teachers and counselors also felt that the high school could not provide the kind of support they offered in the middle school. Reasons cited for the lack of student-centered focus included the size of the high school as compared to the middle school, the changing role of guidance counseling at the high school (e.g., too many students per counselor for the personal attention they received in middle school), and the overall message that being independent is valued in the high school setting. Middle school personnel thought that unless students and families actively seek out the opportunities, the benefits of a smaller learning community, team teaching, and "wrap-around" services for students who need assistance are gone once students enter the high school.

The final theme involved the lack of communication between school personnel at the middle school and the high school. Each group believed that increased frequency and depth of communication around curricular, disciplinary, and organizational issues would help both staff and students in the transition from middle school to high school. For example, guidance counselors were responsible for assisting students with course selection in the high school and providing information about the nuances of course credits, transcripts, and grading policies. Many counselors thought that a more collaborative role between high school and middle school counselors would help alleviate discrepancies in expectations and reality once students move to the high school. Teachers also talked about student perception of rigor in the high school. As a group they were confident that the level of rigor provided in the middle school aligned with high school academic expectations, but felt that students believed that high school was going to be much harder academically. Teachers attempted to provide accurate information about the academic expectations of high school classes, but felt that they lacked definitive information about some logistic policies such as handing in work late, make-ups, or extra credit that might differ from the middle school academic experience.

DISCUSSION

This study represents the second year of a collaborative effort to collect and analyze data related to the perceptions of transition in a large school district in the Midwest. During the first year, we examined students' and parents' perceptions of the transition at the end of their eighth grade year (Smith, Feldwisch, & Abell, 2006). Similar to the current findings, students in the first year held positive perceptions of the social and academic arenas. They looked forward to having more academic choices and to the opportunity to meet and interact with new friends. Students' concerns generally focused on organizational issues such as getting lost or finding their way around the large high school. Parents shared the academic optimism of the students, but were worried about the social issues. Based on feedback and support from the school, the current study expanded to include a posttransition survey and interviews/focus group discussions with school personnel.

The current study explored student and school personnel perceptions of the transition from middle school to high school. Students' perceptions of the academic and social aspects of the two distinct learning environments were generally positive before and after the transition. Eighth grade students' perceptions of the organizational challenges appeared to be resolved early in their ninth grade experience. Students' retrospective reports of the support or help they received from school personnel and family were lower than indicated prior to the transition. Gender differences emerged on the organization subscale. Girls concerns about the organization challenges dissolved early in their ninth grade year. The interaction trend, girls' perceptions increased slightly, while boys' decreased, on the social subscale should be explored further. Analysis of individual items and focus group discussions with boys and girls separately might provide additional insights for this finding. Eighth grade counselors, teachers, and principals presented a more cautious optimism, pointing to the major differences in the ways that the middle school operates. In particular, school personnel were concerned that students would experience challenges negotiating the academic differences. In addition, they felt some students would struggle adhering to the disciplinary procedures in the high school, which they described as less flexible and less personable.

The findings of this study can be interpreted in light of recent studies of the transition from middle school to high school. Expectations of major discrepancies between eighth grade perceptions and ninth grade experiences were not supported by the data. Similar to Akos and Galassi (2004a, 2004b) students in the current study reported generally positive perceptions of high school prior to and after the transition. Akos and Galassi's (2004b) examination of gender differences in the difficulty of transition and school connectedness showed no differences in difficulty, but males reported feeling more connected with school. Boys also reported feeling a greater level of support from peers and family members other than parents. Girls' perceptions of helpful persons declined significantly and more dramatically than boys. The findings are informed by Weinstein et al. (2006) who looked at the impact of peer and family support on mood. Girls in the current study reported slightly more positive perceptions of the social aspects of high school in ninth grade; whereas, the boys' perceptions moved in the opposite direction. Both boys and girls reported a decrease in perceived help by adults (counselors, teachers, and parents). Taken together, looking at the findings around social and helper subscales is informed by a rationale posited by Weinstein et al. (2006). They reported that girls are increasingly looking to their peers for support. Although parents remain the primary influence over major decisions during young adolescence, peers have an increasing impact on the day-to-day decisions and mood. This has particular relevance for the young adolescents experiencing academic transitions because their potential peer networks have expanded numerically and the students in the high school represent a wider continuum of emotional development.

Few studies have examined teachers' perceptions of the transition for their students. Similar to the Akos and Galassi (2004a) finding, teachers expected the transition to be more difficult or challenging than students reported either in eighth grade or ninth grade. Further studies of the counselor, teacher, and principal perspective at both the middle school and high school levels are needed to shed additional light on the distinctive features of the two educational settings (Gibson, 1969).

Limitations

The findings of this study must be considered in the context of the limitations. The study was conducted in a single school district in the Midwest. Also, there was attrition from the pretransition to posttransition survey. Some of the students left the district, moved to private or parochial schools, or were absent on the day of the post-test. The demographic variables are similar for students who participated in both waves of data collection and those who did not complete the posttest. The attrition reduced the sample from 141 to 94, limiting the generalizability of the findings to the district and other similar school districts. Increasing the sample size will increase the statistical power associated with the analysis, particularly with regards to examining differences in gender, race, and/or socioeconomic status. A second limitation has to do with the nature of the single data source for responses. Students reported their perceptions during the pre- and postadministrations of a survey instrument and school staff reported their perceptions in interviews or focus group settings. There were no additional affective or behavioral measures to support or triangulate the findings. Future inquiry will include in-depth interviews with students and additional quantitative analyses, modeling the relationships between perceptions of transition and achievement and behavior indicators.

Implications for Middle-Level Education

Despite the limitations, the study has important implications for middle-level educators. The study represents a transferable process for studying schoolwide issues and provides the field with additional information about how students and school personnel view the transition from middle school to high school.

Employing the translational research framework has resulted in a university-school partnership that spans the middle and high school levels. The study began with understanding parents' and students' perceptions prior to the transition (Smith, Feldwisch, & Abell, 2006) and expanded to include eighth grade school personnel including teachers, school administrators, and guidance counselors. Involving school personnel went beyond including them as participants in the study. Following the data analysis, school personnel were provided with a summary report that showed the results and patterns for their respective school. Meetings were held to discuss the findings and to talk about ways to reduce the gap between parental and student perceptions. Based on these discussions, the school agreed to create a series of intentional transition messages. The decision was based on consensus that school staff had been accustomed to and were more likely to utter a reactive transition message, "You won't be able to get away with that in the high school," or "You will need to learn this for high school," rather than a proactive message in a school newsletter or class discussion/counselor meeting regarding the similarities and differences in middle school and high school homework.

In addition to meaningful involvement of the eighth grade school personnel, the study has grown to include follow-up data on the ninth grade students. This required coordination with the high school principal and staff. The principal has embraced the study and is working to schedule interviews and focus groups with some of the high school teachers and counselors that work primarily or exclusively with ninth graders. The goal of the next phase of the initiative is to compare middle school and high school personnel perceptions of the academic, social, and organization challenges and opportunities facing students in the district. Next, teachers, guidance counselors, and principals from the three middle schools and the high school will be invited to participate in a *transition conference* to share study findings and to develop strategies to further assist students with the transition.

The decrease in scores on the helper subscale may be an indication that information provided by teachers, counselors, and parent while the students were in eighth grade did not align with their students' ninth grade experiences. In order to address the challenges of educational transitions, better communication of school personnel within and between school buildings is essential (Mizelle, 2005). This is true even in a school district that has spent considerable time and effort adopting best practices in transition programming. Even with all of the programs, it is not clear that students are retaining information about the high school. The next steps for the district are to increase the level and depth of communication across middle-level education and high school education.

Based on the findings, we recommend that school districts, regardless of configuration, build in professional development opportunities for cross-building articulation. In particular, counselors, principals, and staff in both buildings should develop intentional transition messages that accurately articulate academic, social, and organizational differences in the two settings. For example, content discussions about homework expectations and sharing exemplary student work afford middle level and high school educators opportunities to learn from one another. In addition to professional development around transition, assessment of transition programs is needed. Schools can use existing surveys or create their own surveys to measure student perceptions of the relative effectiveness of school visits, counselor meetings, orientation programs, and other programs designed to assist students with the transition from middle school to high school. Analysis of the assessments should look closely to see if gender differences are evident. If gender differences are discovered, schools need to think about ways to address the differential impact for boys and girls. Finally, school personnel in middle school and high schools should listen to students and families regarding their feelings and concerns, while at the same time talking to students about the real similarities and differences between middle school and high school. Cushman's (2006) statement, "No one knows better than students themselves what they need from teachers as they move into high school," (p. 47), provides half of the equation guiding this recommendation. The other half comes from teachers, counselors, and principals working together to develop and disseminate accurate information.

REFERENCES

Akos, P., & Galassi, J. P. (2004a). Middle and high school transitions as viewed by students, parents, and teachers. *Professional School Counseling*, 7(4), 212-221.

Akos, P., & Galassi, J. P. (2004b). Gender and race as variables in psychosocial adjustment to middle school and high school. *Journal of Educational Research, 98*(2), 102-108.

Alspaugh, J. W. (1998a). Achievement loss associated with the transition to middle school and high school. *Journal of Educational Research, 92,* 20-25.

Alspaugh, J. W. (1998b). The relationship of school-to-school transitions and school size to high school dropout rates. *High School Journal, 81*(3), 154-160.

Alspaugh, J. W. (2000). The effect of transition grade to high school, gender, and grade level upon dropout rates. *American Secondary Education, 29*(1), 2-9.

Cushman, K. (2006). Help us make the 9th grade transition. *Educational Leadership, 63,* 47-52.

Darling-Hammond, L. (2004.) Standards, accountability, and school reform. *Teachers College Record, 106*(6), 1047-1085.

Eccles, J. S., Midgley, C., Wigfield, A., Buchanan, C. M., Reuman, D., Flanagan, C., et al. (1993). Development during adolescence. *American Psychologist, 48,* 90-101.

Gibson, E. J. (1969). *Principles of perceptual learning and development.* New York: Appleton-Century-Crofts.

Greenwood, D. J., & Levin, M. (2005). Reform of the social sciences and of universities through action research. In N. K. Denzin & Y. S. Lincoln (Eds.), *The Sage handbook of qualitative research* (3rd ed.) (pp. 43-63). Thousand Oaks, CA: Sage.

Hertzog, C. J., & Morgan, P. L. (1998). Breaking the barriers between middle school and high school success: Developing a transition team for student success. *NASSP Bulletin, 82*(597), 94-98.

Hill, C. E., Thompson, B. J., & Nutt Williams, E. N. (1997). A guide to conducting consensual qualitative research. *The Counseling Psychologist, 25,* 517-572.

Isakson, K., & Jarvis, P. (1999). The adjustment of adolescents during the transition into high school: A short-term longitudinal study. *Journal of Youth and Adolescence, 28*(1), 1-26.

Keinholz, K. B. (2001). From Dewey to Beane: Innovation, democracy, and unity characterize middle level education. *Middle School Journal, 32*(3), 20-24.

Kemmis, S., & McTaggart, R. (2005). Participatory action research: Communicative action and the public sphere. In N. K. Denzin & Y. S. Lincoln (Eds.), *The Sage handbook of qualitative research* (3rd ed.) (pp. 559-601). Thousand Oaks, CA: Sage.

Letrello, T. M., & Miles, D. D. (2003). The transition from middle school to high school: Students with and without learning disabilities share their perceptions. *The Clearing House, 76*(4), 212-214.

McIntosh, J., & White, S. H. (2006). Building for freshman success: High schools working as professional learning communities. *American Secondary Education, 34*(2), 40-49.

Miles, M. B., & Huberman, A. M. (1994). *Qualitative data analysis: An expanded sourcebook,* (2nd ed.). Beverly Hill, CA: Sage.

Mizelle, N. B. (1999). Helping middle school students make the transition to high school. *ERIC Clearinghouse on Elementary and Early Childhood Education.*

Retrieved August 4, 2005, from http://www.kidsource.com/education/middlehigh.html

Mizelle, N. B. (2005). Moving out of middle school. *Educational Leadership, 62*(7), 56-60.

Mizelle, N. B., & Irvin, J. L. (2000). Transition from middle school to high school. *Middle School Journal, 31*(5), 57-61.

Morgan, L. P., & Hertzog, C. J. (2001). Designing comprehensive transition plans. *Principal Leadership, 1*(7), 10-18.

National Center for Education Statistics. (2002). *Coming of age in the 1990s: The eighth-grade class of 1988 12 years later.* Retrieved November 17, 2006, from http://nces.ed.gov/programs/quarterly/vol_4/4_2/2-1.asp

Roderick, M., & Camburn, E. (1999). Risk and recovery from course failure in the early years of high school. *American Educational Research Journal, 36*(2), 303-343.

Sanders, D. P. (1981). Educational inquiry as developmental research. *Educational Researcher, 10*(3), 8-13.

Schiller, K. S. (1999). Effects of feeder patterns on students' transition to high school. *Sociology of Education, 72*(4), 216-233.

Seidman, E. L., Allen, L., Aber, J. L., Mitchell, C., & Feinman, J. (1994). The impact of school transitions in early adolescence on the self-system and perceived social context of poor urban youth. *Child Development, 65*(2), 507-522.

Shulman, L. (2000). From Minsk to Pinsk: Why a scholarship of teaching and learning. *The Journal of Scholarship of Teaching and Learning, 1*, 48-52.

Smith, J. B. (1997). Effects of eighth grade transition programs on high school retention and experiences. *Journal of Educational Research, 90*(3), 144-152.

Smith, J. S., Feldwisch, R., & Abell, A. (2006). Similarities and differences in caregivers' and students' perceptions of the transition to high school. *Research in Middle Level Education Online, 29*(10), 1-9.

Weinstein, S. M., Mermelstein, R. J., Hedeker, D., Hankin, B. L., & Flay, B. R. (2006). The time-varying influences of peer and family support on adolescent daily positive and negative affect. *Journal of Clinical Child and Adolescent Psychology, 35*, 420-430.

Zeedyk, M. S., Gallacher, J., Henderson, M., Hope, G., Husband, B., & Lindsay, K. (2003). Negotiating the transition from primary to secondary school: Perceptions of pupils, parents, and teachers. School Psychology International, 24(1), 67-79.

CHAPTER 15

SUICIDE, SCHOOLS, AND THE YOUNG ADOLESCENT

Teresa J. Rishel

ABSTRACT

Haunting realities of a student's life-and-death decision making are discussed as the result of an in-depth lived experience case study to examine the impact of his suicide on school personnel. This chapter exposes how home and school problems contributed to a cycle of despair, depression, and suicide—and illuminates understandings relevant to educational settings. Impacting his decisions were the effects of adolescent development, school climate, and family and social issues, as well as the presence of a monoculturalistic disposition towards acceptance of all students. As such, the resulting alienation, hidden among hegemonic ideologies and practices, becomes an albatross for struggling young adolescents.

INTRODUCTION

Compared with the adolescent years of their parents' generation, young adolescents today face unique challenges. Wading through an erratic and volatile time emotionally, physically, psychologically, and socially, they

The Young Adolescent and the Middle School
pp. 297–322

face fears and worries of dire importance and impending doom. Cultural and global concerns have slowly and disproportionately seeped into their lives, replacing the simplicity of age-appropriate concerns. They fear imminent attack (i.e., 9/11 attacks on NYC), global war, and an economically unstable society—no longer futuristic issues to ponder, but everyday realities. Materialism has caused financial strains on families, creating stressful environments and dysfunctional relationships that impinge upon the adolescent's ability to negotiate their own peer relationships. Fears of school violence and bombings place students in vulnerable positions, which ultimately can impact their willingness and ability to learn (Associated Press, 2006; Dwyer, Osher & Warger, 1998). In 1998, the U.S. Department of Justice reported that over half of all school students witnessed bullying, physical or sexual attacks or robbery at school; and about 1 out of 10 worried about being the victim of an attack. In fact, young adolescents have had to witness this shift as they watch their own peer group become the perpetrators.

At the same time, academic achievement, with an overwhelming focus on standards, testing, and accountability, has forced school success to collide with life issues. Creating a difficult mix for young adolescents to handle, and contributing negatively to adolescent development, they attempt to cope with the barrage of messages of the world as they experience it. Many are living their own form of personal hell where suicide looms as a possible alternative. Wrestling with death and death issues, unlikely components of schooling, necessitates us to pause and reflect on the emotional condition of young adolescents. William Pinar (1992) has suggested that schools must study the meaning of death in order to better understand and contemplate life, stating "Death brings time into focus" (p. 99). As such, an important reminder is the parallel that Schön (1987) drew between the practitioner and the landscape of problem solving in asserting that practitioners do not exist on the high ground where unimportant but manageable problems exist, but on the contrary, they originate in the swamps where human issues reside as "confusing, messy problems" (p. 3).

Questions regarding how young adolescent suicide impacts and affects teacher practices and administrative decision making can only be answered by delving into the swampland of student despair. It requires asking the tough questions and examining the extent to which sufficient, consistent, and knowledgeable interactions prevent exacerbating student circumstances. We might ask if caring for young adolescents is enough. Who is caring? Who is not? How is it shown and do students accept it? To answer these questions, among others, it is important to know the realities of suicide for young adolescents and discard the myths and stigmas that surround it. In order to do this, educators must understand both the overt and hidden ways that the desperate and often hidden lives of young people lead them towards death. We must be cognizant of how young adolescent development affects their decision making and how the structure of schooling—as experienced through peer groups, classroom interactions, and family issues—can intensify problems during this volatile time. In all, we find a clash between the ideologies that anchor educators to traditional ways of acting and believing to those of adolescents who struggle to find meaning in everyday life.

THE REALITY OF YOUNG ADOLESCENT SUICIDE

Suicide is the third leading cause of death for young adolescents, preceded by unintentional injury and malignant tumors (Centers for Disease Control [CDC], 2006a). Young adolescent suicide occurs predominately during after school hours (American Association of Suicidology, [AAS], 2006). A CDC (2006a) report revealed that from 1999-2004, as the third leading cause of death for ages 10-14, there were 1,601 suicides. Statistics show that 966 (60.3%) were suffocation, 521 (32.5%) from firearms, and 66 (4.1%) from poisoning. Other suicide methods included cutting, drowning, fires or burns, transportation related, and unspecified (CDC, 2006a).

According to the AAS (2006), between the years 1981-2004, suicide rates for ages 10-14 increased 51%, with a total of 283 suicides in 2004. Specifically, in 1996, the suicide rate for the same age group was 1.6 per 100,000 compared to 9.5 for 15-19 year olds, showing a significant increase as young adolescents mature (U.S. Public Health, 1999b). Caucasians young adolescents are "far more likely" (AAS, 2006, p. 3) to commit suicide than African Americans, where suicide ranks as the fifth leading cause of death. Caucasian females, aged 10-14, commit suicide less often than Caucasian males, where suicide is 1.8 times "more likely" (AAS, p. 3).

It is important to note that as students enter adolescence, they become more vulnerable to suicide, thus requiring educators to remain proactive in dealing with the problems and situations of young adolescents. The AAS (2006) specifically warns that "*most* attempted suicides by adolescents are the result of interpersonal conflicts" (p. 3) and that any self-destructive behavior should be taken seriously because they often do not tell others' of their intentions.

We cannot be certain why young adolescents kill themselves, as suicide leaves in its wake very few concrete answers and elicits more questions. As Portner (1964) stated in her book, *One in Thirteen: The Silent Epidemic of Teen Suicide*, "Finding an answer to the riddle of self-murder is not like tracing the origins of a disease. There is no one factor that causes suicide" (p. 8). Suicide can occur quickly, with no warning signs or apparent symptoms, but as a result of fragile emotions, impulsivity, and limited decision-making abilities. The danger lies in believing there is safety behind such lists. Relinquishing responsibility to "see" beyond patterns and expected behaviors of a certain group, we overlook those most susceptible to self-death.

Further, child and adolescent depression has reached epidemic proportions, where 10-15% exhibit some symptoms of depression at any given time (U.S. Public Health Service, 1999a). The American Academy of Pediatrics "strongly recommends that education about depression and suicide prevention be integrated into the educational system" (Kirchner, Yoder, Kramer, Lindsey, & Thrush, 2000, p. 238). As a result of the mental health condition of young people in the United States, former Surgeon General Satcher declared suicide a serious national health problem and established a comprehensive suicide prevention and support plan (U. S. Public Health Service, 1999b). For educators, the realities are daunting. Death has become an issue of important consideration in how students view themselves, school success, and whether life is worth living or not.

The issue becomes one of student emotional health and safety in the context of the school environment. We need to understand how school impacts student autonomy, how they function within that view, and the results of negative interaction with teachers and peers. Since a large portion of their lives are in school, the environment "plays a central role in both promoting children's acquisition of knowledge and shaping the ways in which they learn to regulate their attention, emotions, and behavior" (Eccles & Roeser, 1999, p. 504). Considering that nearly all students encounter an average of 50 teachers over a 12-year span, they must learn to adjust to more authority figures than will be required of them at nearly any other time throughout life. The adjustment to differing teacher expectations, attitudes, and instructional methods occurs yearly as students pass from one grade to another (Rishel, 2004). Educators have a moral and ethical responsibility to maintain emotional safety for their students, and when disregarded it "creates a hole in the safety net" (Eccles & Roeser, 1999, p. 516) for students.

THE STIGMA OF SUICIDE—A RESEARCH STUDY

My interest in studying suicide in schools resulted from the suicide of my former student, Dalton, a young adolescent. I was concerned about the lack of research that specifically examined the impact of a student suicide on a school or addressed school issues from a lived experience perspective. Since suicide falls within sensitive topics in educational research, entrance is difficult into settings where the insider's perspective is needed. Because of this, research on school personnel who have experienced losing a student to suicide remains limited, yet is vital in understanding the phenomenon. Researching student suicide is also challenging because suicide is considered a taboo topic that implicitly carries a stigma of silence. Thus, a unique feature of this study was that, as his former administrator, I had the rare opportunity to get an inside view of what occurs in a school after a student commits suicide.

Theoretical Frameworks

Case study research allowed an in-depth examination of Dalton's suicide by examining a specific entity (e.g. a group, event, process, and person), which describes a "particularistic" (Merriam, 1988, p. 11) aspect of the study. The study of Dalton's suicide on the school community was based on two significant areas of research: the fields of social psychology (adolescent theory, identity, moral development) and curriculum theory (ideology, affect, caring curriculums). Social psychology research supplied information about problems that young adolescents incur, while curriculum theory provided an understanding of the ways that school climate can exacerbate a student's propensity towards suicidal behavior. Combined, these two bodies of research established a framework for understanding the impact of schooling in addressing suicide.

Typically, school suicide has been addressed only in terms of aftercare or prevention programs added as curricular components following a suicide (Butler & Novy, 1994). Prevention programs have not been effective and "almost no literature to date has been published about programs designed to train teachers and school personnel" (Kirchner et al., 2000, p. 238). Workshops and in-services, college courses, and video classes are the most common methods used to educate school personnel—none of which address the real needs of the teachers and students (CDC, 2006b; Wilson & Berne, 1999).

Thus, the lived experience perspective emerged as an important and missing piece in understanding student suicide. Since participants had very little or no knowledge about suicide or proactive methods of dealing with it, the purpose was to assess the impact of Dalton's suicide on their professional lives. The study was based on the following research questions: (a) how does a student's suicide impact and/or affect his/her former teachers, their perspectives and instructional practices?, and (b) what are the administrative roles and practices in dealing with a student's suicide? What changes occurred as a result of the death, particularly those related to school climate and culture?

The following combinations of theoretical frameworks were used to answer the research questions: phenomenology (Patton, 1990), heuristic inquiry (Merriam, 1988; Moustakas, 1990; Patton, 1990), lived experience (van Manen, 1990) and case study methodology (Marshall & Rossman, 1999; McMillan & Schumacher, 2001; Merriam, 1988). This eclectic combination allowed a holistic exploration of suicide; however, there none could totally address the issues involved.

The phenomenological approach highlighted suicide as lived experience through heuristic inquiry, where heuristic researchers "*must* have personal experience with and intense interest in the phenomenon under study" (Patton, 1990, p. 71). Phenomenology requires that the researcher discover the meanings and feelings of their own experiences—prior to eliciting the perspectives of the participants'—through writing a full account of the [researcher's] lived experience (Marshall & Rossman, 1999; McMillan & Schumacher, 2001). Understanding how Dalton's suicide affected me as an administrator enabled a more sensitive approach. Since phenomenological research is that which "produces knowledge to disclose what it means to be human" (van Manen, 1990, p.12), I sought to understand how participants made meaning of Dalton's suicide and how it affected their humanness. Positioned within the "web of reality" (Kincheloe, Steinberg, Rodriguez, & Chennault, 1998, p. 3), I negotiated the landscape of discovering painful truths and hidden secrets. Reality was much as Phillion (2002) stated:

> In life, in research, in research-life, we are always in the midst of the story of our life and the stories of others' lives. What we write and what we know is conditional, temporal, situated, fragmented, in transition, in process, in the midst. (p. 146).

Description of Participants and Methods

The study took place in a small, Midwestern community. The school district includes a high school, junior high school, and three elementary schools. Purposeful criterion sampling was used in participant selection, which required that they had sufficient and regular contact with Dalton (McMillan & Schumacher, 2001). Data collection included 18 structured and unstructured interviews of twelve educators and the school nurse: eight participants were Dalton's former elementary and junior high teachers, two were guidance counselors, and two were administrators. Five participants were interviewed twice, two of which were due to a change in the interview questions and three to obtain further information and clarify previous statements. The revised questions elicited more meaningful responses and allowed participants to speak openly about Dalton's death. The school nurse, who was also a county coroner, provided the unique perspective of one who had dealt with suicide.

Data Analysis

Data were analyzed to construct a narrative that merged participant interviews, the researcher's autobiographical narrative, and research literature. Using naturalistic inquiry (Patton, 1990), data unfolded in a manner that was "non-manipulative, unobtrusive, and non-controlling, an openness to whatever emerges" (p. 40). The original plan was to narrow data analysis to four participants; however, since each story added a new layer of understanding, all interviews were included. Interviews were examined using cross-case analysis to extrapolate patterns of perception, knowledge, and beliefs (Miles & Huberman, 1994; Patton, 1990). Narrative analysis was used to decipher ways that participants described Dalton's death (Bernard, 2002; Patton, 1990). Woven throughout the interviews, the interplay of substantial meaning formation was hermeneutic, the process of inferring meaning from actions and speech patterns. Similarities and differences surfaced in how participants reconstructed memories by the words they chose, words left unspoken, and their body language. For example, one guidance counselor repeatedly tapped a pencil anxiously against the desk; a teacher told her story in a matter-of-fact manner without elaboration, opinions, or emotions. Two others (teachers) focused on stories of Dalton's life, school issues, and their feelings about him. Analyzing through "meaning reconstruction" (Carspecken, 1996, pp. 94-95) led to the underpinning of significant themes: guilt, shame, anger, avoidance, and resistance. While, as Patton (1990) suggested, this did not lead to "a single, totally consistent picture" of student suicide (p. 467), it allowed an overarching perspective.

Holistically, emerging as relevant to young adolescent suicide were sociological issues and institutional issues. Sociological issues include the roles and influences of adolescent development, family dynamics, and peer groups, significant in that these issues are socially constructed and impacted from both inside and outside of the school environment. Institutional issues consist of topics that are impacted specifically by the school environment: academic concerns, student behavior, and school culture.

THE STORY

Education is about life, the future, and the quest for career attainment and success. Suicide is a curricular issue hidden among the integration of technology, test scores, standards, and honor rolls. It lies between layers of social interaction in clubs, sports, choir, band, and other activities. Suicide, masked within the ambiguity of the hidden curriculum and ostracized from the overt curriculum, is hidden within the students. It is lived experience, as seen in the following autobiographical synopsis:

> In the midst of a hot, August afternoon, an argument centered on the word "no," broke out between a mother and her 14-year-old son. The teenager ran out the door, making threats as he went. As his mother approached him, he screamed, "I'll see you in hell!" He lit his gasoline soaked body and within seconds, was aflame. His final act was complete. He died two days later. (Rishel, 2003)

I never expected suicide to be a part of my job as a principal. It was not discussed in my teacher or administration preparation and was not a topic generally considered viable for educators, administrators, or educational theorists. Regardless, suicide was a reality for three male students sent to the office for disciplinary action who periodically talked of committing suicide. Talking openly and honestly, they voiced thoughts, problems, and complaints about peers, teachers, parents, and the school, with a resolve that suicide was the answer to their problems. Overwhelmed by their disclosures, I worried how they would cope in a school environment that was not conducive to these types of problems. And I ached for the possibility of the pain their parents could face. From knowledge gained through my own experience with the suicide of a loved one, my heightened sensitivity and awareness made me more receptive to their intentions. Through close work with two of them, their death wishes were channeled away from suicidal thoughts. Dalton, however, was a different story.

Dalton was an extremely complex young adolescent. Although he was a troublemaker, rude to teachers, antisocial, and sarcastic, there was something intriguing and interesting hidden beneath his bravado. His smile could light up a room—or his sinister side could darken the space around him. He appeared generally disgruntled, yet his humor and wit brought laughter among his peers; the school was his stage as he frolicked about in its possibilities for attention. Dalton was exceptionally intelligent, a deep thinker and amazingly verbal, able to solve complex problems years beyond his age. He engaged in conversations that left one to question where he had acquired this vast knowledge. Dalton was also a talented artist whose drawings were morbid and violent, yet detailed and expressive. His artwork was dismissed as unimportant because it did not "fit" into the school's art curriculum. In retrospect, I should have pursued more avenues to help him find utility in creativity and assist teachers to engage him.

Dalton's life had always been difficult. He never knew his father or stepfather; both left while Dalton was still very young. He was raised by his mother, who, without a high school education, struggled to survive. They lived in a house with a dirt floor and no running water, which he termed a "shack." He was responsible for overseeing his younger step-brothers and often told me of his struggles to feed them when there was little or no food in the house. He described his anger toward his mother for the "stupid things" she did, her lack of responsibility and her wild life-style. He often indicated that he did not like his mother, and that he either wanted to kill somebody or himself. However, he never directly referred to her as the target of these threats. Although Dalton's mother and I met several times to discuss his problems, the final time was to discuss his desire to kill himself, his angst with life, and with her. The relationship between Dalton and his mother was severely damaged, which was evident as the meeting reached a turning point. She justified the unfair ways that she treated Dalton, while at the same apologizing for them. Out of nowhere, she shared that it was difficult to love Dalton because he was the product of a rape she incurred at age 16. I reeled from her statement and realized that Dalton had also heard those words. Devastated, broken, and angry, he cried and yelled simultaneously that he hated her, the sinister look invading his face.

From that conversation, I worked diligently with Dalton to create a safe place at school where he felt accepted and cared for. He had the reputation of being a student who did not try hard enough, would not conform to the routine of schooling, and was determined to create trouble, which was unfortunately often true. It was pointed out by school personnel that Dalton created his own problems, or that this "was just the way that family was." Dalton was so desperate that at 12-years-old he wanted to end his life. My office became Dalton's refuge, away from the stresses of school and life. This was often difficult for me, as I alternated between knowing he needed the office time and recognizing that I had to mainstream him into the school environment. I was accused of "making things too easy for him," and letting him manipulate me to get out of class. Some staff members felt that I was "listening to him too much," instead of disciplining him.

The day prior to Dalton's elementary school graduation, he came to say goodbye and that he would not be at his sixth grade graduation because he did not have anything appropriate to wear. Ignorantly, I laughed and said it did not matter what he wore, but what he had accomplished. I will never forget Dalton's words: "Mrs. R, you just don't understand, do you? I am not like the other students; I am different. I do not have clothes to wear to graduation. I have never, ever, had a new shirt, pants, or shoes." I felt foolish and embarrassed for minimizing his reality by simplifying it to fit mine; it was not easy for him to accept that his accomplishments were more worthy than his appearance. I had failed him miserably in my remark and had dismissed his pain, much as a parent would do. I asked him to come to school the following day, at least for the morning, and that I would take him home before graduation.

The next morning, I handed Dalton a bag of clothes and a pair of shoes that he had always wanted—Vans© skateboarding shoes. Words are inadequate to describe that moment. After trying on his new clothes, Dalton returned to my office; he was handsome and for the first time, he looked truly happy. Before Dalton left my office, with tears in his eyes, he thanked me and said, "You are the first person who I think really *likes* me." It was my turn for tears. Dalton attended his graduation—with no family present. That fall Dalton entered junior high school. I introduced him to the junior high principal and explained what had occurred between Dalton and me during my 2 years with him. He guaranteed me that he would look after him and take any suicidal threats seriously. Fifteen months later, Dalton committed suicide, 2 weeks before school started, by dousing himself with gasoline and lighting himself on fire. According to the county coroner, Dalton died 2 days later from "complications due to severe burns," and his death was never recorded as a suicide. The day after he died, I visited his mother to extend my condolences, but also to bring her some pictures of Dalton that she needed, which included Dalton at his graduation. Guilt resurfaced as I pulled away from Dalton's home and questions haunted me. What could I have done to prevent this? Why didn't I do enough? How much of this was my fault?

The funeral was a somber experience with the quietness, fear and disbelief that a suicide brings; muffled sobs, followed by sporadic bellows of grief, gave the room an eerie feeling. Students filled the room and with only standing room available, the line stretched into the street—an ironic scene considering Dalton felt that he had no friends. A few administrators and teachers were present, and as we exchanged the obligatory remarks and reminisced over a few Dalton incidents, we also quickly dismissed the experience as "really sad."

Dalton's Life and Death: Personal Versus Professional

I think of my role as an educator in this tragedy in relationship to Elbaz's (1991) research on how teacher knowledge is gleaned from an inside perspective—the teacher's point of view. My knowledge and understandings of suicide enabled me to see Dalton differently, not from the knowledge I had gained to be an effective principal but from a similar experience in my own life. Similarly, Connelly and Clandinin (1988) addressed educator experiences through the lenses of personal practical knowledge that is derived from lived experience—a combination of theory and practice—resulting in "a moral, affective, and aesthetic way of knowing life's educational situations" (p. 59). Thus, professional practices flow from different types of knowing, fluctuating within the context of the situation, where knowing constitutes not only objective knowing, but the emotionality involved with that knowing. My knowledge of suicide aided in the professional and personal ways I dealt with Dalton's death. However, it was a constant battle to decipher between professional and personal, of which I was only partially aware at the time; I realized it more significantly later, when I reflected on how I *felt* coming to terms with Dalton's death. This tension became an important element of my case study research as I discovered how educational ideology and tradition creates barriers between struggling young adolescents and schooling.

Ideology and Schooling

A distinct understanding of how I processed Dalton's death was based on exploring ideology. Ideology is the foundation of a system of beliefs and values that determine what is acceptable in a given institution, group, or entity in society (Aronowitz & Giroux, 1993). Ideology determines what is considered viable, important, and worthwhile, and also that which is not. Schools, as social communities themselves, mirror the ideologies of society, promoting key values, ideas, and ways of operating. The status quo is incorporated into the rules, customs, and procedures that form school structure and shape school climate. When students' appearance, actions, speech and thoughts mirror dominant ideology, they are validated and accepted. Alternatively, those who differ in these traits are considered outsiders, causing an unwritten—yet practiced—lack of acceptance into the school culture. Grades, rewards, discipline, and ability grouping, among others, complement what the dominant culture values through tracking decisions, leadership opportunities, labeling and so forth, based on both the obvious and hidden aspects evaluations of "who" students are (Apple, 1995; Aronowitz & Giroux, 1993). The rules, interactions, and activities that occur in classrooms and schools are embedded within a "hidden curriculum" that creates a subculture of learning and knowing. Some argue that this has a greater impact on students than the overt (stated) curriculum, an important point when considering adolescent views of schools and schooling (Aronowitz & Giroux, 1993; Beane, 1990; Jackson, 1990).

How did we get to this place where youth are choosing to die as an alternative to dealing with life's problems? What are the influences, situations, experiences, or dynamics that result in suicide? What characteristics of schooling exacerbate an adolescent's inclination toward suicidal behavior? These questions can be answered in three ways: by addressing issues of *adolescent development* that contribute to the despair of youth today; by *critically examining school climate*, where the subtle, often unnoticed and unheard interactions in the environment play a key role in adolescent self-perception; and by *acknowledging family and social issues* that further contribute to the problem.

ROLE OF ADOLESCENT DEVELOPMENT

Young adolescence marks a stage in life where great shifts occur in students' self-concept and identity, where they construct an implicit theory as they begin to question their beliefs, values, opinions, and attitudes towards themselves, their parents, schooling, and life (Beane, 1990; Beane & Lipka, 2000; Elkind, 1988; Schlosser, 1992). As Erikson (1968) posited in his psychoanalytic theory of identity, people develop identity and maturation by dealing with crises as they occur during each stage of life, especially during early adolescence. During this time, children's identity is reconstructed in a type of makeover that helps them transition into this middle ground before adulthood (Erikson, 1968). In fact, Erikson stated that during this transition, as children enter the final stages of identity development during adolescence, one is "apt to suffer more deeply than he ever did before or ever will again from a confusion of roles" (p. 163). One result of this identity crisis is suicide or suicidal tendencies (Eccles & Roeser, 1999; Elkind, 1989; Miller, 1993; Wassef & Ingham, 1995). Kroger (1996), in examining Erikson's psychosocial approach, added:

> Identity formation during adolescence reflects developmental resolutions to all preceding stages and serves as a base for personality developments that lie ahead. In adolescence, identity assumes a change in form ... and now evolves into a new structure, different from (but related to) the sum of its parts. (p. 31)

It is my contention that students such as Dalton are stuck in this empty place where they are looking for something to hang onto, yet having to think and act like an adult. Many young adolescents have adult responsibilities outside of school in caring for younger siblings, caring for dysfunctional or ill parents, or simply operating in the absence of parental or adult guidance, but within the school environment and in all other ways, they are simply young adolescents. As they try to make sense of life and shift from the innocence and protection of elementary school, many are thrown into a cycle of emotional, social, and educational crises with no apparent solutions or sound guidance. If left unresolved, problems eventually surface as critical adult issues such as addictions, alcoholism, drug abuse, dependency on anti-depressants, adultery, gambling, child abuse, and neglect. The cycle repeats itself when the parent, who was once the troubled adolescent, becomes the source of his or her child's problems. Dalton was caught up in the cycle that began with his mother's unfortunate life, rape, and subsequent pregnancy.

We have to wonder how teenagers construct healthy self-images in the midst of this cycle and how they find identity and purpose. Beane and Lipka (2000) addressed how the traditional support systems for young people—home and school—focus more on criticism and disregard their needs, causing an "increased incidence of drug use, eating disorders, early pregnancy, crime activity, and attempted and actual suicide" (p. 5). Poor self-perception manifests itself in these behaviors and are characteristic of self-punishing or suicidal teenagers. As a support system, the school environment, combined with the quality of interactions between school personnel and students, contributes significantly to how adolescents acclimate to this stage of development.

EXAMINING THE SCHOOL CLIMATE

School

As students transition from elementary to middle school, they often have fewer opportunities for decision making and autonomy (Eccles & Roeser, 1999). Underachieving, behavioral, and depressed students find middle schools to be very frustrating especially when attempting to retain their individuality. They learn that participating is not valued by teachers who do not allow them to think for themselves or question the world around them, thereby neutralizing their individuality and encouraging conformity. When problems with peers arise, however, teachers prod students against following the crowd and encourage them to think on their own. They become caught between the two perspectives because they fear being different from their peers and not fitting in.

Beane and Lipka (2000) referred to school as a "place of last resort" (p. 5) in the adolescent's life, where school "may be the last institution where these young people may work with a group of adults who are willing to give them help and guidance, not just criticism" (p. 6). Students like Dalton are caught in a dichotomous relationship between hating school because it is alienating, yet needing it for survival against the pressures of the outside world. Dalton's struggle is described by authors who examined the relationship between students' perceptions of school and their actions at school (Eccles & Roeser, 1999; Elkind, 1988; Schlosser,

1992). They found that regardless of how detached and uncaring a student acts toward teachers and schooling, they regularly think about what goes on in the classroom, what their teachers do and say, and about school life. Although student perceptions are not always based on reality, the result is their inability to learn (Jackson, Boostrom, & Hansen, 1993). Dalton was certainly a detached and uncaring student and probably held many misperceptions about school, yet many of the participants said he really did not hate school; on the contrary, he hated himself and school provided a forum for the attention he sought.

Thus, the atmosphere and situations that occur at school can cause the cycle to continue. When students develop negative attitudes about school, they participate less, allow their grades to decline, and have difficulty adjusting socially. Students begin to skip classes, or school altogether, or they act out while at school which further brings about their desire to withdraw and alienate themselves (Liston, 2000). Dalton's negative attitudes about teachers and schooling were substantial and although he was very bright, he just did not care about school in the ways that are valued—such as academic success. These forms of resistance create an impossible situation for both the student and the teacher. Dalton, as he developed poor relationships with teachers, withdrew academically and socially and further perpetuated his problems. Many students are torn between opposing desires: they want to be loved, to have guidelines and a sense of direction, but on the other hand, they do not want to listen, be loved, or be perceived as being a "good" student. Often misunderstood as rebellion, they are simply reserving the only means available to have power over themselves and their lives. During stressful times, teenagers lose their sense of reality, ability to cope and think rationally. They are consumed with emotional emptiness, which creates further difficulties at home and school. Without adequate coping skills—particularly if they are self-punishing teens—problems with family, peers, or school make them vulnerable to suicide (Eccles & Roeser, 1999). Teenagers, who find themselves deep into depression, or seeking release from it, feel that there is "no way out … they are helpless, hapless, and hopeless" (Elkind, 1989, p. 172).

Teachers and Peers

The social context of schooling—how students fit into the school environment in relationships, comfort, identity, and so on also largely influences a student's emotional health. School is the social mechanism of learning to forge relationships and finding value and acceptance among their peers. Increasingly more important and more influential than parents, peers are considered "the litmus paper of life" (Beane & Lipka, 2000, p. 13). Fitting into the classroom is difficult for many students, particularly as their peer group assesses everything about them, reinforcing the importance of being accepted, popular, and part of the "in" crowd. Unfortunately, peer group interaction is often discouraged at a time when the adolescent needs it most. "When one looks at most middle schools, there seems to be an overriding rule: thou salt not interact with peers" (Beane & Lipka, 2000, p. 38). Research supports that "one of the major factors contributing to youth violence is the impact of peers (National Institute of Mental Health, 2000), a substantial finding in the Columbine shootings. When students do not feel that they fit in, there is a general sense of isolation and alienation, a contributing factor to suicide.

Alongside the pressure to manage peer situations, a main source of stress stems from how teachers treat students within the classroom (Eccles & Roeser, 1999; Elkind, 1989; Wassef & Ingham, 1995). Jackson (1990) posited that the way a classroom is conducted has little to do with the subject matter or the material that is used, but is based on the personality and demeanor of the teacher "mak[ing] even the dullest subject exciting" (p. 108). Two participants shared that Dalton's favorite teachers displayed charisma, patience, and care although they taught what students considered "boring" subjects. In a study by Eccles and Roeser (1999) on the effect of classroom interactions on peer group perceptions, it was found that the students who received the most reproachful remarks from teachers were rated "very negatively" (p. 515) by their classmates in terms of character and social acceptability. Students internalize and are impacted by the negative feedback, criticism, derogatory comments, and facial expressions that their peers receive from the teacher. They interpret the teacher's vocal tone and pitch, body language, and general attitude. Because students are viewed as refusing to acquiesce to authority, further rejection occurs when the student is ostracized by their peers as a result of the teacher's negative interaction with the student (Schlosser, 1992).

A classroom environment that emphasizes discipline, teacher control, and few opportunities for positive student-teacher relationships results in students feeling that the teacher does not like or understand them (Eccles & Roeser, 1999; Elkind, 1988, 1989; Oser, 1991; Schlosser, 1992). Negative teacher communication can indicate to students their "goodness or badness" (Jackson et al., 1993). These teachers are identified by poor classroom management, improper and ineffective disciplinary procedures, and poor attitudes towards students. The usual method of discipline is frequent office referrals and classroom punishments. These public forms of discipline cause students not only to suffer the wrath of the teacher, but also to be seen as troublemakers by their peers. Teacher attention, approval, and grades are used as ways to motivate and reward students, and those with behavior and discipline problems have difficulty once they have crossed the line into this hierarchy of competition. They see no reason to conform to a system that does not work for them.

Henderson and Kesson (2003) described educators as "caught up in the refinement of craft knowledge, the day-to-day business of teaching, and the pressures of the profession" (p.49). These responsibilities often take priority over asking and trying to answer "the more meaningful 'why' questions" (p. 49) or attending to student needs. Some students adapt to facets of classroom life and learn not speak out or question what happens in the classroom, the content under study, or offer a critical perspective, fearing teacher reprisal and humiliation. Ayers (2001) stated that students understand that "in school, a high value is placed on quiet" and in learning to submit to it, they "become passive, quiet, obedient, [and] dull; the environment practically demands it" (p. 51). The cycle further perpetuates itself when the alienated student is unable to perform academically, exhibits consistently poor behavior, or resorts to extraneous methods (i.e., drug or alcohol abuse, sexual experimentation, eating disorders, etc.) to relieve stress. These moral aspects of schooling, where the actions and interactions of individuals affect others, must be recognized as *significant* in how the adolescent views himself within the school environment. They quickly learn "what's good for the group had better be good for me" (Ayers, 2001, p. 50). Educators often fail to realize the impact or importance of their role in these moral decision-making moments. Giroux (1986) pointed out that by maintaining this type of negative classroom interaction, student voice is "reduced to the immediacy of its performance, existing as something to be measured, administered, registered, and controlled" (p. 124). The result is further demise of student self-efficacy.

One participant, Reggie, a middle school teacher, described how he used effective communication and disciplinary methods with Dalton to avoid creating further apathy and alienation:

> It just took a lot of strategies on my part, of getting to know him personally, and it helped because I could relate something on his level. Then, I was much more in tune with him. If I didn't get to know him personally and viewed it as a discipline problem instead of him just trying to be the center of attention, then it would have been different, we would've battled ... everyday.

While it is evident that Reggie worked to develop a relationship with Dalton, some teachers exacerbated his problems. The most common way of handling Dalton's behavior was to send him to the office instead of finding ways to work through situations. Reggie gained Dalton's trust and respect by treating him fairly within the classroom and retaining a relationship outside of it. Reggie felt consistency in the classroom was the key element and that office referrals were temporary fixes, particularly since once the student is kicked out of class, they develop an "I don't care" attitude. Further compounding the problem, students then have to complete work they missed while not in class. Most of them refuse to do it and they receive lower grades. Reggie stated that when this occurs, students "get into that rut and there's nothing you can do. It's a downhill slide." Further, he felt that punishment with Dalton never worked because Dalton simply did not care.

Student apathy, the result of the aforementioned discussion of schooling, creates a broad range of student and school-induced problems. As teachers face an overload of student problems while struggling to meet academic and personal needs, students become apathetic and uncaring. Teachers are considered the front line in handling a large variety of student problems, yet, they understandably feel less competent, are in fact less competent, and are uncomfortable handling situations involving suicide (Davidson & Range, 1999; King, Price, Telljohann, & Wahl, 1999). However, while educators may feel incompetent in handling suicide, their day-to-day choices regarding classroom management remain within their control.

Schoolwork and Homework

Dalton, as the participants attested, was very intelligent. He had the ability; no one ever denied or refuted that. Important to Dalton's reputation and alienation is, unfortunately, the fact that his school career was focused on not completing (on a regular basis) schoolwork or homework. Concerns began in the early elementary grades, as indicated by a participant who stated that she worried about him not completing classroom work or returning his homework: "And he was so smart. If he wanted to have done his work, he could've done it in two minutes time and you know, had umpteen hours of time to do things that he'd wanted to have done." While sympathetic to his needs, alternatives for success, such as differentiated work or getting to the root of his problems, could have replaced what was the beginning of Dalton's propensity to control his environment—and essentially, his life, through schoolwork.

Instead of teachers focusing on ways to tap into Dalton's intelligence in terms of "work," Dalton learned that in the power structure of schooling, he had to succumb to it or resist it. Certainly, Dalton should not have been allowed to circumvent the completion of schoolwork, but instead to have the opportunity for challenging work targeted at his level instead of the repetitive worksheets and drills that were below his level. Dalton's only recourse, his only method of defense, was to resist. Throughout the next 7 years, as teachers continued to prod, reprimand, and eventually retain him, he continued to refuse schoolwork. Dalton used this resistance each year as he encountered a new teacher and the familiar demand that he succumb to doing his work. His low grades did not match his potential, but instead, his lack of surrender. Eventually, this prohibited his participation in advanced placement classes, which may have likewise inspired his interest. In junior high, Dalton's resistance surfaced in acting out and becoming a behavior problem. The school power structure, refusing to be circumvented, resorted to retaining a gifted student because of his lack of performance, yet avoided seeking alternative methods of educating him. Research clearly supports that a child's self-esteem, efficacy, or academic achievement are not enhanced through grade retention (Darling-Hammond, 1998; Jimerson, 2001; Nagaoka & Roderick, 2004), yet remains an institutional exercise of great power (Rishel, in press). At some point, one has to ask, would the decision to retain a student like Dalton suddenly change his academic progress?

In asking one participant, a school guidance counselor, about the circumstances surrounding Dalton's retention, she stated that it was a rare occurrence to retain a student, and that most chose to attend summer school to avoid the retention. Inquiring as to why Dalton refused summer school, she emphatically stated, "Because he hated school! He didn't care what grade he was in." Still faced with how to "deal" with this student and in light of the rarity of retention, decisions were made that once again clearly spoke to power, ideology, and the nature and structure of schooling. Reflecting on Dalton's history of refusing to do his work, I am reminded of a story that one participant, Patsy, a teacher, shared about what she "did" to Dalton, and in the aftermath of his death, what she still relies on to remind herself of what constitutes authentic learning and her role in that process. She had assigned the students to select a research topic to work on primarily outside of class, create an outline, put notes on index cards, and share their findings in a 20-minute oral presentation. As students began handing in their outlines and index cards, Dalton was reminded that he, too, had to follow the procedures of the project; Dalton refused, but did say that he was doing the research. On the day of his presentation, the teacher knew he would show up with nothing prepared and that he would receive an "F."

Dalton's presentation consisted of a 25-minute oration on the Milky Way without using notes. He never wavered, but spoke eloquently and intelligently and fascinated his classmates. Patsy said it was the best presentation ever given. Two days later, while assigning grades to the presentations, Dalton walked passively to her desk, smiled and remarked, "I know I got an A. I did this right." She responded, "No Dalton, you got an F because you didn't follow instructions. You knew what you were supposed to do." He returned to his seat without saying a word, which was unusual for Dalton. She felt that he had "brought this on himself." Years later, she cried as she shared the story. "I know, now, what real learning is. I know that I cheated him and embarrassed him—and I feel guilty." Important to understanding the teacher's actions is the role that power, authority, and ideology played in how she sought to assess student learning. Dalton would not acquiesce to the required steps in the process of research, but clearly resulted in mastering the principle purpose of the assignment; he did not need to follow the intermediary steps and was punished for it. His grade reflected his lack of conformity and his willful desire to do it his own way. Dalton lacked the tools needed to complete the project according to the prescribed methods. He was too poor to buy index cards and had no access to a computer or the internet—yet was resourceful enough to read books from the library and "learn" the information needed.

Academic Angst

In understanding the essential pieces of Patsy's story, students such as Dalton learn not to care about school not only as a result of classroom interactions, but also due to the focus on academic achievement through grading, homework, and assessments. A high negative correlation exists between suicide activity and declined school performance, where academic pressure is the third most significant cause of suicidal behavior, regardless of the intelligence level of the student (Beane & Lipka, 2000; Butler & Novy, 1994). One method of applying academic pressure is through tracking and grouping as a system of competition and reward that further separates students, not only physically, but emotionally and socially as well. Students are keenly sensitive to their academic placement because it determines their peer group. Thus, academic achievement becomes a limited vision for some students due to the preset boundaries of their track, which draws them into passivity and lack of involvement. Dalton was never placed with high-achieving classmates due to his resistance to schooling, his behavioral problems, and his refusal to do schoolwork, which was usually below his level. Beane and Lipka (2000) cautioned that educators must "stare long and hard" (p. 35) at what they do concerning tracking, grouping, and other forms of institutional alienation, which are proven methods of lowering self-esteem, "strip[ping] learners of their personal dignity" (p. 21).

When I think of students such as Dalton who are highly intelligent and creative, yet do not fit within the climate and culture of school and are "different" from other students, I want to believe that they can have successful and meaningful lives in spite of their problems. Then, I realize that intelligence or creativity—or even hope—has nothing to do with success for them. School—with its institutional ideologies— is another representation of all that they cannot have, a place they do not fit in, and another form of oppression. The lack of desire for success and involvement are ways they can act out, resist, and refuse to subscribe to the authoritative framework of schools. By resisting, they have a voice and a way to say, "I know I do not fit into this, and you know it too, so I'm not going to play your game. It won't do me any good because my intelligence does not matter here." The destruction caused by standardized testing also creates emotional damage for many students because the school values something they cannot have. Dalton's failure to perform academically was because there was no *need* to value education. Dalton, and others like him, were not going to college or pursue a career; their future was already determined. Participant Trent felt that the focus on accountability and testing in schools was interfering with the emotional needs of students: "Right now the way we're doing it is 'this' [academics] is making this [emotional] worse because these are the kids who are not passing the test."

Although Dalton's retention was due to his lack of desire for educational success, it was also laced with the ill effects of his home life. Refusing to buy into an ideology to which he had no access, I think Dalton was trying to tell school personnel something that they were not able to see. [Dalton wanted and needed more than what the school or curriculum offered—a climate, culture, and curriculum established for those like him.] He existed in a situation that he did not create but had to accept. From all observations, he was alone to fend for himself when his needs were immense.

ACKNOWLEDGING FAMILY AND SOCIAL ISSUES

While many aspects of schooling impact adolescent development, attitude, and participation, family and social issues bring additional problems. According to the AAS (2006), family conflict is listed among the high risk factors for young adolescent suicide. Many students come to school each day "already victims of injurious conditions" (Dewey, 1938/1997, p. 56) with a heavy load of emotional, physical, and psychological baggage from their lives outside of school. They become withdrawn and passive and suffer the onset of depression or increased depression. Ignoring the difficulties of these students' lives creates further alienation and feelings of hopelessness which can result in suicide or risky behaviors. Part of Dalton's helplessness stemmed from not valuing his intelligence since it was not valued by his mother; it brought no attention, accolades, or acceptance. His efforts to fit in or succeed at school did not prevail over his need to be loved, cared for, and accepted. According to the participants, he wanted his mother to be involved in school event such as parent-teacher conferences and field trips; he wanted love and attention, family, clean clothes, and a normal life, none of which were available to him.

An increase in the number of teenage suicides in a 10-year period was found to be related to stress from what Elkind (1988) termed the "hurrying-related phenomenon." Children receive messages that they are to grow up quickly, achieve, and become successful. Adults encourage and perpetuate the notion that children are cute when they dress and look like miniature adults, participate in adult activities, and train at a young age for a career in sports, music, or drama. Many adults assume that stress is a normal part of adolescence. Although stress levels of children and youth are often greater than those of adults (Elkind, 1994), adults view it as "relatively minor, and that in any case mature children and sophisticated teenagers can handle it" (p. 201). What has occurred, in essence, is the disappearance of viewing children as children, but as more mature and capable than they really are.

Young adolescents often look at the world in disbelief and struggle to make sense of it, battling a state of helplessness and fear, which often results in depression and suicide (Beane, 1990). With the rise in student apathy, increased depression in children, and an increasing suicide rate, there is a need for addressing these issues in education. Noddings (1984), who has devoted much of her work to the concept of caring, has deemed schools in a "crisis of caring" (p. 181). The alienation and isolation suffered by students at home and at school manifests itself in an increase in self-destructive behaviors, offering fewer emotional anchors to which they can cling. Beane (1990), in challenging us to imagine what it must be like for youth today, stated, "Surely the increased incidence of self-destructive behaviors among the young must tell us something of how they view their chances. Surely we must realize that many see little hope for themselves and society" (p. 186).

Students are burdened with issues of loss such as divorce, death, illness, pregnancy, sexual orientation, and poverty, creating a wall between themselves, peers, and teachers. The continued cycle of humiliation, depression, inappropriate behaviors, and poor academic performance causes social isolation, lower self-esteem, and deeper depression (Butler & Novy, 1994; Elkind, 1989; King et al., 1999). Losses also include problems incurred by not only themselves, but when their families cope with loss of jobs, injuries, legal problems or remarriage. Since family or social issues can create situations that require coping skills beyond young people's capabilities, school provides a forum for resistance through misbehavior. Poor behavior increases when student deprivation and lack of identifying with the economic advantages of other classes disallows them to certain aspects of schooling. This "may not be simply a reaction to powerlessness, but might be an expression of power that is fueled by and reproduces the most powerful grammar of domination" (Aronowitz & Giroux, 1993, p. 94). This "counterculture" (Willis, 1989, p. 253) of misbehavior is created by alienated students who resist the code of the school's dominate culture, thus creating a place over which they have control. In sustaining their own class identity, and because school culture is "not real for them" (Beyer, 2000, p. 60), it offers a way to rebel against the dominant ideology both within and outside of school walls.

Dalton and his friends created a similar counterculture by continually breaking rules and resisting authority. Similar to the "lads" in Willis's (1989) study, their behaviors were "lived out in countless small ways ... nstantly recognized by the teachers, and an almost ritualistic part of the daily fabric of life for the kids" (p. 254). Powerless to do anything about his social status, the inequalities he faced, and the lack of a caring environment at home, Dalton found that he could reject schooling and its ideologies as much as it rejected him. Understandably, he became apathetic. And nobody was able to alter his destructive course. His resistance to schooling was his resistance to life. A stalemate had been established: the structure of schooling was not going to change and neither was Dalton. Nothing mattered—and as he uttered, "I'll see you in hell"—he made the decision to quit caring, quit trying, and to quit life.

Dalton's reputation in life followed him into death. The new school year began a week after his burial and once again, he was alienated from the school culture. No announcement was made concerning his death, no assistance was offered to his friends, and no efforts were made to educate the students or staff about suicide. The least of all possible outcomes occurred—a total lack of regard for the student whose locker stood empty, whose name was still on the class rosters, and whose face still haunted the thoughts of his friends. Participants described his friends' anger when they realized that Dalton's suicide would remain an unspoken part of the school culture and that "moving on" was the best choice offered them. Dalton, important to many of the participants, left his mark on their hearts and in their memories. His death was significant, but fleeting. And while the participants have Dalton's suicide as their lived experience—and the possibility of it occurring again—the stinging pain of it quietly subsided.

CONCLUSION

Students at risk of self-destruction are situated amid educational theory where decisions regarding school are made that affect them for a lifetime.

Noddings (1992) suggested, "We need a scheme that speaks to the existential heart of life—one that draws attention to our passions, attitudes, connections, concerns, and experienced responsibilities" (p. 47). While it is understandable and certainly agreeable that educators are not usually prepared for dealing with suicide, knowing the warning signs and how to respond is imperative. Because of this, knowledge about suicide should be an integral and embedded part of school curriculums and teacher education programs. Continued disillusionment and passive resistance intensifies among educators as the increased focus on standardized test scores purports to equal good teachers, good schools, and smarter students. Status, prestige, and reaping monetary rewards leave little hope that there is more to teaching and learning than the school's performance for test-hungry critics.

Upon reflecting on the lack of balance and the irregular flow between the emotional and social needs of students, concern emerges about the extent to which academic achievement can be gained for students whose lives are in turmoil. Dalton served as a prime example of how—by not dealing with the core issues of human problems—test scores will not rise and academic success will remain undesirable or unobtainable. Students who do not feel good about themselves will continue to have difficulties at school and chaotic lives. The issue is how we can improve students' lives enough to give them hope and direction in moving forward with desire and motivation. As educators, I believe it is often difficult for us to remember that our successes are the result of enjoying school, fitting into the school environment, and valuing what it offered.

REFERENCES

American Association of Suicidology. (2006.) *Youth suicide fact sheet*. Retrieved November 18, 2006, from http://www.suicidology.org/associations/1045/files/Youth2003.pdf

Apple, M. W. (1995). Cultural capital and official knowledge. In M. Berube & C. Nelson (Eds.), *Higher education under fire* (pp. 91-106). New York: Routledge.

Aronowitz, S., & Giroux, H. (1993). Education still under siege. *Critical studies in education and culture* (2nd ed.). Westport, CT: Bergin & Garvey.

Associated Press. (Sept 28, 2006). *Details from Colorado school shooting emerge*. Retrieved November 13, 2006, from http://www.msnbc.msn.com/id/15041037/

Ayers, W. (2001). *To teach: The journey of a teacher* (2nd ed.). New York: Teachers College Press.

Beane, J. A. (1990). *Affect in the curriculum: Toward democracy, dignity, and diversity*. New York: Teachers College Press.

Beane, J. A., & Lipka, R. P. (2000). *When the kids come first: Enhancing self-esteem*. New York: Educator's International Press.

Bernard, H. R. (2002). *Research methods in anthropology: Qualitative and quantitative approaches* (3rd ed.). New York: Alta Mira Press.

Beyer, L. E. (2000). *The arts, popular culture, and social change*. New York: Peter Lang.

Butler, J. W., & Novy, D. (1994). An investigation of differences in attitudes between suicidal and nonsuicidal student ideators. *Adolescence, 29,* 623-639.

Carspecken, P. F. (1996). *Critical ethnography in educational research: A theoretical and practical guide*. New York, NY: Routledge.

Centers for Disease Control, (2006a). *Leading cause of death reports.* National Center for Injury Prevention and Control Retrieved January 21, 2007, from http://webappa.cdc.gov/sasweb/ncipc/leadcaus10.html

Centers for Disease Control. (2006b). *Suicide fact sheet.* National Center for Injury Prevention and Control. Retrieved September 9, 2006, from http://www.cdc.gov/ncipc/factsheets/suifacts.htm

Connelly, M. F., & Clandinin, D. J. (1988). *Teachers as curriculum planners: Narratives of experience*. New York: Teachers College Press.

Darling-Hammond, L. (1998). Alternatives to grade retention. *The School Administrator, 55*(7), 18-21.

Davidson, M. W., & Range, L. M. (1999). Are teachers of children and young adolescents responsive to suicide prevention training modules? *Death Studies, 23*(1), 61-71.

Dewey, J. (1997). *Experience and education*. New York: Touchstone. (Original work published 1938)

Dwyer, K., Osher, D., & Warger, C. (1998). *Early warning, timely response: A guide to safe schools.* Washington, DC: U.S. Department of Education.

Eccles, J. S., & Roeser, R. W. (1999). School and community influences on human development. In M. H. Borstein & M. E. Lamb (Eds.), *Developmental psychology: An advanced textbook* (2 ed., pp. 503-546). Mahwah, NJ: Erlbaum.

Elbaz, F. (1991). Research on teacher's knowledge: The evolution of a discourse. *Journal of Curriculum Studies, 23*(1), 1-19.

Elkind, D. (1988). *The hurried child: Growing up too fast too soon*. New York: Addison-Wesley.

Elkind, D. (1989). *All grown up & no place to go: Teenagers in crisis*. New York: Addison-Wesley.

Elkind, D. (1994). *Ties that stress: The new family imbalance*. Cambridge, MA: Harvard University Press.

Erikson, E. H. (1968). *Identity: Youth and crisis.* New York: Norton.

Giroux, H. (1986). Radical pedagogy and the politics of student voice. Pedagogy and the politics of hope: Theory, culture, and schooling. *Interchange, 17*(1) 48-69.

Henderson, J., & Kesson, K. (2003). *Curriculum wisdom: Educational decisions in democratic societies*, New York: Prentice Hall.

Jackson, P. W. (1990). *Life in classrooms*. New York: Teachers College Press.

Jackson, P. W., Boostrom, R. E., & Hansen, D. T. (1993). *The moral life of schools*. San Francisco: Jossey-Bass.

Jimerson, S. (2001). Meta-analysis of grade retention research: Implications for practice in the 21st century. *School Psychology Review, 30*(3), 420-437.

Kincheloe, J. L., Steinberg, S., Rodriguez, N., & Chennault, R. E. (Eds.). (1998). *White reign: Deploying whiteness in America*. New York: St. Martin's Press.

King, K. A., Price, J. H., Telljohann, S. K., & Wahl, J. (1999). High school health teachers perceived self-efficacy in identifying students at risk for suicide. *Journal of School Health, 69*(5), 202-207.

Kirchner, J. E., Yoder, M. C., Kramer, T. L., Lindsey, M. S., & Thrush, C. R. (2000). Development of an educational program to increase school personnel's awareness about child and adolescent depression. *Education, 121*, 235-247.

Kroger, J. (1996). *Identity in adolescence: The balance between self and other* (2nd ed.). New York: Routledge.

Liston, D. P. (2000). Love and despair in teaching. *Educational Theory, 50*(1), 81-102.

Marshall, C., & Rossman, G. B. (1999). *Designing qualitative research* (3rd ed.). Thousand Oaks, CA: McGraw-Hill.

McMillan, J. H., & Schumacher, S. (2001). *Research in education* (5th ed.). New York: Longman.

Merriam, S. B. (1988). *Case study research in education: A qualitative approach*. San Francisco: Jossey-Bass.

Miles, M. B., & Huberman, A. M. (1994). *An expanded sourcebook: Qualitative data analysis* (2nd ed.). Thousand Oaks, CA: Sage.

Miller, P. H. (1993). *Theories of developmental psychology* (3rd ed.). New York: W. H. Freeman.

Moustakas, C. (1990). *Heuristic research: Design, methodology and application*. Newbury Park, CA: Sage.

Nagaoka, J., & Roderick, M. (2004). Ending social promotion: The effects of retention. *Consortium on Chicago School Research,* University of Chicago. Retrieved October 15, 2006, from http://ccsr.uchicago.edu/publications/p70.pdf

National Institute of Mental Health (2000, November). *In harm's way: Suicide in America*. Retrieved July, 2002, from http://www.nimh.nih.gov

Noddings, N. (1984). *A feminine approach to ethics and moral education*. Berkeley: University of California Press.

Noddings, N. (1992). *The challenge to care in schools: An alternative approach to education.* NY: Teachers College Press.

Oser, F. K. (1991). Professional morality: A discourse approach (The case of the teaching profession). In W. M. Kurtines & J. L. Gewirtz (Eds.), *Handbook of moral development* (Vol. 2, pp. 191-226). Boston: Allyn & Bacon.

Patton, M. Q. (1990). *Qualitative evaluation and research methods* (2nd ed.). Newbury Park, CA: Sage.

Phillion, J. (2002). *Narrative inquiry in a multicultural landscape: Multicultural teaching and learning*. Westport CT: Ablex.

Pinar, W. (1992). Cries and whispers. In W. Pinar & W. Reynolds (Eds.), *Understanding curriculum as phenomenological and deconstructed text* (pp. 92-101). New York: Teachers College Press.

Portner, J. (1964). *One in thirteen: The silent epidemic of teen suicide*. Beltsville, MD: Robins Lane Press.

Rishel, T. (2003). *Schoolyard to the graveyard: A curricular study of Dalton's suicide*. Unpublished doctoral dissertation, Purdue University, West Lafayette, Indiana.

Rishel, T. (2004). Maneuvering the emotional and social demands of the classroom. In P. C. Miller (Ed.), *Narratives from the classroom: An introduction to teaching* (pp. 164-182). Thousand Oaks, CA: Sage.

Rishel, T. (in press). From the principal's desk: Alienating Families in the school environment. In T. Turner-Vorbeck & M. Marsh-Miller (Eds.), *Other kinds of families: Diversity in school & culture.* New York: Teachers College Press.

Schön, D. A. (1987). *Educating the reflective practitioner.* San Francisco: Jossey-Bass.

Schlosser, L. K. (1992). Teacher distance and student disengagement: School lives on the margin. *Journal of Teacher Education, 43*(2), 128-140.

U.S. Department of Justice. (1998). *National crime victimization survey, 1995: Preliminary findings.* Bureau of Justice Statistics. Retrieved March 1, 2006, from http://www.ojp.usdoj.gov/bjs/abstract/ncvs95p.htm

U.S. Public Health Service. (1999a). The surgeon general's call to action to prevent suicide. *Mental health: A report of the surgeon general.* Retrieved January 24, 2007, from http://www.surgeongeneral.gov/library/mentalhealth/chapter3/sec5.html

U.S. Public Health Service. (1999b). The surgeon general's call to action to prevent suicide. *Mental health: A report of the surgeon general.* Retrieved May 16, 2006, from http://www.surgeongeneral.gov/library/mentalhealth/home.html

van Manen, M. (1990). *Researching lived experience: Human science for an action sensitive pedagogy.* Albany,: State University of New York Press.

Wassef, A., & Ingham, D. (1995). In search of effective programs to address students' emotional distress and behavioral problems part l: Defining the problem. *Adolescence, 30*, 523-539.

Willis, P. (1989). Class and institutional forms of culture. In J. H. Ballantine (Ed.). *Schools and society: A unified reader* (2nd ed., pp. 251-256). Mountain View, CA: Mayfield.

Wilson, S. M. & Berne, J. (1999). Teacher learning and the acquisition of professional knowledge: An examination of research on contemporary professional development. In A. Iran-Nejad & P. D. Pearson (Eds.), *Review of research in education, 24*, 173-209. Washington, DC: American Educational Research Association.

CHAPTER 16

MIDDLE SCHOOL TEACHER QUALITIES

Looking for Signs of Dignity and Democracy

Mark D. Vagle

ABSTRACT

In this theoretical paper, I explore qualities middle school teachers possess which allow their classrooms to become dignified and democratic. I offer a theoretical perspective for teaching young adolescents by combining aspects of Beane's democratic teaching and Hartoonian's assertion that democracy is essentially an argument between particular value tensions. I focus on 2 tensions: *private wealth and common wealth* and *diversity and unity*. I use this theoretical perspective on democracy to reflect on selected findings from a phenomenological study (Vagle, 2006a), which focused on moments when teachers had recognized and responded to students who did not understand something during an instructional activity.

The Young Adolescent and the Middle School
pp. 323–342

INTRODUCTION

> She needs to spend more time reading and focusing and trying to understand what she's learning.... Here's a great situation ... she's taking the test and [other students] are done with the test in 15 minutes. [They] go hand it in, [and] she's done [too]. She might be on question number 2 but she's done because she can't comprehend or focus anymore ... she's so worried about what her friends ... are going to be doing that she cannot redirect her mind to get back to that piece of paper. So here's what I've done ... to help her out ... talk to her, ask her, I needed her to tell me ... what was not working and she did with a little bit of questioning, never directly saying it, I just kept questioning and then she finally said ... "I can't concentrate, can't read, it doesn't make sense to me. I just, once I get to a certain point I see all this busy-ness coming around, I'll read it and I won't understand what I just read, I don't even know what I just read, I have no idea. (Harry)

Harry, a Grade 7 and 8 science/math teacher with 13 years of teaching experience, describes this moment as a time when he finally recognized precisely what and why one of his students continually turned in assignments quickly, but rarely demonstrated understanding in the assignment (i.e., the final product did not look the way it should have). As a teacher who followed his students from Grade 7 to Grade 8, Harry had not recognized this student's actions when she was in Grade 7. While in the seventh grade, the student demonstrated understanding in her work. However, the following year Harry began to notice that the student tended not to demonstrate understanding in her work. Harry had yet to recognize *what* or *why* the student did not understand—until, on this particular day, the student responded to his questioning. One might wonder, why did this particular student, in this time and space, decide to tell Harry about her lack of understanding? Did Harry simply catch her on a day when she felt like talking? Did Harry catch her on a day when she felt extremely frustrated so that her response erupted, so to speak? Did the student feel safe at this moment—a bit less vulnerable than other moments? Why did this young adolescent's voice speak so clearly to Harry at this moment? What is it about this classroom space that allows this student's voice to speak about something potentially embarrassing for the student—"I ... can't read. It doesn't make sense to me."

It would seem that one possible explanation is that there is something about Harry—a set of qualities perhaps—that creates a safe space for this particular student to say, "it doesn't make sense to me," when she does not want others (especially her peers) to know she does not understand. And perhaps this space—one that allows for young adolescents to say "it doesn't make sense"—can be described as a place of democracy that is marked with dignity.

The purpose of this chapter is to explore what qualities middle school teachers, like Harry, possess that allow their classrooms to become dignified and democratic. I begin with a brief discussion of teacher characteristics deemed essential for effectively working with young adolescents. Then, I offer a theoretical perspective for teaching young adolescents by combining aspects of Beane's (1990, 1997, 2005) notion of democratic teaching and Hartoonian's (2003) assertion that democracy is essentially an argument between particular value tensions. I focus specifically on two tensions: *private wealth and common wealth* and *diversity and unity.* Next, I use this theoretical perspective on democracy to reflect on some of the findings from a phenomenological study (Vagle, 2006a). Essentially, I look for evidence of this theoretical perspective on democracy in a particular aspect in teaching.

In the phenomenological study (Vagle, 2006a), participating teachers were asked—during an unstructured interview or by writing a lived experience description—to describe moments when they had recognized and responded to a student who did not understand something during an instructional activity. Through thoughtful and repeated readings of the data, I identified an essential meaning structure and patterns of meaning which describe the structure. Because this particular chapter is theoretical and conceptual in nature, I do not discuss the research methodology of the phenomenological study. For a more detailed description of the research methodology, please refer to Vagle and the Appendix.

THEORETICAL PERSPECTIVE

In his work on curriculum integration, Beane (1997) reflected on what he had observed in teachers' classrooms as they created places of *high pedagogy.* In these places of high pedagogy teachers respect the dignity of young people, embrace democracy, feel that democratic values and rights should be extended to young people in schools, believe diversity in a classroom is a source of strength, involve young people in significant learning, are interested in excellence and equity, and aim to integrate life inside and outside of school.

Beane (1997) acknowledged that teachers, who may not teach an integrated curriculum, might still hold these same values. However, Beane felt that the teachers he has worked with—those who have committed to an integrated curriculum—integrate these beliefs "into a coherent pedagogy and ... find fulfillment in helping young people pursue *their* interests and ambitions" (p. 70).

Also related to middle school teachers' pedagogy, Roney (2001) examined the characteristics of effective middle school teachers that led to her identification of 34 characteristics. Fifteen of Roney's characteristics of effective middle school teachers had been previously documented in middle grades research (Arth, Lounsbury, McEwin, & Swaim, 1995; Buckner & Bickel, 1991) as well as a position paper (National Middle School Association, 1981). The shared list included, but was not limited to, middle school teachers being positive, showing enthusiasm, demonstrating adaptability and flexibility, and understanding the need for variety of teaching strategies. In addition, Roney referred to Davies (1995) review of quantitative studies, which includes many of the same characteristics with the addition of characteristics such as middle school teachers respecting and accepting others, structuring instruction, and promoting successful experiences.

What appears to be unique about Roney's (2001) study is not only that it resulted in an expanded list of characteristics, but that it also aimed to look at the characteristics in an integrated manner. In short, Roney found there to be a "critical coherence between the [participating teachers'] personal self-awareness ... and the teachers' capacity to relate to the outside world" (p. 100). Teachers felt they needed to know themselves "inside out"—they needed to be inwardly integrated. Roney's use of *integrated* is intriguing because it suggests that lists of characteristics are not experienced or lived as separate entities. Furthermore, it is interesting that both Roney and Beane (1997) stress that what sets the effective middle school teacher apart from the less effective teacher is *not* that he or she does or does not possess some or many of the identified characteristics. Rather it is that the effective middle school teacher (Beane's high pedagogue) integrates these characteristics.

The challenge, of course, is to study and to reflect on this integration, because the integration (the whole) is difficult to access in practice. One way to access this integration is to focus on discrete moments in which the teacher might express certain characteristics. In my study (Vagle, 2006a), I asked participating teachers—during an unstructured interview or by writing a lived experience description—to describe moments when they had recognized and responded to a student who did not understand something during an instructional activity. In a recent article (Vagle, 2006b), I analyzed the response portion of the phenomenon through Beane's notion of high pedagogy by focusing on the degree to which the teachers' responses helped create dignified, democratic learning spaces for their students. In the end, the best I could do was wonder what notions of dignity and democracy really meant in this discrete aspect of teaching. I found these notions to be quite complex. I wondered whether it is a democratic practice for the middle school teacher to let the young adolescent struggle a bit when faced with a difficult task. I wondered if treating students with dignity meant to honor whom the students are, what they are struggling to understand, and what they are interested in exploring. I wondered even more about what it was like for teachers to create dignified, democratic spaces. For the teacher, what are these spaces like? In reflecting upon these questions, I have come to believe that these notions need further consideration.

Beane's Dignity and Democracy

Much of Beane's individual (1990, 1997, 2005) and collaborative (Apple & Beane, 1995) work focused on the notions of dignity and democracy. Consistently, Beane grounded these notions as ways of living with one another and challenged teachers to enact a pedagogy that preserves this way of life. In other words, creating dignified, democratic classrooms was, for Beane, about *being* particular ways. It is about teachers and students living with one another in particular ways. This raised a logical question: What are these particular ways?

Beane (1990) reminded us that human dignity is "the idea that all people, as belonging to humanity, are worthy and have a right to self-respect" (p. 60). Moreover, personal and social efficacy depends, in large part, on the degree to which one feels that they have dignity. Beane went so far as to assert that dignity is the fundamental entitlement of people and that human dignity may be "posited as so fundamental and central that other values and moral principles may be derived from it and, in turn, it may serve as a referent for discourse about the contradictions among the others" (p. 60). It ought not to be surprising that 5 years later, Apple and Beane (1995), in their edited book *Democratic Schools*, included concern for the dignity and rights of individuals and minorities as one of seven conditions on which democracy depends. To say that democracy depends, in part, on treating people with dignity makes dignity a fundamental aspect of democracy.

Describing dignity as a fundamental aspect of democratic teaching continued for Beane (1997) in that he felt that teachers should view their classrooms as places of high pedagogy. As previously mentioned, teachers who aim to exercise Beane's high pedagogy believe a number of things, two of which involve treating students with dignity and believing students should be extended democratic rights. For Beane, teachers respect the *dignity* of young people when they take their students' ideas, hopes, aspirations, and lives seriously and when they listen to young people "whether the message is clear or confused" (p. 68). Listening to young people, for Beane, means listening to young people's concerns, not merely their interests. This pushes teachers to do more than survey students' interests—it asks teachers to engage their students in meaningful discussions about their own learning. Furthermore, treating students with dignity means more than checking in on them or, for example, giving them a choice between one type of assessment or another. It means talking to them about issues. This is not to say that surveying students about their interests or providing students with choices of assessments are bad practices. Rather, the intent is to illustrate the depth of what Beane means when he describes dignity.

This dignified engagement between teacher and student is tied closely to Beane's (1997) notion of actual democracy as opposed to an illusion of democracy where students experience "engineered consent to predetermined plans" (p. 53). Beane's high pedagogues believe in democracy and,

> are interested in and concerned about social issues, enough so that such issues often come to organize work in the classroom. They believe that young people have a right to be well informed and to inquire critically into issues that concern them. (p. 69)

Similar to his notion of dignity, Beane (1997) focused on *issues* that concern students when discussing democracy. In fact, it seems as though these two notions—dignity and democracy—can be considered together as they both focus on the individual student and take the student's concerns seriously. Although Beane referred specifically to curriculum integration at this point, there was also an underlying theme present in how Beane feels teachers should *be* with their students. It is as though integrating curriculum is one practical way for teachers to *be* democratic.

In fact, being democratic appears to be the primary focus of Beane's (2005) most recent book, *A Reason to Teach*, in which he stressed that one should not think of democracy "simply as a form of government where people get to vote, although it is partly that.... But at a deeper level ... regard it as a way of being together, of living, learning, and making our lives better" (pp. 11-12). Beane continued to treat dignity as a central component of democracy, stating that "respect for human dignity is perhaps the most fundamental aspect of democracy, and for this reason it permeates the culture of democratic communities" (p. 71). Moreover, Beane listed dignity as the first of four propositions that might allow for an optimistic and humane view of democracy:

1. all people have an inherent right to dignity,
2. we are capable of caring for and about each other,
3. we can see our own personal fate tied to that of the common good,
4. we have the collective intellectual capacity to resolve the issues we face, and the social capacity to work together in doing so. (p. 12)

If one believes these propositions, then one's view of teaching has the potential of being democratic. Again, it may be ill-advised to reduce democratic teaching to a form of government or a checklist of attributes. "Democracy is a way of life, and when it is thought about and lived long enough, it simply becomes 'what we are about' and 'the way we do things'" (Beane, 2005, p. 15). Of course, as with curriculum integration, Beane's propositions must be lived as well.

The living out of democracy involves multiple voices—individual voices struggling to be heard while working with others. Beane (2005) identified two great social dimensions of democracy. The first is the *common good* and the second is the individual needs, interests, and concerns people bring to the community. While Beane acknowledged that discussions of democracy typically focus on the common good because "there seems to be more than enough self-centered thinking to go around" (p. 73), he simultaneously cautioned educators to not underestimate the role of the individual, because the concerns and interests of the community are formed out of individual concerns.

> And the more diverse the individuals, the richer and more promising the community, since diverse voices bring a wider range of opinions, ideas, and view points. For this reason, diversity in a democratic classroom is seen as a strength rather than a problem. (Beane, p. 73)

The diversity of voices in a community is also part of what Hartoonian (2003), a scholar in social studies education, imagined when he conceptualized democracy. Like Beane, Hartoonian believes democracy is more than a form of government, it is more than freedom, it is more than choice, and it is more than the individual. For Hartoonian, democracy is essentially an argument, marked by four value tensions: *ethics and law*; *private wealth and common wealth*; *freedom and equality*; and *diversity and unity*. Two of these value tensions—*private wealth and common wealth* and *diversity and unity*—help to elucidate further Beane's views of democracy.

Private Wealth and Common Wealth

Hartoonian (2003) emphasized that early in our nation's history people seemed to understand that their personal well-being was connected closely with the welfare of the community. Hence, *happiness* was understood to be a by-product of a good life. It meant living beyond oneself and giving of one's talents to make the community better. The notion of argument, then, is about the struggle to keep a balance between the personal well-being and the welfare of the community. Perhaps this may mean an actual argument—like a debate, a fight, or a protest. However, over time, this might mean a consistent dialogue around issues that are of concern to those in the community. One might imagine Beane's (1997) democratic classroom as a space for this argument or struggle. The teacher and his or her students work through the pendulum swinging action between each individual student's needs and the needs of the entire class. One of the many challenges would be the diversity of individual voices in the classroom.

Diversity and Unity

Hartoonian (2003) stressed that the individual is highly prized in our society, yet a person must exist within the constraints of society—with its obligations and requirements as well as support and enrichment. Again, there is a struggle for balance between what an individual needs and desires and what the larger society will allow. This becomes more complicated when one imagines diversity not only by learning styles, interests, and concerns, but also across lines of gender, race, ethnicity, language, sexual orientation, culture, age, and socioeconomic status. How do individuals desire to live and how does the community in which they live constrain the individual's desire? In Beane's (1997) image of a democratic classroom, he emphasizes that diversity is not seen as a problem, but as a strength because a diversity of voices brings a wider range of opinions, ideas, and viewpoints. It seems that a teacher must trust young adolescents' voices enough to view the diversity as a strength, rather than an obstacle. Moreover, it seems that balancing the diversity of voices with the needs of the group is a challenging endeavor.

Using Hartoonian's (2003) conception of democracy has significant implications for teachers. For example, respecting students' dignity and extending them democratic rights would mean that the teacher creates space for argument around these value tensions or at least allows for these value tensions to be played out, with students as players. This argument, this wrestling, this playing out—is at the core of democracy. One ought to acknowledge that the teacher holds the key, so to speak, to educating students in this manner. The teacher must allow the classroom to become dignified and democratic. The teacher must be willing to exercise a high pedagogy. The teacher must be willing to engage in the struggle between Hartoonian's value tensions.

What does this all mean for teachers of young adolescents? It seems reasonable that teachers of young adolescents would need to believe in Beane's (2005) propositions for an optimistic and humane view of democracy and Hartoonian's (2003) notion of argument among value tensions.

It also seems reasonable that teachers of young adolescents would know and be able to create opportunities for this democracy to be lived out in the classroom. In other words, democracy as argument is not experienced in the abstract. The argument is lived out in unique contexts. It is lived out in Beane's curriculum integration when teachers listen—really listen—to their students' concerns about the world and use these conversations to plan the curriculum. Moreover, this argument is lived out when teachers aim to recognize and respond to students when they do not understand something during an instructional activity (Vagle, 2006a).

TEACHER QUALITIES THAT HELP CREATE DIGNIFIED, DEMOCRATIC SPACES

> The principles of democracy remain our constant, acting as a compass rather than a detailed road map. The point is to keep moving in their direction.... Creating a democratic school begins wherever we think possible and appropriate ... it may mean beginning in our own classroom with some aspect of our own teaching. (Beane, 2005, p. 14)

Ostensibly, one critical aspect of teaching young adolescents is the teacher's recognition of and response to his or her students' understanding. In addition, what qualities a teacher should possess in order to recognize and respond to students in a democratic manner also becomes an important consideration. In this section of the chapter, two such qualities are described, beginning with how some teachers were able to recognize and respond to one student and all students at the same time during instruction and followed by how some teachers experienced recognizing and responding when students did not understand as varied and irregular as opposed to a step-by-step and linear episode. These qualities are discussed using the descriptions of four experienced middle school teachers and by using Beane's (1997) and Hartoonian's (2003) theoretical perspectives on democracy.

Darla, a White female, is a Grade 7 social studies teacher in an urban middle school located in a large Midwestern city; she has taught for 7 years. Garry teaches science in a suburb adjacent to the large Midwestern city in which Darla teaches. He is a White male with 17 years of teaching experience. At Garry's school, all teachers teach the same group of students for 2 years—during Grades 7 and 8—a practice commonly referred to as *looping*. Introduced at the beginning of this paper, Harry, a White male teacher of Grade 7 and Grade 8 science/math, has 13 years of teaching experience. Like Garry, he loops with his students from Grade 7 to Grade 8. Harry teaches in a suburban middle school located outside a midsize Midwestern city. Jackie, a White female, has been teaching Grade 7 social studies in a rural middle school in the Midwest for 16 years.

Recognizing and Responding to One and All

In this particular aspect of teaching, one quality teachers seem to possess is a commitment to recognize one student's lack of understanding while also keeping the rest of the students' understanding in mind during instruction. More specifically, teachers might strive to balance the tension between private and common wealth. In other words, the teacher might aim to protect (in this case recognize) the personal well being of an individual student while also protecting the intimate connection between that individual student's welfare and the welfare of the community (the other students in the classroom). Therefore, the teacher seems committed to recognizing and responding to individual students and many students at the same time. The teacher is concerned about what the individual will gain (i.e., learn) and what the group will gain. A description from Darla helps elucidate this point.

Darla: And there's another student ... very liberal Caucasian male, but he kind of talks over everybody's head.... So he'll say something that's probably in agreement with what the rest of the class is saying but they don't understand what he's saying [be]cause it's at this level that they don't get.... So ... they'll tease him about that and they'll henpeck him about that, you know, [be]cause they don't [understand]

Mark: What will they say to him?

Darla: They don't even know that he's agreeing with them. Well they'll call him brainiac or ... "What did that word mean you freak?" Sometimes they're very merciless.

Mark: Where are you at that point ... and what do you do?

Darla: Typically it's [when] the classroom discussion [is] going on ... I'm ... kind of wandering the horse shoe ... and I'll say, if it's getting out of hand and they're starting to call each other freak ... I [say] "Whoa, whoa, whoa, whoa, wait a minute, now Charlie, can you repeat what you said? What did you mean?" ... to make sure they're understanding each other.... And if I need to, I'll jump in and say what I think he's saying ... or I'll say, "Well it sounds to me like Charlie's agreeing with Tina."

In this case, Darla recognized one student's understanding as being at a high level and simultaneously recognized that the rest of the class did not understand what the one student meant. There are different aspects of recognition that point to different aspects of response. In this case, Darla responded in order to help clarify meaning for all students while reinforcing the understanding the one student already possessed. Darla's actions in this particular case seemed to dignify the individual student who understood at a high level; she also helped the members of the larger classroom community understand what the individual student meant. In effect, Darla strived to balance the tension between the individual and the group's needs simultaneously.

It seems that teachers in a discussion-oriented classroom where students face each other while situated in a circle or horseshoe shape would find themselves in these types of situations quite often. The way students' are organized in the classroom space would both allow for and demand that the teacher recognize and respond to *one and all students* simultaneously because students are oriented to one another and the teacher simultaneously. However, Beane (2005) pointed out that, "Democratic ideas mean little unless we act on them. Nevertheless, methods alone are not enough. There must be intention as well" (p. 15). While the structure of the discussion-oriented classroom might allow for this type of recognition and response, the organization of the classroom space—the method in this case—is not enough. The teacher must intend to be a particular way through this method. Furthermore, this particular type of physical arrangement is not the only *space* where the teacher recognizes and responds to one and all students. Garry disclosed,

> One of the things that I have said to them [is] if I know...a student has a question, there are several of the students with that same question too, so at that point without doing...one to one conversation with her in front of the entire class, I've addressed her concern in front of everybody.

In this case, Garry chose to address one student's question by responding to all students. It is as if Garry had obvious recognition of a lack of understanding with one student because that student directly asked a question. At the same time, Garry recognized the possibility that other students might have the same lack of understanding. He responded to the student who asked the question indirectly by responding to all students—of whom some may or may not have understood. In this respect, Garry recognized and responded (to the individual student) and responded and recognized (to the rest of the class). It is as though Garry combined a reactive response with a *preemptive response*. Even if Garry was just "covering his bases," the important point in relation to the *one-and-all* quality is that his recognition and response were coordinated as he considered one student's understanding and all students' understanding at the same time. Again, there was a balance between the individual student's needs and the entire classroom of students' needs.

This quality is also evident when the teacher recognizes understanding in one student and responds to this recognition to determine if other students understand. This is a variation of an earlier point. Earlier, the consideration focused on how, in a discussion-oriented classroom, the teacher might respond to one student's high level understanding in order to help all students understand. In that case, the teacher recognized, from the start, that no other students understood what the one student was saying. This point can be varied slightly to reveal how the teacher recognizes one student's understanding and uses that recognition and that student's understanding to see if other students understand. Harry recalled,

> I'll try to say 'You know Janet thought this way, do any others see it this way?' And then I'll look at who will kind of chime in and chime out.... Sally and Margaret won't, they'll just write down what the other kids say. I'm not sure if they understand what they're saying but they'll at least write it down because they're supposed to, because it's a social coping skill—so that they're not sought out.

It is not going too far to say that Harry engaged in a recognition-response-recognition process. Harry recognized one student's understanding, which prompted a response to that student and all students, which then prompted recognition of those who understood (chimed in or out) and those who did not "chime in" but did write down what the *understanding* student said. There seems to be a connection to Hartoonian's (2003) value tension between diversity and unity. If one imagines the students as having voices that chime in or out and those voices that do neither, there is a sense of the diversity of understanding in the classroom. Ideally, Harry wants there to be unity. He wants all students to understand. Perhaps using one student's voice to see if other students understand can be interpreted as a way to negotiate this tension between the diversity of the group's understanding and the goal for a unified understanding.

To further complicate matters, there are times when the teacher is certain that a student did not understand before the response and still does not understand after the response. How the teacher comes to know this is important to the *one-and-all students'* quality as well. Garry noted,

> Eventually I went to a different student, got an answer that was more on task or more on topic and then I went back to her to check in ... with her response and have her verbally see what she came in with and she still was having difficulty with it ... she didn't understand, I mean she was verbally saying "You know I'm ... not getting this ... I don't understand ... help me out."

Garry responded to the student who did not understand by turning to another student and then by going back to the first student. This is interesting in that Garry moved back and forth between two students, trying to use another student's understanding to see if the first student would come to understand what should be understood.

In other words, through the response Garry recognized understanding in one student and lack of understanding in another and then tried to use one student's understanding as a response to another student. This response helped Garry recognize that the student who he thought did not understand, really did not understand. In effect, Garry validated his initial recognition. It appears that Garry did not necessarily plan to make these moves prior to the lesson, it just happened during the *living out* of the lesson. What students will or will not understand cannot be programmed. This is, perhaps, one reason why this particular quality is so important—teachers who possess it are able to be democratic in that they can move back and forth along the tension between what is good for one student and the community of students throughout instruction.

Recognition and Response as Irregular Patterns

Related to the *one and all* quality is the teachers' openness to the reality that recognizing and responding when students do not understand varies based on the situation at hand. In other words, the recognition and response, for teachers, has a pattern—first one thing happens, then another, and so on. However, the temporal and spatial dimensions of the pattern vary based on each situation, thus making the pattern unpredictable and often irregular. Rarely, is there a predictable clean and linear pattern that can be applied to all situations. This seems to be an important quality for teachers when they aim to create dignified, democratic spaces because it allows for different recognition and response patterns to take place. The teacher does not force the recognition and response into a predetermined pattern. Rather, the teacher remains open to the possibility that recognition and a response may be necessary at various times and places depending on the situation at hand (e.g., which students do not understand, what they do not understand, at what point in the lesson the recognition takes place).

In fact, a teacher who possesses this quality appears to be navigating Hartoonian's (2003) *diversity and unity* value tension in that he or she acknowledges that particular student's understanding is recognized and responded to in particular ways that vary from other students or from the group as a whole. For instance, Garry described a time when he did not worry "about the fact that [a student's] first response was incorrect."

Instead, Garry used this recognition to inform the types of questions he posed to the student as he "delve[d] into her...understanding." It is as though Garry overlooked the initial misunderstanding in order to learn more about the student's lack of understanding. This involved recognition of the student's understanding throughout his response and demonstrates how recognition has depth, moving from the fact that the student did not understand to more specific recognition of what the student did not understand (e.g. the student's level of understanding). What makes this recognition and response pattern irregular is that Garry did not recognize misunderstanding in an exact manner right away and then lodge a response that settled the matter. Rather, Garry's recognizing and responding were enmeshed with one another.

It is evident that recognizing and responding is not only about what happens at a particular moment in time, but also about what happens over time. Garry described how his response depends on what he has recognized in the student's actions.

> I kind of approached these two different ways. If I have a student that I can tell that they're not understanding because they're not being attentive and it's a ... conscious decision on their part, I will usually try to draw them in by maybe asking a specific question of them concerning the content, "Can you tell me ... the size of the crystals for this particular igneous rock?" If it's a student where I feel they're making the effort but still not understanding ... I'll do [it] privately.

For Garry, these two ways to respond depended on a history of recognitions. For example, if students have been "slumped down in their chair, staring out the window, writing intently—perhaps a note to a friend—at a time when they should be prompted to be thinking" it is likely they are not making the necessary effort. However, Garry also acknowledged that these signs are not absolutes. He must get to know the students over several months to learn which students are truly disengaged, and which only appear to be disengaged but actually have been following along.

Garry's description, again, demonstrates how recognizing and responding have irregular as opposed to predictable patterns. His description suggests that recognition of student understanding is not a fixed, static phenomenon that is void of other recognitions. Rather, an ever-changing phenomenon involves recognition of other phenomena (e.g., effort). It is important to stress that recognition and response are linked carefully to the fact that something is not understood, what is not understood, and *why* something is not understood. This is another important reminder in Garry's description. Garry responded differently to students whom he perceived were not making the effort to understand and those who were making the effort but still did not understand. If the response hinges on these recognitions, then the building up of recognitions and the making up of students over time will continue to make the recognition-response pattern irregular, based on the situation at hand.

Sometimes the recognition-response pattern can span from one day to the next. Jackie described a student who asked a question—during a test—about the central topic being covered on the test. Jackie's response, and depth of recognition, actually came the next day when Jackie and the student met to discuss the student's questions. Jackie remembered,

> One of her problems turned out to be that she didn't know east from west. She knew north and south—but east and west, she was getting mixed up. So we tried to work on that, how to remember that [with] those little memory tricks.

Jackie's recognition that the student did not understand, during the test, was responded to at a different time, in a different place, and in a different context (one-on-one). During the response there was further recognition of what the student did not understand.

In sum, recognition and response must be seen over time and across these contexts. Again, the important point is that recognition-response patterns are not, necessarily, clear and linear, but are irregular in that they involve pauses, emphases, and so on. Of course, one would also not say that all recognition-response patterns have the same irregularity. Rather it is necessary to say that recognition and response when students do not understand have unique patterns, which vary based on the situation, and thus are best described as irregular.

CONCLUDING PERSPECTIVE

Perhaps an effective middle school teacher possesses many of the characteristics which previous studies (Arth et al., 1995; Buckner & Bickel, 1991; Davies, 1995; Roney, 2001) have identified. Perhaps many of these characteristics lead to practices (i.e., methods) which contain signs of democracy, as described by Beane (1997) and supported by Hartoonian (2003). However, as Beane stresses, methods are not enough—there must be intention as well.

One might wonder how conscious middle school teachers are of their intentions— democratic or otherwise. In Vagle's (2006a) study, teachers were not asked directly about their intentions; they were not asked whether they intended to treat their students with dignity or whether they intended to be democratic. Nevertheless, when analyzing their descriptions of a particular aspect of their teaching through a theoretical perspective of democracy there were signs of dignity and democracy. That said, this does not mean that these signs of dignity and democracy cannot be contested. For example, Garry's decision to respond differently to students whom he perceived were making an effort and those who he perceived were not making an effort might be interpreted another way. Is it fair and equitable of Garry to treat these students differently (diversity)? Is this a moment when he should respond "the same way" (unity)? Is it dignified or democratic to afford some students a private response and provide other students with a public response? What is right or wrong?

Perhaps students in a democratic classroom should be held publicly accountable at times, without being publicly ridiculed. Perhaps they should receive subtle reminders (e.g., Garry's questions about course content) which signal that their teacher recognizes that they, for some reason, do not appear to be making the necessary effort to learn the material. In other words, maybe it is part of being a good citizen to participate in what is happening in the classroom. Being given a voice, means using the voice for the good of one's own learning and the community's learning. Of course, answers to these questions are not simple. Perhaps this is the point. Democracy is, in part, a balance between the individual and the community. What happens in the community can be contested.

Identifying signs of democracy is not necessarily about determining whether discrete acts on the part of the teacher are absolutely dignified and democratic (although this is important as well). Rather, the particular signs of democracy in this paper have been signs of the balance—at times struggle—between value tensions. One can see the struggle to recognize the needs of one student, without neglecting the needs of the rest of the students. It would be interesting to ask teachers to reflect upon their attempts to strike a balance between the needs of individual students and the entire classroom and to have them articulate their intentions. It would also be interesting to observe teachers' practice in order to look for signs of democracy (intended or unintended) in other aspects of teaching.

Consider one of Roney's (2001) characteristics of effective middle school teaching—demonstrating *adaptability and flexibility*. If one were to observe experienced teachers being adaptable and flexible, what would be observed? What would teachers be doing? What would their students be doing? If one were to ask experienced teachers to describe moments they were adaptable and flexible, what would they say? Would one see signs of democracy in the teachers' attempts to be adaptable and flexible? Would one see the teacher balancing between the diversity and unity value tension?

Remaining open to the diversity of student understanding in one's classroom means remaining open to how one will recognize and respond to that understanding. This openness allows the response to depend on the nature of the recognition. It allows one response to take place the following day for one student and immediately after the recognition for another student. It allows the response to be tailored to the reason why the student did not understand. Another important point about the signs of democracy is that the diversity of student understanding is seen as a strength rather than a problem. The teachers, in these particular moments, did not appear to force the recognition and the response in a particular direction. They remained open to the possibility of difference.

It seems unreasonable to claim that Harry, Darla, Garry, and Jackie— or any teachers for that matter— are always democratic in their teaching. Furthermore, they do not continuously recognize and respond effectively when students do not understand. Almost assuredly, they, like all those who teach, miss things. That said, there are almost assuredly times they do not miss things. They possess qualities, which allow signs of dignity and democracy to be illuminated. At times, these qualities may even allow a young adolescent to feel safe enough to say to her teacher, "I ... can't read. It doesn't make sense to me."

APPENDIX: RESEARCH METHODOLOGY (VAGLE, 2006A)

In the tradition of van Manen (1990), with some reliance on Dahlberg, Drew, and Nystrom (2001) and Polkinghorne (1989), four research activities constituted the methodological structure:

1. turning to a phenomenon which seriously interests us and commits us to the world,
2. investigating experience as we live it rather than as we conceptualize it,
3. reflecting on the essential themes (meanings) which characterize the phenomenon, and
4. describing the phenomenon through the art of writing and rewriting.

Turning to a Phenomenon Which Seriously Interests Us and Commits Us to the World

The research question. The phenomenon of interest in this study was a pedagogical moment when the teacher recognizes and responds to students who do not understand something during an instructional activity.

Explicating assumptions and predispositions. I attempted to bridle (Dahlberg & Dahlberg, 2003) my preunderstandings of the phenomenon by writing in a research journal prior to and during data collection and throughout data analysis. Bridling, in short, is more about taking a controlled approach and attitude to the research as opposed to the more "mathematical" finitude of bracketing.

Investigating Experience as We Live It Rather Than as We Conceptualize It

The temporality and spatiality of our experiences and the limitation of our language and our faculties in recalling precisely what we experience always hinders us. In that vein, I acknowledge that, at best, I was able to get transformations of the experience (van Manen, 1990) through people who have experienced the phenomenon of interest.

Finding participants. Eighteen participants were identified through a purposive sampling strategy that drew upon Polkinghorne's (1989) participant selection requirements for phenomenological research. First, the participants had to have *experienced the phenomenon under investigation.* I made sure the teachers teach or have taught in a middle school. For the sake of clarity, I defined a middle school as any school that includes students 10-14 years of age and employs at least two structures in support of the middle school philosophy (e.g., interdisciplinary teaming, advisor-advisee, exploratory curriculum). Based on prior interactions with potential participants, I felt safe in saying that all the practicing teachers I contacted had recognized and responded to a student who did not understand something during an instructional activity. That said, Polkinghorne's second requirement—*that the participant have the capacity to provide full and sensitive descriptions of the experience*—became more challenging. I assumed that teachers who had taught longer had more experience recognizing and responding to students who did not understand something during an instructional activity. Therefore, I focused only on teachers who had taught at least three years in a middle school.

Aiming for contextual variation. I anticipated that the context (e.g., years of middle school experience, the grade level, the content area, the geographic locale) likely influenced the teacher's recognition of and response to the moment when a student did not understand. However, my intent was not aimed at isolating these various contextual components and "testing" them. Rather, it was aimed at investigating the meaning of the phenomenon in light of these contextual components, as a whole, as they are lived. Realizing, however, that context does matter, I attempted to attain some contextual variation (Dahlberg et al., 2001) around the phenomenon.

In sum, 12 participants were women and 6 were men, ranging from 4.5 years to 18 years of middle school teaching experience. The group of participants taught across a number of content areas—science and social studies (N = 1), science and math (N = 1), social studies (N = 5), science (N = 4), literacy (N = 5), alternative education (N = 1), and health (N = 1); worked in different geographic locales—rural (N = 4), suburban (N = 13), and urban (N = 1); and taught across a number of grade levels—Grade 6 through Grade 8 (N = 1), Grade 6 (N = 1), Grade 7 (N = 9), Grade 8 (N = 5), and Grade 9 (N = 2).

Data sources. There were two primary sources of lived experience data in this study: the *conversational (unstructured) interview* and the *lived experience written description*. Participants were given the choice of completing one or the other. Fourteen participants chose to be interviewed and four other teachers chose to craft lived-experience descriptions using van Manen's (1990) protocol. The purpose of *the conversational (unstructured) interview* was to gather experiential material about the phenomenon. My goal was to keep the participant close to the experience. This meant that I asked the participant to be as concrete as possible. Throughout each interview, I asked the participant to think of a specific situation, student, and event. Each interview lasted approximately one and a half hours.

The lived experience description provided good access to the experience and served as a second data source. In order to help participants craft a lived experience description, participants were contacted via email, which included a protocol (adapted from van Manen, 1990) for writing lived experience descriptions and one example of a lived experience description.

Data Analysis: Reflecting on the Essential Themes (Meanings) Which Characterize the Phenomenon

Interview data (14 participants) and written lived experience description data (4 participants) were analyzed for their meanings in relation to the phenomenon of interest. Each transcript (or description) was first read in its entirety to get a feel for and a sense of the whole experience—followed by multiple line-by-line readings. Early line-by-line readings included careful note-taking and marking of excerpts that appeared to contain initial meanings, while exercising openness (Dahlberg et al., 2001) to the phenomenon. Final line-by-line readings involved articulating patterns of meaning, based on the markings and margin notes. In order to attend to the participant's descriptions, the researcher attempted to bridle (Dahlberg & Dahlberg, 2003) the researcher's own preunderstandings of the phenomenon by writing in a reflective journal prior to and during data collection and throughout data analysis. A phenomenological description was written based on an essential meaning structure and the identified patterns of meaning.

REFERENCES

Apple, M., & Beane, J. (Eds.). (1995). *Democratic schools.* Alexandria, VA: Association of Supervision and Curriculum Development.

Arth, A. A., Lounsbury, J. H., McEwin, C. K., & Swaim, J. H. (1995). *Middle level teachers: Portraits of excellence.* Columbus, OH: National Middle School Association and National Association of Secondary School Principals.

Beane, J. A. (1990). *Affect in the curriculum: Toward democracy, dignity, and diversity.* New York: Teachers College Press.

Beane, J. A. (1997). *Curriculum integration: Designing the core of democratic education.* New York: Teachers College Press.

Beane, J. A. (2005). *A reason to teach: Creating classrooms of dignity and hope: The power of the democratic way.* Portsmouth, NH: Heinemann.

Buckner, J., & Bickel, F. (1991). If you want to know about effective teaching, why not ask your middle school kids? *Middle School Journal, 22*(3), 26-29.

Dahlberg, H., & Dahlberg, K. (2003). To not make definite what is indefinite: A phenomenological analysis of perception and its epistemological consequences in human science research. *The Humanistic Psychologist, 31*(4), 35-50.

Dahlberg, K., Drew, N., & Nystrom, M. (2001). *Reflective lifeworld research.* Lund, Sweden: Studentlitteratur.

Davies, M. A. (1995). The ideal middle school teacher. In M. Wavering (Ed.), *Educating young adolescents: Life in the middle* (pp. 149-170). New York: Garland.

Hartoonian, H. M. (2003). A conceptual model for democratic citizenship: Arguments, value tensions, and identity. *Pacific-Asian Education, 15*(2), 27-32.

National Middle School Association. (1981). Preparing teachers for the middle grades. *Middle School Journal, 12*(4), 17-19.

Polkinghorne, D. E. (1989). Phenomenological research methods. In R. S. Valle & S. Halling (Eds.), *Existential-phenomenological perspectives in psychology: Exploring the breadth of human experience* (pp. 41-60). New York: Plenum Press.

Roney, K. (2001). The effective middle school teacher: Inwardly integrated, outwardly connected. In V. A. Anfara, Jr., (Ed.), *The handbook of research in middle level education* (pp. 73-105). Greenwich, CT: Information Age Publishing.

Vagle, M. D. (2006a). When students do not understand: Recognition and response in the action present of teaching. (Doctoral dissertation, University of Minnesota, 2006.) *Dissertation Abstracts International, 67*(06), 2043.

Vagle, M. D. (2006b). Dignity and democracy: An exploration of middle school teacher's pedagogy. *Research in Middle Level Education Online, 29*(8), 1-17.

van Manen, M. (1990). *Researching lived experience: Human science for an action sensitive pedagogy.* London, Ontario, Canada: Althouse Press.

CHAPTER 17

A SCHOOL-WIDE APPROACH TO PROMOTING YOUNG ADOLESCENT SOCIAL AND BEHAVIORAL SUCCESS IN MIDDLE SCHOOL

Chris Borgmeier

ABSTRACT

Young adolescents face numerous challenges to healthy social development during the middle school years. Increasing emphasis is expanding the focus of intervention beyond the at-risk student to the entire school context as a focus for intervention. The broader cultural and developmental context of the school environment is particularly important during young adolescence when students are most susceptible to deviant peer influence (Dodge, Dishion & Lansford, 2006). School-wide Positive Behavior Support (SW-PBS) is a research-based framework that has had positive outcomes in middle schools. This chapter will present relevant research on SW-PBS and provide a description of the program.

The Young Adolescent and the Middle School
pp. 343–365

Though recent media attention has seemed to focus more attention on school violence in high schools, studies reveal that middle school students are actually at the highest risk of experiencing school violence (Juvonen, Kaganoff, Augustine, & Constant, 2004). In a review of the literature on the American middle school, Juvonen et al. stated that "school safety is one of the main challenges for the American middle school" (p. 51). The following statistics highlight the safety challenges facing our American middle school:

- During the 2003-2004 school year, there were 53 violent crimes per 1,000 students in middle schools, compared with only 28 violent crimes per 1,000 students in both elementary schools and high schools (National Center for Education Statistics, NCES, 2006).
- Eight percent of middle school teachers (Grades 5-8) reported they had been physically attacked by a student, compared with 6% of high school teachers (Juvonen et al.), and
- Twenty-three percent of middle school teachers reported that a student had threatened them in their current school (Juvonen et al.).

The middle school years are a crucial time in the social and emotional development of young adolescents. Young adolescence is the stage in development when students are most susceptible to deviant peer influence (Dodge et al., 2006). Kazdin (1993) reported that many mental health problems (e.g., anxiety, conduct disorder, depression) increase during the time that adolescents are in their middle school years.

Young adolescents can experience significant emotional distress from attending schools where they feel unsafe, are bullied, or witness others being bullied. A common response to increasing concerns regarding school violence and school safety has been to "get tough" or implement "zero-tolerance" policies. This reactionary approach usually consists of increased reliance on punishment and disciplinary responses that exclude the student from school and/or instruction, such as expulsion, suspension, being sent to the office or the hallway. Research findings have not offered support for the use of "zero tolerance" strategies for reducing student problem behavior (Lewis & Garrison-Harrell, 1999; Turnbull & Turnbull, 2000). In contrast, there is evidence that harsher discipline policies have a negative effect on school climate by decreasing students' feelings of connectedness to the school (McNeely, Nonnemaker, & Blum, 2002; Skiba & Peterson, 1999). Researchers (Alexander, Entwisle, & Kabanni, 2001; Ekstrom, Goetz, Pollack, & Rock, 1986; Wehlage & Rutter, 1985) have further suggested that patterns of disengagement, negative attitudes toward school, and social alienation leading to high school dropout often begin during the middle school experience.

Dodge et al. (2006) suggested that the pervasiveness of these challenges and concerns requires an approach that extends beyond interventions for at-risk individuals to reexamining the school-wide environment and climate. Brand, Felner, Shim, Seitsinger, and Dumas (2003) found that middle school student perceptions of school safety and school climate accounted for about 30% of the variability between student levels of academic aspirations and student depression. Battistitch, Solomon, Watson, and Schaps (1997) reported that positive student outcomes, including reduced problem behavior and increased motivation, are related to a sense of community and a supportive middle school climate. Further research (Eccles et al., 1993; Roeser, Eccles & Freedman-Doan, 1999; Roeser, Eccles & Sameroff, 1998) indicated that a supportive, positive school climate can act as a safeguard to negative student outcomes associated with the challenges of the middle school years. Researchers noted that this is particularly true for students from disadvantaged families (Lee & Smith, 1999; Lee, Smith, Perry, & Smylie, 1999, Midgley & Edelin, 1998). This chapter will introduce School-wide Positive Behavior Support (SW-PBS) as a middle school intervention that can improve the overall school climate, and support the behavioral needs of students who are at-risk. A review of the research on SW-PBS will be provided, as well as an overview and description of the system-wide intervention.

SCHOOL-WIDE POSITIVE BEHAVIOR SUPPORT

Over the past decade, a significant body of research has provided schools with an evidence-based alternative: School-wide Positive Behavior Support (SW-PBS). Dr. Rob Horner and Dr. George Sugai at the University of Oregon were central in the initial development and dissemination of SW-PBS as a systemic intervention (Sugai et al., 2000). SW-PBS is a multifaceted intervention that merges decades of research on (a) effective instruction, (b) behavior management, and (c) systemic school change. What is unique about SW-PBS is not the development of new ideas and interventions for behavior management, but the focus on the systemic implementation of evidence-based instructional and behavior management practices on a school-wide basis.

Instead of waiting for problem behavior to occur and reacting to it or "getting tough" on discipline, SW-PBS focuses schools on taking a proactive approach aimed at promoting socially appropriate behavior and preventing problem behavior. The goal is to create systems in schools that infuse "best practices" in behavior management throughout the school. Instead of stumbling into an occasional classroom in which the teacher is using best practices, schools implement systems to promote strategically the use of proven behavior management practices to all staff, throughout the school day, across all school settings. Some of the best practices that are being promoted in schools through SW-PBS are fairly simple ideas that are best accomplished through a school-wide initiative, which include (a) identifying clear behavioral expectations and school/classroom routines; (b) explicitly teaching expectations and routines; (c) establishing consistent systems for recognizing students for good behavior and academic achievement; and (d) applying consistent, equitable disciplinary responses that are consistent with the behavioral infraction (Cotton, 1995).

SW-PBS has been effectively implemented in schools of all grade levels (from pre-school through high school), but in order to meet the differing developmental needs of students at varying levels of schooling, implementation across schools of the different grade levels can often look dramatically different. Many studies (Kartub, Taylor-Greene, March, & Horner, 2000; Lassen, Steele, & Sailor, 2006; Liuselli, Putnam, & Sunderland, 2002; Metzler, Biglan, Rusby & Sprague, 2001; Oswald, Safran, & Johanson, 2005; Taylor-Greene et al., 1997; Taylor-Greene & Kartub, 2000; Turnbull & Turnbull, 2002; Warren et al., 2003) have documented positive results following SW-PBS implementation in middle school settings including: reduced student discipline referrals, increased attendance, improved perceptions of school climate, and improved academic performance.

In addressing the complex challenges posed by the social development of young adolescents, middle schools must take a sophisticated approach to addressing these challenges. SW-PBS provides a multifaceted approach that starts with a universal intervention designed to improve the overall school climate, then continues to develop increasingly intensive systems of support for serving those students with more persistent behavioral challenges. This approach to school-wide behavior support is most often explained as a three-tiered approach to supporting student behavior. Before beginning to explain specific component interventions of the SW-PBS system, it is important to understand the three-tiered prevention context in which SW-PBS operates.

Three-Tiered Prevention Model

When applying SW-PBS it is understood that different students require different levels of behavioral support. Some students come to school with more challenging problem behaviors that require more sophisticated responses. To effectively serve the needs of all the students, schools must have varying levels of responses for students who present problem behav-

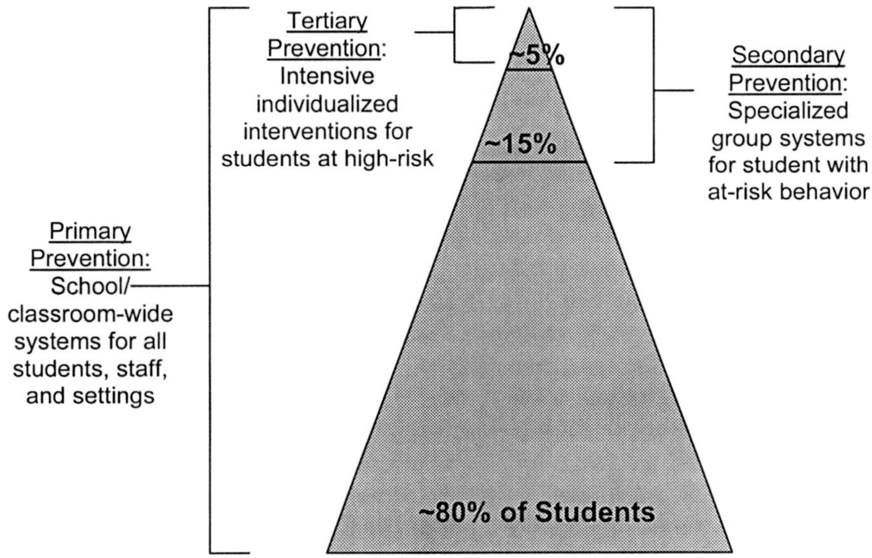

Figure 17.1. Continuum of School-wide Positive Behavior Support.

iors with varying levels of complexity or resistance to common interventions. A visual representation of this is the SW-PBS "triangle" (see Figure 17.1; Walker et al., 1996). This triangle is made up of three levels of support: (1) primary prevention, (2) secondary prevention, and (3) tertiary prevention.

At the level of primary prevention within a SW-PBS model, schools implement a universal or primary intervention. The universal intervention is available to 100% of the students in a school. Though universal system is effective for a majority of students, the system is not expected to be sufficient for the success of every student. Given an effectively implemented primary system of support, it is expected that 80% of the students (represented by the base of the triangle in Figure 17.1) will be successful behaviorally. This is often measured by the percentage of students in a school with zero to one discipline referrals for the year. If fewer than 80% of the students in the school are meeting this criterion, this could be an indication that the focus of intervention should be the improvement of the primary system of support.

As we progress up the triangle, the top two tiers are those students in the school who do not successfully respond to the primary system and require additional interventions and supports to be successful. The goal with students in the top tiers of the triangle is to match them with interventions that will effectively meet their behavioral support needs with the smallest allocation of school time and resources. Maximizing school resources requires that reliance on research-based practices, which is necessary given the challenge of limited resources facing many schools.

The middle tier (represented in Figure 17.1 by 15%) consists of students with at-risk behavior who consistently engage in minor problem behavior. Often times, students in the middle tier have needs or deficits that are common to other students within the tier. This provides the opportunity to implement "group" interventions that can be offered to more than one student at a time, thereby increasing the efficiency of utilizing school resources. To address common needs or deficits of students with at-risk behavior, secondary prevention systems often include interventions that (a) increase student motivation, (b) provide increased monitoring and supervision, (c) teach organizational skills and study skills, and (d) provide academic support. In developing secondary prevention systems, schools are encouraged to develop interventions that address each of these four areas. By identifying students early and providing quick access to such targeted interventions that match the student's needs or deficits, many students will respond successfully.

Finally, there are those students (represented in Figure 17.1 by 5%) at the top of the triangle. These are the students who chronically engage in severe problem behavior and pose the most complex behavioral challenges. Unfortunately, there are few shortcuts with this group of students. Students posing more complex behavioral challenges require increased assessment and more sophisticated solutions. This group of students will require interventions (tertiary prevention) that address their unique individualized needs.

Decades of research have helped to identify a number of specific strategies that have become synonymous with SW-PBS implementation across each of the three tiers. More information about specific interventions within each tier will be provided in the following paragraphs.

Universal Systems: Primary Prevention

An effective school-wide foundation for behavior support is important for a number of reasons. A primary reason is to build a more positive school climate in which students feel safe, supported, and connected. A second reason is to increase behavioral success for the majority of students. If an effective universal system is not in place, the number of students requiring more intensive individual supports can quickly overwhelm a school. Another important result of an effective universal intervention is in removing some of the distractions and "behavioral noise" that can increase the challenging behavior of those students who are at-risk.

Within a middle school, SW-PBS is developed and implemented under the leadership of a school team that is representative of the school staff. The team must include the building administrator, but will include representation of staff across grade levels, subject areas, general education, special education and classified staff. A middle school team will usually consist of six to eight staff members. The team will often attend a series of trainings focused on providing an understanding of SW-PBS and guiding the team through the development of the component parts of the SW-PBS system. The team takes the initiative to develop those components in a way that will best fit the needs of their own school site. Due to the complexities of systemic change, schools will often take the first year to focus on developing the SW-PBS system prior to implementation.

In progressing through training and development, below are the principal components of the universal system of SW-PBS:

creating a common language (three to five positively stated school rules) across staff and students related to student behavioral expectations;

1. creating a common set of behavioral expectations across all school settings for staff and administration;
2. explicitly teaching those behavioral expectations to students on an ongoing basis;
3. creating a system to promote the regular acknowledgment and recognition of students for engaging in positive behavior;
4. implementing a system for tracking student behavioral referrals and using the data to inform decisions related to responses to problem behavior in the school; and
5. creating consistent, fair responses to problem behavior that reduce lost instructional time and focus on the instruction of expected behavior.

While the components listed above are core features of SW-PBS, this is by no means an exhaustive list of universal system interventions that schools have implemented.

It is also important to note that though there are a set of core features that are central to the implementation of SW-PBS; it is not a "canned" program. Since each middle school has different resources, political climates, personalities, and demographics, it is crucial that the school team tailor the development and implementation of SW-PBS to fit the specific needs and character of their school. Throughout the development process, it is important that the team has ongoing dialogue and seeks feedback from the school staff members regarding development of the SW-PBS systems. The nature of a school-wide intervention requires participation and buy-in from 80% of the staff or more, so taking strategic steps to foster buy-in and support is critical. Keeping staff regularly updated through presentations at staff meetings and giving staff members the opportunity to provide feedback (e.g., suggestion boxes or bulletin boards) is important when striving to secure buy-in from staff.

One of the first components of SW-PBS that teams commonly work to develop involves the establishment of school-wide rules. Schools develop a set of three to five "school rules" to guide school expectations and begin to create a common language in the school. Examples are often linked with a school mascot or acronym in an effort to make it more catchy and meaningful to the school. For example, Reynolds Middle School (RMS) adopted rules to match the acronym RMS: *R*espect Others, *M*anage Self, *S*tay Safe. When students, teachers, and others walk down the halls of Reynolds Middle School, they see signs prominently displaying those school-wide rules. The rules are broad enough that any specific behavioral expectations will fall under one of the three broader rules, but by having only three rules, it is easy for students and staff to remember the rules and integrate them into a consistent everyday language in the school. Examples of rules from other middle schools have included (1) respect, relationships, responsibility, results, and (2) be safe, be responsible, be respectful.

After deciding on the school-wide rules, the team, with input from the school staff, identify specific behavioral expectations for each school setting (e.g., hallway, cafeteria, bathroom) that correspond with the three school rules. For example, at Reynolds Middle School, one behavioral expectation for respecting others in the hallway is to move quietly when classes are in session so as not to disrupt others. Managing self in the hallway means to walk directly to your class or destination when you have a hallway pass.

After developing behavioral expectations across all settings, the SW-PBS team begins the task of creating lesson plans for explicitly teaching the rules and behavioral expectations to students for each of the settings. Many middle schools will seek participation from all staff members and even students in developing lesson plans. A variety of formats (e.g., skits, videos) for presenting lessons across school settings can be important for keeping the attention of middle school students. Examples have included skits that staff members perform for students about appropriate behavior in the cafeteria, or videos developed by a group of eighth grade students to teach behavioral expectations in the hallway. It is important that the lessons are entertaining, but also that the behavioral expectations are made clear and linked with the school-wide rules. Schools will usually present the lessons during the first two weeks of school and may revisit lesson periodically throughout the year as needed.

Another primary goal of SW-PBS is to achieve an environment where there are more positive interactions than negative interactions between staff and students. In fact, the goal is to provide attention to positive student behavior five times for every time we respond to student negative behavior. Through implementation of SW-PBS, schools implement an acknowledgement system to encourage staff to increase the frequency of recognizing students doing the right thing.

The positive to negative ratio is getting significant attention not only in schools, but also in the business literature and marital counseling literature. Losada and Heaphy (2004) found that high performance business teams maintained a mean positive to negative ratio of 5.6 to 1, compared with 1.9 to 1 for medium performance and 1 to 3 for low performance teams. In a study of 700 couples, Gottman (1994) was able to predict divorce with 94% accuracy by monitoring the couple's positive to negative ratio. Successful marriages maintained a ratio of about 5 to 1, while marriages ending in divorce had a ratio nearer to 1 to 1. In the busy day of a teacher, one of the first things forgotten is the acknowledgement of those students who are doing the right thing. Some teachers are very proficient in maintaining a 5 to 1 ratio throughout the day, but in most classrooms and schools, teachers fall short (Beaman & Wheldall, 2000).

Implementing a school-wide system that provides a consistent prompt reminding staff to regularly recognize student positive behavior can do a lot to improve the school-wide positive to negative ratio and school climate. Schools are encouraged to develop a token, usually a positive referral form, to hand out to students (and even to other staff) in recognition of positive behavior. The tickets, or positive referral forms, should be very easy for staff to use and hand out—remember the goal is to increase recognition of positive behavior. It is important the positive referrals are easily and frequently accessible to staff and that they are small and easy to carry around. Schools will often link the tickets to a school mascot or theme, such as "Cougar Paws" or "Bravo tickets." The tickets should include the school rules and be easy to fill out, requiring limited writing and information from staff. Remember the goal is to increase recognition of positive behavior, which requires making the tickets very convenient for staff to use.

Schools are further encouraged to hold a regular school-wide event recognizing positive behavior. This event often includes a drawing of a small number of students who received a positive referral. Some schools have awarded students who have their name drawn with movie tickets, tickets to school events, school t-shirts, or a free homework pass. Other schools have invited students who have earned tickets to group social events, such as a special pizza lunch or an ice cream social. Other schools let students redeem positive referrals for items at the school store. An important consideration is developing a system that is financially sustainable for the school. Many schools will seek donations from local businesses in the community to defer costs and other schools creatively use many incentives that do not cost the school money, such as free homework passes. At the middle school level, it is important to change periodically the routine to keep staff and students interested in the acknowledgment system.

The next components of SW-PBS focus on maximizing our responses to student problem behavior. First, it is important that staff and administration are consistent in their understanding of how to respond to student problem behavior. For example, school personnel need to agree upon which behaviors should be sent to the office as a discipline referral and which behaviors the teacher or staff should handle in the setting. This is an important conversation for the staff and administration. Second, the team and administration should evaluate the use of exclusionary or punitive discipline (e.g., detention, suspension) and consider developing a range of alternative responses to problem behavior, which have an instructional or remedial focus and attempt to minimize lost instructional time. Examples include having the student complete a problem solving worksheet, to practice or role-play a more appropriate response to the situation, or to attend a social skills group or "Rule School."

A third focus in responding to problem behavior centers on discipline referral data. Teams implementing SW-PBS need to have a data system for tracking and monitoring discipline referrals. The discipline referral form and data system should collect information about each discipline referral that may be important in guiding decision making. School personnel should develop a process to ensure timely entry of data in to a system that allows for easy examination of the data for team decision-making. In order to provide maximum benefit for decision making, a data system should allow for examining data not only at the level of the individual student, but also at the school level.

An example of one data system that offers that capability is the School-wide Information System (www.swis.org). The School-Wide Information System allows teams quick and easy access to five graphs that can provide a snapshot to guide school-wide decision making related to student behavior in the school. The graphs present the (a) average number of discipline referrals per day for each month, (b) number of referrals by type of problem behavior, (c) number of referrals by school location, (d) number of referrals by time of day, and (e) number of referrals per student. During monthly meetings, the SW-PBS team should review these five graphs for spikes or trends and use the data to guide team decision making. A nice feature of the School-wide Information System is the ability to mine the data if questions come up from the five initial graphs. For example, if there is a spike in the data from 10:15 to 10:30, instead of guessing what might be happening, the team can use the data system to provide data regarding where (e.g., location) or with whom (e.g., grade level, students, staff) the referrals are occurring to pinpoint the source of the problem. The team should then directly use that data to inform intervention planning. Teams are also encouraged to review periodically other forms of data that can be indicators of school behavioral concerns—attendance data, detention, suspension, or expulsion data, school climate data, and academic or achievement data.

Initially, the role of the SW-PBS team is to lead the development and implementation of SW-PBS. Once a school has implemented SW-PBS, the team continues to meet to (a) review school data and make intervention decisions based on the data, (b) sustain the universal system of SW-PBS, and (c) develop additional systems to expand universal systems support. Beyond the previously described core features of SW-PBS, a variety of programs and initiatives can further supplement the SW-PBS foundation. Supplements to SW-PBS foundation have included the implementation of a research-based character education or anti-bullying program, classroom management support, increased parental participation, collaboration with transportation, or supports for substitute teachers. The team will continually have responsibility for maintaining SW-PBS, responding to the data, and striving to create a more positive school climate.

In transitioning to the secondary prevention efforts (see Figure 17.1), it is vital to restate the important role that the universal system (primary prevention) plays in creating an effective "host environment" for intervening with students who are at-risk. It is significantly easier to implement behavioral interventions for students with more challenging behavior in an orderly, academic-focused classroom or school than in a more chaotic setting (Zins & Ponti, 1990). An effective universal system is a key component to maximizing the impact of targeted and individual interventions for students (Sugai et al., 2000; Walker et al., 1996).

To illustrate this point, consider the net impact of a school intervention (such as attending a social skills group or seeing the school counselor every Wednesday for 45 minutes), if the young adolescent spends the remaining 95% of his or her week being regularly disrespected by peers, corrected by staff, and experiencing failure in a negative school environment. Addressing concerns related to young adolescent social and emotional development will require (in some cases) such individual interventions, but of equal, and possibly greater importance, is the accumulation of individual interactions a student has throughout the remainder of his or her days. Establishing explicit consistencies between the targeted interventions and the broader school context should serve to increase the benefit of targeted, time-limited interventions, such as social skills instruction or counseling.

Secondary Prevention: Targeted Interventions

Secondary level prevention provides interventions for students who do not respond successfully to the universal systems. The majority of students who do not respond to an effective universal system (primary prevention) fall within the middle tier of the triangle (see Figure 17.1). These students will frequently respond to minor interventions and supports and will not require intensive individualized supports. The goal of secondary level prevention is to provide support efficiently and effectively to those students who will respond to targeted or group interventions and to refer those students who fail to respond to support that is more intensive. Once again, data is central to this decision making process. Targeted or group interventions are designed with the intention of being quickly accessible, low cost interventions that can be used to support multiple students at one time.

The focus of secondary prevention systems is on the early identification of students with at-risk behavior and a quick turnaround in providing appropriate supports and interventions. Since challenging behavior in schools is so often paired with other school concerns (e.g., academic, attendance) it is important that secondary prevention efforts for behavior are aligned with all intervention and support initiatives in the school including academic and attendance support. Schools often have a team process for identifying students and providing interventions at the prereferral level (e.g., interventions attempted before a referral for special education services). Integrating secondary prevention efforts for behavior into an existing prereferral team process is often a good option. If a prereferral team process is already in place, it may be a matter of reexamining the behavioral assessment and intervention practices of the team to see if there are ways to increase the efficiency and/or efficacy of the team process for providing behavior support.

A goal of the secondary prevention system is to (a) identify students who are at-risk early, (b) conduct a brief assessment to identify factors contributing to or motivating the problem behavior, and (c) match the student with group interventions that address factors directly contributing to the student's problem behavior.

Support for a student referred for targeted interventions should start with a brief functional behavioral assessment (see Crone & Horner, 2003) to determine variables contributing to student problem behavior. This brief assessment might consist of quickly interviewing the staff members at the meeting who have worked with the identified student. The functional behavioral assessment should result in a summary statement identifying (a) the time(s) of day and/or routine(s) during which the behavior occurs, (b) the variables that predictably trigger student problem behavior (antecedents), (c) a description of the problem behavior, and (d) the responses or outcomes of the problem behavior that are benefiting the student (consequences). Once assessment is completed, the student should be matched with the group intervention that is most appropriate for addressing the variables directly contributing to and motivating student problem behavior (an example of matching interventions to the function of student behavior is provided later in this section).

Since students in the middle tier often have needs or deficits that are common to other students, there is an opportunity to offer interventions that are likely to be beneficial for multiple students. To address common needs or deficits of at-risk students, secondary prevention systems often include group interventions that (a) increase student motivation, (b) provide increased monitoring and supervision, (c) teach organizational skills and study skills, and (d) provide academic support. Schools are encouraged to develop a range of interventions that address each of these four areas. The following are examples of some commonly used research-supported, targeted interventions: the Behavior Education Program (Crone, Horner & Hawken, 2004), also referred to as the a Daily Point Card system (Fairchild, 1983; Schumaker, Hovell, & Sherman, 1977); social skills instruction (Brant & Christensen, 2002; Lane, Wehby, Menzies, Doukas, Munton, & Gregg, 2003); mentoring programs (Sinclair, Christenson, Evelo, & Hurley, 1998); and academic support.

Interventions frequently involve incentive programs to increase motivation for students with at-risk behavior. When linked with a point card system an incentive system can provide increased monitoring and supervision. The Behavior Education Program (also known as the Daily Point Card or the Check-In Check-Out program) is an example of a program that combines the use of incentives with a point card that has been implemented successfully in middle school settings (Fairchild, 1983; Hawken & Horner, 2003; Schumaker et al., 1977). Crone et al. (2004) reported that the Behavior Education Program was effective with 60-75% of students who did not respond to universal (primary prevention) systems.

Important components of the Behavior Education Program include:

1. increasing positive attention from an adult in the school through at least two daily contacts, check-in at the beginning of the day and check-out at the end of the school day;

2. increasing frequency of behavioral feedback throughout the day via teacher ratings on the point card at the end of each period;
3. increasing motivation through incentives linked with student behavioral goals; and
4. using a data system featuring a point card for tracking student progress and informing intervention decisions (Crone et al., 2004)

It is important to recognize what distinguishes the Behavior Education Program as a secondary prevention system, rather than simply a point card that any teacher can implement with a student. As a system of prevention, the Behavior Education Program requires systemic level organization and a staff appointed with the responsibility of maintaining the system. As a secondary prevention system, the Behavior Education Program must (a) be readily accessible to any student referred to the program throughout the year; (b) be accessible to multiple students simultaneously; (c) have a pre-established process for referral, introduction of the program, implementation of the program, and data collection; and (d) be understood by all staff members in the event that a student they have contact with is participating in the program (Crone et al., 2004). The team leading implementation of the Behavior Education Program should meet every 2 weeks in order to quickly respond to any new referrals and to review data of those students in the program to inform decision making regarding student interventions.

Other interventions should also be used at schools to provide options for students with varying deficits. In addition to a daily point card system, Sprague, Nishioka, and Stieber (2004) integrate a social skills instructional group, academic instructional group, and mentoring program into the Skills for Success program (a secondary prevention program developed for at-risk middle school students). The following examples are studies illustrating the effectiveness of social skills instruction for at-risk youth as a secondary prevention strategy.

Farrell, Meyer, Sullivan, and Kung (2003) reported that 12 weekly sessions using the Responding in Peaceful and Positive Ways social skills curriculum was effective in reducing discipline referrals for violent behavior in students at risk for problem behavior. The study utilized the curriculum with groups of students consisting of a majority of non-deviant peers. Based on a meta-analysis of the research on social skills instruction, Gresham (1998) provided the following recommendations when providing social skills instruction in schools (1) align social skills instructional content to the targeted skill deficits of the student(s), and (2) train for generalization by linking instruction with naturally occurring behavioral incidents or events. Brant and Christenson (2002) noted improvements in student behavior and reduced off-task behavior following implementation of a social skills group. Consistent with the recommendation to align social skills instructional content with targeted social skill deficits, Brant and Christenson collected assessment data on skill deficits of the targeted students and tailored the social skills curriculum to address those specific deficits.

Another secondary prevention program is mentoring. Sinclair et al. (1998) implemented a dropout prevention program that targeted middle school students at-risk of later high school dropout. Students were selected based on a variety of behavioral and academic indicators, including discipline referrals, attendance, and grades. The authors stated that a primary feature of the program is a mentor who the student and their family knows and trusts, and who demonstrates a persistent concern for the well-being of the student over time. Sinclair et al. reported that students in the mentoring program were significantly more engaged in school, completed more credits, and demonstrated fewer problem behaviors in mainstream settings than students in the comparison group.

Here is an example of a student referral progressing through the second-tier intervention process. Mario, a seventh grade student, was referred to the Student Support Team at the school. The team held a meeting with several of Mario's teachers. After a brief assessment, the team determines that Mario's problems occurred most frequently in classes requiring a lot of reading from textbooks. The team came to the following understanding of the student problem behavior: When asked to respond to questions or complete worksheets based on assigned readings from a text, or if asked to read aloud in class (antecedent), Mario is likely to put his head down and refuse to participate or will talk back to the teacher (behavior) so the teacher calls on someone else (consequence). The team determined that the motivation behind the student's behavior (or function) was to avoid the questions he cannot answer because of his reading difficulties and to avoid the embarrassment of failing in front of his peers. After the initial assessment, the team decided that based on the function of behavior, an intervention needed to include academic supports that addressed his reading failure and his need to avoid the embarrassment of failing in front of his peers. The team looked at the available intervention options for supporting Mario. The school already has some group academic support options in place that the team felt were good options for this student, including (1) a peer tutoring program that could support Mario with reading chapters assigned in class, and (2) a remedial reading program which matches students to one of three leveled reading classes depending on student scores on an initial reading assessment. In addition to the suggested interventions, Mario will be provided with a point card for data collection. The team scheduled to reconvene in two weeks to review Mario's progress.

While targeted interventions will be successful for a large number of those students who do not respond to universal (primary prevention) systems, there will be still be a percentage of students requiring support that is even more intensive. In an effort to maximize school resources, the intention is for the more cost-effective and time-efficient targeted intervention to support effectively as many students as possible. For students requiring supports at the tertiary level, schools are now looking at an increase in the extent of assessment and individualization of intervention plans required to support the more complex concerns presented by these students.

Tertiary Prevention: Individual Student Systems

In any school, there will be students who will require more intensive, individualized supports. The "short-cuts" and "one-size fits all" approach have not been successful for these students. School personnel expend significant time and resources on this group of students. Too commonly, time is spent in frustration by repeatedly using the same punitive disciplinary responses (e.g., suspension, detention, sending to office) with little evidence of student behavioral change. Worse yet, in many cases these punitive responses may contribute to the reoccurrence of the student's problem behavior (e.g., when a student repeatedly engages in problem behavior because he has learned that problem behavior reliably results in being sent to the office—allowing the student to avoid an aversive activity). This is a prime example of using a "one-size fits all" response that is not sophisticated enough to address the complexity of the behavioral challenges posed by the student.

Another common response by schools has been to remove students with significant behavioral challenges from public school settings to alternative settings. In a recent Social Policy Report by the Society for Research in Child Development, Dodge, Dishion, and Lansford (2006) reported strong concerns against placements and treatments that aggregate deviant youth. Dodge et al. stated that placing students in alternate settings or interventions where antisocial peers surround them often exacerbates student problem behavior rather than remediate it. This is especially true in middle school because young adolescents are particularly susceptible to the negative influence of deviant peers. Due to the critical role of positive peer role models, Dodge et al. suggested supporting students with challenging behavior in mainstream school settings within nondeviant peer groups. These suggestions by Dodge et al. occur at a time when many school districts are reevaluating services for students with significant problem behavior due to the high financial cost of removing these students to out-of-district alternative placements (Putnam, Liuselli, Sennett, & Malonson, 2002). The combination of these factors suggests an increasing need to develop effective tertiary systems of behavior support.

A challenge in working with students with significant behavioral concerns is that the treatment manual approach to responding to problem behavior based on the topography of the behavior (e.g., hitting, swearing, defiance) or the student's diagnostic label (e.g., conduct disorder, attention deficit, hyperactivity, emotional disturbance) has been ineffective (Newcomer & Lewis, 2004). Decades of behavioral intervention research have come to the clear conclusion that no single intervention works for all students (Bijou, Peterson, & Ault, 1968). The more important factor in identifying effective behavioral interventions for a student's recurring problem behavior is to clearly understand the context in which the problem behavior occurs and the function served by the student's problem behavior. Functional behavioral assessment (FBA) is the process used to obtain this information (Crone & Horner, 2003; Sugai et al., 2000; Sugai, Lewis-Palmer & Hagan, 1998).

During secondary prevention systems, a brief FBA can be useful. Similar information will be sought at the tertiary level, but the assessment process will become much more comprehensive and formalized. A comprehensive FBA will often consist of many of the following types of data collection (Crone & Horner, 2003; Sugai et al., 1998):

- routines assessment to determine time of day and routines during which student problem behavior regularly occurs,
- staff interviews,
- direct observations of the student,
- student interview,
- review of student records,
- parent interview, and
- academic assessment.

A FBA should result in a summary statement identifying (a) the time(s) of day and/or routine(s) during which the behavior occurs, (b) the variables that predictably trigger student problem behavior (antecedents), (c) a description of the problem behavior, (d) the responses or outcomes of the problem behavior that are benefiting the student (consequences), and (e) any events outside of the student's immediate environment that may be impacting his or her problem behavior (setting events).

Team process and participation is a crucial element of developing a behavior intervention plan based on the FBA information. Team members should include a person with behavioral expertise (referred to hereafter as the behavior specialist), a building administrator, the student's parent or guardian, and the teachers and staff that work with the student on a regular basis. To successfully guide a school-based team through the process of conducting a FBA and implementing a behavior intervention plan, it is essential that the team member serving in the role of behavior specialist have extensive training and experience in behavioral theory, FBA, and behavioral intervention. The teachers, parent, and student play critical role in providing knowledge of the student and because they will also be the persons who will likely be implementing the greatest portion of the intervention plan. The administrator is essential for organizing and confirming the logistical changes (e.g., schedule changes, allocation of resources) that are often required when individualizing student interventions in school systems.

In developing a tertiary system of support, the goal is to use school time and resources most productively to implement a behavioral intervention plan that addresses the unique, individualized needs of the student. Even when supporting students requiring tertiary level support, there will be students of greater and lesser complexity. In progressing through the FBA process, the behavior specialist will make decisions regarding the extent of the assessment information required before progressing to intervention. In some cases, an initial teacher interview and student observation may provide sufficient information to move forward with intervention development. More complex cases may require interviews with multiple people (e.g., teachers, staff, parent, student), multiple student observations, additional records review (e.g., medical history) or assessment data (e.g., student reading level) before moving on to intervention development.

The same is true of the extent of intervention required across students. The resulting behavior intervention plan will be the working document the team constructs that clearly outlines the tasks and responsibilities required for implementation of the plan. The majority of interventions selected for the behavioral plan should occur within the school. Parental/guardian involvement and participation in the behavioral intervention plan is strongly suggested (Dishion & Andrews, 1995; Dishion, Kavanagh, Schnieger, Nelson & Kaufman, 2002), however levels of participation can vary considerably across parents/guardians. Parental participation is particularly important when the student is at-risk of substance use (Dishion & Andrews; Dishion et al.). Outside agencies, including community social services or mental health services, can also be beneficial—especially when there are concerns for the student and the student's family outside of the school context. In such cases, it is important to invite outside participants to collaborate on student behavior intervention planning. Having more members on the team requires a strong leader to keep the team focused and working together effectively.

As in each level of SW-PBS support, decisions must ultimately be driven by data. For each student, the team devises a method of data collection to evaluate student progress. The data collected must be consistent with the goals of the intervention plan. Data collection should target specific behaviors related to reductions in the identified problem behavior(s) and increases in the desired behavior(s). Also, consistent with other levels of SW-PBS support, tertiary support must be a system of support ingrained within the school. The challenges posed by students requiring tertiary system interventions will not allow us devise the plan and walk away. The FBA team must continue to meet regularly to evaluate student progress and modify or revise the plan. When working with students with such intensive needs, changes and improvement to the plan are typical. With young adolescents requiring this level of support, it is important that interventions not be looked at as a way of "curing" a student. These students are often going to require some level of ongoing support to sustain consistent levels of success. It is recommended that at least the core members of the FBA team (i.e., the team member(s) with behavioral expertise and the administrator) meet every two weeks to review referrals and monitor progress on active student behavior plans. If changes to a student behavior plan are required, it is advisable for the entire action team (i.e., participating staff, parent/guardian, students) reconvene to look at the data and make necessary revisions to the plan.

CONCLUSION

Given the many challenges to navigate during young adolescence, it is critical that middle schools provide research-based interventions and supports to guide the way. SW-SW-PBS offers cost-effective, research-based answers at a time when many schools are facing greater demands with more limited resources. SW-PBS is currently being implemented in over 4500 schools across the United States. Many states offer training and technical assistance to school districts through active statewide initiatives supporting the implementation of SW-PBS (Horner & Sugai, 2006). There is no excuse for providing our young adolescents with anything less than a safe and positive trip through the critical crossroads of the middle school years.

AUTHOR'S NOTE

For more information about SW-PBS, or to seek support with SW-PBS implementation within your own state, visit the National Technical Assistance Center on Positive Behavioral Interventions and Supports (PBIS) Web site at www.pbis.org

REFERENCES

Alexander, K. L., Entwisle, D. R., & Kabbani, N. (2001). The dropout process in life course perspective: Early risk factors at home and school. *Teachers College Record, 103*, 760-822.

Battistich, V., Solomon, D., Watson, M., & Schaps, E. (1997). Caring school communities. *Educational Psychologist, 32*, 137-151.

Beaman, R., & Wheldall, K. (2000). Teachers' use of approval and disapproval in the classroom. *Educational Psychology, 20*, 431-446.

Bijou, S. W., Peterson, R. F., & Ault, M. H. (1968). A method to integrate descriptive and experimental field studies at the level of data and empirical concepts. *Journal of Applied Behavior Analysis, 1*, 175-191.

Brand, S., Felner, R., Shim, M., Seitsinger, A., & Dumas, T. (2003). Middle school improvement and reform: Development and validation of a school-level assessment of climate, cultural pluralism, and school safety. *Journal of Educational Psychology, 95*, 570-588.

Brant, M., & Christensen, R. (2002). *Improving student social skills through the use of cooperative learning, problem solving & direct instruction*. Unpublished master's thesis, School of Education, Saint Xavier University, Chicago, IL.

Cotton, K. (1995). *Effective schooling practices: A research synthesis 1995 update*. Portland, OR: Northwest Regional Educational Laboratory.

Crone, D. A., & Horner, R. H. (2003). *Building positive behavior support systems in schools: Functional behavioral assessment*. New York: Guilford Press.

Crone, D. A., Horner, R. H., & Hawken, L. S. (2004). *Responding to misbehavior in schools: The Behavior Education Program*. New York: Guilford Press.

Dishion, T. J., & Andrews, D. W. (1995). Preventing escalation in problem behaviors with high-risk young adolescents: Immediate and 1-year outcomes. *Journal of Consulting and Clinical Psychology, 63*, 538-548.

Dishion, T. J., Kavanagh, K., Schnieger, A., Nelson, S. & Kaufman, N. K. (2002). Preventing early adolescent substance use: A family-centered strategy for the public middle school. *Prevention Science, 3*, 191-201.

Dodge, K. A., Dishion, T. J., & Lansford, J. E. (2006). Deviant peer influences in intervention and public policy for youth. *Social Policy Report, XX* (1), 1-19. Retrieved November 30, 2006, from http://www.srcd.org/spr.html

Eccles, J. S., Midgley, C., Wigfield, A., Buchanan, C. M., Reuman, D., Flanagan, C., et al. (1993). Development during adolescence: The impact of stage-environment fit on adolescents' experiences in schools and families. *American Psychologist, 48*, 90-101.

Ekstrom, R. B., Goertz, M. E., Pollack, J. M., & Rock, D. A. (1986). Who drops out of high school and why? Findings from a national study. *Educational Testing Service, 87*, 356-373.

Fairchild, T. N. (1983). Effects of a daily report card system on an eighth grader exhibiting behavioral and motivational problems. *School Counselor, 31*, 83-86.

Farrell, A. D., Meyer, A. L., Sullivan, T. N., & Kung, E. M. (2003). Evaluation of the Responding in Peaceful and Positive Ways (RIPP) seventh grade violence prevention curriculum. *Journal of Child and Family Studies, 12*, 101-120.

Gresham, F. M. (1998). Social skills training: Should we raze, remodel, or rebuild? *Behavioral Disorders, 24*, 19-25.

Gottman, J. M. (1994). *What predicts divorce: The relationship between marital processes and marital outcomes*. Hillsdale, NJ: Erlbaum.

Hawken, L. S., & Horner, R. H. (2003). Evaluation of a targeted intervention within a schoolwide system of behavior support. *Journal of Behavioral Education, 12*, 225-240.

Horner, R. H., & Sugai, G. (2006, March). *Taking School-wide PBS to scale: District and state level implementation*. Symposium conducted at the 3rd Annual International Association for Positive Behavior Support Conference, Reno, NV.

Juvonen, J., Le, V., Kaganoff, T., Augustine, C., & Constant, L. (2004). *Focus on the wonder years: Challenges facing the American middle school*. Santa Monica, CA: Rand.

Kartub, D., Taylor-Greene, S., Horner, R. H., & March, R. (2000). Reducing hallway noise: A systems approach. *Journal of Positive Behavior Interventions, 2*, 179-182.

Kazdin, A. E. (1993). Adolescent mental health: Prevention and treatment programs. *American Psychologist, 48*(2), 127-141.

Lane, K. L., Wehby, J., Menzies, H. M., Doukas, G. L., Munton, S. M., & Gregg, R. M. (2003). Social skills instruction for students at risk for antisocial behavior: The effect of small group instruction. *Behavioral Disorders, 28*, 229-248.

Lassen, S. R., Steele, M. M., & Sailor, W. (2006). The relationship of school-wide positive behavior support to academic achievement in an urban middle school. *Psychology in the Schools, 43*, 701-712.

Lee, V. E., & Smith, J. B. (1999). Social support and achievement for young adolescents in Chicago: The role of school and academic press. *American Educational Research Journal, 36*, 907-945.

Lee, V. E., Smith, J. B., Perry, T. E., & Smylie, M. A. (1999). *Social support, academic press, and student achievement: A view from the middle grades in Chicago*. Chicago: Consortium on Chicago School Research.

Lewis, T. J., & Garrison-Harrell, L. (1999). Designing setting-specific interventions within school systems of effective behavioral support. *Effective School Practices, 17*, 38-46.

Losada, M., & Heaphy, E. (2004). The role of positivity and connectivity in the performance of business teams: A nonlinear dynamics model. *American Behavioral Scientist, 47*, 740-765.

Luiselli, J. K., Putnam, R. F., & Sunderland, M. (2002). Longitudinal evaluation of behavior support intervention in a public middle school. *Journal of Positive Behavioral Interventions, 4*, 182-188.

McNeely, C. A., Nonnemaker, J. M., & Blum, R. (2002). Promoting school connectedness: Evidence from the national longitudinal study of adolescent health. *Journal of School Health, 72*, 138-146.

Metzler, C. W., Biglan, A., Rusby, J. C., & Sprague, J. R. (2001). Evaluation of a comprehensive behavior management program to improve school-wide positive behavior support. *Education & Treatment of Children, 24*, 448-479.

Midgley, C., & Edelin, K. (1998). Middle school reform and early adolescent well-being: The good news and the bad. *Educational Psychologist, 33*, 195-206.

National Center for Education Statistics. (2006). *Crime, violence, discipline and safety in U.S. Public Schools: Findings from the School Survey on Crime and Safety: 2003-04*. (Publication No. NCES 2007302). Retrieved December 19, 2006, from, http://nces.ed.gov/pubsearch/pubsinfo.asp?pubid=2007302

Newcomer, L. L., & Lewis, T. J. (2004). Functional behavioral assessment: An investigation of assessment reliability and effectiveness of function-based interventions. *Journal of Emotional and Behavioral Disorders, 12*, 168-181.

Oswald, K., Safran, S., & Johanson, G. (2005). Preventing trouble: Making schools safer places using Positive Behavior Support. *Education and Treatment of Children, 28*, 265-278.

Putnam, R. F., Liuselli, J. K., Sennett, K., & Malonson, J. (2002). Cost-efficacy analysis of out-of-district special education placements: An evaluative measure of behavior support interventions in public schools. *Journal of Special Education Leadership, 15*, 17-24_

Roeser, R. W., Eccles, J. S., & Freedman-Doan, C. (1999). Academic functioning and mental health in adolescence: Patterns, progressions, and routes from childhood. *Journal of Adolescent Research, 14*, 135-174.

Roeser, R. W., Eccles, J. S., & Sameroff, A. J. (1998). Academic and emotional functioning in early adolescence: Longitudinal relations, patterns, and prediction by experience in middle school. *Developmental Psychopathology, 10*, 321-352.

Schumaker, J. B., Hovell, M. F., & Sherman, J. A. (1977). An analysis of daily report cards and parent-managed privileges in the improvement of adolescents' classroom performance. *Journal of Applied Behavior Analysis, 10*, 449-464.

Sinclair, M. F., Christenson, S. L., Evelo, D. L., & Hurley, C. M. (1998). Dropout prevention for youth with disabilities: Efficacy of a sustained school engagement procedure. *Exceptional Children, 65*, 7-21.

Skiba, R., & Peterson, R. (1999). The dark side of zero tolerance: Can punishment lead to safe schools? *Phi Delta Kappan, 80*, 1-12.

Sprague, J. R., Nishioka, V. M., & Stieber, S. (2004, October). Skills for success: A multi-level school violence prevention intervention. Proceedings of Persistently Safe Schools, 11-24. Washington, DC: Hamilton Fish Institute, The George Washington University.

Sugai, G., Horner, R. H., Dunlap, G., Heineman, M., Lewis, T. J., Nelson, C. M., et al. (2000). Applying positive behavior support and functional behavioral assessment in schools. *Journal of Positive Behavioral Interventions, 2*, 131-143.

Sugai, G., Lewis-Palmer, T., & Hagan, S. (1998). Using functional assessment to develop behavior intervention plans. *Preventing School Failure, 43*, 6-13.

Taylor-Greene, S., Brown, D., Nelson, L., Longton, J., Gassman, T., Cohen, J., et al. (1997). School-wide behavioral support: Starting the year off right. *Journal of Behavioral Education, 7*, 99-112.

Taylor-Greene, S. J., & Kartub, D. T. (2000). Durable implementation of school-wide behavior support: The high five program. *Journal of Positive Behavior Interventions, 2*, 233-245.

Turnbull, A. P., Edmonson, H., Griggs, P., Wickham, D., Sailor, W., Freeman, R., et al. (2002). Positive behavior support: Implementation of three components. *Exceptional Children, 68*, 377-402.

Turnbull, H. R., & Turnbull, A. P. (with Stowe, M., & Wilcox, B. L.). (2000). *Free appropriate public education: The law and children with disabilities* (6th ed.). Denver, CO: Love.

Walker, H. M., Horner, R. H., Sugai, G., Bullis, M., Sprague, J. R., Bricker, D., et al. (1996). Integrated approaches to preventing antisocial behavior patterns among school-age children and youth. *Journal of Emotional and Behavioral Disorders, 4*, 194-209.

Warren, J. S., Edmonson, H. M., Griggs, P., Lassen, S., McCart, A., Turnbull, A., et al. (2003). Urban applications of school-wide positive behavior support: Critical issues and lessons learned. *Journal of Positive Behavior Interventions, 5*, 80-91.

Wehlage, G. G., & Rutter, R. A. (1985). *Dropping out: How much do schools contribute to the problem?* Madison, WI: Wisconsin Center for Educational Research, University of Wisconsin-Madison.

Zins, J. E., & Ponti, C. R. (1990). Best practices in school-based consultation. In A. Thomas & J. Grimes (Eds.), *Best practices in school psychology—II* (pp. 673-694). Washington, DC: National Association of School Psychologists.

ABOUT THE CONTRIBUTORS

Patrick Akos is an associate professor of school counseling in the School of Education at the University of North Carolina at Chapel Hill. He is a former college, elementary and middle school counselor and was recognized in 2004 as the American School Counselor Association's Counselor Educator of the Year. Dr. Akos's research focuses on the transition into and out of middle school and strengths-based school counseling. More information can be located at: http://soe.unc.edu/fac_research/profile/akos.php

Garet Allen-Malley is a lecturer in The Middle Level Teacher Education in the College of Education and Social Services at the University of Vermont in Burlington, VT. Her teaching responsibilities range from introductory courses, practicum supervision and graduate level courses. Her research interests include effective teaming practices, early adolescent development and student identification of effective teaching practices. Her research has been published by the National Middle School Association and the National Association of Secondary School Principals.

Lynley H. Anderman is an associate professor and the director of graduate studies in the Department of Educational and Counseling Psychology at the University of Kentucky. Her research interests focus on student motivation and the ways in which it is fostered within adaptive instructional and social-relational contexts, including aspects of teachers' instructional practices, teacher-student relationships, peer relationships, and students' sense of school belonging. Much of her research focuses on motivation in the middle school grades.

Vincent A. Anfara, Jr. is associate professor of educational administration and supervision at The University of Tennessee, Knoxville. He received the PhD in educational administration from the University of New Orleans in 1995. Before entering the professorate, he taught for 23 years in both middle and high schools in Louisiana and New Mexico. His research interests focus on middle school reform, school improvement planning, leadership in middle schools, issues related to student achievement, and qualitative research approaches. He is past chair of the National Middle School Association's (NMSA) Research Advisory Board and past-president of the American Educational Research Association's (AERA) Middle Level Education Research Special Interest Group. He has authored over 60 articles published in journals including *Middle School Journal, Research in Middle Level Education Annual, Education and Urban Society, The Journal of School Leadership, NASSP Bulletin*, the *International Journal of Leadership in Education*, and *Educational Researcher*. Vincent is also the author/editor of nine books related to middle grades education. Recent works include *The Encyclopedia of Middle Grades Education* (with Andrews & Mertens, 2005) and *The Developmentally Responsive Middle Level Principal: A Leadership Model and Measurement Instrument* (with Roney, Smarkola, DuCette, & Gross, 2006).

Penny Bishop is an assistant professor in the College of Education and Social Services at the University of Vermont in Burlington, VT, where she directs the Middle Level Teacher Education Program. Her teaching and research interests lie in developmentally responsive schooling for young adolescents. Her research has been published in *Middle School Journal*; *Research in Middle Level Education Online*; *Current Issues in Middle Level Education*; and *Journal of Adolescent and Adult Literacy*.

Chris Borgmeier is an assistant professor of special education at Portland State University. Dr. Borgmeier's professional and research interests include working with schools to improve school climate and reduce student behavior problems. He is working with several school districts on district-wide initiatives to implement School-wide Positive Behavior Support in schools. At PSU, he leads a Positive Behavior Support Focus Area and teaches classes related behavior management.

Kathleen Brinegar is currently pursuing her EdD in educational leadership and policy studies at the University of Vermont. As a Graduate Teaching Fellow in the Middle Level Teacher Education Program, she teaches graduate and undergraduate courses on adolescent literacy, middle grades organization and pedagogy and middle grades curriculum and assessment. Her current research interests include the schooling experiences of middle level refugee and immigrant students and young adolescent perceptions of school engagement.

Thomas M. Brinthaupt, professor of psychology at Middle Tennessee State University, received his PhD from the University of Pittsburgh in 1989. His primary research interests include self and identity, personality and health psychology, and teaching with instructional technologies. He is the coeditor of five volumes in the SUNY Press "Studying the Self" series, including *The Role of Self in Teacher Development* (1999) and *Understanding Early Adolescent Self and Identity: Applications and Interventions* (2002).

Dave F. Brown is the coauthor of the second edition of *What Every Middle School Teacher Should Know* (with Knowles, 2007), and author of *Becoming A Successful Urban Teacher* (2002). He frequently conducts research with middle level teachers and young adolescents on identity development, advisories, and flexible scheduling. He was recently presented with the William Alexander Award by the Pennsylvania Middle School Association for his outstanding contributions to middle level education in Pennsylvania.

Micki M. Caskey is an associate professor in the Department of Curriculum and Instruction within the Graduate School of Education at Portland State University. She holds a PhD in curriculum and instruction with an emphasis in interdisciplinary education from the University of South Florida. She draws on more than 20 years of teaching in both middle and high schools in inner city schools. Her areas of specialization include middle grades education, content area literacy, learning strategies and content enhancements, action research, and teacher education. She is president-elect of the Middle Level Education Research Special Interest Group of the American Education Research Association (AERA), chair of the National Middle School Association's (NMSA) Research Advisory Board, editor of *Research in Middle Level Education Online*, professional developer for the Center for Research on Learning's Strategic Instruction Model (SIM), board member of the Portland Council of the International Reading Association, higher education representative to the Oregon Middle Level Association, and past-chair of the Oregon Middle Level Consortium. She edited *Making a Difference: Action Research in Middle Level Education* (Volume V in *The Handbook of Research in Middle Level Education* series), coauthored *Reading and Learning Strategies: Middle Grades through High School*, and has written numerous journal articles and book chapters.

Francine Falk-Ross is an associate professor in the Department of Literacy Education at Northern Illinois University. She teaches courses in reading methods for grades K-12 to preservice and practicing teachers at the undergraduate and graduate levels. She has published articles and book chapters focusing on middle level reading issues, such as the integration of media into literacy lessons and modifications for struggling readers, as well as on topics related to language factors in literacy achievement.

Leslee A. Fisher is an associate professor in the Department of Exercise, Sport, and Leisure Studies at the University of Tennessee, Knoxville. She teaches undergraduate and graduate courses in sport and exercise psychology with primary research interests in gender identity development in sport, feminist theory, cultural studies of sport, and positive psychology. Dr. Fisher is currently the Secretary-Treasurer of the Association of Applied Sport Psychology (AASP). She also holds state counseling licensure and national certification.

Heather L. Leaman is an assistant professor of elementary education at West Chester University of Pennsylvania. She taught sixth grade in a Pennsylvania public middle school for eleven years prior to joining the West Chester faculty. She has a PhD in curriculum and instruction from Penn State University. Research interests include: teacher professional development, middle level students and teaching and social studies instruction.

Sungtaek Lim is an assistant professor in the Department of Education at Sunchon National University in South Korea. He teaches educational psychology and human development. His research interests are the areas of achievement motivation, moral development, creativity, and teacher efficacy.

Richard P. Lipka is a professor of education at Pittsburg State University in Kansas. A graduate of the State University of New York College at Buffalo (BS & MS) and the University of Illinois (PhD), he taught sixth grade as a member of a four person team in Amherst, New York. His primary research interest is affective development with an emphasis upon self-concept and self-esteem. To that end, he serves as coeditor (with Tom Brinthaupt) of the *Studying The Self* book series for SUNY press. In addition, he has written book chapters and articles for a variety of professional journals.

Melissa N. Madeson is a PhD student in sport studies at the University of Tennessee, Knoxville. She earned her BA in psychology and MS in kinesiology from California State University, Sacramento and her current research interests involve various aspects of sport and exercise psychology. Melissa works with female athletes on developing psychological skills to enhance performance as an intern for the Mental Training Center at the University of Tennessee. With a passion for health and fitness, she also works as an instructor and personal trainer at a local gym.

Molly M. Mee is an assistant professor in the College of Education at Towson University, Baltimore. She received her EdD in curriculum and instruction from the George Washington University, Washington DC in 2000. In her current position, she teaches a variety of education courses and operates a professional development school program. She taught middle school language arts for 8 years in Maryland. Research interests include middle level instruction, Socratic Seminar, student motivation, and professional development communities.

Steven B. Mertens is a senior research scientist at the Center for Prevention Research and Development at the University of Illinois. For the past decade he has served as the project director for the design, research, and evaluation of several large-scale evaluations and research studies of comprehensive middle-grades reform projects, including Michigan Middle Start, Mid South Middle Start, and Turning Points. He and his colleagues have published over 30 research articles, book chapters, and reports addressing varying aspects of middle-grades school reform and improvement; recent books include the *Encyclopedia of Middle Grades Education* (with Anfara and Andrews, 2005) and *A Practitioner's Guide to Understanding and Applying Middle Grades Research* (with Flowers and Mulhall, 2007). Currently Steve serves as a board member of the National Forum to Accelerate Middle-Grades Reform, Council Member for the American Educational Research Association's (AERA) Middle Level Education Research Special Interest Group, as well as several editorial board positions. He recently completed a 6-year term as a member of the National Middle School Association's (NMSA) Research Advisory Board.

Peter Mulhall is the director of Center for Prevention Research and Development, and adjunct faculty member at the University of Illinois. He has more than 20 years experience in school and community health education with a special interest in adolescent health and education, and published papers on adolescent health, preventive interventions, and evaluation methods. He recently worked with state and federal agencies developing performance measures assessing capacity, process and outcomes for prevention and early intervention programs.

Maureen Murphy is a doctoral student in gifted education at the University of Virginia. Before moving to Virginia, she served as a middle school language arts teacher in California, Maryland, and Pennsylvania. She is currently studying advanced readers in Reading First classrooms.

Teresa J. Rishel is an assistant professor in middle childhood education and curriculum and instruction at Kent State University. She taught for 15 years in elementary and middle schools, and served as an elementary principal, and received a PhD from Purdue University. Dr. Rishel focuses on preparing effective middle level teachers by connecting theory to practice. Specifically, she researches young adolescent/adolescent suicide in terms of sociocultural relationships, hidden curriculum and student performance.

Barbara Ruben is an assistant professor in the Curriculum and Instruction Department at Portland State University. She earned an education administrator license in 1995 and a doctorate in education leadership in 2004. Her impressive educational background includes teaching every level from kindergarten through eighth grade and working as a math consultant, a science teacher, and reading tutor. Her area of specialization is teacher education. She currently works with preservice teachers in the Graduate School of Education.

Joshua S. Smith is an assistant professor of educational psychology at Indiana University-Purdue University Indianapolis and associate director in the Center for Urban and Multicultural Education in the School of Education. His research interests involve the study of educational transitions including the transition from middle school to high school and the transition from high school to college. Dr. Smith also works with schools and community-based organization to evaluate educational programs on student and organizational outcomes.

Frances Spielhagen is an assistant professor of education at Mount Saint Mary College, Newburgh, New York. From 2003-2006, she was an AERA/IES Post-Doctoral Research Fellow and affiliated with the Center for Gifted Education at the College of William and Mary in Williamsburg, Virginia. Dr. Spielhagen is a career educator with over 30 years experience in secondary schools. She has also engaged in funded and published educational research, as well as grant writing and program evaluation.

Carol Ann Tomlinson is professor of educational leadership, foundations, and policy at the University of Virginia's Curry School of Education where she is also codirector of Curry's Institutes on Academic Diversity. Prior to joining the UVA faculty, she was a middle school teacher for 20 years. Carol is author of over 200 books, chapters, articles, and other materials. She works throughout the United States and around the world with teachers who work to create more academically responsive classrooms.

Mark D. Vagle, assistant professor of middle school education at The University of Georgia, taught in elementary and middle schools and was a middle school assistant principal. He received his PhD from The University of Minnesota-Twin Cities in 2006. His dissertation study focused on middle school teachers' recognition and response to students who did not understand something during instruction. Currently, his research focuses on relational and technical dimensions of teachers' pedagogy.

David C. Virtue is an assistant professor in the middle level education program at the University of South Carolina, where he teaches courses in social studies methods and middle level organization and philosophy. David also works with the State Department of Education as the director of ML-TEACH, a project designed to help middle level teachers become properly certified and highly qualified. David's research interests include middle level teacher preparation and middle level certification policy.

Monica A. Wallace, assistant professor of psychology at Middle Tennessee State University, received her PhD from The University of Tennessee in 2003. Her primary research interests are related to the use of operant procedures to promote behaviors and academic skills that support learning and issues related to the teaching of psychology. She currently teaches in the school psychology graduate program.

Printed in the United States
201703BV00005B/280-324/A